法王子無憂藏法王子大辯藏法王子弥勒
菩薩導首菩薩藥王菩薩藥上菩薩花幢菩
薩華光幢菩薩陀羅尼自在王菩薩觀世音
菩薩大勢至菩薩常精進菩薩寶印首菩薩
寶積菩薩寶杖菩薩越三界菩薩毗摩颰羅
菩薩香象菩薩大香象菩薩師子吼王菩薩
師子遊戲世菩薩師子奮迅菩薩師子精進
菩薩勇鋭力菩薩師子威猛伏菩薩莊嚴菩
薩大莊嚴菩薩如是等菩薩摩訶薩八万人

如是我聞一時佛住王舍城耆闍崛山中與
大比丘衆万二千人俱菩薩摩訶薩八萬人
天龍夜叉乾闥婆阿修羅迦樓羅緊那羅摩
睺羅伽諸比丘比丘尼及優婆塞優婆夷俱
大轉輪王小轉輪王金輪銀輪諸輪之王國
王王子國臣國民國士國女國大長者各與
眷屬百千万數而自圍遶來詣佛所頭面礼
足遶百千匝燒香散華種種供養已退一面

The Threefold Lotus Sutra

THE  THREE

THE LOTUS

and MEDITATION ON THE

translated by BUNNŌ

with revisions by W. E. SOOTHILL,

FOLD LOTUS SUTRA

INNUMERABLE MEANINGS,
FLOWER OF THE WONDERFUL LAW,
BODHISATTVA UNIVERSAL VIRTUE

KATŌ, YOSHIRŌ TAMURA, *and* KŌJIRŌ MIYASAKA

WILHELM SCHIFFER, *and* PIER P. DEL CAMPANA

KOSEI PUBLISHING CO. • *Tokyo*

THE ENDPAPER DESIGN: Reproduced on the endpapers is a portion of a ten-scroll copy of the entire Threefold Lotus Sutra written in gold ink on dark blue paper by the Japanese nobleman Fujiwara no Motohira in the early twelfth century. As was the custom of the time, Motohira copied the sutras as a devotional act, in this case following the death of his father in about 1128. For many centuries stored in Chūson-ji temple in Iwate Prefecture, northeastern Japan, the scrolls are now in the collection of Nikkyō Niwano, Tokyo. They have been designated an Important Cultural Property by the Japanese government.

First edition, 1975
Tenth printing, 1988

Published by Kōsei Publishing Co., Kōsei Building, 2-7-1 Wada, Suginami-ku, Tokyo 166; and John Weatherhill Inc., of New York and Tokyo.

ISBN 4-333-00208-7

Contents

THE SUTRA OF
THE LOTUS FLOWER OF THE WONDERFUL LAW
page 31

THE SUTRA OF
MEDITATION ON THE BODHISATTVA UNIVERSAL VIRTUE
page 347

Preface

IT HAS LONG BEEN MY DESIRE to see the entire Threefold Lotus Sutra, consisting of the Sutra of the Lotus Flower of the Wonderful Law and its two related, shorter sutras, the Sutra of Innumerable Meanings and the Sutra of Meditation on the Bodhisattva Universal Virtue, published in English translation. Revered since ancient times as "the king of all sutras" and "the most excellent sutra," the Threefold Lotus Sutra contains the essence of the teaching of Sakyamuni Buddha. This teaching we wished to share with people the world over. Finally, in the autumn of 1967, our wish began to be realized as work started on a new English-language version of the Lotus Sutra.

The first English version of this sutra was undertaken by H. Kern. His translation from the Sanskrit, entitled *Saddharma-Puṇḍarīka, or The Lotus of the True Law,* was published in 1884 as volume 21 of Max Müller's monumental Sacred Books of the East series. An English translation of Kumārajīva's great fifth-century translation from Sanskrit into Chinese was later made by Bunnō Katō and revised by Professor William Edward Soothill of Oxford University. Portions of this version were published in 1930 as *The Sutra of the Lotus Flower of the Wonderful Law.*

Our own English edition, entitled *Myōhō-Renge-Kyō: The Sutra of the Lotus Flower of the Wonderful Law,* published by the Kōsei Publishing Company in 1971, was based on the Katō/Soothill version as further revised by the late Dr. Wilhelm Schiffer, director of research of the International Institute for the Study of Religions, Tokyo, with the assistance of Professor Yoshirō Tamura of Tokyo University. This edition has received wide acclaim from scholars, religious leaders, critics, and the media. In recognition of its cultural contribution and its merits as a translation, the book received the seventh Japan Translation Award in 1971.

The Sutra of Innumerable Meanings, popularly known as the "opening sutra" of the three-part scripture, and the Sutra of Meditation on the Bodhisattva Universal Virtue, the "closing sutra," had never been made available in English before the former was translated by Professor Tamura and the latter by Kōjirō Miyasaka; these two works were published together by the Kōsei Publishing Company in 1974 under the title *Muryōgi-Kyō and Kanfugen-Gyō*. It is indeed unfortunate that Dr. Schiffer died in 1972 while revising the translation manuscript of the Sutra of Innumerable Meanings, but happily the task of revising this and the Sutra of Meditation on the Bodhisattva Universal Virtue was continued and completed by his close friend and colleague Dr. Pier P. Del Campana, professor at Sophia University, Tokyo.

Because of the close connection of the opening and closing sutras with the Lotus Sutra, from the very beginning it had been our wish and intention eventually to publish the English translation of all three sutras in a single volume. We are most grateful for the cooperation of John Weatherhill, Inc., joint publishers with the Kōsei Publishing Company of this new one-volume edition, *The Threefold Lotus Sutra.*

In order to make *The Threefold Lotus Sutra* the best and most reliable English edition possible, the translators, revisers, and Suzanne Trumbull, editor in charge of the book at Weatherhill, worked together closely in the reediting of the manuscripts. In addition, the footnotes have been revised and a glossary has been provided especially for this edition.

We sincerely hope that this book will help people the world over to understand the true spirit of Buddhism, thus contributing to the cultural exchange and mutual understanding of East and West. At the same time, I wish to extend my sincere thanks to the translators, revisers, and editors, who gave so much of their time and energy to this project.

NIKKYŌ NIWANO
President, Risshō Kōsei-kai
An Organization of Buddhist Laymen

Introduction

SINCE ANCIENT TIMES the Sutra of Innumerable Meanings, the Sutra of the Lotus Flower of the Wonderful Law, and the Sutra of Meditation on the Bodhisattva Universal Virtue have been known collectively in China and Japan as the Threefold Lotus Sutra 法華三部經, and have been highly esteemed not only in the Buddhist world but also in the literary world.

THE SUTRA OF THE LOTUS FLOWER OF THE WONDERFUL LAW, or Lotus Sutra, is recorded by Seng-yu 僧祐 (445–518) in volume two of the *Ch'u-san-tsang-chi-chi* 出三藏記集, the oldest extant catalogue of Buddhist scriptures, as follows: "*Cheng-fa-hua-ching* 正法華經, 10 fascicles, 27 chapters, translated by Dharmaraksha [Chu-fa-hu 竺法護] in 286, and *Miao-fa-lien-hua-ching* 妙法蓮華經 [*Hsin-fa-hua-ching* 新法華經], 7 fascicles, translated by Kumārajīva [Chiu-ma-lo-shih 鳩摩羅什; 344–413] in 406." According to the *K'ai-yüan-shih-chiao-lu* 開元釋教錄 written by Chih-sheng 智昇 in 730, six complete Chinese translations of the Lotus Sutra had been undertaken, of which three still exist. The three extant versions are *Cheng-fa-hua-ching*, 7 or 10 fascicles and 27 chapters, translated by Dharmaraksha in 286;

Miao-fa-lien-hua-ching, 7 fascicles and 27 chapters or 8 fascicles and 28 chapters, translated by Kumārajīva in 406; and *T'ien-pen-miao-fa-lien-hua-ching* 添品妙法蓮華經, 7 or 8 fascicles and 27 chapters, translated by Jñānagupta (She-na-chüeh-to 闍那崛多) and Dharmagupta (Ta-ma-chi-to 達摩笈多) in 601. This last is a revision of Kumārajīva's version.

Dharmaraksha's version is the oldest Chinese translation of the sutra. However, this does not necessarily mean that the Sanskrit original of his version is the oldest Sanskrit text of the sutra itself. Because all the Sanskrit originals are lost, we cannot know which was the oldest. Recently, however, relatively old manuscripts of the Sanskrit text of the Lotus Sutra, or *Saddharma-puṇḍarīka Sūtra,* have been discovered in Nepal, Central Asia, and Kashmir. It is estimated that the Nepalese manuscripts were copied during and after the eleventh century, while the Central Asian manuscripts were copied earlier. Some are thought to have been copied as early as the seventh or eighth century. The text that was discovered in 1931 at Gilgit in Kashmir is estimated to have been copied still earlier, in the fifth or sixth century. If this estimate is correct, it is older than any other known extant Sanskrit version.

The translator Kumārajīva was born in Kucha, an important trade center in ancient Central Asia, and the Sanskrit original of his Chinese version is thought to be allied to the recently discovered Central Asian manuscripts. Because these are older than the Nepalese texts, Kumārajīva's version is thought to be relatively close to the original form of the Lotus Sutra. However, the age of a specific copy of the sutra and the contents of the Sanskrit manuscripts are not necessarily related. Future investigation should shed new light on this question.

Kumārajīva's version consisted of 7 fascicles and 27 chapters at the time that he translated the sutra. Around the time of T'ien-t'ai Chih-i 天台智顗 (538–97), the founder of the T'ien-t'ai school of Buddhism, the chapter "Devadatta" (*Ti-p'o-ta-to-p'in* 提婆達多品) was added to Kumārajīva's version, so that the sutra came to consist of 7 fascicles and 28 chapters. In the *Fa-hua-wen-kou* 法華文句, a commentary by Chih-i on the Kumārajīva version of the Lotus Sutra, the chapter on Devadatta is inserted as the twelfth chapter. By the first half of the eighth century, around the middle of the T'ang dynasty, the sutra had been divided into 8 fascicles and 28 chapters, for these figures can be seen in the *K'ai-yuan-shih-chiao-lu.*

According to extant commentaries on the Lotus Sutra, Tao-sheng 道生 (d. 434) and Fa-yün 法雲 (Kuan-chai-ssu 光宅寺; 467–529) drew a line between chapter 13 (14), "A Happy Life" (*An-lao-hang-p'in* 安樂行品), and chapter 14 (15), "Springing Up out of the Earth" (*Ts'ung-ti-yung-ch'u-p'in* 從地涌出品); they regarded the first half of the sutra, thus divided, as belonging to the realm of cause, which reveals the unity of the Dharma, and the latter half as belonging to the realm of effect, which reveals the eternity of the Buddha. Chih-i, who followed this division, defined the first half of the sutra as the realm of trace (*chi-men* 迹門) and the latter half as the realm of origin (*pen-men* 本門). His classification has been generally accepted since. The nucleus of the first half is chapter 2, "Tactfulness" (*Fang-pien-p'in* 方便品), in which the Wonderful Law as the One-vehicle, that is, the unifying truth of the universe, is explained. The nucleus of the latter half is chapter 16, "Revelation of the [Eternal] Life of the Tathāgata" (*Ju-lai-shou-liang-p'in* 如來壽量品), in which the eternal life of the Buddha is revealed.

There is also another way of dividing the Lotus Sutra. In accordance with the history of the formation of the sutra, it is considered that the section from chapter 10, "A Teacher of the Law" (*Fa-shih-p'in* 法師品), to chapter 20 (21), "The Divine Power of the Tathāgata" (*Ju-lai-shen-li-p'in* 如來神力品), and chapter 21 (22), "The Final Commission" (*Chu-lei-p'in* 囑累品), constitute another group, although this grouping overlaps both divisions of Chih-i's classification. In this third group, the practice of the bodhisattvas as apostles or deputies of the Buddha is stressed. For example, the following expressions are found: "the entrusting" (*nikshepa,* 付屬, or *parindanā,* 囑累) of the Law; "the apostle of the Tathāgata" (*tathāgata-dūta,* 如來使); "one sent by the Tathāgata" (*tathāgata-saṃpreshita,* 如來所遣); and "the message" (*preshaṇa,* 使) or "the command" (*ājñā,* 勅) of the Tathāgata. In chapter 14 (15) and chapter 21 (22) the Bodhisattva Eminent Conduct (Viśishṭacāritra, 上行) acts as the representative of such bodhisattvas. He is a leader of those bodhisattvas who live in the actual world and who have been given the mission of propagating the Law in the corrupt Latter Days.

In conclusion, it may be stated that the Lotus Sutra can be classified into three divisions, including both the traditional and historically defined classifications.

Of all the Chinese texts of the Lotus Sutra, Kumārajīva's translation is the only version that has been widely used, because it is both an excellent and an elegant translation. Almost all commentaries on the Lotus Sutra written in China and Japan have used Kumārajīva's version. In Japan especially, not only religious movements but also literary works concerning the Lotus Sutra have become popular through this version.

MAJOR DIFFERENCES AMONG THE VARIOUS TEXTS of the sutra are listed below.

Abbreviations used: Skt = extant Sanskrit text; Tib = Tibetan version; Cheng = *Cheng-fa-hua-ching;* T'ien = *T'ien-pen-miao-fa-lien-hua-ching;* Miao = *Miao-fa-lien-hua-ching;* extant Miao = extant *Miao-fa-lien-hua-ching*

1. The latter part of "The Parable of the Herbs": included in Skt, Tib, Cheng, T'ien; not in Miao, extant Miao
2. The first part of "The Five Hundred Disciples Receive the Prediction of Their Destiny" and "A Teacher of the Law": only in Cheng
3. "Devadatta": included in the latter part of "Beholding the Precious Stupa" in Skt, Tib, Cheng, T'ien; not in Miao; the chapter following "Beholding the Precious Stupa" in extant Miao
4. "The Final Commission": included as the final chapter (27) in Skt, Tib, Cheng, T'ien; included as the chapter following "The Divine Power of the Tathāgata" in Miao, extant Miao
5. The verse portion of "The All-Sidedness of the Bodhisattva Regarder of the Cries of the World": included in Skt, Tib, T'ien, extant Miao; not in Cheng, Miao
6. The psalm to Amita in the above verse portion: included only in Skt and Tib
7. "Dhāraṇīs": included as the chapter following "The Divine Power of the Tathāgata" in Skt, Tib, T'ien; included as the chapter following "The All-Sidedness of the Bodhisattva Regarder of the Cries of the World" in Cheng, Miao, extant Miao

In addition to the above major discrepancies, there are two or three minor differences among the texts.

The Sutra of Innumerable Meanings is also listed by Seng-yu in volume two of his *Ch'u-san-tsang-chi-chi,* as follows: "*Wu-liang-i-ching* 無量義經, 1 fascicle, translated by Dharmajātayaśas [T'an-ma-chia-t'o-yeh-she 曇摩伽陀耶舍] in the age of the emperor Kao-ti of the Ch'i dynasty." Volume nine of the same catalogue also lists the *Wu-liang-i-ching-hsü* 無量義經序, the Introduction to the Sutra of Innumerable Meanings, written by Liu-ch'iu 劉虬 (438–95). According to this introduction, in the third year of Chien-yüan 建元 (481) of the Ch'i dynasty a priest by the name of Hui-piao 慧表 received the Sutra of Innumerable Meanings from Dharmajātayaśas and gave it to Liu-ch'iu in the third year of Yung-ming 永明 (485). Liu-ch'iu presumed this to be "the Great-vehicle sutra called Innumerable Meanings" mentioned in chapter one of Kumārajīva's version of the Lotus Sutra.

All succeeding Buddhist scholars, including T'ien-t'ai Chih-i, believed Liu-ch'iu's presumption to be correct, and consequently the Sutra of Innumerable Meanings came to be regarded as a preface to the Lotus Sutra and was known as the "opening sutra." Moreover, the expression "In forty years and more, the truth has not been revealed yet," in chapter two of the Sutra of Innumerable Meanings, was interpreted as relating to the Lotus Sutra, that is, as meaning that the Lotus Sutra is "the truth" revealed by Sakyamuni after his expedient preaching of more than forty years. However, the Lotus Sutra is never mentioned by name in the Sutra of Innumerable Meanings, so that it remains for further research to ascertain whether this sutra has a direct connection with the Lotus Sutra.

The Sutra of Meditation on the Bodhisattva Universal Virtue is recorded in volume two of the *Ch'u-san-tsang-chi-chi* as follows: "*Kuan-p'u-hsien-p'u-sa-hsing-fa-ching* 觀普賢菩薩行法經 or *P'u-hsien-kuan-ching* 普賢觀經, *Ch'u-shen-kung-te-ching* 出深功德經, 1 fascicle, translated by Dharmamitra [T'an-ma-mi-to 曇摩密多; 356–442] during the Yüan-chia 元嘉 era [424–53] in the age of the emperor Wen-ti of the Sung dynasty." According to the *K'ai-yüan-shih-chiao-lu,* there were three different versions of this sutra: *P'u-hsien-kuan-ching* 普賢觀經, 1 fascicle, translated by Gītamitra (Chih-to-mi-to 祇多密多) in the Eastern Chin dynasty (317–420); *Kuan-p'u-hsien-p'u-sa-ching* 觀普賢菩薩經, 1 fascicle, translated by Kumārajīva; and

Kuan-p'u-hsien-p'u-sa-hsing-fa-ching 觀普賢菩薩行法經, 1 fascicle, translated by Dharmamitra. However, only the third version is extant.

In the Sutra of Meditation on the Bodhisattva Universal Virtue, not only is the Lotus Sutra mentioned by name, but the same teaching as found in the Lotus Sutra can be seen. Therefore it is unquestionable that the Sutra of Meditation on the Bodhisattva Universal Virtue was composed following chapter 28 of the Lotus Sutra, "Encouragement of the Bodhisattva Universal Virtue." Hence this sutra came to be regarded as the epilogue of the Lotus Sutra, or the "closing sutra."

The central theme of the sutra is an exhortation to the practice of repentance. The so-called repentance of reality, or meditation on reality, is especially emphasized. In the sutra this practice is also called "the repentance of the non-sin aspect," signifying that this repentance originates in the concept of *śūnyatā,* voidness or nonattachment. T'ien-t'ai Chih-i greatly valued this repentance and advocated it as the *fa-hua-san-mi* 法華三昧, "the contemplation of the Lotus." Since his time the "repentance of reality" has become popular in both China and Japan.

There is no extant Sanskrit text of either the Sutra of Innumerable Meanings or the Sutra of Meditation on the Bodhisattva Universal Virtue, a fact that indicates the importance of further investigation of the origins of these two scriptures.

Yoshirō Tamura
Professor, Tokyo University

EDITORIAL NOTE

THE GUIDING PRINCIPLE in the revision and editing of the Katō/Soothill translation of the Sutra of the Lotus Flower of the Wonderful Law and its two companion sutras, Innumerable Meanings and Meditation on the Bodhisattva Universal Virtue, has been the desire to produce a text that would be easy to read and at the same time maintain a high level of scholarship. To this end, all notes that do not lead to a better understanding of the text and all notes containing sectarian interpretations of the text have been eliminated. Other notes have been deleted when it was felt that the information therein would be more appropriately included in the glossary prepared for this edition.

Wherever possible, words left in Sanskrit by the translators have been translated into English. Only words like *pāramitā,* for which no adequate English equivalents exist, have been left in Sanskrit. All Sanskrit words in the text are in roman type for smoother reading; the spelling of words no longer considered foreign to English has been anglicized, and diacritical marks have been removed. The plural of all Sanskrit words has been formed in the English way, by adding *s.*

The Sutra of Innumerable Meanings

translated by
Yoshiro Tamura
with revisions by
Wilhelm Schiffer
Pier P. Del Campana

CHAPTER I

Virtues

THUS HAVE I HEARD. Once[1] the Buddha was staying at the City of Royal Palaces on Mount Gṛdhrakūṭa with a great assemblage of great bhikshus, in all twelve thousand. There were eighty thousand bodhisattva-mahāsattvas. There were gods, dragons, yakshas, gandharvas, asuras, garuḍas, kiṃnaras, and mahoragas, besides all the bhikshus, bhikshuṇīs, upāsakas, and upāsikās. There were great wheel-rolling kings, small wheel-rolling kings, and kings of the gold wheel, silver wheel, and other wheels; further, kings and princes, ministers and people, men and women, and great rich persons, each encompassed by a hundred thousand myriad followers. They went up to the Buddha, made obeisance at his feet, a hundred thousand times made procession around him, burned incense, and scattered flowers. After they variously worshiped, they retired and sat to one side.

Those bodhisattvas' names were the Son of the Law-king Mañjuśrī, the Son of the Law-king Great Dignity Treasury, the Son of the Law-king Sorrowlessness Treasury, the Son of the Law-king Great

1. The "I" is Ānanda (Joy), so called because he was born on the night that Sakyamuni attained buddhahood. Famous for his memory, Ānanda contributed to the compilation and editing of many sutras.

Eloquence Treasury, the Bodhisattva Maitreya, the Bodhisattva Leader, the Bodhisattva Medicine King, the Bodhisattva Medicine Lord, the Bodhisattva Flower Banner, the Bodhisattva Flower Light Banner, the Bodhisattva King Commanding Dhāraṇīs at Will, the Bodhisattva Regarder of the Cries of the World, the Bodhisattva Great Power Obtained, the Bodhisattva Ever Zealous, the Bodhisattva Precious Seal, the Bodhisattva Precious Store, the Bodhisattva Precious Stick, the Bodhisattva Above the Triple World, the Bodhisattva Vimabhara,[2] the Bodhisattva Scented Elephant, the Bodhisattva Great Scented Elephant, the Bodhisattva King of the Lion's Roar, the Bodhisattva Lion's Playing in the World, the Bodhisattva Lion's Force, the Bodhisattva Lion's Assiduity, the Bodhisattva Brave Power, the Bodhisattva Lion's Overbearing, the Bodhisattva Adornment, and the Bodhisattva Great Adornment: such bodhisattva-mahāsattvas as these, eighty thousand in all.

Of these bodhisattvas there is none who is not a great saint of the Law-body. They have attained commands, meditation, wisdom, emancipation, and the knowledge of emancipation. With tranquil minds, and constantly in contemplation, they are peaceful, indifferent, nonactive, and free from desires. They are immune from any kind of delusion and distraction. Their minds are calm and clear, profound and infinite. They remain in this state for hundreds of thousands of koṭis of kalpas, and all the innumerable teachings have been revealed to them. Having obtained the great wisdom, they penetrate all things, completely understand the reality of their nature and form, and clearly discriminate existing and nonexisting, long and short.

Moreover, well knowing the capacities, natures, and inclinations of all, with dhāraṇīs and the unhindered power of discourse, they roll the Law-wheel just as buddhas do. First, dipping the dust of desire in a drop of the teachings, they remove the fever of the passions of life and realize the serenity of the Law by opening the gate of nirvana and fanning the wind of emancipation. Next, raining the profound Law of the Twelve Causes, they pour it on the violent and intense rays of sufferings—ignorance, old age, illness, death, and so on; then pouring abundantly the supreme Mahayana, they dip all the good roots of living beings in it, scatter the seeds of goodness over the field of merits,

2. A mechanical restoration of the Chinese phonetic transliteration of the Sanskrit. This name is not found in any other sutra.

and make all put forth the sprout of buddhahood. With their wisdom [brilliant] as the sun and the moon, and their timely tactfulness, they promote the work of the Mahayana and make all accomplish Perfect Enlightenment speedily; and with eternal pleasure wonderful and true, and through infinite great compassion, they relieve all from suffering.

These are the true good friends for all living beings, these are the great field of blessings for all living beings, these are the unsummoned teachers[3] for all living beings, and these are the peaceful place of pleasure, relief, protection, and great support for all living beings. They become great good leaders or great leaders for living beings everywhere. They serve as eyes for blind beings, and as ears, nose, or tongue for those who are deaf, who have no nose, or who are dumb; make deficient organs complete; turn the deranged to the great right thought. As the master of a ship or the great master of a ship, they carry all living beings across the river of life and death to the shore of nirvana. As the king of medicine or the great king of medicine, they discriminate the phases of a disease, know well the properties of medicines, dispense medicines according to the disease, and make people take them. As the controller or the great controller, they have no dissolute conduct; they are like a trainer of elephants and horses who never fails to train well, or like a majestic and brave lion that inevitably subdues and overpowers all beasts.

Bodhisattvas, playing in all pāramitās, being firm and immovable at the stage of tathāgata, and purifying the Buddha-country with the stability of their vow power, will rapidly accomplish Perfect Enlightenment. All these bodhisattva-mahāsattvas have such wonderful merits as seen above.

Those bhikshus' names were Great Wisdom Śāriputra, Supernatural Power Maudgalyāyana, Wisdom Life Subhūti, Mahā-Kātyāyana, Maitrāyaṇī's son Pūrṇa, Ājñāta-Kauṇḍinya, Divine Eye Aniruddha, Precept-keeping Upāli, Attendant Ānanda, Buddha's son Rāhula, Upananda, Revata, Kapphiṇa, Vakkula, Acyuta,[4] Svāgata, Dhūta Mahā-Kāśyapa, Uruvilvā-Kāśyapa, Gayā-Kāśyapa, and Nadī-Kāśyapa. There are twelve thousand bhikshus such as these. All are

3. Those who are ready to help living beings on their own initiative, even if they are not asked.

4. Chapter 8 of the Lotus Sutra gives "Cunda," which may be correct.

arhats, unrestricted by all bonds of faults, free from attachment, and truly emancipated.

At that time the Bodhisattva-Mahāsattva Great Adornment, seeing that all the groups sat in settled mind, rose up from his seat, went up to the Buddha with the eighty thousand bodhisattva-mahāsattvas in the assembly, made obeisance at his feet, a hundred thousand times made procession round him, burned celestial incense, scattered celestial flowers, and presented the Buddha with celestial robes, garlands, and jewels of priceless value which came rolling down from the sky and gathered all over like clouds. The celestial bins and bowls were filled with all sorts of celestial delicacies, which satisfied just by the sight of their color and the smell of their perfume. They placed celestial banners, flags, canopies, and playthings everywhere; pleased the Buddha with celestial music; then went forth to kneel with folded hands, and praised him in verse, saying with one voice and one mind:

"Great! The Great Enlightened, the Great Holy Lord,
In him there is no defilement, no contamination, no
  attachment.
The trainer of gods and men, elephants and horses,
His moral breeze and virtuous fragrance
Deeply permeate all.
Serene is his wisdom, calm his emotion,
And stable his prudence.
His thought is settled, his consciousness is extinct,
And thus his mind is quiet.
Long since, he removed false thoughts
And conquered all the laws of existence.
His body is neither existing nor nonexisting;
Without cause or condition,
Without self or others;
Neither square nor round,
Neither short nor long;
Without appearance or disappearance,
Without birth or death;
Neither created nor emanating,
Neither made nor produced;
Neither sitting nor lying,

Neither walking nor stopping;
Neither moving nor rolling,
Neither calm nor quiet;
Without advance or retreat,
Without safety or danger;
Without right or wrong,
Without merit or demerit;
Neither that nor this,
Neither going nor coming;
Neither blue nor yellow,
Neither red nor white;
Neither crimson nor purple,
Without a variety of color.
Born of commandments, meditation,
Wisdom, emancipation, and knowledge;
Merit of contemplation, the six divine faculties,
And the practice of the way;
Sprung of benevolence and compassion,
The ten powers, and fearlessness;
He has come in response
To good karmas of living beings.
He reveals his body,
Ten feet six inches in height,
Glittering with purple gold,
Well proportioned, brilliant,
And highly bright.
The mark of hair curls as the moon,
In the nape of the neck there is a light as of the sun.
The curling hair is deep blue,
On the head there is a protuberance.
The pure eyes, like a stainless mirror,
Blink up and down.
The eyebrows trail in dark blue,
The mouth and cheeks are well formed.
The lips and tongue appear pleasantly red,
Like a scarlet flower.
The white teeth, forty in number,
Appear as snowy agate.

Broad the forehead, high-bridged the nose,
And majestic the face.
The chest, with a swastika mark,
Is like a lion's breast.
The hands and feet are flexible,
With the mark of a thousand spokes.
The sides and palms are well rounded,
And show in fine lines.
The arms are elongated,
And the fingers are straight and slender.
The skin is delicate and smooth,
And the hair curls to the right.
The ankles and knees are well defined,
And the male organ is hidden
Like that of a horse.
The fine muscles, the collarbone,
And the thigh bones are slim
Like those of a deer.
The chest and back are shining,
Pure and without blemish,
Untainted by any muddy water,
Unspotted by any speck of dust.
There are thirty-two such signs,
The eighty kinds of excellence are visible,
And truly, there is nothing
Of form or nonform.
All visible forms are transcended;
His body is formless and yet has form.
This is also true
Of the form of the body of all living beings.[5]
Living beings adore him joyfully,
Devote their minds to him,
And pay their respects wholeheartedly.
By cutting off arrogance and egotism,
He has accomplished such a wonderful body.
Now we, the assemblage of eighty thousand,

5. That is, the Buddha and men are fundamentally nonsubstantial.

Making obeisance all together,
Submit ourselves to the saint of nonattachment,
The trainer of elephants and horses,
Detached from the state of thinking,
Mind, thought, and perception.
We make obeisance,
And submit ourselves to the Law-body,
To all commands, meditation, wisdom,
Emancipation, and knowledge.
We make obeisance,
And submit ourselves to the wonderful character.
We make obeisance,
And submit ourselves to the unthinkable.
The sacred voice sounds eight ways,[6]
As the thunder sounds.
It is sweet, pure, and greatly profound.
He preaches the Four Noble Truths,
The Six Pāramitās, and the Twelve Causes,
According to the working of the minds of living beings.
One never hears without opening one's mind
And breaking the bonds of the infinite chain of life and death.
One never hears without reaching srota-āpanna,
Sakṛdāgāmin, anāgāmin, and arhat;
Reaching the state of pratyekabuddha,
Of nonfault and noncondition;
Reaching the state of bodhisattva,
Of nonlife and nondeath;
Of obtaining the infinite dhāraṇī
And the unhindered power of discourse,
With which one recites profound and wonderful verses,
Plays and bathes in the pure pond of the Law,
Or displays supernatural motion
By jumping and flying up,
Or freely goes in or out of water and fire.
The aspect of the Tathāgata's Law-wheel is like this.
It is pure, boundless, and unthinkable.

6. This refers to the eight excellent qualities of the voice of the Buddha.

Making obeisance all together,
We submit ourselves to him
When he rolls the Law-wheel.
We make obeisance,
And submit ourselves to the sacred voice.
We make obeisance,
And submit ourselves to the Causes, Truths, and Pāramitās.
For infinite past kalpas,
The World-honored One has practiced
All manner of virtues with effort
To bring benefits to us human beings,
Heavenly beings, and dragon kings,
Universally to all living beings.
He abandoned all things hard to abandon,
His treasures, wife, and child,
His country and his palace.
Unsparing of his person as of his possessions,
He gave all, his head, eyes, and brain,
To people as alms.
Keeping the buddhas' precepts of purity,
He never did any harm,
Even at the cost of his life.
He never became angry,
Even though beaten with sword and staff,
Or though cursed and abused.
He never became tired,
In spite of long exertion.
He kept his mind at peace day and night,
And was always in meditation.
Learning all the law-ways,
With his deep wisdom
He has seen into the capacity of living beings.
As a result, obtaining free power,
He has become the Law-king,
Who is free in the Law.
Making obeisance again all together,
We submit ourselves to the one
Who has completed all hard things."

CHAPTER II

Preaching

AT THAT TIME the Bodhisattva-Mahāsattva Great Adornment, with the eighty thousand bodhisattva-mahāsattvas, finished praising the Buddha with this verse and said to the Buddha in unison: "World-honored One, we, the assemblage of the eighty thousand bodhisattvas, want to ask you about the Tathāgata's Law. We are anxious that the World-honored One should hear us with sympathy."

The Buddha addressed the Bodhisattva Great Adornment and the eighty thousand bodhisattvas: "Excellent! Excellent! Good sons, you have well known that this is the time. Ask me what you like. Before long, the Tathāgata will enter parinirvāṇa. After nirvana, there shall be not a doubt left to anybody. I will answer any question you wish to ask."

Thereupon the Bodhisattva Great Adornment, with the eighty thousand bodhisattvas, said to the Buddha in unison with one voice: "World-honored One! If the bodhisattva-mahāsattvas want to accomplish Perfect Enlightenment quickly, what doctrine should they practice? What doctrine makes bodhisattva-mahāsattvas accomplish Perfect Enlightenment quickly?"

The Buddha addressed the Bodhisattva Great Adornment and the eighty thousand bodhisattvas: "Good sons, there is one doctrine which makes bodhisattvas accomplish Perfect Enlightenment quickly. If a bodhisattva learns this doctrine, then he will accomplish Perfect Enlightenment."

"World-honored One! What is this doctrine called? What is its meaning? How does a bodhisattva practice it?"

The Buddha said: "Good sons! This one doctrine is called the doctrine of Innumerable Meanings. A bodhisattva, if he wants to learn and master the doctrine of Innumerable Meanings, should observe that all laws[1] were originally, will be, and are in themselves void in nature and form; they are neither great nor small, neither appearing nor disappearing, neither fixed nor movable, and neither advancing nor retreating; and they are nondualistic, just emptiness. All living beings, however, discriminate falsely: 'It is this' or 'It is that,' and 'It is advantageous' or 'It is disadvantageous'; they entertain evil thoughts, make various evil karmas, and [thus] transmigrate within the six realms of existence; and they suffer all manner of miseries, and cannot escape from there during infinite koṭis of kalpas. Bodhisattva-mahāsattvas, observing rightly like this, should raise the mind of compassion, display the great mercy desiring to relieve others of suffering, and once again penetrate deeply into all laws. According to the nature of a law, such a law emerges. According to the nature of a law, such a law settles. According to the nature of a law, such a law changes. According to the nature of a law, such a law vanishes. According to the nature of a law, such an evil law emerges. According to the nature of a law, such a good law emerges. Settling, changing, and vanishing are also like this. Bodhisattvas, having thus completely observed and known these four aspects from beginning to end, should next observe that none of the laws settles down even for a moment, but all emerge and vanish anew every moment; and observe that they emerge, settle, change, and vanish instantly. After such observation, we see all manner of natural desires of living beings. As natural desires are innumerable, preaching is immeasurable, and as preaching is immeasurable, meanings are innumerable. The Innumerable Meanings originate from one law. This one law is, namely, nonform. Such nonform is form-

1. Or "all existences."

less, and not form. Being not form and formless, it is called the real aspect [of things]. The mercy which bodhisattva-mahāsattvas display after stabilizing themselves in such a real aspect is real and not vain. They excellently relieve living beings from sufferings. Having given relief from sufferings, they preach the Law again, and let all living beings obtain pleasure.

"Good sons! A bodhisattva, if he practices completely the doctrine of the Innumerable Meanings like this, will soon accomplish Perfect Enlightenment without fail. Good sons! The Sutra of Innumerable Meanings, such a profound and supreme Great-vehicle, is reasonable in its logic, unsurpassed in its worth, and protected by all the buddhas of the three worlds. No kind of demon or heretic can break into it, nor can any wrong view or life and death destroy it. Therefore, good sons! Bodhisattva-mahāsattvas, if you want to accomplish supreme buddhahood quickly, you should learn and master the Sutra of Innumerable Meanings, such a profound and supreme Great-vehicle."

At that time the Bodhisattva Great Adornment said to the Buddha again: "World-honored One! The preaching of the World-honored One is incomprehensible, the natures of living beings are also incomprehensible, and the doctrine of emancipation is also incomprehensible. Though we have no doubt about the laws preached by the Buddha, we repeatedly ask the World-honored One for fear that all living beings should be perplexed. For more than forty years since the Tathāgata attained enlightenment, you have continuously preached all the laws to living beings—the four aspects, suffering, voidness, transience, selflessness, nonlarge, nonsmall, nonbirth, nondeath, one aspect, nonaspect, the nature of the law, the form of the law, void from the beginning, noncoming, nongoing, nonappearance, and nondisappearance. Those who have heard it have obtained the law of warming, the law of the highest, the law of the best in the world,[2] the merit of srota-āpanna, the merit of sakṛdāgāmin, the merit of anāgāmin, the merit of arhat, and the way of pratyekabuddha; have aspired to enlightenment; and ascending the first stage, the second stage, and the third stage, have attained the tenth stage. Because of what difference

2. The law of warming, the law of the highest, and the law of the best in the world are three stages to be passed through by the disciple who is not yet free of desire when he tries to understand fully the Four Noble Truths.

between your past and present preaching on laws do you say that if a bodhisattva practices only the Sutra of Innumerable Meanings, a profound and supreme Great-vehicle, he will soon accomplish supreme buddhahood without fail? World-honored One! Be pleased to discriminate the Law widely for living beings out of compassion for all, and to leave no doubt to all Law-hearers in the present and future."

Hereupon the Buddha said to the Bodhisattva Great Adornment: "Excellent! Excellent! Great good sons, you have well questioned the Tathāgata about such a wonderful meaning of the profound and supreme Great-vehicle. Do know that you will bring many benefits, please men and gods, and relieve living beings from sufferings. It is truly the great benevolence, and the truth without falsehood. For this reason you will surely and quickly accomplish supreme buddhahood. You will also make all living beings in the present and future accomplish supreme buddhahood.

"Good sons! After six years' right sitting under the Bodhi tree of the wisdom throne, I could accomplish Perfect Enlightenment. With the Buddha's eye I saw all the laws and understood that they were inexpressible. Wherefore? I knew that the natures and desires of all living beings were not equal. As their natures and desires were not equal, I preached the Law variously. It was with tactful power that I preached the Law variously. In forty years and more, the truth has not been revealed yet. Therefore living beings' powers of attainment are too different to accomplish supreme buddhahood quickly.

"Good sons! The Law is like water that washes off dirt. As a well, a pond, a stream, a river, a valley stream, a ditch, or a great sea each alike effectively washes off all kinds of dirt, so the Law-water effectively washes off the dirt of all delusions of living beings.

"Good sons! The nature of water is one, but a stream, a river, a well, a pond, a valley stream, a ditch, and a great sea are different from one another. The nature of the Law is like this. There is equality and no differentiation in washing off the dirt of delusions, but the three laws, the four merits, and the two ways[3] are not one and the same.

"Good sons! Though each washes equally as water, a well is not a

3. The three laws are the Four Noble Truths, the Twelve Causes, and the Six Pāramitās (see Glossary); the four merits are srota-āpanna, sakṛdāgāmin, anāgāmin, and arhat (see Glossary); and the two ways are the Great-vehicle, or Mahayana, and the lesser vehicle, or Hinayana.

pond, a pond is not a stream or a river, nor is a valley stream or a ditch a sea. As the Tathāgata, the world's hero, is free in the Law, all the laws preached by him are also like this. Though preaching at the beginning, in the middle, and at the end all alike effectively wash off the delusions of living beings, the beginning is not the middle, and the middle is not the end. Preaching at the beginning, in the middle, and at the end are the same in expression but different from one another in meaning.

"Good sons! When I rolled the Law-wheel of the Four Noble Truths for the five men, Ājñāta-Kauṇḍinya and the others, at the Deer Park in Vārāṇasī after leaving the king of trees, I preached that the laws are naturally vacant, ceaselessly transformed, and instantly born and destroyed. When I discoursed explaining the Twelve Causes and the Six Pāramitās for all the bhikshus and bodhisattvas in various places during the middle period, I preached also that all laws are naturally vacant, ceaselessly transformed, and instantly born and destroyed. Now in explaining the Sutra of Innumerable Meanings, a Great-vehicle, at this time, I preach also that all laws are naturally vacant, ceaselessly transformed, and instantly born and destroyed. Good sons! Therefore the preaching at the beginning, in the middle, and at the end are the same in expression but different from one another in meaning. As the meaning varies, the understanding of living beings varies. As the understanding varies, the attainment of the law, the merit, and the way also varies.

"Good sons! At the beginning, though I preached the Four Truths for those who sought to be śrāvakas, eight koṭis of heavenly beings came down to hear the Law and raised the desire for enlightenment. In the middle, though I preached in various places the profound Twelve Causes for those who sought to be pratyekabuddhas, innumerable living beings raised the aspiration for enlightenment or remained in the stage of śrāvaka. Next, though I explained the long-term practice[4] of bodhisattvas, through preaching the twelve types of sutras of Great Extent, the Mahā-Prajñā, and the voidness of the Garland Sea, a hundred thousand bhikshus, myriad koṭis of men and gods, and innumerable living beings could remain in the merits of srota-āpanna, sakṛdāgāmin, anāgāmin, and arhat or in the law appropriate

4. Religious exercises extending over many kalpas.

to the pratyekabuddha. Good sons! For this reason, it is known that the preaching is the same, but the meaning varies. As the meaning varies, the understanding of living beings varies. As the understanding varies, the attainment of the law, the merit, and the way also varies. So good sons! Since I attained the way, and stood to preach the Law for the first time, till I spoke the Sutra of Innumerable Meanings, the Great-vehicle, today, I have never ceased from preaching suffering, voidness, transience, selflessness, nontruth, nonreality, nonlarge, nonsmall, nonbirth in origin, and also nondeath at present, one aspect, nonaspect, the form of the law, the nature of the law, noncoming, nongoing, and the four aspects by which all the living are driven.

"Good sons! For this reason, all the buddhas, without a double tongue, answer widely all voices with one word; though having one body, reveal bodies innumerable and numberless as the sands of the Ganges of a hundred thousand myriad koṭis nayutas; in each body, display various forms countless as the sands of some hundred thousand myriad koṭis nayutas asaṃkhyeya Ganges, and in each form show shapes countless as the sands of some hundred thousand myriad koṭis nayutas asaṃkhyeya Ganges. Good sons! This is, namely, the incomprehensible and profound world of buddhas. Men of the two vehicles cannot apprehend it, and even bodhisattvas of the ten stages cannot attain it. Only a buddha together with a buddha can fathom it well.[5]

"Good sons! Thereupon I say: the Sutra of Innumerable Meanings, the wonderful, profound, and supreme Great-vehicle, is reasonable in its logic, unsurpassed in its worth, and protected by all the buddhas of the three worlds. No kind of demon or heretic can break into it, nor can any wrong view or life and death destroy it. Bodhisattva-mahāsattvas, if you want to accomplish supreme buddhahood quickly, you should learn and master the Sutra of Innumerable Meanings, such a profound and supreme Great-vehicle."

After the Buddha had finished explaining this, the three-thousand-great-thousandfold world was shaken in the six ways; various kinds of celestial flowers, such as utpala, padma, kumuda, and puṇḍarīka, rained down naturally from the sky; and innumerable kinds of celestial perfumes, robes, garlands, and treasures of priceless value also

5. It can only be comprehended by one who has reached the buddha degree, that is, the highest degree of enlightenment.

rained and came rolling down from the sky, and they were offered to the Buddha, all the bodhisattvas and śrāvakas, and the great assembly. The celestial bins and bowls were filled with all sorts of celestial delicacies; celestial banners, flags, canopies, and playthings were placed everywhere; and celestial music was played in praise of the Buddha.

Also the buddha-worlds, as many as the sands of the Ganges, in the direction of the east were shaken in the six ways; celestial flowers, perfumes, robes, garlands, and treasures of priceless value, celestial bins, bowls, and all sorts of celestial delicacies, celestial banners, flags, canopies, and playthings rained down; and celestial music was played in praise of those buddhas, those bodhisattvas, the śrāvakas, and the great assembly. So, too, was it in the southern, western, and northern quarters, in the four intermediate directions, in the zenith and nadir.

At this time thirty-two thousand bodhisattva-mahāsattvas in the assembly attained to the contemplation of the Innumerable Meanings. Thirty-four thousand bodhisattva-mahāsattvas obtained the numberless and infinite realms of dhāraṇī and came to roll the never retrogressing Law-wheel of buddhas all over the three worlds. All the bhikshus, bhikshuṇīs, upāsakas, upāsikās, gods, dragons, yakshas, gandharvas, asuras, garuḍas, kiṃnaras, mahoragas, great wheel-rolling kings, small wheel-rolling kings, kings of the silver wheel, iron wheel, and other wheels, kings and princes, ministers and people, men and women, and great rich persons, and all the groups of a hundred thousand followers, hearing together the Buddha Tathāgata preaching this sutra, obtained the law of warming, the law of the highest, the law of the best in the world, the merit of srota-āpanna, the merit of sakṛdāgāmin, the merit of anāgāmin, the merit of arhat, and the merit of pratyekabuddha; attained to the bodhisattva's assurance of the law of no birth;[6] acquired one dhāraṇī, two dhāraṇīs, three dhāraṇīs, four dhāraṇīs, five, six, seven, eight, nine, ten dhāraṇīs, a hundred thousand myriad koṭis of dhāraṇīs, and asaṃkhyeya dhāraṇīs as innumerable as the sands of the Ganges; and all came to roll the never-retrogressing Law-wheel rightly. Infinite living beings gained the aspiration to Perfect Enlightenment.

6. Transcendence of life and death.

CHAPTER III

Ten Merits

AT THAT TIME the Bodhisattva-Mahāsattva Great Adornment said to the Buddha again: "World-honored One! The World-honored One has preached this Sutra of Innumerable Meanings, a wonderful, profound, and supreme Great-vehicle. It is truly profound, profound, and profound. Wherefore? In this assembly, all the bodhisattva-mahāsattvas, all the four groups, gods, dragons, demons, kings, subjects, and all the living beings, hearing this Sutra of Innumerable Meanings, a profound and supreme Great-vehicle, never fail to obtain the realm of dhāraṇīs, the three laws, the four merits, and the aspiration to enlightenment. It should be known that this Law is reasonable in its logic, unsurpassed in its worth, and protected by all the buddhas of the three worlds. No kind of demon or heretic can break into it, nor can any wrong view or life and death destroy it. Wherefore? Because hearing [it] but once is keeping all the laws.

"If a living being can hear this sutra, he will acquire a great benefit. Wherefore? If he practices it sincerely, he will quickly accomplish supreme buddhahood without fail. If a living being cannot hear [it], it should be known that he loses a great benefit. He will never accomplish supreme buddhahood even after a lapse of infinite, boundless, inconceivable asaṃkhyeya kalpas. Wherefore? Because he does not know the great direct way to enlightenment, he meets with many sufferings in walking steep ways.

"World-honored One! This sutra is inconceivable. World-honored One! Be pleased to explain the profound and inconceivable matter of this sutra out of benevolence for all the people. World-honored One! From what place does this sutra come? For what place does it leave? At what place does it stay? Whereupon does this sutra make people quickly accomplish Perfect Enlightenment, having such infinite merits and inconceivable powers?"

At that time the World-honored One addressed the Bodhisattva-Mahāsattva Great Adornment: "Excellent! Excellent! Good sons; just so, just so, just as you say. Good sons! I preach this sutra as profound, profound, and truly profound. Wherefore? Because it makes people quickly accomplish supreme buddhahood; hearing [it] but once is keeping all the laws; it greatly benefits all the living; there is no suffering in practicing the great direct way. Good sons! You ask where this sutra comes from, where it leaves for, and where it stays. Do listen attentively. Good sons! This sutra originally comes from the abode of all the buddhas, leaves for the aspiration of all the living to buddhahood, and stays at the place where all the bodhisattvas practice. Good sons! This sutra comes like this, leaves like this, and stays like this. Therefore this sutra, having such infinite merits and inconceivable powers, makes people quickly accomplish supreme buddhahood.

"Good sons! Do you want to hear how this sutra has ten inconceivable merit-powers?" The Bodhisattva Great Adornment said: "We heartily want to hear." The Buddha said: "Good sons! First, this sutra makes the unawakened bodhisattva aspire to buddhahood, makes a merciless one raise the mind of mercy, makes a homicidal one raise the mind of great compassion, makes a jealous one raise the mind of joy, makes an attached one raise the mind of detachment, makes a miserly one raise the mind of donation, makes an arrogant one raise the mind of keeping the commandments, makes an irascible one raise the mind of perseverance, makes an indolent one raise the mind of assiduity, makes a distracted one raise the mind of meditation, makes an ignorant one raise the mind of wisdom, makes one who lacks concern for saving others raise the mind of saving others, makes one who commits the ten evils raise the mind of the ten virtues, makes one who wishes for existence aspire to the mind of nonexistence, makes one who has an inclination toward apostasy build the mind of nonretrogression, makes one who commits defiled acts raise the mind of undefilement, and makes one who suffers from delusions raise the mind of detachment. Good sons! This is called the first inconceivable merit-power of this sutra.

"Good sons! Secondly, the inconceivable merit-power of this sutra is as follows: if a living being can hear this sutra but once, or only one verse and phrase, he will penetrate into a hundred thousand koṭis of meanings, and the law kept by him cannot be explained fully even in infinite kalpas. Wherefore? It is because this sutra has innumerable meanings.

"Good sons! Suppose that from one seed a hundred thousand myriad seeds grow, from each of a hundred thousand myriad seeds another hundred thousand myriad seeds grow, and in such a process seeds increase to an unlimited extent. This sutra is like this. From one law a hundred thousand meanings grow, from each of a hundred thousand meanings a hundred thousand myriad meanings grow, and in such a process meanings increase to an unlimited and boundless extent. Such being the case, this sutra is called Innumerable Meanings. Good sons! This is the second inconceivable merit-power of this sutra.

"Good sons! Thirdly, the inconceivable merit-power of this sutra is as follows: if a living being can hear this sutra but once, or only one verse and phrase, he will penetrate into a hundred thousand myriad koṭis of meanings. After that, his delusions, even though existent, will become as if nonexistent; he will not be seized with fear, though he moves between birth and death; and he will raise the mind of compassion for all the living, and obtain the spirit of bravery to obey all the laws. A powerful wrestler can shoulder and hold any heavy thing. The keeper of this sutra is also like this. He can shoulder the heavy treasure of supreme buddhahood, and carry living beings on his back out of the way of birth and death. He will be able to relieve others, even though he cannot yet relieve himself. Just as a ferry master, though he stays on this shore owing to his serious illness and unsettled body, can be made to cross over by means of a good and solid ship that has the quality of carrying anyone without fail, so also is it with the keeper of this sutra. Though he stays on this shore of ignorance, old age, and death owing to the hundred and eight kinds of serious illness,[1] with which his body under the existence of all the five states is seized and ever afflicted, he can be delivered from birth and death through practicing this strong Mahayana Sutra of Innumerable Meanings as it is preached, which realizes the deliverance of living beings. Good sons! This is called the third inconceivable merit-power of this sutra.

"Good sons! Fourthly, the inconceivable merit-power of this sutra is as follows: if a living being can hear this sutra but once, or only one verse and phrase, he will obtain the spirit of bravery, and relieve others, even though he cannot yet relieve himself. He will become the attendant [of the buddhas] together with all the bodhisattvas, and all the buddha-tathāgatas will always preach the Law to him. On hearing [it], he will keep the Law entirely and follow it without disobeying. Moreover, he will interpret it for people extensively as occasion calls.

"Good sons! Suppose that a new prince is born of a king and a queen. A day, two days, or seven days, and a month, two months, or seven months passing away, he will attain the age of one, two, or seven. Though he cannot yet manage national affairs, he will come to be revered by people and take all the great king's sons into his company. The king and the queen will always stay and converse with him with special and deep affection because he is their little child. Good sons! The keeper of this sutra is also like this. The king—the buddha—and the queen—this sutra—come together, and this son—a bodhisattva—is born of them. If the bodhisattva can hear one phrase or verse of this sutra once, twice, ten times, a hundred times, a thousand times, myriad times, myriad koṭis of times, or innumerable and numberless times like the sands of the Ganges, he will come to shake the three-thousand-great-thousandfold world, though he cannot yet realize the ultimate truth, and will take all great bodhisattvas into his attendance, while being admired by all of the four classes and the eight guardians, though he cannot yet roll the great Law-wheel with the sacred voice like the roll of thunder. Entering deeply into the secret law of the buddhas, he will interpret it without error or fault. He will always be protected by all the buddhas, and especially covered with affection,

1. The one hundred and eight illusions, or obstacles to enlightenment.

because he is a beginner in learning. Good sons! This is called the fourth inconceivable merit-power of this sutra.

"Good sons! Fifthly, the inconceivable merit-power of this sutra is as follows: if good sons or good daughters keep, read, recite, and copy the Sutra of Innumerable Meanings, such a profound and supreme Great-vehicle, either during the Buddha's lifetime or after his extinction, they will realize the way of great bodhisattvas though they cannot yet be delivered from all the faults of an ordinary man and are still wrapped in delusions. They will fill with joy and convince those living beings, extending a day to a hundred kalpas, or shortening a hundred kalpas to a day. Good sons! These good sons or good daughters are just like a dragon's son who can raise clouds and cause a rainfall seven days after his birth. Good sons! This is called the fifth inconceivable merit-power of this sutra.

"Good sons! Sixthly, the inconceivable merit-power of this sutra is as follows: if good sons or good daughters keep, read, and recite this sutra either during the Buddha's lifetime or after his extinction, even though clothed in delusions, they will deliver living beings from the life and death of delusions, and make them overcome all sufferings, by preaching the Law for them. After hearing it, living beings will put it into practice, and attain the law, the merit, and the way, where there will be equality and no difference from the Buddha Tathāgata. Suppose that a king, in journeying or falling ill, leaves the management of national affairs to his prince, though he is an infant. Then the prince, by order of the great king, leads all the government officials according to the law, and propagates the right policy, so that every citizen of the country follows his orders exactly as if the king were governing. It is the same with good sons or good daughters keeping this sutra. During the Buddha's lifetime or after his extinction, these good sons will propagate the doctrine, preaching exactly as the Buddha did, though they themselves cannot yet live in the first stage of immobility, and if living beings, after hearing [their preaching], practice it intently, they will cut off delusions and attain the law, the merit, and the way. Good sons! This is called the sixth inconceivable merit-power of this sutra.

"Good sons! Seventhly, the inconceivable merit-power of this sutra is as follows: if good sons or good daughters, hearing this sutra either during the Buddha's lifetime or after his extinction, rejoice, believe, and raise the rare[2] mind; keep, read, recite, copy, and expound it; practice it as it has been preached; aspire to buddhahood; cause all the good roots to sprout; raise the mind of great compassion; and want to relieve all living beings of sufferings, the Six Pāramitās will be naturally present in them, though they cannot yet practice the Six Pāramitās. They will attain the assurance of the law of no birth in their bodies; life and death, and delusions will be instantly destroyed; and they will rise to the seventh stage of bodhisattva.

"Suppose there is a vigorous man who tries to destroy an enemy on behalf of his king and after the enemy has been destroyed, with great joy, the king gives him half the kingdom as a prize. Good sons or good daughters who keep this sutra are like this. They are the most vigorous of all ascetics. They come to attain the Law-treasure of the Six Pāramitās even though they are not consciously seeking it. The enemy of death and life will be naturally destroyed, and they will be made comfortable by the prize of a fief, realizing the assurance of no birth as the treasure of half the buddha-country. Good sons! This is called the seventh inconceivable merit-power of this sutra.

"Good sons! Eighthly, the inconceivable merit-power of this sutra is as follows: if good sons or good daughters, either during the Buddha's lifetime or after his extinction, see someone who has received this sutra, they will make him revere and believe it exactly as if he saw the body of the Buddha; they will keep, read, recite, copy, and worship this sutra with joy; serve and practice it as the Law; firmly keep the commandments and perseverance; they will also practice almsgiving; raise a deep benevolence; and explain the Sutra of Innumerable Meanings, this supreme Great-vehicle, widely to others. To one who for a long time does not at all recognize the existence of sinfulness and blessedness, they will show this sutra, and force him to have faith in it with all sorts of expedients. By the strong power of the sutra, he will be made to stir up faith and to convert suddenly. After stirring up faith, he will endeavor so valorously that he can acquire the virtue and power of this sutra, and attain the way and the merit. In this way, these good sons or good daughters will attain the assurance of the law of no birth in their bodies of men or women by the merit of having

2. Rare because extraordinary.

been enlightened, reach the upper stage, become the attendants [of the buddhas], together with all the bodhisattvas convert living beings quickly, purify buddha-lands, and attain supreme buddhahood before long. Good sons! This is called the eighth inconceivable merit-power of this sutra.

"Good sons! Ninthly, the inconceivable merit-power of this sutra is as follows: if good sons or good daughters, receiving this sutra either during the Buddha's lifetime or after his extinction, leap for joy; acquire the unprecedented; keep, read, recite, copy, and adore this sutra; and explain its meaning discriminatingly and widely for living beings, they will instantly destroy the heavy barrier of sins resulting from previous karma and become purified, acquire great eloquence, gradually realize all pāramitās, accomplish all samādhis and śūraṃgama-samādhi, enter the great gate of dhāraṇī, and rise up to the upper stage quickly with strenuous efforts. They will spread their divided bodies in all the lands of ten directions, and relieve and emancipate entirely all living beings who suffer greatly in the twenty-five abodes. Thus such a power can be seen in this sutra. Good sons! This is called the ninth inconceivable merit-power of this sutra.

"Good sons! Tenthly, the inconceivable merit-power of this sutra is as follows: if good sons or good daughters, receiving this sutra either during the Buddha's lifetime or after his extinction, greatly rejoice; raise the rare mind; keep, read, recite, copy, and adore this sutra of their own accord; practice it as it has been preached; also induce many monks and lay people to keep, read, recite, copy, adore, and expound this sutra, and practice it as the Law, these good sons or good daughters will obtain the innumerable realms of dhāraṇī in their bodies because it is wholly by the merciful and friendly instruction of these good sons or good daughters that other people attain the way and the merit through the power of the practice of this sutra. They will make vast oaths and great vows of numberless asaṃkhyeya naturally and from the beginning in the stage of ordinary men, and raise a deep desire to relieve all living beings. They will realize the great compassion, thoroughly abolish all sufferings, gather many good roots, and bring benefit to all. They will explain the favor of the Law and greatly enliven the withered; give all living beings the medicine of the Law, and set all at ease; gradually elevate their view to live in the stage of the Law-cloud.[3] They will spread favor extensively, grant mercy to all suffering living beings, and lead them into the [Buddha-] way. Thereupon these persons[4] will accomplish Perfect Enlightenment before long. Good sons! This is called the tenth inconceivable merit-power of this sutra.

"Good sons! The Sutra of Innumerable Meanings, such a supreme Great-vehicle, has an extremely great divine power and is unsurpassed in its worth. It makes all ordinary men accomplish the sacred merit, and makes them free from life and death forever. Thereupon this sutra is called Innumerable Meanings. It makes all the living sprout the innumerable ways of all the bodhisattvas in the stage of ordinary men, and makes the tree of merit grow dense, thick, and tall. Therefore this sutra is called inconceivable merit-power."

At that time the Bodhisattva-Mahāsattva Great Adornment, with the eighty thousand bodhisattva-mahāsattvas, said to the Buddha with one voice: "World-honored One! The Sutra of Innumerable Meanings, such a profound, wonderful, and supreme Great-vehicle preached by the Buddha, is reasonable in its logic, unsurpassed in its worth, and protected by all the buddhas of the three worlds. No kind of demon or heretic can break into it, nor can any wrong view or life and death destroy it. Thereupon this sutra has ten such inconceivable merit-powers. It greatly benefits innumerable living beings, makes all bodhisattva-mahāsattvas attain the contemplation of Innumerable Meanings, a hundred thousand realms of dhāraṇī, all the stages and assurances of bodhisattva, and the accomplishment of the four way-merits of pratyekabuddha and arhat. The World-honored One has preached such a Law willingly for us in compassion, and made us obtain the benefits of the Law abundantly. This is immensely marvelous and unprecedented. It is difficult to repay the merciful favor of the World-honored One."

At the close of these words, the three-thousand-great-thousandfold world was shaken in the six ways;[5] various kinds of celestial flowers,

3. The stage of the Law-cloud is the tenth and highest of the ten stages of the bodhisattva-way.

4. Good sons and daughters.

5. The six ways are moving, rising, springing, trembling, reverberating, and thudding.

such as utpala, padma, kumuda, and puṇḍarīka, rained down from the sky; and numberless kinds of celestial perfumes, robes, garlands, and treasures of priceless value also rained and came rolling down from the sky, and they were offered to the Buddha, all the bodhisattvas and śrāvakas, and the great assembly. The celestial bins and bowls were filled with all manner of celestial delicacies, which gave satisfaction naturally to anyone who [just] saw them and smelled their perfume. The celestial banners, flags, canopies, and playthings were placed everywhere, and celestial music was played in praise of the Buddha.

Also the buddha-worlds, as numerous as the sands of the Ganges, in the east were shaken in the six ways; celestial flowers, perfumes, robes, garlands, and treasures of priceless value rained down; the celestial bins and bowls, and all sorts of celestial delicacies gave satisfaction naturally to anyone who [just] saw them and smelled their perfume. The celestial banners, flags, canopies, and playthings were placed everywhere, and celestial music was played in praise of those buddhas, those bodhisattvas and śrāvakas, and the great assembly. So, too, was it in the southern, western, and northern quarters, in the four intermediate directions, in the zenith and nadir.

At that time the Buddha addressed the Bodhisattva-Mahāsattva Great Adornment and the eighty thousand bodhisattva-mahāsattvas: "You should entertain a deep respect for this sutra, practice it as the Law, instruct all widely, and propagate it earnestly. You should protect it heartily day and night, and make all living beings obtain the benefits of the Law. This is truly great mercy and great compassion, so, offering the divine power of a vow, you should protect this sutra and not let anybody put obstacles in its way. Then you should have it practiced widely in Jambudvīpa, and make all the living observe, read, recite, copy, and adore it without fail. Because of this you will be made to attain Perfect Enlightenment rapidly."

At this time the Bodhisattva-Mahāsattva Great Adornment rose up from his seat, went up to the Buddha with the eighty thousand bodhisattva-mahāsattvas, made obeisance at his feet, a hundred thousand times made procession round him, and then going forth to kneel, said to the Buddha with one voice: "World-honored One! We have been placed under the mercy of the World-honored One to our delight. The Sutra of Innumerable Meanings, this profound, wonderful, and supreme Great-vehicle, has been preached for us. We will widely propagate this sutra after the Tathāgata's extinction in obedience to the Buddha's command, and let all keep, read, recite, copy, and adore it. Be pleased to have no anxiety! With the vow-power, we will let all the living observe, read, recite, copy, and adore this sutra, and acquire the marvelous merit of this sutra."

At that time the Buddha said in praise: "Excellent! Excellent! All good sons; you are really and truly the Buddha's sons. You are persons who abolish sufferings and remove calamities thoroughly with great mercy and great compassion. You are the good field of blessings for all living beings. You have been the great good leaders extensively for all. You are the great support for all living beings. You are the great benefactors of all living beings. Always bestow the benefits of the Law extensively on all."

At that time all in the great assembly, greatly rejoicing together, made salutation to the Buddha and, taking possession [of the sutra], withdrew.

The Sutra of the Lotus Flower of the Wonderful Law

translated by
Bunno Kato
with revisions by
W. E. Soothill
Wilhelm Schiffer
Yoshiro Tamura

CHAPTER I

Introductory

THUS HAVE I HEARD. Once the Buddha was staying at the City of Royal Palaces on Mount Gṛdhrakūṭa with a great assemblage of great bhikshus, in all twelve thousand; all [of them] arhats, faultless, free from [earthly] cares, self-developed, emancipated from all bonds of existence, and free in mind. Their names were Ājñāta-Kauṇḍinya, Mahā-Kāśyapa, Uruvilvā-Kāśyapa, Gayā-Kāśyapa, Nadī-Kāśyapa, Śāriputra, Mahā-Maudgalyāyana, Mahā-Kātyāyana, Aniruddha, Kapphiṇa, Gavāṃpati, Revata, Pilindavasta, Vakkula, Mahā-Kaushthila, Nanda,[1] Sundara-Nanda, Pūrṇa son of Maitrāyaṇī,[2] Subhūti, Ānanda, and Rāhula—all such great arhats are well known to everybody. In addition there were two thousand under training and no longer under training;[3] the bhikshuṇī Mahāprajāpatī, with six thousand followers; the bhikshuṇī Yaśodharā, the mother of

The title of this chapter consists of the two words *hsü* 序, "introduction," and *p'in* 品, "grade, degree, kind." As an introduction to the entire sutra this chapter includes (1) the order of the sutra, (2) the origin or scene of the revelation, and (3) the statement of the doctrine of the sutra. Each chapter is styled a *p'in,* as each treats of its own subject.

1. Or Mahā-Nanda. 2. Or "Pūrṇa Maitrāyaṇī *putra.*"

3. *Śaiksha* and *aśaiksha,* that is, undergraduates and graduates.

Rāhula, also with her train; there were eighty thousand bodhisattva-mahāsattvas, all free from backsliding in regard to Perfect Enlightenment, all having obtained dhāraṇī, [all] endowed with knowledge of eloquent discourse,[4] and rolling the never-retrogressing wheel of the Law; who had paid homage to countless hundreds of thousands of buddhas, under whom they had planted all the roots of virtue, constantly being extolled by them; who cultivated themselves by charity, entered well into the Buddha-wisdom, penetrated the greatest knowledge, and reached the other shore;[5] whose fame became universally heard in innumerable worlds, they being able to save numberless hundreds of thousands of living beings. Their names were the Bodhisattva Mañjuśrī, the Bodhisattva Regarder of the Cries of the World, the Bodhisattva Great Power Obtained, the Bodhisattva Ever Zealous, the Bodhisattva Never Stopping, the Bodhisattva Precious Palm [of the Hand], the Bodhisattva Medicine King, the Bodhisattva Bold Almsgiver, the Bodhisattva Precious Moon, the Bodhisattva Moon Light, the Bodhisattva Full Moon, the Bodhisattva Great Power, the Bodhisattva Infinite Power, the Bodhisattva Above the Triple World, the Bodhisattva Bhadrapāla, the Bodhisattva Maitreya, the Bodhisattva Precious Store, and the Bodhisattva Leader: such bodhisattva-mahāsattvas as these, eighty thousand in all. At that time there was Śakra Devendra with his following of twenty thousand divine sons; there were also the Divine Son Excellent Moon, the Divine Son Universal Fragrance, the Divine Son Precious Light, and the four great heavenly kings with ten thousand divine sons in their train; the god Sovereign and the god Great Sovereign,[6] followed by thirty thousand divine sons; Brahma Heavenly King,[7] the lord of the sahā-world, Great Brahma Śikhin[8] and Great Brahma Light,[9] and others, with their following of twelve thousand divine sons. There were [also] the

4. One of the four *pratisaṃvids,* or four unlimited forms of wisdom: (1) *dharma-pratisaṃvid,* unlimited knowledge of the Law; (2) *artha-pratisaṃvid,* unlimited knowledge of principles; (3) *nirukti-pratisaṃvid,* unlimited knowledge of terms or arguments; and (4) *pratibhāna-pratisaṃvid,* unlimited knowledge of pleasant discourse.

5. The shore of enlightenment beyond the sea of mortality.

6. The deities in the fifth and the sixth (and highest) heavens of the Realm of Desire, respectively.

7. The deity in the first of the four meditation heavens in the Realm of Form.

8. Śikhin is another name of Brahma Heavenly King.

9. The deity in the second of the four meditation heavens in the Realm of Form.

eight dragon kings:[10] Nanda Dragon King, Upananda Dragon King, Sāgara Dragon King, Vāsuki Dragon King, Takshaka Dragon King, Anavatapta Dragon King, Manasvin Dragon King, and Utpalaka Dragon King, each with some hundred thousand followers: further, the four kiṃnara kings: Law Kiṃnara King, Mystic Law Kiṃnara King, Great Law Kiṃnara King, and Law-maintaining Kiṃnara King, each with some hundred thousand followers; besides, the four gandharva kings: Pleasing Gandharva King, Pleasant Sound Gandharva King, Charming Gandharva King, and Charming Sound Gandharva King, each with some hundred thousand followers; further, the four asura kings: Balin Asura King, Kharaskandha Asura King, Vemacitri Asura King, and Rāhu Asura King, each with some hundred thousand followers; also the four garuḍa kings: the Garuḍa King Great in Dignity, the Garuḍa King Great in Body, the Garuḍa King Great in Fullness, and the Garuḍa King Absolute at Will, each with some hundred thousand followers; and King Ajātaśatru, son of Vaidehī,[11] with some hundred thousand followers. Each worshiped at the Buddha's feet, retired, and sat to one side.

At that time the World-honored One, surrounded, worshiped, revered, honored, and extolled by the four groups, preached, for the sake of all the bodhisattvas, the Great-vehicle sutra called Innumerable Meanings, the Law by which bodhisattvas are instructed and which the buddhas watch over and keep in mind. Having preached this sutra, the Buddha sat cross-legged and entered the contemplation termed the station of innumerable meanings,[12] in which his body and mind were motionless. At this time the sky rained mandārava, mahā-mandārava, mañjūshaka, and mahā-mañjūshaka flowers over the Buddha and all the great assembly, while the universal buddha-world shook in six ways. Then in the congregation bhikshus, bhikshuṇīs, upāsakas, upāsikās, gods, dragons, yakshas, gandharvas, asuras, garuḍas, kiṃnaras, mahoragas, human and nonhuman beings, as well as minor kings and the holy wheel-rolling kings: all of this assembly, obtaining that which had never been before, with joy and folded hands and with one mind looked up to the Buddha. Then the Buddha

10. Rulers of the waters.

11. The wife of King Bimbisāra.

12. Here the Buddha contemplates the truth that the boundless principles come forth from the one Law, that is, the Wonderful Law revealed in the Lotus Sutra.

sent forth from the circle of white hair between his eyebrows[13] a ray of light, which illuminated eighteen thousand worlds in the eastern quarter, so that there was nowhere it did not reach, downward to the Avīci hell and upward to the Akanishthā heaven. In this world were seen in those lands all their living creatures in the six states of existence; likewise were seen the buddhas existing at present in those lands; and there could be heard the sutra-laws those buddhas were preaching; there could also be seen there bhikshus, bhikshuṇīs, upāsakas, and upāsikās who had practiced and attained the Way; further were seen the bodhisattva-mahāsattvas, who walked the bodhisattva-way from various causes, with various discernments in faith, and with various appearances;[14] likewise were seen the buddhas who had entered final nirvana; and there were seen the stupas made of the precious seven for the relics of the buddhas, which were erected after the buddhas entered final nirvana.

At that time Maitreya Bodhisattva reflected thus: "Now does the World-honored One display an appearance so marvelous. What is the cause and reason of this auspicious sign? Now that the Buddha, the World-honored One, has entered into his contemplation and such inconceivable and unprecedented [wonders] appear, of whom shall I inquire, and who will be able to answer?" Again, he reflected thus: "Here is Mañjuśrī, the son of the Law-king, who has been in close contact with and paid homage to former innumerable buddhas, and who must have witnessed such unprecedented signs as these. Let me now ask him."

Then [also] the bhikshus, bhikshuṇīs, upāsakas, upāsikās, and all the heavenly beings, dragons, and other spirits reflected thus: "Of whom shall we now inquire concerning this shining spiritual sign of the Buddha?"

Then Maitreya Bodhisattva, desiring to resolve his own doubts and observing the thoughts [arising] in all the assembly of the four groups of bhikshus, bhikshuṇīs, upāsakas,and upāsikās, as well as the heavenly beings, dragons, and other spirits, inquired of Mañjuśrī, saying: "What are the cause and reason of this auspicious and spiritual sign, shedding so great a luminous ray, lighting up the eighteen thousand

13. The *ūrṇa*. This circle of hair issues rays of light that illuminate every universe. It is one of thirty-two signs possessed by every buddha.

14. The various aspects of practice.

eastern lands, revealing in detail the splendor of those buddha-realms?"

Thereupon Maitreya Bodhisattva, desiring to announce this meaning over again, inquired thus in verse:

"Mañjuśrī!
Why does [our] master
From the white hair between his eyebrows
Universally radiate so great a ray?
The rain of mandārava
And mañjūshaka flowers
And fragrant breezes of sandal
Delight [our] every heart.
By reason of this
All the earth is replete with splendor,
While this [whole] world
Shakes in six [different] ways.
At this moment the four groups
Are all full of joy,
Glad in body and in mind
To obtain [a sign so] unprecedented.
The ray between his brows
Illuminates the eastern quarter
Of the eighteen thousand lands,
Coloring them all with gold.[15]
From the Avīci hell
Up to the Summit of All Existence,
[The dwellers] in all the worlds,
The living beings in their six states,
The progress of those being born and of the dying,
Their good and evil karma and environment,[16]
The retribution, good or evil,
I see them all from here.
I see also the buddhas,
The holy masters, the lions,[17]

15. Gold is a symbol of enlightenment.

16. Karma is the immediate cause of weal or woe in any succeeding state. Environment is the secondary cause. 17. *Vādisimha,* "holy lion lord"; also translated as "lion of the Law," meaning fearless in teaching the Law; an epithet of the Buddha.

Expounding the sutra,
Mystic and supreme;
Their voices clear and pure
Send forth softly sounding tones,
Teaching the bodhisattvas
In numberless myriad koṭis;
Their sacred voices, deep and mystic,
Cause men to rejoice in hearing;
Each in his own world,
Proclaiming the good Law
By various reasonings
And innumerable illustrations,
Reveals the Buddha-law
And opens the understanding of all creatures.
If any have met with distress
And are weary of age, disease, and death,
For these they announce nirvana
To bring to an end all distresses.
If any are in a happy estate,
Having paid homage to buddhas,
Devoted to seeking the victorious Law,
For these they announce pratyekabuddhahood.
If any Buddha-sons
Have carried out their various duties,
Seeking after the supreme wisdom,
For those they announce the pure way.
Mañjuśrī!
Abiding here,
I see and hear such things as these
And thousands of koṭis of things;
These things so numerous
Let me now briefly describe.
I see in those lands
Bodhisattvas like the sands of the Ganges,
Who in various degrees
Seek after the Buddha-way.
Some there are who give alms of

Gold, silver, and coral,
Pearls[18] and jewels,
Moonstones and agates,[19]
Diamonds and precious stones,
Male and female slaves, carriages and animals to ride,
Wagons and litters gem-adorned.
They give all these alms with joy
And, turning toward the Buddha-way,
Seek to gain this vehicle,
The supreme in the triple world,
Magnified by the buddhas.
Besides, there are bodhisattvas
Who give precious four-horse carriages
With railed [seats] and ornate covers
And [other] adorned vehicles as alms.
Also I see bodhisattvas
Who give their own flesh, hands, and feet,
And their wives and children, as alms,
To seek after the supreme Way.
Again I see bodhisattvas
Who give their own heads, eyes, and bodies,
Cheerfully and gladly, as alms,
To seek after the wisdom of the Buddha.
Mañjuśrī!
I see many kings
Who go to visit the buddhas
To ask about the supreme Way,
And then abandon their pleasant lands,
Palaces, ministers, and concubines,
And shaving beard and hair,
Put on the robes of the Law.
I see also bodhisattvas
Who become bhikshus,

18. Literally, "felicitous pearls"; pearls are always bright and luminous, therefore a symbol of the Buddha and of his doctrines.

19. These constitute the so-called precious seven, of which several combinations exist. See Glossary.

Live alone in seclusion and quiet,
And take their joy in reciting sutras.
And I see bodhisattvas
Who in their zeal and earnestness
Enter the depths of the mountains
To ponder the Buddha-way.
I see also those who, renouncing [all] desires,
Constantly dwell in the seclusion of the wilds,
Profoundly to practice meditation
And obtain the five transcendent faculties.
Further I see bodhisattvas
Peacefully meditating with folded hands
And in myriads of stanzas
Extolling the kings of the Law.
Again I see bodhisattvas,
Profound in wisdom, firm in will,
Able to question the buddhas
And receive and retain all they hear.
And I see Buddha-sons,
Perfect in meditation and wisdom,
With innumerable illustrations
Proclaiming the Law for the multitude,
Cheerfully and gladly preaching the Law
To transform bodhisattvas,
And, destroying the army of Māra,
Strike the drum of the Law.
I see also bodhisattvas,
Calm in perfect meditation,
Who, though honored by gods and dragons,
Count it not a joy.
Again I see bodhisattvas
Who, dwelling in forests, emit radiance
That saves the sufferers in hell
And causes them to enter the Buddha-way.
I see also Buddha-sons
Who, unsleeping,
Walk about in the forest,
Diligently seeking the Buddha-way.

Further I see perfect [observers of the] commandments,
In strictness without flaw,
Pure as precious pearls,
Who thereby seek the Buddha-way.
And I see Buddha-sons
Who, abiding in the power of perseverance,
[Though] men of the utmost arrogance
Hate, abuse, and beat them,
Are able to endure all of these
In order to seek the Buddha-way.
I see also bodhisattvas
Who leave all play and laughter
And all foolish companions,
Who seek association with the wise,
And with all their mind get rid of distraction,
Concentrating their thoughts in mountain forests
For myriads of koṭis of years,
To seek the Buddha-way.
Or I see bodhisattvas
Who bestow edibles, dainties, drink and food,
And all kinds of medicaments
On buddhas and monks as alms;
Who give famous clothes and superior garments
Worth thousands and myriads,
Or clothes of priceless value,
To buddhas and monks as alms;
Who give myriads of koṭis of kinds
Of precious buildings built of sandalwood,
With all sorts of wonderful bed furniture,
To buddhas and monks as alms;
Who give immaculate gardens
Abounding with flowers and fruits,
With flowing springs and bathing pools,
To buddhas and monks as alms;
Who give alms like these,
Every kind most wonderful,
Joyfully without grudging,
Seeking after the supreme Way.

Moreover, there are bodhisattvas
Who preach the Law of tranquillity,
Teaching in various ways
The numberless living beings.
Also I see bodhisattvas
Who observe that the nature of all laws
Is not in two [opposing] forms,[20]
But like space.
Again I see Buddha-sons,
With minds free from attachments,
By this mystic wisdom
Seeking after the supreme Way.
Mañjuśrī!
There are also bodhisattvas
Who, after the extinction of buddhas,
Pay homage to [their] relics.
Also I see Buddha-sons
Who build numerous stupas,
Innumerable as the sands of the Ganges,
Splendidly adorning the domains,
Precious stupas of height most wonderful,
Five thousand yojanas,
Their height and breadth proportionate,
Two thousand yojanas [around];
Each of those stupas
Has thousands of banners and flags,
Curtains decorated with jewels,
And precious bells harmoniously sounding;
Gods, dragons, and other spirits,
Human beings and beings not human
With perfumes, flowers, and music
Are always paying homage [to them].
Mañjuśrī!
All the Buddha-sons
For worshiping the relics
So splendidly adorn the stupas

20. The two forms are existence and nonexistence. These bodhisattvas realize the law of undifferentiation, or the Middle Path.

That all the domains are thereby
Made extraordinarily wonderful and fine,
Like the king of celestial trees
In full bloom.
The Buddha sends forth but a single ray
And I with all the assembly
See that these domains
Are extraordinarily wonderful.
Rare are the divine powers
And wisdom of the buddhas;
Sending forth a single pure ray,
They illuminate innumerable domains.
We, beholding this,
Attain that which has never been before.
Son of Buddha, Mañjuśrī,
Do you resolve all their doubts!
All of the four groups, joyfully expecting,
Gaze on [thee], O virtuous one, and on me.
Why has the World-honored One
Emitted such a ray of light?
Son of Buddha! Now give answer;
Remove our doubts and make us glad.
For what abundant benefits
Has he spread such a ray of light?
Seated on the wisdom throne,
The Wonderful Law which he has obtained—
Does the Buddha [now] wish to preach it?
Is he [now] going to prophesy?[21]
He shows us all the buddha-lands,
Ornate and pure with precious things,
And we see the buddhas [there];
This is not for any trivial reason.
Know, Mañjuśrī!
All the four groups, the dragons and spirits
Are gazing on and questioning thee
As to what thou wilt say."

21. This refers to the Buddha's prediction of future recompense for those who are endeavoring to attain buddhahood.

At that time Mañjuśrī spoke to Maitreya Bodhisattva-Mahāsattva and all the other leaders:[22] "All ye good sons! According to my consideration, the Buddha, the World-honored One, is now intending to preach the great Law, to pour the rain of the great Law, to blow the conch of the great Law, to beat the drum of the great Law, and to expound the meaning of the great Law. All ye good sons! Whenever from any of the former buddhas I have seen this auspice, after emitting such a ray, they have thereupon preached the great Law. Because of this, know ye that now the Buddha, having displayed this ray, in like manner intends to cause all creatures to hear and know the Law which all the worlds will find hard to believe. That is why he displays this auspice.

"All ye good sons! In time of yore, infinite, boundless, inconceivable asaṃkhyeya kalpas ago, there then was a buddha styled Sun Moon Light Tathāgata, Worshipful, All Wise, Perfectly Enlightened in Conduct,[23] Well Departed,[24] Understander of the World, Peerless Leader,[25] Controller,[26] Teacher of Gods and Men, Buddha, World-honored One.[27] He proclaimed the Right Law, which is good at its commencement, good in its middle, and good at the end; which is profound in its meaning, subtle in its terms, pure and unadulterated, perfect, flawless, and noble in practice.[28] For those who sought to be śrāvakas he preached response to the Law of the Four Noble Truths for the overcoming of birth, old age, disease, and death, and finally [leading to] nirvana; for those who sought pratyekabuddhahood he preached response to the Law of the Twelve Causes; for the bodhisattvas he preached response to the Six Pāramitās to cause them to attain Perfect Enlightenment and to accomplish perfect knowledge.

"Next again there was a buddha, also named Sun Moon Light, and again a buddha, also named Sun Moon Light; and in like manner there

22. Literally, "great men," or *mahāsattvas*.

23. One who has perfected the three clear views: (1) the clear view of destiny, (2) the clear view of supernatural insight, and (3) the clear view of faultlessness (or perfection of character).

24. Rightly going (to final nirvana).

25. The supreme noble man. 26. The noble man who controls (all evil).

27. From "Tathāgata" to "Buddha" comprise the ten titles of a buddha, while "World-honored One" is the general title of a buddha.

28. Here the seven good characteristics of a buddha's preaching are described: (1) good as to time, (2) good in meaning, (3) good in terms, (4) good in its purity, (5) good in its perfection, (6) good in its flawlessness, and (7) good in the nobility of its practice.

were twenty thousand buddhas all bearing the same name Sun Moon Light and the same surname Bharadvāja.[29] Know, Maitreya! All these buddhas, from the first to the last, bore the same name Sun Moon Light and perfectly possessed the ten titles. The Law which they should preach was good at its commencement, in its middle, and at the end.

"Before the last of these buddhas left his home, he had eight royal sons: the first was named Possessing the Will, the second named Excellent Will, the third named Infinite Will, the fourth named Precious Will, the fifth named Increasing Will, the sixth named Undoubting Will, the seventh named Echoed Will, and the eighth named Law Will.

"These eight princes in their honorable estate were independent, each having dominion over four continents. All these princes, hearing that their father had left his home and attained Perfect Enlightenment, renounced the royal position and, following him, left home, resolute on the Great-vehicle; they constantly practiced noble deeds, and all became teachers of the Law, having planted all roots of goodness under thousands of myriads of buddhas.

"At that time the Buddha Sun Moon Light preached the Great-vehicle sutra called Innumerable Meanings, the Law by which bodhisattvas are instructed and which the buddhas watch over and keep in mind. Having preached this sutra, he at once, amidst the great assembly, sat cross-legged and entered the meditation [termed] the station of innumerable meanings, in which his body and mind were motionless. At this moment the sky rained mandārava, mahā-mandārava, mañjūshaka, and mahā-mañjūshaka flowers over the buddha and all the great assembly, while the universal buddha-world shook in six ways.

"Then, in the congregation, bhikshus, bhikshuṇis, upāsakas, upāsikās, gods, dragons, yakshas, gandharvas, asuras, garuḍas, kiṃnaras, mahoragas, human and nonhuman beings, as well as minor kings and the holy wheel-rolling kings, all of this assembly, obtaining that which had never been before, with joy and folded hands and with one mind looked up to the buddha.

"Then the tathāgata sent forth, from the circle of white hair be-

29. One of the eighteen Brahmanic families.

tween his eyebrows, a ray of light, which illuminated eighteen thousand buddha-lands in the eastern quarter, so that there was nowhere it did not reach, just like all these buddha-lands which now are seen.

"Know, Maitreya! At that time in the assembly there were twenty koṭis of bodhisattvas who joyfully desired to hear the Law. All these bodhisattvas, beholding this ray of light illuminating the buddha-lands universally, and obtaining that which they had never had before, desired to know the causes of and reasons for that ray.

"Then there was a bodhisattva named Mystic Light, who had eight hundred disciples. When the Buddha Sun Moon Light arose from his contemplation, he preached, by means of the Bodhisattva Mystic Light, the Great-vehicle sutra called the Lotus Flower of the Wonderful Law, by which bodhisattvas are instructed and which the buddhas watch over and keep in mind. During sixty minor kalpas he rose not from his seat and during [these] sixty minor kalpas his hearers in that assembly remained seated in their places, motionless in body and mind, listening to the buddha's preaching and deeming it but the length of a meal. During that time there was no one in the assembly who felt fatigue in either body or mind.

"The Buddha Sun Moon Light, for sixty minor kalpas having preached this sutra, at once proclaimed these words to the host of Brahmas, Māras, śramaṇas, Brahmans, gods, men, and asuras: 'Today, at midnight, will the tathāgata enter the nirvana of no remains.'[30]

"Thereupon there was a bodhisattva named Virtue Treasury. The Buddha Sun Moon Light then spoke to all the bhikshus, foretelling[31] [thus]: 'This Bodhisattva Virtue Treasury will become the next buddha and his name will be Pure Body Tathāgata, Arhat, Samyaksaṃbodhi.'

"The buddha, having predicted him, at midnight entered the nirvana of no remains. After the buddha's extinction, the Bodhisattva Mystic Light, having retained [in memory] the Sutra of the Lotus Flower of the Wonderful Law, expounded it for men during fully eighty minor kalpas. All the eight sons of the Buddha Sun Moon Light took Mystic Light as their teacher. Mystic Light taught and influenced them to be firm in Perfect Enlightenment. All these princes paid homage to innumerable hundred thousand myriad koṭis of bud-

30. Entering the nirvana of no remains means entering Perfect Enlightenment at death.

31. Predicting the bodhisattva's destiny.

dhas and accomplished the Buddha-way. The last to become a buddha was named Burning Light.[32]

"He had eight hundred disciples, one of whom was named Fame Seeker. This one was greedily attached to the development of gain, and though he read and recited many sutras repeatedly, none of them penetrated and stuck, for he forgot and lost almost all. So he was named Fame Seeker. This man also, because he had planted many roots of goodness, was able to meet innumerable hundred thousand myriad koṭis of buddhas, whom he worshiped, revered, honored, and extolled.

"Know, Maitreya! The Bodhisattva Mystic Light of that time, was it some other person? [No,] it was I myself, [while] the Bodhisattva Fame Seeker was you yourself. Now I see that this auspice is no different from the former one.

"Therefore I consider that the present Tathāgata will preach the Great-vehicle sutra called the Lotus Flower of the Wonderful Law, by which bodhisattvas are instructed and which the buddhas watch over and keep in mind."

Then Mañjuśrī in the great assembly, desiring to announce this meaning over again, spoke thus in verse:

"I remember a past age,
Infinite and numberless kalpas ago;
There was a buddha, the most honored of men,
Named Sun Moon Light.
That world-honored one preached the Law
To save innumerable creatures
And countless koṭis of bodhisattvas
And cause them to enter the Buddha-wisdom.
Before that buddha left his home
The eight princes born to him,
Having seen the great sage leave his home,
Also followed him and practiced the noble life.
Then that buddha preached the Great-vehicle,
The sutra called Innumerable Meanings,
Amongst the hosts of living beings,

32. Or "Burning Lamp"; so named because when he was born a ray of light issued from his body.

And in detail defined it for them.
When the buddha had preached this sutra
He then, on the seat of the Law,
Sat cross-legged in the contemplation
Termed the station of innumerable meanings.
The sky rained mandārava flowers,
[While] the heavenly drums sounded of themselves;
Gods, dragons, and spirits
Worshiped the most honored of men.
All of the buddha-lands
At that moment trembled greatly.
The ray sent forth from the buddha's brows
Revealed unprecedented wonders.
This ray, illuminating the eastern quarter
Of eighteen thousand buddha-lands,
Showed everywhere all living creatures
In the state of their mortal karmas.
Some of the buddha-lands were seen
Adorned with every precious thing,
Many-hued with lapis lazuli and crystal,
From the shining of the buddha's ray.
Besides I saw gods, men,
Dragons, spirits and yakshas,
Gandharvas and kiṃnaras,
Each of them worshiping that buddha.
Further I saw tathāgatas
Who of themselves had accomplished the Buddha-way,
Their appearance like mountains of gold,
Very wonderful in their majesty.
As within pure lapis lazuli
A real golden image is made apparent,
So the world-honored one in the great assembly
Expounded the meaning of the profound Law.
In each of the buddha-lands
Were śrāvakas innumerable;
By the shining of the buddha's ray
Their great host was completely visible.
Besides there were the bhikshus

Who, having dwelt in the mountain forests,
Had zealously advanced and kept the pure commandments
As if they were protecting bright jewels.
And I also saw bodhisattvas
Who practiced donations and perseverance,
As the sands of the Ganges in number,
By the radiance of the buddha's ray.
I saw also bodhisattvas
Who, entering into deep meditation,
Were at rest, motionless in body and mind,
Seeking the supreme Way.
Again I saw bodhisattvas
Who, knowing the nirvana-nature of the Law,
Each in his own domain
Preached the Law and sought the Buddha-way.
Thereupon all of the four groups,
Seeing the Buddha Sun Moon Light
Display great supernatural powers,
With joy in all their minds
Each asked one of another:
'For what reason are these things?'
He who is honored by gods and men
Soon rose from his contemplation,
[Thus] extolling the Bodhisattva Mystic Light:
'Thou art the eye of the world,
To whom all turn in faith,
Able to keep the treasury of the Law.
Such a law as I preach,
Thou alone art able to bear it witness.'
The world-honored one, having [thus] praised him
And caused Mystic Light to rejoice,
Then preached this Law-Flower Sutra
During full sixty minor kalpas,
Never rising from his seat.
The supreme and wonderful Law so preached,
This Mystic Light, Teacher of the Law,
Was wholly able to receive and retain.
When the buddha had preached this Law-Flower

And caused all of them to rejoice,
Then he, on that very day,
Proclaimed to the hosts of gods and men:
'The Truth of the Reality of All Existence
Has [just] been preached for all of you.
I now, at midnight,
Must enter into nirvana.
Do you, with all your mind, advance zealously
And depart from all slackness;
Buddhas are very rarely encountered;
In koṭis of kalpas but one is met.'
The sons of the world-honored one,
Hearing that the buddha was entering nirvana,
Every one felt grieved and distressed:
'How sudden is the buddha's extinction!'
The holy lord, the king of the Law,
Comforted the countless multitude:
'Even when I am extinct,
Be ye not sad and afraid!
This Bodhisattva Virtue Treasury,
In the realization of faultlessness,
Has gained complete understanding.
He will become the next buddha,
Whose name will be called Pure Body;
He, too, will save innumerable creatures.'
That night the buddha became extinct,
As [when] firewood is finished the fire dies out.
His relics were distributed
And innumerable stupas erected.
Bhikshus and bhikshuṇis,
Numerous as the sands of the Ganges,
Doubled their zealous advance,
Seeking the supreme Way.
This Mystic Light, Teacher of the Law,
Having kept the treasury of the Law,
During eighty minor kalpas
Widely proclaimed the Law-Flower Sutra.
All these eight princes,

Converted by Mystic Light,
Kept firmly the supreme Way
And would see countless buddhas.
Having worshiped the buddhas
And followed them, walking the Great Way,
In succession they could become buddhas,
And one by one they were foretold.
The last, the god of gods,[33]
Was called the Buddha Burning Light.
He, the leader of all the sages,[34]
Saved innumerable living beings.
This Mystic Light, Teacher of the Law,
At that time had a pupil
Who was always of a lazy spirit,
Greedily attached to fame and gain,
Tireless in seeking fame and gain,
Addicted to enjoyment in noble families,
Casting aside that which he had learned,
Forgetting everything and dull of apprehension,
Who because of these things[35]
Was called Fame Seeker.
He also by practicing good works
Was enabled to see numberless buddhas,
Also to pay homage to buddhas
And to follow them, walking the Great Way,
Perfecting the Six Pāramitās,
And now has seen Śākya, the Lion.
He will afterward become a buddha
And will be named Maitreya,
Who shall widely save living creatures
Countless in number.
He who, after the extinction of the other buddha,
Was the slothful one was yourself.
And Mystic Light, Teacher of the Law,

33. "God of gods" is (1) an epithet of the Buddha and (2) the supreme heaven of the four heavens of the Realm of Form.
34. *Rishis,* men transformed into immortals through asceticism and meditation.
35. Literally, "causes and reasons."

Was I myself who now am [here].
Having seen the Buddha of Light[36]
Of yore [send forth] a like auspicious ray,
I therefore know that the present Buddha
Desires to preach the Law-Flower Sutra.
The present sign is like the former auspice;
It is the tactful method of buddhas.
Now the Buddha sends forth a ray
To help reveal the Truth of Reality.
Be aware, all of you!
Fold your hands and with all your mind await!
The Buddha will pour the rain of the Law
To satisfy those who seek the Way.
If those who seek after the three vehicles
Have any doubts or regrets,
The Buddha will rid them of them
So that none whatever shall remain."

36. In full, "the Buddha Sun Moon Light."

CHAPTER II

Tactfulness

AT THAT TIME the World-honored One, rising quietly and clearly from contemplation, addressed Śāriputra: "The wisdom of buddhas is very profound and infinite. Their wisdom-school is difficult to understand and difficult to enter, so that the śrāvakas and pratyekabuddhas cannot apprehend it. Wherefore? [Because] the buddhas have been in fellowship with countless hundred thousand myriad koṭis of buddhas, perfectly practicing the infinite Law of all buddhas, boldly and zealously advancing and [making] their fame universally known, perfecting the very profound, unprecedented Law and preaching, as opportunity served, its meaning [so] difficult to understand. Śāriputra! Ever since I became Buddha, with various reasonings and various parables I have widely discoursed and taught, and by countless tactful methods have led living beings, causing them to leave all attachments. Wherefore? [Because] the Tathāgata is altogether perfect in his tactfulness and pāramitā of wisdom. Śāriputra! The wisdom of the Tathāgata is broad and great, profound

The title of this chapter in Chinese, *Fang-pien* 方便 (Sanskrit *Upāya-kauśalya*), means an appropriate, expedient, or tactful method.

and far-reaching; [his mind] is infinite;[1] [his expositions] are unimpeded;[2] [his] powers,[3] [his] fearlessness,[4] [his] meditations,[5] [his] emancipations,[6] [his] contemplations have enabled him to enter into the boundless [realms] and to accomplish all the unprecedented Law. Śāriputra! The Tathāgata is able to discriminate everything, preach the laws skillfully, use gentle words, and cheer the hearts of all. Śāriputra! Essentially speaking, the Buddha has altogether fulfilled the infinite, boundless, unprecedented Law. Enough, Śāriputra, there is no need to say more. Wherefore? [Because] the Law which the Buddha has perfected is the chief unprecedented Law, and difficult to understand. Only a buddha together with a buddha can fathom the Reality of All Existence, that is to say, all existence[7] [has] such a form, such a nature, such an embodiment, such a potency, such a function, such a primary cause, such a secondary cause, such an effect, such a recompense, and such a complete fundamental whole."[8]

1. "Infinite" indicates the four kinds of infinite mind or infinite virtues: benevolence (or kindness), compassion, joy, and indifference. See also p. 209, fn. 5.

2. "Unimpeded" (or "unlimited") indicates the four unlimited forms of wisdom listed on p. 32, fn. 4.

3. The ten powers. See Glossary.

4. The four kinds of fearlessness of a buddha: (1) fearlessness in proclaiming all truth; (2) fearlessness in proclaiming the truth of perfection, or freedom from faults; (3) fearlessness in exposing obstacles to the truth; and (4) fearlessness in proclaiming the way to end all suffering.

5. *Dhyāna,* literally, "fixed abstraction": contemplation or exercises in reflection; one of the Six Pāramitās. See Glossary.

6. The eight emancipations. See Glossary.

7. All laws or all existences. The word "Reality" does not occur in the extant Sanskrit text.

8. These ten categories, termed the Ten Suchnesses, are fundamental to the T'ien-t'ai sect of Buddhism. The most important doctrine of its founder, Chih-i (538–97), that of "three thousand [worlds] in one thought," arises from these categories. The extant Sanskrit text has only the following sentences corresponding to these ten categories: (1) *ye ca te dharmā,* or "what those laws are," "such a nature"; (2) *yāthā ca te dharmā,* or "how those laws are," "such a function"; (3) *yādṛśaś ca te dharmā,* or "like what those laws are," "such a complete fundamental whole"; (4) *yallakshaṇāś ca te dharmā,* or "of what forms [or characteristics] those laws are," "such a form"; (5) *yatsvabhāvāś ca te dharmaḥ,* or "of what self-natures those laws are," "such an embodiment"; (6) *ye ca,* or "what"; (7) *yathā ca,* or "how"; (8) *yādṛśaś ca,* or "like what"; (9) *yallakshaṇāś ca,* or "of what forms"; (10) *yatsvabhāvāś ca,* or "of what self-natures." These seem to correspond to the ten categories, but the sixth to the tenth, which are not found in Kern's translation, may be only a repetition of the first five. This extant Sanskrit original may be different from that which Kumārajīva used, or Kumārajīva may have translated these words according to their inner, esoteric meanings.

At that time the World-honored One, desiring to proclaim this teaching over again, spoke thus in verse:

"Immeasurable are the world's heroes.
[Embracing] gods and men in the world
[Among] all the living creatures,
None can know the buddhas.
The Buddha's powers and fearlessness,
Emancipations and contemplations,
And the Buddha's other laws
No one is able to measure.
Of yore I followed countless buddhas,
And perfectly trod the [right] ways
Of the profound and wonderful Law,
Which are difficult to perceive and perform.
During infinite koṭis of kalpas,
After pursuing all those ways,
Having obtained the perfect fruit on the wisdom throne,
I was able perfectly to understand.
Such great effects as these,
The meaning of every nature and form:
I and other buddhas in the universe
Alone can understand these things.
This Law is inexpressible,
It is beyond the realm of terms;
Among all the other living beings
None can apprehend it
Except the bodhisattvas
Who are firm in the power of faith.
The disciples of all the buddhas
Who have offered worship to the buddhas
And have ended all their faults
And dwell in this last bodily state,
Such men as these
Have not powers equal [to such knowledge].
Though the world were full
Of beings like Śāriputra
Who with utmost thought combined to measure it,

They could not fathom the Buddha-wisdom.
Indeed though the universe were full
Of beings like Śāriputra,
And the rest of [my] disciples
Filled the world in every quarter,
[Who] with utmost thought combined to measure it,
They also could not understand.
Though pratyekabuddhas of keen intelligence,
In their last faultless bodily stage,
Also filled every region of the universe,
Numerous as bamboo in the woods,
[If] these with united mind
Through infinite koṭis of kalpas
Wished to ponder the Buddha's real wisdom,
[They] could not know the least part.
Though newly vowed bodhisattvas
Who have worshiped countless buddhas,
Have penetrated all meanings,
And can ably preach the Law,
[Abounding] as rice and hemp, bamboo and reeds,
Filled the world in every quarter,
[If] with one mind by mystic wisdom,
Through kalpas like the sands of the Ganges,
All these were to ponder together,
They could not know the Buddha-wisdom.
Though bodhisattvas, free from falling back,
Numerous as the sands of the Ganges,
With one mind investigated together,
They too could not understand.
Again I say to Śāriputra:
'The faultless and inscrutable,
Profound and mysterious Law
I now have wholly attained.
Only I know these truths,
As also do the buddhas of the universe.
Know, Śāriputra!
The words of buddhas do not differ.
In the laws preached by the Buddha

[You] should beget great strength of faith,
For at length after the Buddha's [preparatory] teaching
He must [now] proclaim the [perfect] Truth.'
I address all the śrāvakas
And seekers after the vehicle of pratyekabuddhas,
Those whom I have freed from the bondage of suffering
And who have reached nirvana:
'The Buddha employs his tactful powers;
He shows [the Way] by the three-vehicle teaching.
All beings have various attachments;
He leads them to obtain escape.' "

At that time in the great assembly there were śrāvakas and faultless arhats, Ajñāta-Kauṇḍinya and others, twelve hundred in number, and bhikshus, bhikshuṇīs, upāsakas, and upāsikās, who had vowed to be śrāvakas and pratyekabuddhas—all these reflected thus: "For what reason does the World-honored One now extol the tactful way so earnestly and say these words: 'The Law which the Buddha has obtained is very profound and difficult to comprehend. That which he proclaims has a meaning so hard to understand that all the śrāvakas and pratyekabuddhas are unable to attain it'? [As yet] the Buddha has declared only one principle of emancipation, and we also, obtaining this Law, reach nirvana. But now we do not know where this principle leads."

At that time Śāriputra, apprehending the doubt in the minds of the four groups and also himself not having mastered [the meaning], spoke to the Buddha, saying: "World-honored One! What is the cause and what the reason for so earnestly extolling the paramount tactful method and the very profound, mysterious Law, difficult to understand, of the buddhas? From of yore I have never heard such a discourse from the Buddha. At present these four groups are altogether in doubt. Will the World-honored One be pleased to explain these things, why the World-honored One extols so earnestly the very profound and mysterious Law, [so] difficult to understand."

Then Śāriputra, desiring to announce this meaning over again, spoke thus in verse:

"O Wisdom Sun! Great Holy Honored One!
At length thou hast preached this Law,

[And] declared thyself to have obtained such
Powers, fearlessness, and contemplations,
Meditations, emancipations, and other
Inconceivable laws.
About the Law obtained on the wisdom throne
No one [has been] about to utter any question,
And I find it hard to fathom [the meaning]
And also am unable to ask questions.
Without being asked thou thyself hast spoken,
Extolling the way thou hast walked,
That thy most mysterious wisdom
Is that which the buddhas obtained.
All the faultless arhats
And those who are seeking nirvana
Have now fallen into nets of doubt.
Why does the Buddha speak thus?
Seekers after pratyekabuddhahood,
Bhikshus and bhikshuṇīs,
Gods, dragons, and spirits,
Gandharvas and other beings
Scan each other in perplexity,
And look expectant to the Honored of Men.[9]
What may be [the meaning of] this matter?
We would the Buddha will explain.
In [this] assembly of śrāvakas
The Buddha says I am the chief [of the disciples],
But I, now, of my own wisdom
Am in doubt and cannot understand
Whether it is the final Law
Or is the Way to progress [there].
The sons born of the Buddha's mouth
With folded hands wait expectantly.
Be pleased to send forth the mystic sound
And now proclaim the truth as it is.

9. Literally, "the honored biped," or the most honored of living beings that have two legs; another epithet of the Buddha. The two legs indicate virtuous happiness and wisdom, commandments and meditation, and so on—the means by which the Buddha works in the universe.

Gods, dragons, spirits, and others,
Numerous as the sands of the Ganges;
Bodhisattvas aspiring to be buddhas,
Fully eighty thousand in number;
Also, from myriads of koṭis of countries,
Holy wheel-rolling kings are here,
With folded hands and reverent hearts,
Desiring to hear the perfect Way."

At that time the Buddha said to Śāriputra: "Enough, enough, there is no need to say more. If I explain this matter, all the worlds of gods and men would be startled and perplexed."

Śāriputra again said to the Buddha: "World-honored One! Be pleased to explain it! Be pleased to explain it! Wherefore? [Because] in this assembly there are numberless hundred thousand myriad koṭis of asaṃkhyeya living beings who have already seen the buddhas, whose perceptions[10] are keen and whose wisdom is clear. If they hear the Buddha's teaching, they will be able to believe it respectfully."

Then Śāriputra, desiring to announce this meaning over again, spoke thus in verse:

"King of the Law, Most High Honored One!
Be pleased to explain without misgiving!
In this assembly are countless beings
Who can respectfully believe."

The Buddha again [said]: "Enough, Śāriputra! If I explained this matter, all the worlds of gods, men, and asuras would be startled and perplexed, and haughty[11] bhikshus might fall into the great pit."[12]

Then the World-honored One once again spoke in verse:

"Enough, enough, no need to say more.
My Law is subtle and inscrutable;

10. Literally, "roots." Usually there are considered to be six roots, or sense organs: eyes, ears, nose, tongue, body, and mind. But here the "five roots" are meant, the roots of faith, zealous progress, memory, meditation, and wisdom. The five roots are also called the five powers.

11. Utmost haughtiness or arrogance, which possesses those who mistakenly think they have obtained the perfect Law.

12. This refers to hell.

Those who are haughty
On hearing would not believe it respectfully."

Then Śāriputra once again said to the Buddha: "World-honored One! Be pleased to explain it! Be pleased to explain it! In this present assembly there are, equal with me, hundreds of thousands of myriads of koṭis who, in former lives, have followed the Buddha and been transformed by him. Such men as these can certainly believe respectfully and throughout the night will peacefully rest and in various ways be abundantly benefited."

Then Śāriputra, desiring to announce this meaning over again, spoke thus in verse:

"Most High and Honored of the Living!
Be pleased to explain the paramount Law!
I am the eldest son of the Buddha.
Condescend to explain it discriminately.
In this assembly countless beings
Are able respectfully to believe this Law.
The Buddha already in his former lives
Has taught such living beings.
All with one mind, folding their hands,
Desire to hear the Buddha's words.
There are twelve hundred of us
And others aspiring to be buddhas.
Be pleased, for the sake of these beings,
To condescend to explain it discriminately.
If these hear this Law,
They will beget great joy."

At that time the World-honored One addressed Śāriputra: "Since you have already thrice earnestly repeated your request, how can I refuse to speak? Do you now listen attentively to, ponder, and remember it! I will discriminate and explain it for you."

When he had thus spoken, in the assembly some five thousand bhikshus, bhikshuṇīs, upāsakas, and upāsikās straightway rose from their seats and, saluting the Buddha, withdrew. Wherefore? [Because] the root of sin in these beings was so deep and their haughty spirit so enlarged that they imagined they had attained what they had not attained and had proved what they had not proved. In such error as this they would not stay; and the World-honored One was silent and did not stop them.

Thereupon the Buddha addressed Śāriputra: "Now in this congregation I am free from [useless] twigs and leaves, and have nothing but all that are purely the true and real. It is good, Śāriputra, that such extremely haughty ones as those are gone away. Now carefully listen and I will expound [the matter] for you." Śāriputra said: "So be it, World-honored One; I desire joyfully to listen."

The Buddha addressed Śāriputra: "Such a wonderful Law as this is [only] preached by the buddha-tathāgatas on [rare] occasions, just as the udumbara flower is seen but once in [long] periods. Śāriputra, believe me, all of you; in the Buddha's teaching no word is false. Śāriputra, the meaning of the laws which the buddhas expound as opportunity serves is difficult to understand. Wherefore? [Because] I expound the laws by numberless tactful ways and with various reasonings and parabolic expressions. These laws cannot be understood by powers of thought or discrimination; only the buddhas can discern them. Wherefore? [Because] the buddhas, the world-honored ones, only on account of the one [very] great cause appear in the world. Śāriputra, why [do I] say that the buddhas, the world-honored ones, only on account of the one [very] great cause appear in the world? Because the buddhas, the world-honored ones, desire to cause all living beings to open [their eyes] to the Buddha-knowledge so that they may gain the pure [mind], [therefore] they appear in the world; because they desire to show all living beings the Buddha-knowledge, they appear in the world; because they desire to cause all living beings to apprehend the Buddha-knowledge, they appear in the world; because they desire to cause all living beings to enter the way of the Buddha-knowledge, they appear in the world.[13] Śāriputra, this is why

13. To open, to show, to apprehend, and to enter the perception of the Buddha-knowledge are termed the four perceptions of the Buddha-knowledge. Every creature originally has the buddha-nature, but buried beneath his ignorance and earthly cares it is invisible. In this sutra the Buddha teaches that all creatures can realize their own buddha-nature and teaches these four perceptions of the Buddha-knowledge.

it is [only] on account of the one [very] great cause that buddhas appear in the world."

The Buddha addressed Śāriputra: "The buddha-tathāgatas teach only bodhisattvas. Whatever they do is always for one purpose, that is, to take the Buddha-knowledge and reveal it to all living beings. Śāriputra! The Tathāgata, by means of the One Buddha-vehicle,[14] preaches to all living beings the Law; there is no other vehicle, neither a second nor a third. Śāriputra! The laws of all the buddhas in the universe also are like this. Śāriputra! The buddhas in times past, by infinite, numberless tactful ways and with various reasonings and parabolic expressions, expounded the laws for the sake of all living beings. All these laws are for the One Buddha-vehicle, [so that] all those living beings, who have heard the Law from the buddhas, might all finally obtain perfect knowledge.

"Śāriputra! The future buddhas who are to appear in the world will also, by infinite, numberless tactful ways and with various reasonings and parabolic expressions, expound the laws for the sake of all living beings. All these laws are for the One Buddha-vehicle, [so that] all those living beings who hear the Law from the buddhas shall finally obtain perfect knowledge.

"Śāriputra! The buddhas, the world-honored ones, at present in innumerable hundred thousand myriad koṭis of buddha-lands in the universe, who are so greatly benefiting and rejoicing all living beings, these buddhas, by infinite, numberless tactful ways and with various

14. Also called the One-vehicle and the Buddha-vehicle. "Vehicle" (Sanskrit *yāna*) means a vehicle by which one reaches the goal, the Law taught and practiced by the Buddha. It is interpreted as (1) the Law by which one obtains buddhahood and (2) those who practice that Law. The Buddha spoke of many kinds of vehicles—the two vehicles, the three vehicles, the five vehicles, and so on. The One Buddha-vehicle means the Law taught and practiced as the one and only Buddha-way, and also refers to those who follow that Law. This teaching includes two concepts of the vehicle, as relative and as absolute. The One Buddha-vehicle, considered as relative, is a vehicle that is explained correlatively with other kinds of vehicles. In such cases the One Buddha-vehicle refers to one of those vehicles; the term used in this sense is found in all the Mahayana sutras. In this chapter, however, the Buddha proclaims that such teachings are all temporary and expedient, for use only until he reveals the final truth. Here the absolute One Buddha-vehicle is shown as the final truth, comprehending all temporary and expedient teachings. After this absolute One Buddha-vehicle has been revealed, none of the other vehicles is to exist independently; all Buddhism is to depend upon and be unified in it. Only this sutra contains this doctrine, and is therefore known as the One-vehicle sutra.

reasonings and parabolic expressions, also expound the laws for the sake of all living beings. All these laws are for the One Buddha-vehicle, [so that] all those living beings who hear the Law from the buddhas finally obtain perfect knowledge.

"Śāriputra! All these buddhas teach only bodhisattvas, desiring to show all living beings the Buddha-knowledge, desiring to cause all living beings to apprehend the Buddha-knowledge, and desiring to cause all living beings to enter the Way of the Buddha-knowledge. Śāriputra! I, at the present time, am also like them. Knowing that all living beings have many kinds of desires deeply attached in their minds, I have, according to their capacity, expounded the laws by various reasonings, parabolic expressions, and tactful powers. Śāriputra! Such [teachings] all are in order to secure perfect knowledge of the One Buddha-vehicle. Śāriputra! In the whole universe there are not even two vehicles,[15] how much less a third.[16]

"Śāriputra! The buddhas appear in the evil ages of the five decays, that is to say, decay of the kalpa, decay through tribulations, decay of all living creatures, decay of views, and decay of lifetime. Thus, Śāriputra! Because in the disturbed times of kalpa decay all living beings are very vile, being covetous and envious, bringing to maturity every root of badness, the buddhas by tactful powers in the One Buddha-vehicle discriminate and expound the three. Śāriputra! If my disciples who call themselves arhats or pratyekabuddhas [will] neither hear nor understand that the buddha-tathāgatas teach only bodhisattvas, these are not the Buddha's disciples nor arhats nor pratyekabuddhas.

"Again, Śāriputra! [If] those bhikshus and bhikshuṇīs who claim that they have already become arhats [and say]: 'This is our last bodily state [before] final nirvana,' and thereupon do not again devote themselves to seek after Perfect Enlightenment, you must know that this class are all extremely conceited. Wherefore? [Because] there is no such thing as a bhikshu who has really obtained arhatship if he has not believed this Law. [But] there is an exceptional case when, after the Buddha's extinction, there is no [other] buddha present. Wherefore? [Because] after the Buddha's extinction it is hard to find persons who [can] receive and keep, read and recite, and explain the meaning

15. The vehicles of the śrāvaka and pratyekabuddha. See Glossary.
16. The third vehicle is that of the bodhisattva.

of such sutras as these. [Only] if they meet other buddhas can they, in this [same] Law, obtain [the] solution. Śāriputra! You should with all your heart believe and discern, receive and keep the word of the Buddha. No word of the buddha-tathāgatas is false; there is no other vehicle, but only the One Buddha-vehicle."

At that time the World-honored One, desiring to proclaim this teaching over again, spoke thus in verse:

"Bhikshus and bhikshuṇīs
Obsessed by utmost arrogance,
Upāsakas [filled with] self-conceit,
Upāsikās with unbelief,
Four groups such as these,
Five thousand in number,
Perceiving not their errors
And faults in the commandments,
Careful only of their flaws:
Such small wit they showed,
These dregs of the assembly, who
Because of the Buddha's splendid virtue withdrew;
These men of little virtuous happiness
Are incapable of receiving this Law.
[Now] this assembly has no twigs and leaves,
But only those who are true and real.
Śāriputra! Listen carefully to
The laws obtained by the buddhas, which,
By infinite tactful powers,
They expound for all creatures.
What they all entertain in their minds,
All the ways they practice,
How many kinds are their desires,
And their former karmas, good and evil,
The Buddha knows all these perfectly.
With various reasonings and parables,
Terms and tactful powers,
He causes them all to rejoice,
Preaching either sutras,

Or gāthās, or former things,[17]
Or birth stories,[18] or the unprecedented,[19]
And also preaching by reasonings,[20]
By parables[21] and geyas,
And by upadeśa scriptures.
The dull who delight in petty rules,[22]
Who are greedily attached to existence,
Who, under innumerable buddhas,
Do not walk the profound and mystic Way,
Who are harassed by all the sufferings—
Because of these I preach nirvana.
I [have] set up such tactful ways
To enable them to enter the Buddha-wisdom.
[But] I have never said: 'You all
Shall accomplish the Buddha-way.'
The reason why I have never [so] said
Is that the time for saying it had not arrived.
[But] now is the very time,
And I have resolved to preach the Great-vehicle.
These nine divisions[23] of my Law
Preached according to [the capacity] of all creatures
Are [but] the introduction to the Great-vehicle,
Hence I preach this sutra.
There are sons of the Buddha whose minds are pure,
Who are gentle and clever-natured,

17. Literally, "original events"; stories of previous lives of saints, such as śrāvakas and bodhisattvas.
18. Stories detailing the former lives of the Buddha.
19. Literally, "what never took place before," that is, marvels.
20. Literally, "causes and reasons," or primary and secondary causes; the chain of cause and effect of all existence, in which there are twelve links (see Glossary). This also refers to the three classes of sutras: those written because of a request or query, those written because of certain violated precepts, and those written because of special events that demand doctrinal clarification.
21. Literally, "comparisons of parables."
22. Literally, "small law." Here it means the Hinayana.
23. The nine divisions of Hinayana texts, arranged according to subject. The nine divisions are sutras, stanzas, former things, birth stories, the unprecedented, reasonings, parables, chants, and doctrinal discourses.

And who, in innumerable buddha-regions,
Have walked the profound and mystic Way;
On behalf of these sons of the Buddha
I preach this Great-vehicle sutra.
And I predict that such men as these
In the world to come will accomplish the Buddha-way.
Through their deep-hearted mindfulness of the Buddha
And observance of the pure commandments,
These, hearing that they may become buddhas,
Are filled throughout with great joy.
The Buddha knows their mind and conduct,
And therefore preaches to them the Great-vehicle.
[If] śrāvakas or bodhisattvas
Hear the Law which I preach,
Even be it but one verse,
All, without doubt, become buddhas.
In the buddha-lands of the universe
There is only the One-vehicle Law,
Neither a second nor a third,
Except the tactful teachings of the Buddha.
But by provisional expressions
He has led all living creatures,
Revealing the Buddha-wisdom.
In the appearing of buddhas in the world
Only this One is the real fact,
For the other two are not the true.
They never by a smaller vehicle[24]
Save all living creatures.
The Buddha himself abides in the Great-vehicle,
In accordance with the Law he has attained,
Enriched with powers of meditation and wisdom,
And by it[25] he saves all creatures.
I, proving the supreme Way,
The Great-vehicle, the universal Law,
If I convert by a smaller vehicle
Even but one human being,

24. The Hinayana.
25. The Great-vehicle, or Mahayana.

I shall fall into grudging—
A thing that cannot be.
If men turn in faith to the Buddha,
The Tathāgata will not deceive them,
[For he] has no covetous and envious desires
And is free from all the sins of the laws.
So the Buddha, in the universe,
Is the one being perfectly fearless.
I, by my signs-adorned body,[26]
With their shining illuminate the world,
And am worshiped by countless multitudes,
For whom I preach the seal of reality.[27]
Know, Śāriputra!
Of yore I made a vow,
Wishing to cause all creatures
To rank equally without difference with me.
According to the vow I made of old,
Now [all] has been perfectly fulfilled
For converting all living beings
And leading them to enter the Buddha-way.
Whenever I meet any creatures
I teach them all by the Buddha-way.
[But] the unwitting [remain] confused
And, going astray, never accept my teaching.
I know that all these creatures
Have never practiced the fundamental goodness,
Are firmly attached to the five desires,
And through infatuation are in distress;
By reason of these desires,
They have fallen into the three evil paths;
Transmigrating in the six states of existence,
They suffer the utmost misery.
Received into the womb in minute form,
Life after life they ever increase and grow,
Poor in virtue and of little happiness.

26. This refers to the thirty-two signs that distinguish a buddha. See Glossary.
27. The seal of the Law, a system of magic gesticulation. Here it means that the teaching of the Reality of All Existence in this sutra is the Buddha's seal.

They are oppressed by all the distresses;
They have entered the thickets of heretical views,
Such as 'existence' or 'nonexistence';[28]
Relying on these [false] views,
Altogether sixty-two,[29]
They are deeply attached to these false laws,
Firmly holding, unable to give them up,
Self-sufficient and self-inflated,
Suspicious, crooked, and faithless in mind;
During thousands and milliards of kalpas
They have not heard the name of a buddha,
Nor have they heard the True Law;
Men such as these can hardly be saved.
For this reason, Śāriputra,
I set up a tactful way for them,
Proclaiming the way to end sufferings,
Revealing it through nirvana.
Though I proclaim nirvana,
Yet it is not real extinction.
All existence,[30] from the beginning,
Is ever of the nirvana-nature.
When a son of the Buddha has fulfilled his course,
In a world to come he becomes a buddha.
[Only] by my powers of tactfulness
Do I manifest the three-vehicle Law.
[For] all the world-honored ones
Expound the One-vehicle Way.
Now let all in this great assembly
Be free from doubts and perplexities.
The buddhas do not differ in their statements;
There is One only and no second vehicle.
In the past countless kalpas

28. "There is," or being, existence, and "There is not," or nonbeing, nonexistence. The former is the view that all is real, the latter that all is unreal. These are two schools of non-Buddhist thought.
29. The sixty-two views arise out of the above two views, that is, of existence and nonexistence.
30. Or "laws." These two lines may be read: "All and any laws from the very first have always been those of nirvana."

Innumerable extinct buddhas,
In hundreds, thousands, and milliards,
Whose numbers cannot be counted,
All such world-honored ones as these
With various reasonings and parables
And innumerable tactful powers
Have proclaimed the various laws.
[But] all these world-honored ones
Proclaimed the One-vehicle Law,
Converting numberless creatures
To enter the Buddha-way.
Moreover, the great holy masters,
Knowing that which all the worlds
Of gods, men, and other creatures
Deeply desire in their hearts,
In addition, by varying tactfulness,
Assist in revealing the first principles.
If there are any beings
Who have met the former buddhas;
If, having heard the Law, they have given donations;
If they have kept the commandments and been persevering,
Been assiduous, meditative, and wise;
Having kept these various ways of happiness and virtue,
Such beings as these
Have all attained the Buddha-way.
After the extinction of buddhas,
Men with good and soft minds for the truth,
Such living beings as these
Have all attained the Buddha-way.
After the extinction of buddhas,
Those who worshiped their relics
And built many koṭis of sorts of stupas,
With gold, silver, and crystal,
With moonstone and agate,
With jasper and lapis lazuli,
Clearly and broadly decorated,
Handsomely displayed on every stupa;
Or those who built stone shrines

Of sandalwood and aloes,
Eaglewood and other woods,
Of brick, tiles, and clay;
Or those who in the wilds
Raised earth for buddhas' shrines;
Even children, in their play,
Who gathered sand for a buddha's stupa:
All such beings as these
Have attained the Buddha-way.
If men for the sake of buddhas
Have erected images
Carved with the [characteristic] signs,
[They] have all attained the Buddha-way.
Or those who with the precious seven,
With brass, red and white copper,
With wax, lead, and tin,
With iron, wood, and clay,
Or with glue and lacquer
Have adorned and made buddhas' images,
All such ones as these
Have attained the Buddha-way.
Those who have painted buddhas' images
With the hundred blessing-adorned signs,
Whether done by themselves or by employing others,
Have all attained the Buddha-way.
Even boys in their play
Who with reed, wood, or pen
Or with the fingernail
Have drawn buddhas' images,
All such ones as these,
Gradually accumulating merit
And perfecting hearts of great pity,
Have attained the Buddha-way;
Indeed, by influencing the bodhisattvas,
Have saved countless creatures.
If men to the stupas and shrines,
To the precious images and paintings,
With flowers, incense, flags, and umbrellas

Have paid homage with respectful hearts;
Or employed others to perform music,
Beat drums, blow horns and conchs,
Panpipes and flutes, play lutes, harps,
Guitars, gongs, and cymbals,
Such mystic sounds as these,
All played by way of homage;
Or with joyful hearts
By singing have extolled the merits of buddhas
Even though in but a low voice,
[These too] have attained the Buddha-way.
Even anyone who, with distracted mind,
With but a single flower
Has paid homage to the painted images
Shall gradually see countless buddhas.
Or those who have offered worship,
Were it by merely folding the hands,
Or even raising a hand,
Or by slightly bending the head,
By thus paying homage to the images
Gradually see innumerable buddhas,
Attain the supreme Way,
Extensively save countless creatures,
And enter the formless nirvana,
As [when] firewood is finished the fire dies out.
If any, [even] with distracted mind,
Enter a stupa or temple
And cry but once 'Namaḥ Buddha,'
They have attained the Buddha-way.
If any from the buddhas of the past,
Whether in existence or already extinct,
Have heard this Law,
They have all attained the Buddha-way.
All the future world-honored ones,
Infinite in their number,
All these tathāgatas
Also by tactful ways preach the Law.
All of the tathāgatas

By infinite tactful ways
Save all living creatures
To enter the Buddha's faultless wisdom.
Of those who hear the Law
Not one fails to become a buddha.
[This is] the original vow of the buddhas:
'By the Buddha-way which I walk,
I desire universally to cause all creatures
To attain the same Way along with me.'
Though the buddhas in future ages
Proclaim hundreds, thousands, koṭis,
Countless schools of doctrine,
In reality they are [but] the One-vehicle.
The buddhas, the honored ones,
Know that nothing has an independent existence[31]
And that buddha-seeds[32] spring from a cause,[33]
So they reveal the One-vehicle.
All things abide in their fixed order,
[Hence] the world abides forever.[34]

31. Literally, "laws [or beings] are always non-nature." This means that no existing thing has its own fixed or independent nature and body. That is to say, all existing things are inconceivable and mysterious.
32. The buddha-seed is the buddha-nature possessed by all things. This includes two concepts: (1) the natural seed, or nature-seed, is the buddha-seed that all existing things, even beings in hell, originally possess, but it has no independent power to appear of itself; (2) the vehicle-seed is the buddha-seed by which the natural seed is caused to appear. The latter is the Law of the One Buddha-vehicle revealed in this sutra.
33. The natural seed can only be developed through the teaching and practice of the Law of the One Buddha-vehicle. The buddha-nature of all beings depends upon this Law, climbs up by it, and appears through its help or by reason of it. Here "cause" may be read as "providence." The two lines from "Know" to "cause" differ from the extant Sanskrit text, probably because of a difference in the original texts used.
34. This translation follows the interpretation of the T'ien-t'ai sect, but it may also be read: "These stable laws and order [are] / Immovable [and] ever abide in the world," because the extant Sanskrit text reads: *"dharma-sthitiṃ dharma-niyāmatāṃ ca / nitya-sthitāṃ loki imām akampyām."* According to Chih-i, *dharma-niyāmatā,* law-order or fixed position, indicates suchness. That is, every law (or being) abides in suchness or reality. Because of standing on reality, all laws (or beings) abide forever, and therefore every phenomenon also has an unshakable and everlasting existence.

Having apprehended this on the wisdom throne,
The leaders proclaim it in tactful ways.
Whom gods and men pay homage to,
The present buddhas in the universe,
Whose number is as the sands of the Ganges,
And who appear in the world
For the relief of all creatures,
These also proclaim such a Law as this.
Knowing the supreme nirvana,
Though by reason of their tactful powers
They display various kinds of ways,
Really they are [but] the [One] Buddha-vehicle.
Knowing the conduct of all creatures,
What they entertain in their deepest minds,
The karma they have developed in the past,
Their inclinations and zeal,
And their capacities, keen or dull,
With various kinds of reasonings,
Parables, and narrations,
As they could respond, so have they tactfully taught.
Now I also in like manner
For the relief of all creatures
By various kinds of doctrine
Promulgate the Buddha-way.
I, by my power of wisdom,
Knowing the natures and inclinations of creatures,
Tactfully proclaim the laws
[Which] cause all to obtain gladness.
Know, Śāriputra!
I, observing with the Buddha's eyes,
See the creatures in the six states of existence,
Poor and without happiness and wisdom,
In the dangerous path of mortality,
In continuous, unending misery,
Firmly fettered by the five desires
Like the yak caring for its tail,
Smothered by greed and infatuation,
Blinded and seeing nothing;

They seek not the Buddha, the mighty,
And the Law to end sufferings,
But deeply [fall] into heresies,
And seek by suffering to be rid of suffering.
For the sake of all these creatures,
My heart is stirred with great pity.
When I first sat on the wisdom throne,
Looking at [that] tree and walking about it
During thrice seven days,
I pondered such matters as these:
'The wisdom which I have obtained
Is wonderful and supreme.
[But] all creatures are dull in their capacities,
Pleasure-attached and blind with ignorance.
Such classes of beings as these,
[I saw,] how can they be saved?'
Thereupon all the Brahma kings
And Lord Śakra of all the gods,
The four heavenly beings who protect the worlds,
Also the god Great Sovereign
And all the other heavenly beings,
With hundreds of thousands of myriads of followers,
Respectfully saluted with folded hands,
Entreating me to roll the wheel of the Law.[35]
Then I pondered within myself:
'If I only extol the Buddha-vehicle,
All creatures, being sunk in suffering,
Will not be able to believe this Law,
And by breaking the Law through unbelief
Will fall into the three evil paths.
I had rather not preach the Law,
But instantly enter nirvana.'
Then, on remembering what former buddhas
Performed by their tactful powers,
[I thought:] 'The Way which I have now attained
I must preach as the tripartite vehicle.'

35. "To roll the wheel of the Law" means to teach the Law. The first sermon of the Buddha in particular is designated by this term.

While I was pondering thus,
All the buddhas in the universe appeared
And, with sacred voice, cheered me in response:
'Excellent! Sakyamuni!
The first of leaders!
Having attained this supreme Law,
Thou art following after all the buddhas
In using tactful powers.
We, too, have all attained
This most wonderful, supreme Law,
[But] for the sake of the many kinds of creatures,
We divide and preach [it] in three vehicles.
Those of little wisdom delight in petty laws,
Not believing that they can become buddhas,
Hence we, by tactful ways,
Divide and preach the [natural] results.
Though we also proclaim the three vehicles,
It is only for teaching the bodhisattvas.'
Know, Śāriputra!
Hearing the voices of the Holy Lions,
Profoundly clear and mystic,
I saluted them, 'Namaḥ buddhas,'[36]
And again reflected thus:
'Having come forth into the disturbed and evil world,
I, according to the buddhas' behest,
Will also obediently proceed.'
Having finished pondering this matter,
I instantly went to Vārāṇasī.
The nirvana-nature of all existence,
Which is inexpressible,
I by [my] tactful ability
Preached to the five bhikshus.[37]
This is called [the first] rolling of the Law-wheel,
Whereupon there was the news of nirvana[38]

36. This may be translated "Hail to the buddhas!"
37. The five ascetics who had been Sakyamuni's companions before his enlightenment: Ājñāta-Kauṇḍinya, Aśvajit, Vāshpa, Mahānāman, and Bhadrika.
38. Literally, "nirvana-sound" or "voice of nirvana"; that is, the term "nirvana" (enlightenment) was uttered.

And also the separate names of Arhat,
Of Law, and of Saṃgha.[39]
From distant kalpas onward
I have extolled and indicated the Law of nirvana
For the perpetual end of mortal distress;
Thus have I continuously spoken.
Know, Śāriputra!
When I saw the Buddha-sons
Bent on seeking the Buddha-way,
In countless thousands and myriads of koṭis,
All, with reverent hearts,
Draw near to [me] the Buddha;
They had already heard from the buddhas
The Law which they tactfully explained.
Then I conceived this thought:
'The reason why the Tathāgata appears
Is for preaching the Buddha-wisdom;
Now is the very time.'
Know, Śāriputra!
The stupid and those of little wit,
The tied to externals and the proud
Cannot believe this Law.
But now I am glad and fearless;
In the midst of the bodhisattvas
Frankly put aside tactfulness
And only proclaim the supreme Way.
[You] bodhisattvas hearing this Law,
Having all got rid of the nets of doubts,
[You] twelve hundred arhats
Will all become buddhas.
In the same fashion that the buddhas,
Past, present, and future, preach the Law,
So also will I now
Proclaim the undivided Law.
The appearing of buddhas in the world
Is far apart and of rare occurrence,

39. That is, the terms "Arhat" (Buddha), "Dharma" (Law or Teaching), and "Saṃgha" (assemblage of monks) successively came into being.

And when they do appear in the world,
With [equal] rareness do they proclaim this Law.
Even in infinite countless kalpas,
Rarely may this Law be heard;
And those who are able to listen to this Law,
Men such as these are also rare.
It is like the udumbara flower,
Which all love and enjoy,
Seldom seen by gods and men,
Appearing but once in [long] periods.
So he who, hearing the Law, extols it joyfully
And utters but one single word of it
Has already paid homage to
All the buddhas in the three worlds.
Such a one is exceedingly rare,
[Rarer] than the udumbara flower.
Be you free from doubts;
I am the king of the Law[40]
And declare to all the assembly:
'I, only by the One-vehicle Way,
Teach the bodhisattvas,
And have no śrāvaka disciples.'
Know, all of you, Śāriputra,
Śrāvakas, and bodhisattvas,
That this Wonderful Law
Is the mystery of all the buddhas.
Because the evil world of the five decadences
Only delights in sensual attachments,
[Its] creatures such as these
Never seek the Buddha-way.
The wicked in generations to come,
Who hear the One-vehicle preached by the Buddha,
In their delusion and unbelief
Will break the Law and fall into evil ways.
[But] there are beings, modest and pure,
Devoted to seeking the Buddha-way;

40. "King of the Law" is an epithet of every buddha.

For such as these [I] must
Widely extol the One-vehicle Way.
Know, Śāriputra!
The Law of the buddhas is thus:
By myriads of koṭis of tactful ways
They proclaim the Law as opportunity serves.
[But] those who will not learn
Are not able to discern it.
[But] you already know
The expedient tactful ways of
The buddhas, the leaders of the world.
Have no further doubts;
Rejoice greatly in your hearts,
Knowing that you will become buddhas."

HERE ENDS
THE FIRST FASCICLE

CHAPTER III

A Parable

AT THAT TIME Śāriputra, ecstatic with joy, instantly rose up, folded his hands, and looking up at the honorable face, spoke to the Buddha, saying: "Now, hearing the sound of the Law from the World-honored One, I am filled with ecstasy, obtaining that which I have never experienced before. Wherefore? Because of yore when I heard of such a Law as this from the Buddha and saw bodhisattvas who were predicted to become buddhas, we were never prepared for these things and greatly distressed ourselves at having lost the Tathāgata's infinite knowledge. World-honored One! Constantly when dwelling alone in mountain forests or under trees, whether sitting or walking, I was occupied with this thought: 'We equally have entered the Law-nature.[1] [But] why does the Tathāgata save us by the small-vehicle law?' This is our own fault, not the World-honored One's. Wherefore? [Because] had we attended to his preaching in regard to the accomplishment of Perfect Enlightenment, we should certainly have been delivered by the Great-vehicle. Whereas we, not understanding [his] tactful method of opportune preaching, on first

1. "Law-nature" here means the mind-emptiness that is sought by śrāvakas and pratyekabuddhas.

hearing the Buddha-law [only] casually believed, pondered, and bore witness to it. World-honored One! Ever since then I have passed whole days and nights in self-reproach. But now, on hearing from the Buddha the unprecedented Law which I have never before heard, I have ended all my doubts and regrets, am at ease in body and mind, and am happily at rest. Today I indeed know that I am really a son of the Buddha, born from the mouth of the Buddha, evolved from the Law, and have obtained a place in the Buddha-law."

At that time Śāriputra, desiring to announce this meaning over again, spoke thus in verse:

"I, hearing the voice of the Law,
Have obtained the unprecedented;
My heart is full of joy
And all nets of doubts are gone.
From of yore have I received the Buddha's teaching
And shall not miss the Great-vehicle.
The voice of the Buddha is very precious,
Able to rid all creatures of distress.
I, now freed from imperfections,
Hearing it, am also rid of anxiety.
When dwelling in mountain valleys
Or abiding under forest trees,
Whether sitting or walking to and fro,
I ever pondered on this matter
And deeply accused myself, lamenting:
'Why am I [so] self-deluding?
We also are Buddha-sons
Who have equally entered the faultless Law,
[Yet] we cannot, in the future,
Proclaim the supreme Way.
The golden thirty-two [signs],
The ten powers and [eight] emancipations
Are all included in the one Law,
Yet [I] do not attain them.
The eighty kinds of excellence,[2]

2. The eighty kinds of physical beauty and other special characteristics of a buddha.

The eighteen unique characteristics,
Merits such as these
I have entirely missed.'
When alone I was walking to and fro
And saw the Buddha in the great assembly,
His fame filling the universe,
Abundantly benefiting all creatures,
I thought I had lost this advantage
And that I had deluded myself.
Always by day and by night
I ever pondered these things,
Desiring to ask the World-honored One
Whether I had lost [my opportunity] or not.
Ever did I see the World-honored One
Extolling the bodhisattvas;
Therefore by day and night
I have pondered such things as these.
Now I hear the voice of the Buddha
Opportunely preaching the Law,
Faultless and inscrutable,
Which causes all to reach the wisdom throne.
Formerly I was attached to heretical views,
Being a teacher of heretical mendicants.[3]
The World-honored One, knowing my heart,
Uprooted my heresy and taught me nirvana.
[Thus] having completely freed myself from heretical views
And obtained proof of the Law of the Void,
Then in my mind I said to myself:
'I have attained extinction.'
But now I have perceived
This is not the real extinction.
Whenever one becomes a buddha,
He possesses all the thirty-two signs;
Gods, men, and yakshas,

3. The Chinese translation uses the equivalent of the Sanskrit *brahmacārin,* literally, "descendant of purity": a young Brahman who is a student of the Vedas under a preceptor or who practices chastity; a young Brahman before marriage, that is, in the first period of his life.

Dragons and other spirits revere him.
Then it may be said:
'Extinction is forever complete, nothing remaining.'
The Buddha in the great assembly
Proclaims [that] I shall become a buddha.
Hearing such a voice of the Law,
All doubts and regrets have been removed.
On first hearing the Buddha's preaching,
In my mind there was fear and doubt
Lest it might be Māra acting as Buddha,
Distressing and confusing my mind.
[But when] the Buddha, with various reasonings
And parables, speaks so skillfully,
One's heart is peaceful as the sea.
On hearing, my nets of doubts were broken.
The Buddha preaches that the infinite, extinct
Buddhas of past worlds
Calmly established [and] in tactful ways
All likewise expounded this Law.
The present and future buddhas,
Countless in their numbers,
Also with tactful ways
Proclaim such a Law as this.
The present World-honored One,
After his birth and leaving home,
Having gained the Way and rolled the Law-wheel,
Also has preached with tactfulness.
It is the World-honored One who preaches the true Way;
The Evil One[4] has no [such] truths [as] these.
Hence I know for certain that
This is not Māra acting as Buddha,
But because I had fallen into nets of doubts,
I conceived it as the doing of Māra.
Hearing the gentle voice of the Buddha,
Profound and very refined,
Expounding the pure Law,

4. Sanskrit "Pāpiyas," another name for Māra, "the Evil One" or "the Evil of Evils."

My heart is filled with joy,
My doubts and regrets are forever ended,
[I am] at rest in real wisdom.
I am sure I shall become a buddha,
Revered by gods and men,
And rolling the supreme Law-wheel,
Shall teach many bodhisattvas."

At that time the Buddha said to Śāriputra: "Now I declare in this great assembly of gods, men, ascetics, Brahmans, and others. Of yore, in the presence of twenty thousand koṭis of buddhas, for the sake of the supreme Way, I continuously taught you, while you also for long nights [and days] have followed me and received my teaching. By reason of my tactful guidance, you have been born into my Law. Śāriputra! Of yore I caused you to resolve on the Buddha-way. But you have now entirely forgotten it and so consider that you have attained extinction. Now again desiring to cause you to recollect the Way which you originally resolved to follow, I preach for all the śrāvakas this Great-vehicle sutra called the Lotus Flower of the Wonderful Law, by which bodhisattvas are instructed and which the buddhas watch over and keep in mind.

"Śāriputra! In a world to come, after infinite, boundless, and inconceivable kalpas, when you shall have served some thousand myriad koṭis of buddhas, maintained the Right Law, and completed the way which bodhisattvas walk, you shall become a buddha whose title will be Flower Light Tathāgata, Worshipful, All Wise, Perfectly Enlightened in Conduct, Well Departed, Understander of the World, Peerless Leader, Controller, Teacher of Gods and Men, Buddha, World-honored One, and whose domain shall be named Undefiled, whose land will be level and straight, pure and ornate, peaceful and prosperous, replete with celestial people; with lapis lazuli for earth, having eight intersecting roads with golden cords to bound their cities, and by each road a line of precious-seven trees always [filled] with flowers and fruits. The Tathāgata Flower Light also will teach and convert all living creatures by the three vehicles.

"Śāriputra! When that buddha appears, though it is not in an evil age, he will preach the three-vehicle Law because of his original vow. Its kalpa will be named Ornate with Great Jewels. For what reason is it named Ornate with Great Jewels? Because in that domain the bodhisattvas are considered the great jewels. These bodhisattvas will be infinite, boundless, inconceivable, beyond computation or compare, such as none can apprehend who has not a buddha's wisdom. Whenever they walk, jewel flowers will receive their feet. These bodhisattvas will not have started in this conception for the first time, for all of them will have cultivated the roots of virtue for a long time, purely performing noble deeds under infinite hundred thousand myriad koṭis of buddhas, being always praised by buddhas, constantly practicing the Buddha-wisdom, perfecting the great spiritually pervading [power], knowing well the way of all the laws, and being upright and genuine [in character], firm in will and thought. Such bodhisattvas as these will fill that domain.

"Śāriputra! The lifetime of the Buddha Flower Light will be twelve minor kalpas, except the time during which he, being a prince, has not yet become a buddha. And the lifetime of the people of his domain will be eight minor kalpas. The Tathāgata Flower Light, at the expiration of twelve minor kalpas, will predict the future destiny of the Bodhisattva Full of Firmness[5] to Perfect Enlightenment and will declare to all the bhikshus: 'This Bodhisattva Full of Firmness shall next become a buddha, whose title will be Calmly Walking on Flowery Feet Tathāgata, Arhat, Samyaksaṃbodhi. The domain of the buddha also will be of like character.'

"Śāriputra! After the extinction of this Flower Light Buddha, the Righteous Law will abide in the world during thirty-two minor kalpas and [then] the Counterfeit Law will also abide in the world during thirty-two minor kalpas."

At that time the World-honored One, desiring to proclaim this teaching over again, spoke thus in verse:

"Śāriputra! In an age to come,
You shall become a buddha, honored for universal wisdom,[6]
By name and title Flower Light,
And you shall save innumerable creatures.
Paying homage to numberless buddhas,

5. Or "Full of Perseverance."
6. Or "honored [attainer] of universal wisdom."

Perfecting bodhisattva-actions
And the merits of the ten powers and so on,
It shall be evident that [you have attained] the supreme Way.
After infinite kalpas have passed
There will be a kalpa named Ornate with Great Jewels,
And a world named Undefiled,
Pure and flawless,
With lapis lazuli for its ground,
With golden cords defining its ways,
With trees variegated by the precious seven,
Always having flowers and fruits.
All the bodhisattvas of that domain,
Ever firm in will and thought,
Of supernatural powers and pāramitās
All in complete possession,
Under numberless buddhas
Having well learned the bodhisattva-way:
Such leaders as these
Shall be converted by the Buddha Flower Light.
[That] buddha, when he is a prince,
Will abandon his domain and give up earthly glory,
And in his last bodily existence
Will leave home and achieve the Buddha-way.
The Buddha Flower Light will dwell in the world
For a lifetime of twelve minor kalpas,
And the people of his domain
Will live for eight minor kalpas.
After that buddha's extinction
The Righteous Law will abide in the world
For thirty-two minor kalpas,
Widely saving living creatures.
At the expiration of the Righteous Law,
The Counterfeit Law [will abide] for thirty-two [minor kalpas].
His relics will be widely dispersed,
Universally worshiped by gods and men.
The doings of the Buddha Flower Light,
Such as these will be his deeds.
That most holy honored of men,

Most excellent and incomparable,
He is really you yourself;
Therefore rejoice and be glad."

At that time all the four groups of bhikshus, bhikshuṇīs, upāsakas, and upāsikās, and gods, dragons, yakshas, gandharvas, asuras, garuḍas, kiṃnaras, mahoragas, and others, all the great assembly, seeing that Śāriputra in the presence of the Buddha had received his prediction of Perfect Enlightenment, rejoiced greatly in unbounded ecstasy, each divesting himself of the robe he wore and offering it in homage to the Buddha, while Śakra Devendra, the Lord Brahma, and others, with countless divine sons, also paid homage to the Buddha with wonderful heavenly robes and celestial mandārava flowers, mahā-mandārava flowers, and so on. The celestial robes bestrewed, remaining in the sky, whirled round of themselves and hundreds of thousands of myriads of sorts of heavenly musical instruments all at once made music in the sky. And, raining numerous heavenly flowers, they uttered these words: "Of old at Vārāṇasī the Buddha first rolled the wheel of the Law and now again rolls the supreme and greatest Law-wheel."

Thereupon all the divine sons, desiring to announce this meaning over again, spoke [thus] in verse:

"Of old, at Vārāṇasī,
[Thou] didst roll the Law-wheel of the Four Noble Truths
And discriminately preach the laws
Of the rise and extinction of the five aggregates,
And now again thou dost roll the most wonderful,
Supreme, great wheel of the Law,
The Law which is extremely profound
And which few are able to believe.
We for a long time past
Have often heard the World-honored One preach,
[But] we have never before heard such
A profound, mystic, and supreme Law.
The World-honored One preaching this Law,
We all follow it with joy.
The great wise Śāriputra
Now has received the Honored One's prediction.

We also in like manner
Must certainly become buddhas,
Who in all worlds
Are the most honored and peerless.
The Buddha-way is beyond conception
And is preached by opportune tactful methods.
May all our happy karma
In the present world or past worlds,
And the merit of seeing the Buddha,
All turn to the Way of buddhahood."

Thereupon Śāriputra spoke to the Buddha, saying: "World-honored One! I now have no doubts or regrets. In person, before the Buddha, I have received my prediction of Perfect Enlightenment. [But] these twelve hundred self-controlled ones, who of yore abode in the [four] stages of learning,[7] were always instructed by the Buddha, saying: 'My Law is able to give freedom from birth, decrepitude, disease, and death, and the final attainment of nirvana.' Each of these who are under training and no longer under training is also free from [false] views about the self and about 'existence' or 'nonexistence,' and considers he has attained nirvana. But now, in the presence of the Buddha, hearing that which they have never heard before, they have all fallen into doubts and perplexities. Good! World-honored One! Please state the reasons to the four groups so that they may be free from doubts and regrets."

Then the Buddha spoke to Śāriputra: "Have I not before said that the buddhas, the world-honored ones, by various reasonings, parables, and terms preach the Law tactfully, all for the purpose of Perfect Enlightenment? All these teachings are for the purpose of transforming bodhisattvas. But Śāriputra! Let me now again in a parable make this meaning still more clear, [for] intelligent people through a parable reach understanding.

"Śāriputra! Suppose in a [certain] kingdom, city, or town there is a great elder, old and worn, of boundless wealth, and possessing many fields, houses, slaves, and servants. His house is spacious and large, having only one door, and with many people dwelling in it, one

7. Also called the four holy stages, or the four fruits, of śrāvakas. See Glossary.

hundred, two hundred, or even five hundred in number. Its halls and chambers are decayed and old, its walls crumbling, the bases of its pillars rotten, the beams and rooftree toppling and dangerous. On every side at the same moment fire suddenly starts and the house is in flames. The sons of the elder, say ten, twenty, or even thirty, are in this dwelling. The elder, on seeing this conflagration spring up on every side, is greatly startled and reflects thus: 'Though I am able to get safely out of this burning house, yet my children in the burning house are pleasurably absorbed in amusements, without apprehension, knowledge, surprise, or fear. Though the fire is pressing upon them and pain and suffering are imminent, they do not mind or fear and have no impulse to escape.'

"Śāriputra! This elder ponders thus: 'I am strong in my body and arms. Shall I get them out of the house by means of a flower vessel,[8] or a bench,[9] or a table?'[10] Again he ponders: 'This house has only one gate; moreover, it is narrow and small; [my] children are young, knowing nothing as yet and attached to their place of play; perchance they will fall into and be burned in the fire. I must speak to them on this dreadful matter, [warning them] that the house is burning and that they must come out instantly lest they be burned and injured by the fire.' Having reflected thus, according to his thoughts, he notifies his children: 'Come out quickly, all of you!'

"Though the father, in his pity, lures and admonishes with kind words, yet the children, joyfully attached to their play, are unwilling to believe him and have neither surprise nor fear, nor any mind to escape; moreover, they do not know what is the fire [he means], or what the house, and what he means by being lost, but only run hither and thither in play, glancing at their father. Then the elder reflects thus: 'This house is burning in a great conflagration. If I and my children do not get out at once, we shall certainly be burned up by it. Let me now by some tactful means cause my children to escape this disaster.' Knowing that to which each of his children is predisposed and all the various attractive playthings and curiosities to which their natures will joyfully respond, the father informs them, saying: 'The things with which you are fond of playing, so rare and precious—if

8. A symbol of the wisdom of the Buddha.
9. A symbol of the four fearlessnesses of the Buddha. See Glossary.
10. A symbol of the ten powers of the Buddha. See Glossary.

you do not [come and] get them, you will be sorry for it afterward. Such a variety of goat carts, deer carts, and bullock carts is now outside the gate to play with. All of you must come quickly out of this burning house, and I will give you whatever you want.' Thereupon the children, hearing of the attractive playthings mentioned by their father, and because they suit their wishes, every one eagerly, each pushing the other and racing against each other, comes scrambling out of the burning house.

"Then the elder, seeing his children have safely escaped and are all in the square, sits down in the open, no longer troubled but with a mind at ease and ecstatic with joy. Then each of the children says to their father: 'Father! Please now give us those lovely things you promised us to play with, goat carts, deer carts, and bullock carts.' Śāriputra! Then the elder gives to each of his children equally a great cart, lofty and spacious, adorned with all the precious things, surrounded with railed seats, hung with bells on its four sides, and covered with curtains, splendidly decorated also with various rare and precious things, linked with strings of precious stones, hung with garlands of flowers, thickly spread with beautiful mats, supplied with rosy pillows, yoked with white bullocks of pure [white] skin, of handsome appearance, and of great muscular power, which walk with even steps and with the speed of the wind, having also many servants and followers to guard them. Wherefore? Because this great elder is of boundless wealth and all his various treasuries and granaries are full to overflowing. So he reflects thus: 'My possessions being boundless, I must not give my children inferior small carts. All these children are my sons, whom I love without partiality. Having such great carts made of the precious seven, infinite in number, I should with equal mind bestow them on each one without discrimination. Wherefore? Because if I gave them to the whole nation, these things of mine would not run short—how much less to my children!' Meanwhile each of the children rides on his great cart, having got that which he had never had before and never expected to have. Śāriputra! What is your opinion? Has that elder, in giving great carts of the precious substances to his children equally, been somewhat guilty of falsehood?"

Śāriputra said: "No, World-honored One! That elder only caused his children to escape the disaster of fire and preserved their bodies alive—he committed no falsity. Why? He has in such a manner preserved their bodies alive and also they have obtained those playthings; how much more by tactful means has he saved them from that burning house! World-honored One! Even if that elder did not give them one of the smallest carts, still he is not false. Wherefore? [Because] that elder from the first formed this intention: 'I will by tactful means cause my children to escape.' For this reason he is not false. How much less [so] seeing that this elder, knowing his own boundless wealth and desiring to benefit his children, gives them great carts equally!"

The Buddha said to Śāriputra: "Good! Good! It is even as you say. Śāriputra! The Tathāgata is also like this, for he is the father of all worlds, who has forever entirely ended all [his] fear, despondency, distress, ignorance, and umbrageous darkness and has perfected [his] boundless knowledge, powers, and fearlessness; is possessed of great spiritual power and wisdom; has completely attained the pāramitās of tactfulness and wisdom; who is the greatly merciful and greatly compassionate, ever tireless, ever seeking the good, and benefiting all beings. And he is born in [this] triple world, the old decayed burning house, to save all living creatures from the fires of birth, old age, disease, death, grief, suffering, foolishness, darkness, and the three poisons, and teach them to obtain Perfect Enlightenment. He sees how all living creatures are scorched by [the fires of] birth, old age, disease, death, grief, and sorrow, and suffer various kinds of distress by reason of the five desires and the [greed for] gain; and how, by reason of the attachments of desire and [its] pursuits, they now endure much suffering and hereafter will suffer in hell, or as animals or hungry spirits; even if they are born in a heaven, or amongst men, there are such various kinds of sufferings as poverty, distress, separation from loved ones, and union with hateful beings. Absorbed in these things, all living creatures rejoice and take their pleasure, while they neither apprehend nor perceive, are neither alarmed nor fear, and are without satiety, never seeking to escape but in the burning house of this triple world running about hither and thither, and although they will meet with great suffering, count it not a cause for anxiety.

"Śāriputra! The Buddha, having seen this, then reflects thus: 'I am the father of all creatures and I must snatch them from suffering and give them the bliss of the infinite, boundless Buddha-wisdom for them to play with.'

"Śāriputra! The Tathāgata again reflects thus: 'If I only use spiritual power and wisdom, casting aside every tactful method, and extol for the sake of all living creatures the wisdom, powers, and fearlessness of the Tathāgata, living creatures cannot by this method be saved. Wherefore? As long as all these creatures have never escaped birth, old age, disease, death, grief, and suffering, but are being burned in the burning house of the triple world, how can they understand the Buddha-wisdom?'

"Śāriputra! Even as that elder, though with power in body and arms, yet does not use it but only by diligent tact resolutely saves [his] children from the calamity of the burning house and then gives each of them great carts made of precious things, so is it with the Tathāgata; though he has power and fearlessness, he does not use them, but only by his wise tact does he remove and save all living creatures from the burning house of the triple world, preaching the three vehicles: the śrāvaka, pratyekabuddha, and Buddha vehicles. And thus he speaks to them: 'All of you! Do not delight to dwell in the burning house of the triple world. Do not hanker after [its] crude forms, sounds, odors, flavors, and contacts. [For] if, through hankering, you beget a love [of it], then you will be burned by it. Get you out of the triple world and attain to the three vehicles, the śrāvaka, pratyekabuddha, and Buddha vehicles. I now give you my pledge for this, and it will never prove false. Do you only be diligent and zealous!' By these tactful means does the Tathāgata lure all creatures forth, and again speaks thus: 'Know ye! All these three vehicles are praised by sages; [in them you will be] free and independent, without wanting to rely on anything else. Riding in these three vehicles, by means of perfect faculties,[11] powers,[12] perceptions,[13] ways,[14] concentrations, emancipations, and contemplations, you will as a matter of course be happy and gain infinite peace and joy.'

"Śāriputra! If there are living beings who have a spirit of wisdom within and, following the Buddha, the World-honored One, hear the Law, receive it in faith, and zealously make progress, desiring speedily to escape from the triple world and seeking nirvana for themselves, these will [have the vehicle] named the śrāvaka-vehicle, just as some of those children come out of the burning house for the sake of a goat

11. The five roots. See p. 57, fn. 10. 12. The five powers. See p. 57, fn. 10.
13. The seven degrees of intelligence.
14. The Eightfold Path. See Glossary.

cart. If there are living beings who, following the Buddha, the World-honored One, hear the Law, receive it in faith, and zealously make progress, seeking self-gained wisdom,[15] delighting in the tranquillity of [their] individual goodness, and deeply versed in the causes and reasons of the laws, these will [have the vehicle] named the pratyekabuddha-vehicle, just as some of those children come out of the burning house for the sake of a deer cart. If there are living beings who, following the Buddha, the World-honored One, hear the Law, receive it in faith, diligently practice, and zealously advance, seeking the complete wisdom, the wisdom of the Buddha, the natural wisdom, the wisdom without a teacher, and the knowledge, powers, and fearlessness of the Tathāgata, who take pity on and comfort innumerable creatures, benefit gods and men, and save all [beings], these will [have the vehicle] named the Great-vehicle. Because the bodhisattvas seek this vehicle, they are named mahāsattvas. They are like those children who come out of the burning house for the sake of a bullock cart.

"Śāriputra! Just as that elder, seeing his children get out of the burning house safely to a place free from fear, and, pondering on his immeasurable wealth, gives each of his children a great cart, so also is it with the Tathāgata. Being the father of all living creatures, if he sees infinite thousands of koṭis of creatures by the teaching of the Buddha escape from the suffering of the triple world, from fearful and perilous paths, and gain the joys of nirvana, the Tathāgata then reflects thus: 'I possess infinite, boundless wisdom, power, fearlessness, and other Law-treasuries of buddhas. All these living creatures are my sons to whom I will equally give the Great-vehicle, so that there will be no one who gains an individual nirvana,[16] but all [gain] nirvana by the same nirvana as the Tathāgata. All these living creatures who escape the triple world are given the playthings of buddhas, concentrations, emancipations, and others, all of one form and one kind, praised by sages and able to produce pure, supreme pleasure.' Śāriputra! Even as that elder at first attracted his children by the three carts and afterward gave them only a great cart magnificently adorned with precious things and supremely restful, yet that elder is not guilty of

15. Natural wisdom, obtained without a teacher.
16. Literally, "gain extinction [nirvana] alone," that is, individualism as contrasted with the universalism of Mahayana.

falsehood, so also is it with the Tathāgata: there is no falsehood in first preaching three vehicles to attract all living creatures and afterward saving by the Great-vehicle only. Wherefore? Because the Tathāgata possesses infinite wisdom, power, fearlessness, and the treasury of the laws, and is able to give all living creatures the Great-vehicle Law, but not all are able to receive it. Śāriputra! For this reason know that the buddhas, by their tactful powers, in the One Buddha-vehicle discriminate and expound the three."

The Buddha, desiring to proclaim this teaching over again, spoke thus in verse:

"Suppose there is an elder
Who has a large house,
And for long this house has been old,
Is also falling and decayed,
With lofty halls in dangerous condition,
Pillar bases broken and rotten,
Beams and rooftree toppling and leaning,
Foundation and steps in a state of collapse,
Walls and partitions ruined and cracked,
Their plaster crumbling away,
Thatch in disorder and dropping,
Rafters and eaves awry and slipping,
Its surrounding fences bent and distorted,
Filled with all kinds of refuse.
Five hundred people
Are dwelling within it.
Owls, hawks, and vultures,
Crows, magpies, pigeons, doves,
Black snakes, vipers, scorpions,
Centipedes, millipedes,
Geckos, galley worms,
Weasels, ferrets, rats, and mice,
All sorts of evil creatures,
Run about in every direction;
There are places stinking with excrement and urine,
Overflowing with uncleanliness,
Where dung beetles and worms

Flock together.
Foxes, wolves, and jackals
Bite and trample each other
To gnaw [human] carcasses,
Scattering their bones and flesh.
Following these, packs of dogs
Come, striving to snatch and grab,
And gaunt with hunger skulk about
Seeking food everywhere,
Quarreling and scuffling,
Snarling and barking.
Such is the fearfulness of that house
Full of variety.
In every direction there are
Goblins and ogres,[17]
Yakshas and malign demons,
Who devour the flesh of men;
All sorts of venomous insects
And evil birds and brutes
Hatch or suckle their broods,
Each hiding and protecting its own;
Yakshas come striving with each other
To seize and eat them;
When they have eaten their fill,
Their evil minds become inflamed,
And the sound of their quarreling
Is dreadful in the extreme.
Kumbhāṇḍa demons
Crouch on the earth and mold,
Sometimes springing from the ground
A foot or two high,
Wandering about to and fro,
Giving full rein to their sports;
Seizing dogs by their feet,
Striking them so that they lose their voices,
Twisting their legs around their necks,

17. Hill demons, house demons, and water demons.

Frightening dogs for their own amusement.
Also there are demons
Tall of stature,
Naked, black, and lean,
Always dwelling in that [house],
Who emit great and dreadful sounds,
Bellowing in search of food.
Again there are demons
With throats [narrow] as a needle.
And there are demons
With heads like a bullock's.
Some eat human flesh,
Some devour dogs;
Their locks are all disheveled,
They are cruel and fiendish,
And, oppressed by hunger and thirst,
Race about crying and calling.
Yakshas and hungry ghosts,
Evil birds and brutes
Hungrily hurry in all directions,
Peeping and looking through window and lattice.
Such are its plagues,
Terrible beyond measure.
This decaying old house
Belongs to a man
Who has just gone outside
But a little while ago,
Whereupon that house
Of a sudden catches fire.
All at once, in every direction,
Its flames are in full blaze;
Rooftree, beams, rafters, pillars
With cracking sound burst open,
Break, split, and topple down;
Walls and partitions crumble.
Demons and spirits
Bellow and cry aloud;
Hawks, vultures, and other birds,

Kumbhāṇḍa demons and others
Hurry about in alarm,
Powerless to escape.
Evil beasts and venomous insects
Hide away in holes and cavities;
Piśācaka demons
Also take up their abode therein.
For lack of merits
They are driven by the fire,
Cruelly hurting each other,
Supping and devouring each other's flesh and blood.
Creatures of the jackal tribe
Are already dead in herds.
The bigger evil beasts
Come striving to devour [them].
Fetid smoke and bursting flames
Fill and choke the surrounding [air].
Centipedes and millipedes
And all kinds of venomous snakes,
Burned by the fire,
Run contending from their holes.
Kumbhāṇḍa demons
Thereon seize and eat them.
And hungry demons,
Their heads ablaze with fire,
Tormented with hunger, thirst, and heat,
Rush about confused and in distress.
Such is the state of that house,
Dreadful in the extreme,
With horrid calamities and conflagration
And disasters not a few.
At this very time the master of the house
Is standing outside the gate,
When he hears someone saying:
'All of your children
A little while ago in their play
Came into this house
In their youth and ignorance,

Enjoying themselves with their amusements.'
On hearing this, the elder
In alarm enters the burning house,
With intent to save them
From the harm of burning.
So he tells his children
Of all the [impending] dangers, saying:
'There are evil demons and venomous worms,
And calamitous fire is spreading;
Sufferings upon sufferings
Follow each other unceasing;
Venomous snakes and vipers,
All kinds of yakshas,
Kumbhāṇḍa demons,
Jackals, foxes, and dogs,
Hawks, vultures, owls,
And all sorts of galley worms
Are tormented by hunger and thirst
And to be feared in the extreme.
Even these distresses are hard to deal with;
How much more this conflagration?'
The children, unheeding,
Though they hear their father's admonition,
Remain attached to their pleasures
And do not stop their play.
Thereupon the elder
Begins to reflect thus:
'My children, [acting] in this manner,
Add to my anxiety and distress.
Now this house [really]
Has nothing to delight in,
Yet all my children,
Bewitched by their play,
Take no notice of my instructions
And will be injured by the fire.'
Instantly he ponders,
Arranges a device,
And says to his children:

'I have many varieties
Of rare playthings,
Excellent carts wonderfully bejeweled,
Goat carts and deer carts
And great bullock carts,
Now all just outside the door;
Come out, all of you!
I, for your sakes,
Have made these carts.
You may roam and play with them
At your own will and pleasure.'
When the children hear him tell
Of such carts as these,
They immediately rush in rivalry,
Scampering forth,
And reach the open ground,
Away from harm.
The elder, seeing his children
Escape from the burning house,
Takes his place in the square,
Sitting on the lion throne,
And congratulates himself, saying:
'Now I am joyful.
All these children,
Brought up with so much difficulty,
Stupid, little, and ignorant,
Entered this dangerous house,
Abounding with venomous worms
And fearful goblins.
Conflagrations and raging flames
Broke out on every side,
But all these children were
Fascinated by their play.
Now I have rescued them
And caused them to escape from harm.
Therefore, all you people!
Now I am joyful.'
Then the children,

Knowing their father is sitting at ease,
All come to the father
And speak to the father, saying:
'Please give to us
The three kinds of precious carts
As you promised, [saying]:
"If you children come out,
I will give you three carts
And you can [choose] whichever you like."
Now is the very time;
Be pleased to give them [to us].'
The elder is very rich
And has treasuries full of
Gold, silver, lapis lazuli,
Moonstone, and agate.
With all kinds of precious things
[He has] made great carts,
Magnificently adorned and splendidly decorated,
Surrounded with railed seats,
Hung with bells on every side,
Strung with golden cords,
And with networks of pearls
Spread over them;
Festoons of golden flowers
Hang down here and there;
Many colors and varied decorations
Surround and encircle;
Soft silks and silk floss
Make the cushions;
The best quality of fine felt,
Worth thousands of koṭis,
Snow white and pure,
Is spread above [the cushions].
There are great white bullocks,
Sleek, strong, and active,
Of finest shape,
Yoked to the precious carts;
There are numerous retinues

Tending and guarding them.
These excellent carts
Are equally given to all the children.
Then the children,
Ecstatic with joy,
Riding these precious carts,
Roam in every direction,
Playing joyfully
Just as they wish, without hindrance.
I tell you, Śāriputra!
I also am like this,
The most honored of all the sages,
The father of the world;
All living beings
Are my sons
[But] are deeply attached to earthly pleasures
And without wisdom.
The triple world is not safe,
Just as the burning house,
Full of all kinds of sufferings,
Was greatly to be feared.
Ever there are distresses of birth,
Old age, disease, and death;
Such fires as these
Are burning ceaselessly.
The Tathāgata, freed from
The burning house of the triple world,
Tranquilly lives in seclusion,
Abiding in peace in the woodland.
Now this triple world
All is my domain;
The living beings in it
All are my sons.
But now this place
Abounds with distresses;
And I alone
Am able to save and protect them.[18]

18. The passage "Now this triple world . . . protect them" is called the

Though I taught and admonished them,
Yet they did not believe,
For they were imbued with desires
To which they were greedily attached.
Therefore, tactfully
I tell them of the three vehicles
Which cause all living beings
To know the sufferings of the triple world,
And reveal and expound
The way of escaping from the world.
If all these sons
Are resolved in their minds,
They will perfectly have the three clear views
And the six transcendent faculties,
And will become pratyekabuddhas
Or bodhisattvas who never slide back.[19]
Śāriputra!
I, for the sake of all beings,
By means of this parable
Preach the One Buddha-vehicle.
If all of you are able
To receive these words in faith,
You shall all be able
To accomplish the Buddha-way.
This vehicle is wonderful,
Pure, and supreme;
In all the worlds
There is nothing more exalted;
It is that which the Buddha rejoices in
And which all living creatures

---

preaching of the Three Merits of Sakyamuni Buddha: (1) his merit as lord, because the triple world is his possession or domain; (2) his merit as leader or teacher, because he alone saves all living creatures; and (3) his merit as father, because all are his sons.

19. The lines "If all these sons . . . who never slide back" are translated according to the Japanese rendering but can also be translated as follows: "If all these sons / Are resolved in their minds, / Perfect in the three clear views / And the six transcendent faculties, / Becoming pratyekabuddhas / Or never-backsliding bodhisattvas . . ."

Should praise,
Worship, and adore.
Infinite thousands of koṭis
Of powers, emancipations,
Meditations, and wisdom,
And the Buddha's other laws:
Such is the vehicle provided[20]
To cause all my sons,
Night and day for many kalpas,
Ever to take their recreation in it,
With bodhisattvas
As well as śrāvakas
Riding in this precious vehicle
Directly to the wisdom throne.
For these causes and reasons,
[Though] one searches in every direction,
There is no other vehicle
Except the Buddha's device.[21]
I tell you, Śāriputra!
All you people
Are my sons;
I then am father.
You, for successive kalpas
Burning in many sufferings,
Have I wholly rescued,
That you may escape the triple world.
Though I previously preached that
You [would attain] extinction,
You have only become free from birth and death,
And have not [attained] real extinction.
What you have now to do
Is only [to attain] the Buddha-wisdom.
If there be any bodhisattvas
Amongst this assembly,
Be you able wholeheartedly to obey
The real Law of the buddhas.

20. This line can also be translated "obtain such a vehicle as this."
21. The Buddha's tactfulness.

Though buddhas, world-honored ones,
[Convert] by tactful methods,
[Yet] living creatures transformed by them
Are all bodhisattvas.
If there are any of little wit
Who are deeply attached to desires and passions,
[The Buddha] for their sake
Preaches the truth of suffering.
All the living with joyful hearts
Attain the unprecedented.
The truth of suffering preached by the Buddha
Is real without differentiation.
If there are any living beings
Who do not know the source of suffering,
Deeply attached to the cause of suffering,
And unable to forsake it even for a moment,
[The Buddha] for the sake of them
Preaches the Way[22] by tactful methods, [saying]:
'The cause of all suffering
Is rooted in desire.'
If desire be extinguished,
[Suffering] has no foothold.
To annihilate all suffering
Is called the third truth.
For the sake of the truth of extinction
To observe and walk in the Way,
Forsaking all bonds of suffering,
This is called the attaining of emancipation.
From what have these people
Attained emancipation?
Merely to depart from the false
Is called emancipation.
But they have not yet really attained
Entire emancipation.
[So] the Buddha declares that these people
Have not yet really reached extinction.

22. The Eightfold Path. See Glossary.

Because these people have not yet gained
The supreme Way,
I am unwilling [to declare]
That they have attained extinction.
I am the king of the Law,
Absolute in regard to the Law,
Pacifying all creatures,
And therefore appear in the world.
Śāriputra!
This my seal of the Law,[23]
Because of my desire to benefit
All the world, is [now] expounded
Wherever you roam;
Do not recklessly proclaim it.
If there be any hearers
Who joyfully receive with profound obeisance,[24]
You may know these people
Are of avivartika.
If there be any who receive
This sutra-law in faith,
These people must have already
Seen buddhas of past times,
Revered and worshiped them,
And heard this Law.
If there be any people who are able
To believe your preaching,
They must have seen me
And also seen you
And these bhikshus,
As well as [these] bodhisattvas.[25]
This Law-Flower Sutra
Is preached for [men of] profound wisdom.[26]
Men of shallow knowledge, hearing it,

23. The seal of the Law is the same as the seal of reality. See p. 65, fn. 27.
24. To receive, carrying the folded hands to the top of the head as a sign of utmost reverence.
25. Or "[As I] also have been seen by you and the bhikshus and bodhisattvas."
26. Or "For its profound wisdom is preached."

Go astray, not understanding.
All the śrāvakas
And pratyekabuddhas
Cannot by their powers
Attain this sutra.
Śāriputra!
Even you into this sutra
Can [only] enter by faith;
How much [more difficult] for the other śrāvakas.
All the other śrāvakas,
Because of believing the Buddha's words,
Obediently follow this sutra;
But it is not that they themselves have knowledge.
Again, Śāriputra!
To those who are haughty and lazy[27]
And to those with self-centered views,
Do not preach this sutra.
Common shallow people
Deeply attached to the five desires,
Who on hearing cannot apprehend,
Do not preach it to them.
If any people do not believe in
And vilify this sutra,
Then they cut [themselves] off [from] all
The buddha-seeds in the worlds;[28]
Or if again they sullenly frown,
And cherish doubts and perplexities,
Listen to my declaration
Concerning the recompense of such people's sin:
Whether during the Buddha's lifetime
Or after his extinction,
If there be any who slander
Such a sutra as this,

27. In the following passage the so-called "fourteen sins of slandering the Law" are expounded. These are fundamental causes of falling into the Avīci hell: haughtiness, neglect, self-centeredness, shallowness, sensuality, irrationality, unbelief, sullenness, doubting, slander, scorning goodness, hating goodness, jealousy of goodness, and grudging goodness.

28. Or "Then they cut off / The buddha-seeds in all the worlds."

Who, seeing those who read and recite,
Write or hold this sutra,
Scorn and despise, hate and envy them
And bear them a tenacious grudge.
Concerning the recompense of such people's sin,
Listen now again:
After their lifetimes end
They will enter into the Avīci hell
For a complete kalpa,
Being born again at each kalpa's end
And thus revolving
In innumerable kalpas;
When they come out of hell,
They will be degraded to animals,
Such as dogs or jackals,
With lean-cheeked forms,
Blue-black, with scabs and sores,
Knocked about by men;
Moreover, by men
Hated and scorned,
Constantly suffering hunger and thirst,
Bones and flesh withered.
During life beaten with thorns[29]
And after death with potsherds and stones,
Because of cutting [themselves] off from the buddha-seed
They receive such recompense for their sin.
Perhaps they become camels,
Or are born amongst asses,
Always carrying burdens on their backs,
Being beaten with sticks,
Thinking only of water and grass,
Knowing nothing else.
Because of slandering this sutra,
Such is their punishment.
Some[times] becoming jackals,
They enter a village,

29. Literally, "Alive receiving thorn poison."

Their bodies scabbed with sores,
Having not even an eye,
By all the boys
Beaten and stoned,
Suffering bitter pains,
At times even [beaten] to death.
When they have thus died,
Again they each receive a serpent's body
Of a shape as long as
Five hundred yojanas.
Deaf and stupid, without feet,
They wriggle about on their bellies,
By many kinds of insects
Stung and devoured,
Day and night in misery,
With never any rest.
Because of slandering this sutra,
Such is their punishment.
Should they become human beings,
Their powers [of life] are blunted,
Short and ugly, palsied and lame,
Blind, deaf, and humpbacked;
Whatever they may say,
People do not believe;
Their breath is vile,
They are possessed by demons,
They are needy and menial,
Ordered about by others,
Often ill and emaciated,
Having none on whom to rely;
Though they are dependent on others,
These take no notice of them;
Even if they gain anything,
They instantly forget and lose it;
If they make use of means of healing
And follow the usual methods of treatment,
Other ailments will only be added,
Or, again, they will cause [their patients] to die;

If they themselves are ill,
None will save and cure them;
Though they take good medicine,
[Their disease] becomes increasingly severe;
If other people cause rebellion,
And plunder and rob,
For such crimes as these
The retribution pervertedly falls on them.
Such sinners as these
Never see the Buddha,
The king of all the holy ones,
Who preaches the Law, instructs, and transforms.
Such sinners as these
Are always born in distress;
Mad, deaf, and confused in mind,
They never hear the Law;
During kalpas innumerable
As the sands of the Ganges,
Whenever they are born they are deaf and dumb
And with deficient natural powers;
They constantly dwell in the hells
As their pleasure gardens,
Or in other evil states
As their dwellings;
Among asses, hogs, and dogs
Are the places where they [must] go.
Because of slandering this sutra,
Such is their punishment.
If they become human beings,
They are deaf, blind, and dumb,
Poor, needy, and feeble,
As their own ornament;
Dropsy and scurf,
Scabs, sores, and abscesses,
All such ills as these
Will be their apparel.
Their bodies are always fetid abodes,
Filthy and unclean;

They are deeply absorbed in themselves,
They become angrier and angrier,
Their carnal passions are utterly inflamed,
They are no better than animals;
Because of slandering this sutra,
Such is their punishment.
I say [to you], Śāriputra!
Those who slander this sutra,
If I told the tale of their evils,
I could not exhaust them in a whole kalpa.
For this cause and reason
I especially say to you:
Amongst undiscerning people,
Do not preach this sutra.
If there be any who are clever,
Of clear wisdom,
Learned and of strong memory,
Who seek after the Buddha-way,
To such people as these,
Then, you may preach it.
If any have ever seen
Hundreds of thousands of koṭis of buddhas,
Cultivated many roots of goodness,
And been firm in their inmost minds,
To such people as these,
Then, you may preach it.
If any have zealously progressed,
Constantly maintained kindly hearts,
And never spared body and life,
Then you may preach it to them.
If any have been reverent,
With unvarying mind,
Having left all the ignorant
And dwelt alone in mountains and swamps,
To such people as these,
Then, you may preach it.
Again, Śāriputra!
If you see any

Who give up bad friends
And make friends of the good,
To such people as these,
Then, you may preach it.
If you see Buddha-sons
Who keep the commands in purity,
Like pure bright jewels,
Who seek the Great-vehicle sutra,
To such people as these,
Then, you may preach it.
If any be free from irascibility,
Of upright character and patient,
Always compassionate to all beings
And reverent to the buddhas,
To such people as these,
Then, you may preach it.
Further, if there be Buddha-sons
Who, in the general assembly,
With pure hearts,
By various reasonings,
Parables, and expressions,
Expound the Law without hesitation,
To such people as these,
Then, you may preach it.
If there be bhikshus
Who, for the sake of perfect knowledge,
Seek the Law in every direction,
Folding their hands in profound obeisance,
Only pleased to receive and keep
The Great-vehicle sutra,
Even without accepting
A single verse of any other sutra,
To such people as these,
Then, you may preach it.
Like a man who with all his mind
Seeks for the Buddha's relics,
So those who seek the sutra and,
Having obtained it, receive it with profound obeisance,

And who are not again
Bent on seeking other sutras,
And also have never minded
Books of other philosophies,
To such people as these,
Then, you may preach it.
I say to you, Śāriputra!
Were I to speak [in detail] of [all] these kinds
Of seekers after the Buddha-way,
In a whole kalpa I could not finish.
Such people as these
Are able to believe and discern.
You should to them preach
The Sutra of the Flower of the Wonderful Law."

CHAPTER IV

Faith Discernment

AT THAT TIME the wisdom-destined Subhūti, Mahā-Kātyāyana, Mahā-Kāśyapa, and Mahā-Maudgalyāyana, hearing from the Buddha the unprecedented Law and the prediction by the World-honored One of Śāriputra's [future destiny of] Perfect Enlightenment, were struck with wonder and ecstatic with joy. Thereupon they rose from their seats, and, arranging their garments, humbly baring their right shoulders, placing their right knees on the ground, with one mind folding their hands, bending their bodies in reverence, and gazing upon his honored face, addressed the Buddha, saying:

"We, heads of the monks, in years moreover worn out, consider that we have attained nirvana, and that there is nothing more we are able to undertake, so we do not press forward to seek after Perfect Enlightenment. The World-honored One for a long time has been preaching the Law, and we all the time seated in our places have become weary in our bodies and neglectful, only thinking of the void,

The title of this chapter can also be translated "Discernment Resulting from Faith" or "Discernment by Faith."

of the formless, and of nonfunction,[1] but in regard to the bodhisattva-laws, their supernatural displays, the purifying of the buddha-lands, and the perfecting of all living beings, our hearts have not taken delight. Wherefore? [Because we have fancied that] the World-honored One had caused us to escape the triple world and to obtain [proof of] nirvana, and besides, now we are [so] worn with age that in regard to Perfect Enlightenment, for which the Buddha instructs bodhisattvas, we have not conceived a single fond thought of joy. Now we, in the presence of the Buddha, hearing that śrāvakas are predicted to [attain] Perfect Enlightenment, are extremely glad in our minds and have obtained that which we have never experienced before. Unexpectedly we now of a sudden hear this rare Law. Profoundly do we congratulate ourselves [on] having acquired so great and good a gain, an inestimable jewel, without the seeking. World-honored One! Now let us have the pleasure of speaking in a parable to make plain this meaning.

"It is like a man who, in his youth, leaves his father and runs away. For long he dwells in some other country, for ten, twenty, or fifty years. The older he grows, the more needy he becomes. Roaming about in all directions to seek clothing and food, he gradually wanders along till he unexpectedly approaches his native country. From the first the father searched for this son, but in vain, and meanwhile settled in a [certain] city. His home became very rich, his goods and treasures incalculable: gold, silver, lapis lazuli, coral, amber, crystal, and other gems, so that his granaries and treasuries overflow; he has many youths and slaves, retainers and attendants, and numberless elephants, horses, carriages, animals to ride, cows, and sheep. His revenues and investments spread to other countries, and his traders and customers are many in the extreme.

"At this time the poor son, wandering through village after village and passing through countries and cities, at last reaches the city where his father has settled. The father has always been thinking of his son, and though he has been parted from him over fifty years, he has never spoken of the matter to anyone, only pondering it himself and cherishing regret in his heart as he reflects: 'Old and worn, I

1. These are three Hinayana ideas, called "the three gates of emancipation [or freedom]" or "the three samādhis": to contemplate the fundamental nature of all existence (1) as void or immaterial, (2) as formless, and (3) as functionless.

own much wealth—gold, silver, and jewels, granaries and treasuries overflowing—but I have no son. Someday my end will come and my wealth will be scattered and lost, for there is no one to whom I can leave it.' Thus does he earnestly, whenever he thinks of his son, repeat this reflection: 'If I could only get [back] my son and commit my wealth to him, how contented and happy should I be, with never any more anxiety!'

"World-honored One! Meanwhile the poor son, hired for wages here and there, unexpectedly arrives at his father's house. Standing by the gate, he sees from afar his father seated on a lion couch, his feet on a jeweled footstool, revered and surrounded by Brahmans, Kshatriyas, and citizens, and with strings of pearls worth thousands and myriads adorning his body; attendants and young slaves with white fly whisks wait upon him right and left; he is covered by a precious canopy from which hang streamers of flowers; perfume is sprinkled on the earth, all kinds of famous flowers are scattered around, and precious things are placed in rows; some he accepts, others he rejects. Such is his glory, and the honor of his dignity. The poor son, seeing his father possessed of [such] great power, was seized with fear, regretting that he had come to [this] place, and secretly reflected thus: 'This must be a king or someone of royal rank; it is no place for me to obtain anything for the hire of my labor. I had better go to some poor hamlet, where there is a place to hire out my labor, and food and clothing are easier to get. If I tarry here long, I may suffer oppression and forced labor.'

"Having reflected thus, he hastily runs away. Meanwhile the rich elder on his lion seat has recognized his son at first sight and with great joy in his mind has thus reflected: 'Now I have the one to whom my treasuries of wealth are to be made over. Always have I been thinking of this [my] son, with no means of seeing him; but suddenly he himself has come and my longing is satisfied. Though worn with years, I still yearn [for him].'

"Instantly he dispatches his attendants to rush after him and fetch him back. Thereupon the messengers hasten forth to seize him. The poor son, surprised and scared, loudly cries his complaint: 'I have committed no offence against you; why should I be arrested?' The messengers all the more hasten to lay hold of him and compel him to go back. Thereupon the poor son thinks to himself that [though] he is innocent yet he will be imprisoned, and that will certainly mean his death, so that he is all the more terrified, faints away, and falls on the ground. The father, seeing this from afar, gives the messengers his word: 'There is no need for this man. Do not fetch him by force. Sprinkle cold water on his face to restore him to consciousness and do not speak to him any further!'[2] Wherefore? The father, knowing that his son's disposition is inferior, knowing that his own lordly position has caused distress to his son, yet profoundly assured that he is his son, tactfully says nothing to others that this is his son. A messenger says to the son: 'I now set you free; go wherever you will.' The poor son is delighted, [thus] obtaining the unexpected. He rises from the ground and goes to a poor hamlet in search of food and clothing.

"Then the elder, desiring to attract his son, sets up a device. Secretly he sends two men of doleful and undignified appearance, [saying]: 'You go and visit that place and gently say to the poor man: "There is a place for you to work here; you will be given double wages." If the poor man agrees, bring him back and give him work. If he asks what work do [you] wish him to do, then you may say to him: "It is for removing [a heap of] dirt that we hire you, and we both also would work along with you."' Then the two messengers went in search of the poor son and, having found him, placed [before him] the above proposal. Thereupon the poor son, having received his wages beforehand, joins with them in removing the dirt [heap]. His father, beholding the son, is struck with compassion for and wonder at him.

"Another day he sees at a distance through a window his son's figure, gaunt, lean, and doleful, filthy and unclean from the piles of dirt and dust; thereupon he takes off his strings of jewels, his soft attire and ornaments, and puts on again a coarse, torn, and dirty garment, smears his body with dust, takes a dustpan in his right hand, and with an appearance of fear[3] says to the laborers: 'Get on with your work, don't be lazy.' By [such] a device he gets near his son, to whom he soon afterward says: 'Aye, [my] man, you stay and work here, do not go again elsewhere; I will increase your wages; whatever you need, bowls, utensils, rice, wheat flour, salt, vinegar, and so on; have no hesitation; besides, there is [an] old and worn-out servant

2. Or "He sprinkles cold water . . . does not speak . . ." and so on.

3. The probable meaning is "with an appearance of sternness," but the Japanese rendering is as above.

whom you shall be given if you need him. Be at ease in your mind; I am as it were your father; do not be worried again. Wherefore? I am old and advanced in years, but you are young and vigorous; all the time you have been working, you have never been deceitful, lazy, angry, or grumbling; I have never seen you have such vices as these, like the other laborers. From this time forth you shall be as my own begotten son.'

"Thereupon the elder gives him a name anew and calls him a son. Then the poor son, though he rejoices at this happening, still thinks of himself as a humble hireling. For this reason, for twenty years he continues to be employed for removing dirt. After this period, there is confidence between them and he goes in and out and at his ease, though his abode is still the original place.

"World-honored One! Then the elder becomes ill and, knowing that he will shortly die, says to the poor son: 'Now I possess abundant gold, silver, and precious things, and my granaries and treasuries are full to overflowing. The quantities of these things, and the [amounts] which should be received and given, [I want] you to understand in detail. Such is my mind. Do you agree to this my will. Wherefore? Because now I and you are of the same mind. Be increasingly mindful so that there be no waste.'

"Then the poor son accepts his instructions and commands, and becomes acquainted with all the goods, gold, silver, and precious things, as well as all the granaries and treasuries, but has no idea of expecting to receive [as much as] a meal, while his abode is still the original place and his sense of inferiority too he is still unable to abandon.

"After a short time has passed, again the father, knowing that his son's ideas have gradually been enlarged and his will well developed, and that he despises his previous [state of] mind, on seeing that his own end is near, commands his son [to come] and at the same time gathers together his relatives, and the kings, ministers, Kshatriyas, and citizens. When they are all assembled, he thereupon addresses them, saying: 'Know, gentlemen, this is my son begotten by me. It is over fifty years since, from a certain city, he left me and ran away to endure loneliness and misery. His former name was so and so and my name is so and so. At that time in that city I sought him sorrowfully. Suddenly in this place I met and regained him. This is really my son and I am really his father. Now all the wealth which I possess belongs entirely to my son, and all my previous disbursements and receipts are known by this son.'

"World-honored One! When the poor son heard these words of his father, great was his joy at such unexpected [news], and thus he thought: 'Without any mind for or effort on my part these treasures now come of themselves to me.'

"World-honored One! The very rich elder is the Tathāgata and we all are as the Buddha's sons. The Tathāgata has always declared that we are his sons. World-honored One! Because of the three sufferings, in the midst of births and deaths we have borne all kinds of torments, being deluded and ignorant and enjoying [our] attachment to trifles. Today the World-honored One has caused us to ponder over and remove the dirt of all diverting discussions of [inferior] laws [or things]. In these we have been diligent to make progress and have got [but] a day's pay [for our effort] to reach nirvana.[4] Having got this, we greatly rejoiced and were contented, saying to ourselves: 'For our diligence and progress in the Buddha-law what we have received is ample.' But the World-honored One, knowing beforehand that our minds were attached to low desires and delighted in inferior things, lets us go our own way and does not discriminate against us, [saying]: 'You shall [yet] have control of the treasury of Tathāgata-knowledge.' The World-honored One by his tactful power tells of the Tathāgata-wisdom, [but] we, [though] following the Buddha and receiving [but] a day's wage of nirvana, have deemed it a great gain and never devoted ourselves to seeking after this Great-vehicle. We also have declared and expounded the Tathāgata-wisdom to bodhisattvas, but in regard to this [Great-vehicle] we have never had a longing for it. Wherefore? The Buddha, knowing that our minds delight in inferior things, by his tactful power teaches according to our [capacity], but still we do not perceive that we are really Buddha-sons. Now we have just realized that the World-honored One does not begrudge the Buddha-wisdom. Wherefore? From of old we are really sons of the Buddha, but only have taken pleasure in minor matters; if we had had a mind to take pleasure in the great, the Buddha would have preached the Great-vehicle Law to us. Now he in this sutra preaches only the

4. Or "[to make progress and] reach nirvana as our day's hire."

One-vehicle; and though formerly in the presence of bodhisattvas he spoke disparagingly of śrāvakas who were pleased with minor matters, yet the Buddha had in reality been instructing them in the Great-vehicle. Therefore we say that though we had no mind to hope or expect it, [yet] now the great treasure of the King of the Law has of itself come to us, and such things that Buddha-sons should obtain we have all obtained."

Then Mahā-Kāśyapa, desiring to proclaim this meaning over again, spoke [thus] in verse:

"We on this day
Have heard the Buddha's voice teach
And are ecstatic with joy at
Having obtained the unprecedented.
The Buddha declares that [we] śrāvakas
Will become buddhas;
[His] peerless collection of treasures
We have received without seeking.
It is like a youth,
Immature and ignorant,
Who leaves his father and runs away
To other lands far distant,
Wandering about in many countries
For over fifty years.
His father, with anxious care,
Searches in all directions.
Wearied with his search,
He abides in a certain city.
Where he builds a house,
Enjoying the pleasures of life;[5]
Very rich is his house,
With abundance of gold and silver,
Moonstones and agates,
Pearls and lapis lazuli,
Elephants, horses, oxen, and sheep,
Palanquins, litters, carriages,

5. Literally, "enjoying the five desires." See Glossary.

Husbandmen, young slaves,
And a multitude of people;
His revenues and investments
Spread even to other countries;
His traders and customers
Are found everywhere;
A thousand myriad koṭis of people
Surround and honor him;
Constantly by the king
He is held in affection;
All the ministers and noble families
Honor him highly;
For all these reasons
His guests are many;
Such are the abundance of his wealth
And the greatness of his power.
But his years are wearing away
And he grieves the more over his son;
Morning and night he ponders:
'The time of my death is approaching;
My foolish son has left me
For over fifty years;
These things in my storehouses—
What shall I do [with them]?'
At that time the poor son
Seeks food and clothing
From city to city,
From country to country,
Sometimes getting something,
Sometimes nothing;
Famished, weak, and gaunt,
Covered with scabs and sores,
Gradually he passes along
To the city where his father dwells.
Hired for wages he roams about,
At last reaching his father's house.
At that very hour the elder
Within his gates

Has set up a great jeweled curtain
And sits on a lion seat
Surrounded by his attendants,
Everybody taking care of him.
Some are counting
Gold, silver, and precious things,
[Others] incoming and outgoing goods,
Noting and recording bonds.
The poor son, seeing his father
So noble and splendid,
Thinks: 'This must be a king
Or one of royal rank.'
Alarmed and wondering, [he says]:
'Why have I come here?'
Again he thinks to himself:
'If I tarry [here] long,
I may suffer oppression
And be driven to forced labor.'
Having pondered thus,
He runs off in haste
In search of some poor place,
That he may go and hire his labor.
At that time the elder
On the lion seat,
Seeing his son from afar,
Secretly recognizes him
And instantly orders servants
To pursue and fetch him back.
The poor son cries in alarm,
Faints away, and falls on the ground, [saying]:
'These men have caught me;
I shall certainly be killed.
Why, for food and clothing,
Did I come here?'
The elder, knowing that his son,
Being foolish and inferior,
Will not believe in his word,
Nor believe that he is his father,

With tactful method
Again dispatches other men,
One-eyed, squat, common,
And unimposing, [saying]:
'You [go and] tell him,
Saying: "You be hired along with us
To remove dirt and rubbish
And you shall be given double wages." '
The poor son hearing this
Is glad, and comes with them,
For the purpose of removing dirt
And cleansing outhouses.
The elder, through a lattice,
Continually sees his son,
And thinks of him as foolish
And pleased with humble things.
Then the elder,
Donning a tattered dirty garment,
Takes a dirt hod,
Goes to where his son is,
And by [this] device gets near him,
Bidding him be diligent, [saying]:
'I have [decided to] increase your wages,
Besides oil for your feet,
And plenty of food and drink,
And thick warm mats.'
Then with sharp words he thus chides:
'Get you on with the work.'
Again he speaks gently:
'You are as if you were my son.'
The elder, being wise,
Gradually causes him to go in and out,
And after twenty years
Employs him in house affairs,
Showing him gold and silver,
Pearls and crystal,
And the incoming and outgoing of things;
All these he makes him know.

Still he dwells without,
Lodging in a hovel,
For himself thinking of penurious things,
[Saying]: 'These things are not mine.'
The father, knowing his son's mind
Has gradually developed,
And wishing to give him his wealth,
Gathers together his relatives,
Princes and ministers,
Kshatriyas and citizens.
In this great assembly,
He announces: 'This is my son,
Who left me and went elsewhere
Fifty years ago;
Since I saw my son arrive,
Twenty years have passed.
Long ago in a certain city
I lost this son;
In wandering round in search of him,
At last I arrived here.
All that I have,
Houses and people,
I entirely give to him;
He is free to use them as he will.'
The son thinks of his former poverty
And inferior disposition,
[Yet] anew from his father
Obtains such great treasures,
Together with houses and buildings
And all this wealth,
[And so] rejoices greatly
On receiving such unexpected [fortune].
So it is with the Buddha;
Knowing that we are pleased with trifles,
He did not before proclaim,
'You will become buddhas,'
But said that we
Who are attaining faultlessness

And perfect in Hinayana
Are his śrāvaka disciples.
The Buddha commands us:
'Preach the most high Way,
And that these who practice it
Will become buddhas.'
We, receiving the Buddha's teaching,
For the sake of great bodhisattvas,
By numerous reasonings,
By various parables,
And by so many expressions,
Preach the supreme Way.
The sons of the Buddha,
Hearing the Law from us,
Day and night ponder over
And with unflagging zeal practice it.
Then the buddhas
Will predict of them:
'You, in a future generation,
Shall become buddhas.'
The mystic Law
Of all the buddhas
[Can] only to bodhisattvas
Be expounded in full reality,
So not to us [till now]
Was this truth preached.
Just as that poor son
Who came to be near his father,
Though he knew all the goods,
Had no hope of possessing them,
[So] we, though we proclaimed
The treasury of the Buddha-law,
Yet had no will or wish for it,
Being also like him.
We, with the extinction of inward [fires],[6]
Considered ourselves satisfied;

6. Literally, "inside extinction," that is, the annihilation of all the earthly cares in one's mind.

Having thus settled this matter,
Nothing more remained to be done.
Even if we had heard
Of the purification of buddha-lands
And the conversion of living beings,
We would never have rejoiced.
And wherefore?
[Because we fancied that] all things
Were altogether void,
Without birth, without extinction,
Nothing large, nothing small,
Without fault, without effort.
Thinking thus,
With no conception of joy,
We, for long,
Neither coveted nor were attached
To the Buddha-wisdom,
Nor had we any will or wish [for it].
But we, in regard to the Law,
Considered we had reached finality.
We, for a long time
Practicing the Law of the Void,
Obtained release from the triple world's
Distressing troubles,
Dwelling in the final bodily state
Of nirvana [in which form still] remains;
Being instructed by the Buddha, [we thought]
We had, without a doubt, attained the Way
And that we had therefore
Repaid the Buddha's grace.
Though we, for the sake
Of all Buddha-sons,
Have preached the Bodhisattva-law
That they should seek the Buddha-way,
Yet we, in regard to this Law,[7]
Had never any wish or pleasure.

7. Some Chinese copies do not have this line, but the Japanese copies do.

Our Leader saw and let us alone,
Because he looked into our minds;
[So] at first he did not stir up our zeal
By telling of the true gain.
Just as the rich elder,
Knowing his son's inferior disposition,
By his tactfulness
Subdues his mind,
And afterward gives him
All his wealth,
So is it with the Buddha
In his display of rarities.
Knowing those who delight in trifles,
And by his tactfulness
Subduing their minds,
He instructs them in the greater wisdom.
Today we have obtained
That which we have never had before;
What we have not previously looked for
Now we have unexpectedly obtained,
Just as that poor son
Obtained inestimable treasures.
World-honored One! Now we
Have got the Way and got the fruit,
And, in the faultless Law,
Attained to clear vision.[8]
We for long
Having kept the Buddha's pure commands,
Today for the first time
Obtain their fruit and reward.
In the Law of the Law-king,
Having long practiced holy deeds,[9]
Now we have attained to the faultless,
Peerless great fruit;
Now we are

8. The Buddha-wisdom.
9. Literally, "brahma-conduct."

Really hearers of the sound,[10]
Who cause all beings to hear
The sound of the Buddha-way.
Now we are
Really arhats,
Who, in all the worlds
Of gods, men, Māras, and Brahmans,
Universally by them
Are worthy of worship.
The World-honored One, in his great grace,
By things which are rare
Has compassion for and instructs
And benefits us;
Through countless koṭis of kalpas,
Who could repay him?
Service by hands and feet,
Homage with the head,
All kinds of offerings,
Are all unable to repay him.
If one bore [him] on one's head,[11]
Or carried [him] on one's shoulders
Through kalpas [numerous] as the sands of the Ganges;
Or revered him with one's whole mind,
Or with the best of food,
Or garments of countless value
And all kinds of bed things,
Or every sort of medicament;
Or with ox-head sandalwood[12]
And all kinds of jewels
Erected stupas and monasteries;
Or carpeted the ground with precious garments;
With such things as these
To pay homage
Through kalpas as the sands of the Ganges,

10. Śrāvakas.
11. Perhaps as a crown.
12. Sandalwood from Uttarakuru (see p. 258, fn. 3); this continent is said to be shaped like the head of an ox.

Yet one would be unable to repay.
Buddhas rarely [appear with their]
Infinite and boundless,[13]
Inconceivably
Great transcendent powers;
They are faultless and effortless,
The kings of the Law,
Who are able, for inferior [minds],
Patiently [to bide their time] in this matter,
And for common folk attached to externals
To preach as is befitting.
Buddhas in the Law
Attain to supreme power.
Knowing all living beings,
With their various desires and pleasures,
And their powers,
[So] according to their capacities,
By innumerable parables,
They preach the Law to them.
According as all living beings
In past lives [have planted] good roots,
[The buddhas,] knowing the mature
And the immature,
And taking account of each,
Discriminating and understanding,
In the One-vehicle, as may be befitting,
They preach the three."

HERE ENDS
THE SECOND FASCICLE

13. Or "Buddhas [possess] rare, infinite . . ."

CHAPTER V

The Parable of the Herbs

AT THAT TIME the World-honored One addressed Mahā-Kāśyapa and the [other] great disciples: "Good! Good! Kāśyapa; you have well proclaimed the real merits of the Tathāgata. Truly they are as you have said. The Tathāgata, in addition, has infinite, boundless, innumerable merits, [which] if you spoke of for infinite koṭis of kalpas you could not fully express. Know, Kāśyapa! The Tathāgata is the king of the Law. Whatever he declares is wholly free from falsity. He expounds all the laws by wise tactfulness. The Law preached by him all leads to the stage of perfect knowledge. The Tathāgata sees and knows what is the good of all the laws and also knows what all living beings in their inmost hearts are doing; he penetrates them without hindrance. Moreover, in regard to all laws, having the utmost understanding of them, he reveals to all living beings the wisdom of perfect knowledge.[1]

"Kāśyapa! Suppose, in the three-thousand-great-thousandfold world there are growing on the mountains, along the rivers and

The "herbs" of this chapter title can be translated as "medicinal herbs." Kern has "plants."

1. The state of all-knowing intelligence, that is, the Buddha-wisdom.

streams, in the valleys and on the land, plants, trees, thickets, forests, and medicinal herbs of various and numerous kinds, with names and colors all different. A dense cloud, spreading over and everywhere covering the whole three-thousand-great-thousandfold world, pours down [its rain] equally at the same time. Its moisture universally fertilizes the plants, trees, thickets, forests, and medicinal herbs, with their tiny roots, tiny stalks, tiny twigs, tiny leaves, their medium[-sized] roots, medium stalks, medium twigs, medium leaves, their big roots, big stalks, big twigs, and big leaves; every tree big or little, according to its superior, middle, or lower [capacity], receives its share. From the rain of the one cloud [each] according to the nature of its kind acquires its development, opening its blossoms and bearing its fruit. Though produced in one soil and moistened by the same rain, yet these plants and trees are all different.

"Know, Kāśyapa! The Tathāgata is also like this; he appears in the world like the rising of [that] great cloud. Universally he extends his great call over the world of gods, men, and asuras, just as that great cloud everywhere covers the three-thousand-great-thousandfold region. In the great assembly he sounds forth these words: 'I am the Tathāgata, the Worshipful, the All Wise, the Perfectly Enlightened in Conduct, the Well Departed, the Understander of the World, the Peerless Leader, the Controller, the Teacher of Gods and Men, the Buddha, the World-honored One. Those who have not yet been saved I cause to be saved; those who have not yet been set free to be set free; those who have not yet been comforted to be comforted; those who have not yet obtained nirvana to obtain nirvana.[2] I know the present world and the world to come as they really are. I am the All Knowing, the All Seeing, the Knower of the Way, the Opener of the Way, the Preacher of the Way. Come to me, all you gods, men, and asuras, to hear the Law.' At that moment numberless thousand myriad koṭis of classes of living beings came to the Buddha to hear the Law. Thereupon the Tathāgata, observing the natural powers of all these beings, keen or dull, zealous or indifferent, according to their [capacity] preached to them the Law in varying and unstinted ways,

2. These four acts correspond with the four universal vows of a bodhisattva: (1) "I vow to save all living beings without limit"; (2) "I vow to end the numberless distresses"; (3) "I vow to know all laws without end"; (4) "I vow to accomplish the supreme Buddha-way."

causing them all to rejoice and joyfully obtain much profit. All these living beings, having heard this Law, [are] comforted in the present life and afterward [will be] born in happy states, [where they will be] made joyful by the Truth and also hear the Law. Having heard the Law, they are freed from hindrances, and according to their capacity in all the laws, they gradually enter the Way.

"Just as that great cloud, raining on all the plants, trees, thickets, forests, and medicinal herbs, and according to the nature of their seed perfectly fertilizing them so that each grows and develops, [so] the Law preached by the Tathāgata is of one form[3] and flavor,[4] that is to say, deliverance,[5] abandonment,[6] extinction,[7] and finally the attainment of perfect knowledge.[8] If there be living beings who hear the Law of the Tathāgata and keep, read, recite, and practice it as preached [by him], their achievements will not [enable them] to understand their own [nature]. Wherefore? [Because] there is only the Tathāgata who knows the seed, the form, the embodiment, and the nature of all these living beings, what things they are reflecting over, what things they are thinking, what things practicing, how reflecting, how thinking, how practicing, by what laws reflecting, by what laws thinking, by what laws practicing, and by what laws attaining to what laws. There is only the Tathāgata who in reality sees, clearly and without hindrance, the stages in which all living beings are, just as those plants, trees, thickets, forests, medicinal herbs, and others do not know their own natures, superior, middle, or inferior. The Tathāgata knows this unitary essential Law, that is to say, deliverance, abandonment, extinction, final nirvana of eternal tranquillity, ending in return to the void. The Buddha, knowing this and observing the dispositions of all living beings, supports and protects them. For this reason he does not immediately declare to them the complete and perfect wisdom. Kāśyapa! All of you! A most rare thing it is that you should be able to know the Law preached by the Tathāgata as he sees fit, and be able to believe

3. "One form" means that all forms or appearances are manifestations of reality.

4. "One flavor" is interpreted as the One-vehicle Law, or the Law of Equality.

5. Deliverance from mortality.

6. Abandonment of attachments or abandonment of the view that nirvana means total extinction.

7. Extinction here means the Middle Path, that is, neither mortal existence nor total extinction.

8. Perfect knowledge is the wisdom concerning all seeds.

and able to receive it. Wherefore? [Because] the Law preached by buddhas, the world-honored ones, as they see fit is difficult to discern and difficult to know."

At that time the World-honored One, desiring to proclaim this teaching over again, spoke thus in verse:

"The Law-king who destroys existence
Appears in this world;
According to the natures of all living beings,
He preaches the Law discriminately.
The Tathāgata is greatly to be honored
And profound in wisdom;
For long has he kept secret this essential [truth],
Not endeavoring hastily to declare it.
The wise, if they hear it,
Are able to believe and discern;
The ignorant doubt and turn away,
Losing it perpetually.
Therefore, Kāśyapa,
According to their powers I preach to them
With varied reasonings
To bring them to right views.
Know, Kāśyapa!
It is like a great cloud
Rising above the world,
Covering all things everywhere,
A beneficent cloud full of moisture;
Flashes of lightning shine and glint,
The voice of thunder vibrates afar,
Bringing gladness and ease to all.
The sun's rays are veiled,
And the earth is cooled;
The cloud lowers and spreads
As if it might be caught and gathered;
Its rain everywhere equally
Descends on all sides,
Streaming and pouring without stint,
Enriching all the land.

On mountains, by rivers, in steep valleys,
In hidden recesses, there grow
The plants, trees, and herbs;
Trees, big or small,
The shoots of all the ripening grain,
Sugar cane and grapevine,
All these by the rain are fertilized
And abundantly enriched.
The dry ground is all soaked,
And herbs and trees flourish together.
From the one water which
Issued from that cloud,
Plants, trees, thickets, forests,
According to their need, receive moisture.
All the trees,
Superior, middle, inferior, all,
Each according to its size,
Grow and develop
Roots, stalks, branches, and leaves,
Blossoms and fruits in their brilliant colors;
By the pouring of the one rain,
All become fresh and glossy.
Just as their bodies, forms,
And natures are divided into great and small,
So the enriching [rain], though one and the same,
Yet makes each flourish.
In the same manner the Buddha also
Appears in the world,
Like a great cloud
Universally covering all things;
And having appeared in the world,
He, for the sake of all living beings,
Discriminates and proclaims
The reality of all the laws.
The great holy World-honored One
Among the gods and men
And all the other beings
Proclaims this, saying:

'I am the Tathāgata,
The most honored among men;
I appear in the world
Just like a great cloud,
To pour enrichment on all
Parched living beings,
To free them all from misery
And so attain the joy of peace,
Joy in the world,
And the joy of nirvana.
Gods, men, and all!
With all your mind hearken to me.
Come all of you here
And behold the peerless honored one.
I am the World-honored One,
Who cannot be equaled.
To give peace to all creatures
I appear in the world,
And for the hosts of the living
Preach the Law, pure as sweet dew:
The one and only Law
Of emancipation and nirvana.'
With one transcendent voice
I proclaim this meaning,
Constantly taking the Great-vehicle
As my subject.
I look upon all [living beings]
Everywhere [with] equal [eyes],
Without distinction of persons,
Or mind of love or hate.
I have no predilections
Nor limitations [or partiality];
Ever to all [beings]
I preach the Law equally;
As [I preach] to one person,
So [I preach] to all.
Constantly I proclaim the Law,
Never occupied with aught else;

Going or coming, sitting or standing,
I never weary of
Pouring it abundantly upon the world,
Like the rain enriching universally.
Honored and humble, high and low,
Law-keepers and law-breakers,
Those of perfect character
And those of imperfect,
Orthodox and heterodox,
Quick-witted and dull-witted,
[With] equal [mind] I rain the rain of the Law
Unwearyingly.
All living creatures
On hearing my Law,
According to their receptive powers,
[Find their] abode in their several places;
Some dwell [amongst] gods or men
Or holy wheel-rolling kings,
Or Śakra, Brahma, or other kings;
These are [like] smaller herbs.
[Those who] know the faultless Law
[And are] able to attain nirvana,
[Who] cultivate the six transcendent [faculties]
And obtain the three clear [views],
Who dwell alone in mountain forests,
Ever practicing meditation,
And obtain pratyekabuddhahood—
These are the larger herbs.
Those who seek the World-honored One,
[Resolving,] 'We will become buddhas,'
And practice zeal and meditation—
These are the superior herbs.
And these Buddha-sons
Who single-minded [walk] the Buddha-way,
Ever practicing compassion,
Assured that they will become buddhas
Certainly and without doubt—
These are named shrubs.

The firmly settled in the transcendent [faculties],
Who roll the unretreating wheel
And save infinite hundred
Thousand koṭis of the living,
Such bodhisattvas as these
Are named trees.
The Buddha's equal preaching
Is like the one rain;
[But] beings, according to their nature,
Receive it differently,
Just as the plants and trees
Each take a varying supply.
The Buddha by this parable
Tactfully reveals
And with various expressions
Proclaims the One Law;
[But of] the Buddha-wisdom
It is as a drop in the ocean.
I rain down the rain of the Law,
Filling the whole world,
The one essential Law,
To be practiced according to ability,
Just as those thickets, forests,
Herbs, and trees,
According to their size,
Luxuriantly develop.
The Law of all buddhas
Ever by its essential oneness
Causes all the worlds
Universally to gain perfect weal.
Gradually by its observance
All attain the Way's fruition.
Śrāvakas and pratyekabuddhas
Who dwell in the mountain forests,
Are in the final bodily state,
And, hearing the Law, reach fruition
Are named herbs,
Each progressing in growth.

As to the bodhisattvas
Who are firm in wisdom,
Penetrate the triple world,
And seek the highest vehicle,
These are named shrubs
Which gain increasing growth.
Again, those who practice meditation
And gain transcendent powers,
Who, hearing the doctrine of the Void,
Greatly rejoice in their minds,
And emitting innumerable rays
Save all living beings,
These are named trees
Which gain increasing growth.
Like this, Kāśyapa,
Is the Law preached by the Buddha.
It is just like a great cloud
Which with the same kind of rain
Enriches men and blossoms,
So that each bears fruit.
Know, Kāśyapa!
By numerous reasonings
And various parables
I reveal the Buddha-way;
This is my tactful method.
All buddhas do the same.
What I have now said to you all
Is the veriest truth.
All śrāvakas
[Have] not [yet] attained nirvana.[9]
The Way in which you walk
Is the bodhisattva-way;
By gradually practicing and learning,
All [of you] will become buddhas."

9. According to the extant Sanskrit original, this line can be translated "come to attain nirvana."

CHAPTER VI

Prediction

AT THAT TIME the World-honored One, after pronouncing this verse, addressed all the great assembly, uttering words like these: "This my disciple Mahā-Kāśyapa in the world to come shall do homage to three hundred myriad koṭis of world-honored buddhas, serving, revering, honoring, and extolling them and widely proclaiming the infinite great Law of the buddhas. In his final bodily state he will become a buddha, whose name will be called Radiance Tathāgata, Worshipful, All Wise, Perfectly Enlightened in Conduct, Well Departed, Understander of the World, Peerless Leader, Controller, Teacher of Gods and Men, Buddha, World-honored One, whose domain is named Radiant Virtue, and whose kalpa is named Great Magnificence. The lifetime of [that] buddha will be twelve minor kalpas, his Righteous Law will abide in the world for twenty minor kalpas, and the Counterfeit Law will also abide for twenty minor kalpas. His domain will be beautiful, devoid of dirt, potsherds, thorns, and unclean ordure; its land will be level and straight, with no uneven places, neither pitfalls nor mounds, its ground

This chapter contains the announcement of the future destinies of the four great disciples of Sakyamuni Buddha, Kāśyapa, Maudgalyāyana, Subhūti, and Kātyāyana.

of lapis lazuli, lines of jewel trees, golden cords to bound the ways, strewn with precious flowers, and purity [reigning] everywhere. In that domain the bodhisattvas will be infinite thousand koṭis, with śrāvakas numberless. No Māra deeds will be there, and though there are Māra and Māra's people, they all will protect the Buddha-law."

At that time the World-honored One, desiring to proclaim this teaching over again, spoke thus in verse:

"I say to you bhikshus
That with my Buddha-eyes
I see that this Kāśyapa
In the world to come,
After innumerable kalpas,
Will become a buddha,
And that in the world to come
He will serve and pay homage to
Three hundred myriad koṭis
Of world-honored buddhas;
For the sake of the Buddha-wisdom
He will purely practice the brahma-life,
Serving the highest
And most honored of men,
Putting into practice all
The peerless wisdom,
And in his final bodily state
Become a buddha.
His land will be pure,
With lapis lazuli for ground,
Abundance of jewel trees
Lining the roadsides,
Golden cords to bound the ways,
Rejoicing the beholders,
Ever-pervading fragrance,
Rare flowers strewn everywhere,
Every kind of rarity
Adding to its splendor;
Its land will be level,

Free from mounds and hollows.
Many bodhisattvas,
Of untold number
And gentle mind,
Will attain great transcendent powers
And reverently keep the Buddha's
Great-vehicle sutras.
His multitude of śrāvakas,
Of faultless final form,
Sons of the Law-king,
Will be beyond count;
Even the eyes of the gods
Cannot know their number.
That buddha's lifetime will be
Twelve minor kalpas;
His Righteous Law will abide in the world
For twenty minor kalpas;
The Counterfeit Law will abide
For twenty minor kalpas.
Such will be the history of
The Radiant World-honored One."

Thereupon Mahā-Maudgalyāyana, Subhūti, Mahā-Kātyāyana, and others all tremblingly folded their hands with one mind, and gazing up into the World-honored One's face, not for an instant lowering their eyes, with united voice spoke thus in verse:

"Great Hero, World-honored One,
Law-king of the Śākyas!
Out of compassion for us
Grant us the Buddha-announcement!
If thou dost know the depths of our minds
And predict our future destinies,
It will be like pouring sweet dew
To change the heat to coolness,
Like one from a famine land
Suddenly finding a royal repast,

Yet cherishing doubt and fear,
Not daring at once to eat,
But when instructed by the king,
Then daring to eat.
Thus it is with us;
While minding Hinayana error,
We know not how to obtain
The supreme wisdom of the Buddha.
Though we hear the voice of the Buddha,
Who says we shall become buddhas,
Our hearts are still anxious and afraid,
Like him who dare not eat.
But if we receive the Buddha's prediction,
Then shall we be happy and at ease.
Great Hero, World-honored One!
Thou dost ever desire to pacify the world;
Be pleased to bestow our prediction,
Like bidding the famished to feast!"

Thereupon the World-honored One, knowing the thoughts in the minds of those senior disciples, addressed all the bhikshus: "This Subhūti, in the world to come, shall do homage to three hundred myriad koṭis of nayutas of buddhas, serving, revering, honoring, and extolling them, practicing the brahma-life, and perfecting the bodhisattva-way. In his final bodily state he will become a buddha whose title will be Name Form[1] Tathāgata, Worshipful, All Wise, Perfectly Enlightened in Conduct, Well Departed, Understander of the World, Peerless Leader, Controller, Teacher of Gods and Men, Buddha, World-honored One, whose kalpa is named Possessing Jewels, and whose domain is named Jewel Producing. His land will be level and straight, with crystal for ground, adorned with jewel trees, devoid of mounds and pits, gravel, thorns, and unclean ordure, the earth covered with precious flowers, and purity [reigning] everywhere. All the people in that land will dwell on jeweled terraces and in pearly palaces. Śrāvaka disciples will be innumerable and limitless, they can be made

1. The Sanskrit is *śaśiketu,* "harelike," that is, moonlike, moon-shaped, or moon-sign, but the Chinese version gives "namelike" or "name-form"; the characters 兔 (hare) and 名 (name) do bear a resemblance to each other.

known neither by figures nor by metaphors, and the bodhisattva host will be numberless thousand myriad koṭis of nayutas. The lifetime of [that] buddha will be twelve minor kalpas, his Righteous Law will abide in the world for twenty minor kalpas, and the Counterfeit Law will also abide for twenty minor kalpas. That buddha will always dwell in the empyrean, preaching the Law to living beings and delivering innumerable bodhisattvas and śrāvakas."

At that time the World-honored One, desiring to proclaim this teaching over again, spoke thus in verse:

"All you host of bhikshus!
I have something to tell you.
All with one mind
Listen to what I say!
My senior disciple
Subhūti
Will become a buddha
Whose title will be Name Form.
He will serve numberless
Myriad koṭis of buddhas,
And following the practice of the buddhas,
Will become perfect in the Great Way.
In his final bodily state
He will obtain the thirty-two signs,
And be erect and beautiful
As a mountain of jewels.
The domain of that buddha
Will be peerless in pure splendor,
So that all who behold [it]
Will love and delight in it.
The buddha in its midst
Will save innumerable beings;
In his Buddha-law
Many will be the bodhisattvas,
All of keen faculties,
Who roll the never-receding wheel.
His domain is ever
Ornate with bodhisattvas;

His śrāvaka host is
Beyond expression and count,
Who all attain the three clear [views],
Perfect the six transcendent [faculties],
Abide in the eight emancipations,
And are greatly awe-inspiring.
That buddha preaches the Law,
Revealing himself in infinite
Supernatural transformations
Beyond conception.
Gods and people
As the sands of the Ganges in number
All with folded hands
Hearken to that buddha's words.
That buddha's lifetime will be
Twelve minor kalpas,
His Righteous Law will abide in the world
For twenty minor kalpas,
And the Counterfeit Law will also abide
For twenty minor kalpas."

At that time the World-honored One again addressed all the assembly of bhikshus, [saying]: "Now I announce to you that this Mahā-Kātyāyana, in the world to come, will worship and serve eight thousand koṭis of buddhas with many kinds of offerings, revering and honoring them. After those buddhas are extinct he for each [of them] will erect stupas a thousand yojanas in height, of equal length and breadth, five hundred yojanas, composed of the precious seven—gold, silver, lapis lazuli, moonstone, agate, pearl, and carnelian—and will serve those stupas with garlands of flowers, perfume,[2] sandal powder,[3] burning incense, silk canopies, flags, and banners. After this he will again similarly serve two myriad koṭis of buddhas; and, having served these buddhas, he will complete his bodhisattva-way and become a buddha whose title will be Jambūnada Golden Light[4] Tathāgata,

2. Perfumed ointment made of ground sandalwood or aloes and water. It is used for painting or oiling.

3. Ground sandalwood used for sprinkling.

4. Literally, "Luster of the Jambū River." The Jambū River is supposed to flow from the *jambū* trees on Mount Sumeru over golden sands.

Worshipful, All Wise, Perfectly Enlightened in Conduct, Well Departed, Understander of the World, Peerless Leader, Controller, Teacher of Gods and Men, Buddha, World-honored One. His land will be level and straight, with crystal for ground, adorned with jewel trees, with golden cords to bound the ways, its ground covered with wonderful flowers, and purity [reigning] everywhere, so that beholders rejoice. The four evil conditions will not be there—hells, hungry spirits, animals, and asuras—[but] gods and men will be many, and infinite myriad koṭis of śrāvakas and bodhisattvas will adorn his domain. The lifetime of that buddha will be twelve minor kalpas, his Righteous Law will abide in the world for twenty minor kalpas, and the Counterfeit Law will also abide for twenty minor kalpas."

At that time the World-honored One, desiring to proclaim this teaching over again, spoke thus in verse:

"All of you host of bhikshus!
Listen to me with one mind!
The words that I speak
Are true and infallible.
This Kātyāyana
Will, with various kinds
Of excellent offerings,
Pay homage to buddhas.
After the buddhas are extinct
He will erect stupas of the precious seven
And also, with flowers and perfumes,
Pay homage to their relics;
In his final bodily state
He will obtain the Buddha-wisdom
And accomplish Perfect Enlightenment.
His land will be pure
And he will save innumerable
Myriad koṭis of the living,
Being worshiped by all
In every direction.
His buddha-luster
None can surpass,
And his buddha-title will be

Jambūnada Golden Light.
Bodhisattvas and śrāvakas
Free from all existence,
Numberless, uncountable,
Will adorn his domain."

Thereupon the World-honored One again addressed the great assembly, [saying]: "Now I announce to you that this Mahā-Maudgalyāyana will, with various kinds of offerings, serve eight thousand buddhas, revering and honoring them. After the extinction of these buddhas he for each [of them] will erect stupas a thousand yojanas in height, of equal length and breadth, five hundred yojanas, composed of the precious seven, gold, silver, lapis lazuli, moonstone, agate, pearl, and carnelian, and will serve them with garlands of flowers, perfume, sandal powder, burning incense, silk canopies, flags, and banners. After this he will again similarly serve two hundred myriad koṭis of buddhas, and then become a buddha, whose title will be Tamālapattra Sandal Fragrance Tathāgata, Worshipful, All Wise, Perfectly Enlightened in Conduct, Well Departed, Understander of the World, Peerless Leader, Controller, Teacher of Gods and Men, Buddha, World-honored One. His kalpa will be named Joyful and his domain named Glad Mind. Its land will be level and straight, with crystal for ground, adorned with jewel trees, strewn with pearly flowers, and purity [reigning] everywhere, so that beholders rejoice. There will be gods, men, bodhisattvas, and śrāvakas, countless in number. The lifetime of that buddha will be twenty-four minor kalpas, his Righteous Law will abide in the world for forty minor kalpas, and the Counterfeit Law will also abide for forty minor kalpas."

Thereupon the World-honored One, desiring to proclaim the teaching over again, spoke thus in verse:

"This my disciple
Mahā-Maudgalyāyana,
After casting aside this body,
Will see eight thousand
Two hundred myriads of koṭis
Of world-honored buddhas,
And, for the sake of the Buddha-way,

Will serve and revere them.
Among these buddhas,
Ever practicing the brahma-life
For innumerable kalpas,
He will keep the Buddha-law.
After these buddhas are extinct,
He will erect stupas of the precious seven,
Displaying afar their golden spires,
And, with flowers, perfumes, and music
Pay homage to
The stupas of the buddhas.
Having gradually accomplished
The bodhisattva-way,
In the domain Glad Mind
He will become a buddha,
Styled Tamālapattra
Sandal Fragrance.
The lifetime of that buddha
Will be twenty-four kalpas.
Constantly to gods and men
He will preach the Buddha-way.
Śrāvakas will be innumerable
As the sands of the Ganges,
Having the three clear [views], the six transcendent [faculties],
And awe-inspiring powers.
Bodhisattvas will be numberless,
Firm in their will, and zealous
In the Buddha-wisdom,
Who never backslide.
After this buddha is extinct,
His Righteous Law will abide
For forty minor kalpas
And the Counterfeit Law the same.
[You] my disciples
Of perfect powers,
Five hundred in number,
All will receive their prediction
To become buddhas

In the world to come.
Of my and your
Development in previous worlds
I will now make declaration.
Do you all listen well!"

CHAPTER VII

The Parable of the Magic City

THE BUDDHA addressed the bhikshus, [saying]: "Of yore in the past, infinite, boundless, and inconceivable asaṃkhyeya kalpas ago, there was then a buddha named Universal Surpassing Wisdom[1] Tathāgata, Worshipful, All Wise, Perfectly Enlightened in Conduct, Well Departed, Understander of the World, Peerless Leader, Controller, Teacher of Gods and Men, Buddha, World-honored One, whose domain was named Well Completed,[2] and whose kalpa was named Great Form. Bhikshus! Since that buddha became extinct, a very long time has passed. For instance, suppose the earth element in a three-thousand-great-thousandfold world were by someone ground into ink, and he were to pass through a thousand countries in an eastern direction, and then let fall one drop as large as a grain of dust; again, passing through [another] thousand countries, again let fall one drop; [suppose] he thus proceeds until he has finished the ink [made] of the earth element—what is your opinion? All these

1. "Great Pervading Surpassing Wisdom," or "He Whose Surpassing Wisdom Reaches Everywhere."

2. Or "Well Accomplished." Many copies have 好城 "excellent city" instead of 好成 "well completed." Nanjio's translation has 集有 "assembled existence."

countries—is it possible for mathematicians or their disciples to find their end or confines so as to know their number?"

"No, World-honored One!"

"Bhikshus! [Suppose] all those countries which that man has passed, where he has dropped [a drop] and where he has not, ground to dust, and let one grain of the dust be a kalpa—[the time] since that buddha became extinct till now still exceeds those numbers by innumerable, unlimited hundred thousand myriad koṭis of asaṃkhyeya kalpas. By the power of my Tathāgata-wisdom, I observe that length of time as if it were only today."

At that time the World-honored One, desiring to proclaim this teaching over again, spoke thus in verse:

"I remember in a past world,
Immeasurable infinite kalpas ago,
A buddha, a [most] honored man,
Named Universal Surpassing Wisdom.
Suppose someone by his power
Ground a three-thousand-great-thousandfold world
With its entire earth element
Entirely into ink,
And, passing a thousand countries,
Then lets fall one drop;
Proceeding in a like manner
He drops all this atomized ink;
[Suppose] all such countries as these,
Those ink-dropped and those undropped,
Again are entirely ground to dust,
And a grain be as a kalpa—
The number of those grains
Are exceeded by his kalpas.
Since that buddha became extinct,
Such are the measureless kalpas.
[I,] the Tathāgata, by unhindered wisdom
Know the extinction of that buddha
And his śrāvakas and bodhisattvas
As if it were now occurring.
Know, bhikshus!

The Buddha-wisdom is pure and minute,
Faultless and unhindered,
Penetrating through infinite kalpas."

The Buddha [then] addressed all the bhikshus, [saying]: "The lifetime of the Buddha Universal Surpassing Wisdom is five hundred and forty myriad koṭis of nayutas of kalpas. At the beginning when that buddha, seated on the wisdom throne, had destroyed the army of Māra, [though] he was on the point of attaining Perfect Enlightenment, the Buddha-laws were not yet revealed to him. So for a minor kalpa and then onward for ten minor kalpas he sat cross-legged with body and mind motionless; but the Buddha-laws were not yet revealed to him.

"Then the gods of the thirty-three heavens[3] spread for that buddha a lion throne a yojana high under a Bodhi tree so that the buddha on this throne should attain Perfect Enlightenment. No sooner had he sat on that throne than the Brahma heavenly kings rained down celestial flowers over an area of a hundred yojanas. A fragrant wind from time to time arose, sweeping away the withered flowers and raining fresh ones. Thus incessantly during full ten minor kalpas they paid honor to the buddha and even till his extinction they constantly rained those flowers, while the gods [belonging to] the four [heavenly] kings to honor the buddha constantly beat celestial drums and other gods performed celestial music during fully ten minor kalpas and continued so to do until his extinction.

"Bhikshus! After the lapse of ten minor kalpas, the Buddha Universal Surpassing Wisdom attained the Buddha-laws, and Perfect Enlightenment was revealed to him. Before that buddha left home he had sixteen sons, the eldest of whom was named Wisdom Store. Each of his sons had various kinds of valued amusements, [but] on hearing that their father had accomplished Perfect Enlightenment, they all gave up the things they valued and went to pay their regards to the buddha, their weeping mothers escorting them. Their grandfather,

3. The second highest of the six heavens of the Realm of Desire. The thirty-three heavens are situated on top of Mount Sumeru, eighty thousand yojanas above this world. They are ruled by Indra, whose own heaven is located on the central peak of Mount Sumeru; of the thirty-two other heavens, eight are located at each of the four cardinal points on the top of Mount Sumeru.

Sacred Wheel-rolling King, with his one hundred ministers and also a hundred thousand myriad koṭis of his people, all surrounded and followed them to the terrace of enlightenment, all desiring to draw near to the Tathāgata Universal Surpassing Wisdom and to serve, revere, honor, and extol him. After their arrival they did homage before his feet with their heads, and after making procession around him, with folded hands and in one mind, they gazed up to the world-honored one and praised him in verse, saying:

'The World-honored One of Great Might,
To save all living beings,
After measureless koṭis of years
Thou hast now become a buddha
And perfected all thy vows.
Good indeed is our fortune unsurpassed,
For rarely do world-honored ones appear.
At one sitting ten minor kalpas have passed,
Thy body and limbs
Still, peaceful, and motionless,
And with mind ever tranquil,
Never distracted;
Thou hast completed eternal nirvana
And dost calmly dwell in the faultless Law.
Now, seeing the world-honored one
Who has calmly accomplished the Buddha-way,
We have attained good fortune
And congratulate ourselves with great joy.
All the living are ever suffering,
Blind and without a leader,
Unaware of the way to end pain,
Knowing not to seek deliverance.
Through the long night evil ways have increased,
Diminishing the heavenly throng;
[The world] has passed from darkness into darkness,
Never hearing a buddha's name.
[But] now the Buddha has attained the supreme,
Pacific, faultless Law,
And we as well as gods and men

Gain the greatest fortune.
Therefore we all prostrate ourselves
And offer our lives to the peerless honored one.'

"Thereupon all these sixteen royal sons, when they had extolled the buddha in verse, entreated the world-honored one to roll the Law-wheel on, saying: 'World-honored One! Preach the Law, and abundantly comfort, have compassion for, and benefit both gods and men!' Repeating it in verse, they said:

'Hero of the world! Incomparable!
Adorned with a hundred auspicious signs!
Who has attained to supreme wisdom:
Be pleased to preach to the world,
For deliverance to us
And to all classes of the living;
Discriminate and reveal it
So that we may obtain this wisdom!
If we attain buddhahood,
All other living beings will also [attain it].
World-honored One! Thou knowest what the living
In their deepest minds are thinking,
The ways in which they walk,
Their capacities for wisdom,
Their pleasures and past good works,
The karma their former lives produced.
World-honored One! Thou knowest all these;
[Pray] roll along the peerless wheel.' "

The Buddha [then] said to the bhikshus: "When the Buddha Universal Surpassing Wisdom attained Perfect Enlightenment, the five hundred myriad koṭis of buddha-worlds in all directions were each shaken in [different] ways; [even] the dark places between those realms, where the august light of the sun and moon could not shine, all became brilliant. All the living beings in their midst could see each other and unitedly exclaimed: 'From where have all these living beings suddenly come?' Moreover, the palaces of the gods in all those regions, even Brahma palaces, shook in six [different] ways and a great light universally shone, filling all the worlds, surpassing the light of heaven.

"Then eastward, all the palaces of the Brahma heavens in five hundred myriad koṭis of domains were brilliantly illuminated with double their normal brightness. And each of those Brahma heavenly kings reflected thus: 'For what reason does this sign appear, that our palaces are now illuminated as never of yore?' Then those Brahma heavenly kings all visited each other to discuss this affair. Meanwhile, amongst those assembled there was a great Brahma heavenly king named Savior of All, who addressed the host of Brahmas in verse:

'In all our palaces
Never has there been such shining;
What can be its cause?
Let us together investigate it.
Is it that a great virtuous god is born,
Is it that a buddha appears in the world,
That this great shining
Everywhere illuminates the universe?'

"Thereupon the Brahma heavenly kings in five hundred myriad koṭis of domains, with all their palace train,[4] each taking a sack filled with celestial flowers, went together to visit the western quarter to investigate this sign. [There] they saw the Tathāgata Universal Surpassing Wisdom on the wisdom terrace under the Bodhi tree, seated on the lion throne, surrounded and revered by gods, dragon kings, gandharvas, kiṃnaras, mahoragas, human and nonhuman beings, and others. And they saw his sixteen royal sons entreating the buddha to roll along the Law-wheel. Then all the Brahma heavenly kings bowed to the ground before the buddha, made procession around him hundreds and thousands of times, and then strewed the celestial flowers upon him. The flowers they strewed [rose] like Mount Sumeru and were offered also to the buddha's Bodhi tree. That Bodhi tree was ten yojanas in height. When they had offered the flowers, each of them presented his palace to the buddha and spoke thus: 'Out of compassion for us and for our good, condescend to accept the palaces we offer!'

4. The Sanskrit version has "aerial cars" (Kern) instead of "palaces," and the Chinese commentaries describe them as being mobile like carriages.

"Thereupon all the Brahma heavenly kings, before the buddha, with one mind and voice praised him in verse, saying:

'Rare is a world-honored one,
Hard it is to meet him,
Perfect in infinite merit,
Able to save all.
Great teacher of gods and men,
He has compassion for the world.
All the living in the universe
Everywhere receive his aid.
The [distance] we have come
Is five hundred myriad koṭis of domains,
Leaving deep meditative joys
For the sake of serving the buddha.
As rewards for our former lives
Our palaces are magnificently adorned;
Now we offer them to the world-honored one
And beg him in mercy to accept.'

"Then, when the Brahma heavenly kings had extolled the buddha in verse, each spoke thus: 'Be pleased, World-honored One, to roll the Law-wheel, deliver all the living, and open the nirvana-way!'

"Then the Brahma heavenly kings with one mind and voice spoke in verse, saying:

'Hero of the world! Honored of men!
Be pleased to proclaim the Law!
By the power of thy great compassion,
Save wretched living beings!'

"Then the Tathāgata Universal Surpassing Wisdom silently gave assent.

"Again, bhikshus! The great Brahma kings in the southeastern quarter of five hundred myriad koṭis of domains, each seeing his own palace radiant with light as never before, were ecstatic with joy and amazed. And instantly all visited each other to discuss together this affair. Meanwhile amongst those assembled there was a great Brahma heavenly king whose name was Most Merciful, who addressed the host of Brahmas in verse:

'What is the cause of this affair,
That such a sign should appear?
In all our palaces
Never has there been such shining.
Is it that a great virtuous god is born?
Is it that a buddha appears in the world?
We have never yet seen such a sign.
Let us with one mind investigate it.
Let us pass through a thousand myriad koṭis of lands
In search of the light and together explain it.
It must be that a buddha has appeared
In the world to save suffering beings.'

"Thereupon the five hundred myriad koṭis of Brahma heavenly kings, with all their palace train, each taking a sack filled with celestial flowers, went together to visit the northwestern quarter to investigate this sign. There they saw the Tathāgata Universal Surpassing Wisdom on the wisdom terrace under the Bodhi tree, seated on the lion throne, surrounded and revered by gods, dragon kings, gandharvas, kiṃnaras, mahoragas, human and nonhuman beings, and others. And they saw the sixteen royal sons entreating the buddha to roll along the Law-wheel. Then all the Brahma heavenly kings bowed to the ground before the buddha, made procession around him hundreds and thousands of times, and then strewed the celestial flowers upon him. The flowers they strewed [rose] like Mount Sumeru and were offered also to the buddha's Bodhi tree. When they had offered the flowers, each of them presented his palace to the buddha and spoke thus: 'Out of compassion to us and for our good, condescend to accept the palaces we offer!' Thereupon all the Brahma heavenly kings, before the buddha, with one mind and voice praised him in verse, saying:

'Holy lord, king among gods,
With voice [sweet as] the kalavinka's,
Who has compassion for all living beings!
We now respectfully salute thee.

Rarely does a world-honored one appear,
But once in long ages;
One hundred and eighty kalpas
Have passed away empty, with never a buddha,
The three evil regions becoming replete,
While heavenly beings decreased.
Now the buddha has appeared in the world
To become the eye of all living beings,
The resort of all the world,
Savior of all,
Father of all the living,
Who has compassion for and does good [to all].
Happy through our former destinies,
We now meet the world-honored one.'

"Then, when the Brahma heavenly kings had extolled the buddha in verse, each spoke thus: 'Be pleased, World-honored One, to have compassion for all [beings], roll the Law-wheel, and deliver the living!'

"Then the Brahma heavenly kings with one mind and voice spoke in verse, saying:

'Most holy! Roll on the Law-wheel;
Reveal the nature of thy laws;
Deliver suffering beings,
That they may obtain great joy.
All the living, hearing this Law,
Obtain the Way as if born in heaven;
Evil processes [of karma] decrease,
While endurers of goodness[5] increase.'

"Then the Tathāgata Universal Surpassing Wisdom silently gave assent.

"Again, bhikshus! The great Brahma kings in the southern quarter of five hundred myriad koṭis of domains, each seeing his own palace radiant with light such as never was before, were ecstatic with joy and

5. Those who restrain bad thoughts and strive after good things.

amazed. And instantly all visited each other to discuss together this affair, [asking]: 'What is the cause of this radiant light in our palaces?' In that assembly there was a great Brahma heavenly king whose name was Wonderful Law, who addressed the host of Brahmas in verse:

'That all our palaces
Scintillate with brilliant rays
Cannot be without reason.
Let us investigate this sign!
Through hundreds of thousands of kalpas,
Never has such a sign been seen.
Is it that a great virtuous god is born?
Is it that a buddha appears in the world?'

"Thereupon the five hundred myriad koṭis of Brahma heavenly kings, with all their palace train, each taking a sack filled with celestial flowers, went together to visit the northern quarter to investigate this sign. [There] they saw the Tathāgata Universal Surpassing Wisdom on the wisdom terrace under the Bodhi tree, seated on the lion throne, surrounded and revered by gods, dragon kings, gandharvas, kiṃnaras, mahoragas, human and nonhuman beings, and others. And they saw [his] sixteen royal sons entreating the buddha to roll along the Law-wheel. Then all the Brahma heavenly kings bowed to the ground before the buddha, made procession around him hundreds and thousands of times, and then strewed the celestial flowers upon him. The flowers they strewed [rose] like Mount Sumeru and were offered also to the buddha's Bodhi tree. When they had offered the flowers, each of them presented his palace to the buddha and spoke thus: 'Out of compassion to us and for our good, condescend to accept the palaces we offer!'

"Thereupon all the Brahma heavenly kings, before the buddha, with one mind and voice praised [him] in verse, saying:

'How hard it is to get sight of a world-honored one,
Who destroys all earthly cares!
After a hundred and thirty kalpas,
Now at length we have obtained the sight.
To hungry and thirsty creatures
He pours forth the rain of the Law.

He whom we have never seen before,
The possessor of infinite wisdom,
Rare as the udumbara flower,
Today has been met by us.
All our palaces are
Made beautiful by [thy] light,
World-honored One! In thy great mercy,
We pray thou wilt condescend to accept [them].'

"Thereupon, when the Brahma heavenly kings had extolled the buddha in verse, each spoke thus: 'Be pleased, World-honored One, to roll the Law-wheel, and cause all the worlds of gods, Māras, Brahmas, monks, and Brahmans to be comforted and delivered!'

"Then all the Brahma heavenly kings with one mind and voice praised him in verse, saying:

'Be pleased, honored of gods and men,
To roll the supreme Law-wheel,
To beat the drum of the Great Law,
To blow the conch of the Great Law,
Universally to pour the rain of the Great Law,
And save innumerable creatures!
We all devote ourselves to thee.
Proclaim the reverberating news!'[6]

"Then the Tathāgata Universal Surpassing Wisdom silently gave assent.

"The southwestern quarter down to the nadir also [responded] in like fashion.

"Then, in the upper quarter, the great Brahma kings of five hundred myriad koṭis of domains, all beholding the palaces in which they rested become augustly radiant with light such as never was before, were ecstatic with joy and amazed. At once they visited each other to discuss together this affair, [asking]: 'What is the cause of this light in our palaces?' In that assembly there was a great Brahma heavenly king whose name was Śikhin, who addressed the host of Brahmas in verse:

'What is now the cause

6. Literally, "deep far-reaching sound."

That all our palaces
Are radiant with such august light
And made beautiful as never before?
Such a wonderful sign as this
Of old we have never heard nor seen.
Is it that a great virtuous god is born?
Is it that a buddha appears in the world?'

"Thereupon the five hundred myriad koṭis of Brahma heavenly kings, with all their palace train, each taking a sack filled with celestial flowers, went together to visit the nadir quarter to investigate this sign. [There] they saw the Tathāgata Universal Surpassing Wisdom on the wisdom terrace under the Bodhi tree, seated on the lion throne, surrounded and revered by gods, dragon kings, gandharvas, kiṃnaras, mahoragas, human and nonhuman beings, and others. And they saw [his] sixteen royal sons entreating the buddha to roll along the Law-wheel. Then all the Brahma heavenly kings bowed to the ground before the buddha, made procession around him hundreds and thousands of times, and then strewed the celestial flowers upon him. The flowers they strewed [rose] like Mount Sumeru and were also offered to the buddha's Bodhi tree. When they had offered the flowers, each of them presented his palace to the buddha and spoke thus: 'Out of compassion to us and for our good, condescend to accept the palaces we offer!'

"Thereupon all the Brahma heavenly kings, before the buddha, with one mind and voice praised [him] in verse, saying:

'How good it is to see the buddhas,
Holy honored ones who save the world,
Who can compel the hells of the triple world
To deliver up the living.
The all-wise, honored of gods and men,
Out of compassion for the crowds of young buds
Can open the doors of the sweet dews
For the extensive relief of all.
Innumerable kalpas of yore
Have emptily passed without buddhas;

While world-honored ones did not appear,
Darkness has everywhere reigned.
Thriving were the three evil states,
Flourishing also the asuras,
While the heavenly host dwindled,
And dying, fell into evil estates;
Not hearing the law from buddhas,
Ever following improper ways,
Their bodies, strength, and wisdom,
These all dwindled away;
Because of sinful karma
They lost their joy and joyful thoughts;
Fixed in heretical views,
Unconscious of the rules of goodness,
Not receiving the correction of buddhas,
They ever fell into evil ways.
The buddha is the eye of the world,
[And] after long ages appears.
Through pity for the living
He is revealed in the world,
Surpassing in his Perfect Enlightenment.
Great is our felicity,
And all other beings
Rejoice as never before.
All our palaces,
Made beautiful through this light,
Now we offer the World-honored One.
Condescend in compassion to accept them!
May this [deed of] merit
Extend to all [creatures]
That we with all the living
May together accomplish the Buddha-way!'

"Thereupon, when the five hundred myriad koṭis of the Brahma heavenly kings had extolled the buddha in verse, each said to him: 'Be pleased, World-honored One, to roll the Law-wheel; abundantly comfort; abundantly deliver!'

"Then all the Brahma heavenly kings spoke in verse, saying:

'World-honored One, roll the Law-wheel,
Beat the drum of the Law, sweet as dew,
Save the suffering living,
Reveal the nirvana-way!
Be pleased to receive our entreaty
And with thy great, mystic voice,
Out of compassion spread abroad
The Law thou hast practiced for infinite kalpas.'

"At that time the Tathāgata Universal Surpassing Wisdom, receiving the entreaty of the Brahma heavenly kings of the ten regions and of [his] sixteen royal sons, at once thrice rolled the Law-wheel[7] of twelve divisions,[8] which neither śramaṇas, Brahmans, gods, Māras, Brahmas, nor other beings of the world are able to roll. His discourse was: 'This [is] suffering; this the accumulation of suffering; this the extinction of suffering; this the way to extinction of suffering'; and he extensively set forth the Law of the Twelve Causes, namely: 'Ignorance causes action; action causes consciousness; consciousness causes name and form; name and form cause the six entrances [or sense organs]; the six entrances cause contact; contact causes sensation; sensation causes desire [or love]; desire causes clinging; clinging causes existence; existence causes birth; birth causes old age and death, grief, lamentation, suffering, and distress. Ignorance annihilated, then action is annihilated; action annihilated, then consciousness is annihilated; consciousness annihilated, then name and form are annihilated; name and form annihilated, then the six entrances are annihilated; the six entrances annihilated, then contact is annihilated; contact annihilated, then sensation is annihilated; sensation annihilated, then desire is annihilated; desire annihilated, then clinging is annihilated; clinging annihilated, then existence is annihilated; existence annihilated, then birth is annihilated; birth being annihilated, then are annihilated old age and death, grief, lamentation, suffering, and distress.'

"When the buddha preached this Law amidst the gods, men, and the great host, six hundred myriad koṭis of nayutas of people, without

7. To roll the Law-wheel three times means (1) to show what the Four Noble Truths are, (2) to exhort others to practice the Four Noble Truths, and (3) to witness or prove that the Buddha has accomplished the Four Noble Truths.

8. According to the T'ien-t'ai sect this is interpreted as "twelve turns" because of the three forms of presentation of each of the Four Noble Truths (see fn. 7 above).

being subject to all the [temporary] laws, had their minds freed from faults, all obtaining the profound, mystic meditations, the three clear [views], and the six transcendent [faculties], and accomplishing the eight emancipations. Likewise at a second, a third, and a fourth time of preaching the Law, thousands of myriads of koṭis of nayutas of living beings, [numerous] as the sands of the Ganges, without being subject to all the [temporary] laws, had their minds freed from all faults. From this time forth the host of [his] śrāvakas was immeasurable and boundless, beyond expression in numbers.

"Meanwhile the sixteen royal sons, all being youths, left their home and became śrāmaṇeras of keen natural powers, wise and intelligent. They had already served hundreds of thousands of myriads of koṭis of buddhas, purely practiced brahma-conduct, and sought Perfect Enlightenment. Together they addressed the buddha, saying: 'World-honored One! All these innumerable thousand myriad koṭis of great virtuous śrāvakas have already become perfect. World-honored One! Preach also to us the Law of Perfect Enlightenment! And when we have heard it we will all put the lesson into practice. World-honored One! We are longing for the tathāgata's knowledge. The thought of our inmost hearts thou dost prove and know.'

"Then amongst the throng whom the holy wheel-rolling king led, eight myriad koṭis of people, seeing that the sixteen royal sons had gone forth from their home, also sought to leave their homes, whereupon the king permitted them.

"Then that buddha, on the entreaty of the śrāmaṇeras, when two myriad kalpas had passed, in [the presence of] the four groups preached this Great-vehicle Sutra named the Lotus Flower of the Wonderful Law, the Law by which bodhisattvas are instructed and which the buddhas watch over and keep in mind. When he had preached this sutra, the sixteen śrāmaṇeras, for the sake of Perfect Enlightenment, all received, kept, recited, and penetrated it.

"While this sutra was being preached, the sixteen bodhisattva-śrāmaṇeras all received it in faith, and amongst the host of śrāvakas there were also [those who] believed and discerned it, but the other living beings of thousands of myriad koṭis of kinds all cherished doubts and perplexities.[9]

9. Kern's translation reads: ". . . the disciples as well as the sixteen novices were

"The buddha preached this sutra for eight thousand kalpas without cessation. When he had finished preaching it, he then entered a quiet room and remained in meditation for eighty-four thousand kalpas.

"Thereupon the sixteen bodhisattva-śrāmaṇeras, knowing that the buddha had entered the room and was absorbed in meditation, each ascended a Law throne and also for eighty-four thousand kalpas extensively preached and expounded to the four groups the Sutra of the Flower of the Wonderful Law. Each of them saved six hundred myriad koṭis of nayutas of living beings, [as many] as the sands of the Ganges, showing, teaching, benefiting, and gladdening them, and leading them to develop a mind of Perfect Enlightenment.

"The Buddha Universal Surpassing Wisdom, after eighty-four thousand kalpas had passed, arose from his meditation, went up to the Law throne, and quietly sat down on it.

"Universally addressing the great assembly, [he said]: 'Rare are such bodhisattva-śrāmaṇeras as these sixteen, keen in their natural powers and clear in their wisdom, who have paid homage to infinite thousand myriad koṭis of buddhas, constantly practiced brahma-conduct under those buddhas, received and kept the Buddha-wisdom, and revealed it to living beings, leading them to enter into it. Do you all, again and again, draw nigh and worship them. Wherefore? Because if śrāvakas, pratyekabuddhas, and bodhisattvas are able to believe the Law of the sutra preached by these sixteen bodhisattvas, and receive and keep it without spoiling it, all those people will attain the Tathāgata-wisdom of Perfect Enlightenment.' "

The Buddha addressed all the bhikshus, [saying]: "These sixteen bodhisattvas ever take delight in preaching this Sutra of the Lotus Flower of the Wonderful Law. The six hundred myriad koṭis of nayutas of living beings, like the sands of the Ganges, whom each of these bodhisattvas converted, born generation by generation, all following [these] bodhisattvas, heard the Law from them and all believed and discerned it. For this cause they succeeded in meeting

---

full of faith, and many hundred thousand myriads of koṭis of beings acquired perfect certainty" (SBE vol. 21, p. 175). Dharmaraksha reads as Kern does, but Nanjio follows Kumārajīva's version, stating that he cannot find the prefix *nir* (not) in any of the extant Sanskrit texts that he has read, but only the word *vicikitsā* (doubt or perplexity). (See Nanjio's Japanese translation from the Sanskrit, p. 207 n.) Oka agrees with Nanjio in his translation from the Sanskrit. Kern notes this as a variant reading.

four myriad koṭis of buddhas, world-honored ones, and at the present time have not ceased [to do so].

"Bhikshus! I tell you now: that buddha's disciples, the sixteen śrāmaṇeras, have all attained Perfect Enlightenment, and in all countries in every direction are at the present time preaching the Law and have infinite hundred thousand myriad koṭis of bodhisattvas and śrāvakas as their followers. Two of those śrāmaṇeras became buddhas in the eastern quarter, one named Akshobhya in the Kingdom of Joy, the other named Sumeru Peak; of the two buddhas in the southeastern quarter, one is named Lion Voice, the other Lion Ensign; of the two buddhas in the southern quarter, one is named Space Dweller, the other Eternal Extinction; of the two buddhas in the southwestern quarter, one is named Imperial Ensign, the other Brahma Ensign; of the two buddhas in the western quarter one is named Amita, the other He Who Has Passed Through All the Sufferings of the World; of the two buddhas in the northwestern quarter, one is named Tamālapattra Spiritually Pervading Sandal Odor, the other Sumeru Sign; of the two buddhas in the northern quarter, one is named Sovereign Cloud, the other named Sovereign Cloud King; the buddha in the northeastern quarter is named Destroyer of All the World's Fear; and the sixteenth is I myself, Sakyamuni Buddha, who have accomplished Perfect Enlightenment in the sahā-domain.

"Bhikshus! When we were śrāmaṇeras, each of us taught and converted infinite hundred thousand myriad koṭis of living beings, [numerous] as the sands of the Ganges; and those who heard the Law from me [attained] Perfect Enlightenment. Amongst these living beings down to the present there are some who [still] remain in the stage of śrāvakas. I constantly instruct them in Perfect Enlightenment, so that all these people will through this Law gradually enter the Way of buddhahood. Wherefore? Because the Tathāgata-wisdom is hard to believe and hard to understand. All those living beings, innumerable as the sands of the Ganges, whom I converted at that time are yourselves, bhikshus, and will be my śrāvaka-disciples in future worlds after my extinction.

"After my extinction there will also be disciples of mine who, not hearing this sutra, nor knowing nor apprehending the course which bodhisattvas pursue, will by their own merits conceive the idea of extinction and enter [what they think is] nirvana. [But] in other domains [wherever they may go] I shall [still] be Buddha though under different names. These people, though they conceive the idea of extinction and enter [what they call] nirvana, yet in those lands will seek after the Buddha-wisdom and succeed in hearing this sutra. Only by the Buddha-vehicle will they attain [real] extinction. There is no other vehicle except the tactful teachings of the Tathāgata. Bhikshus! If the Tathāgata himself knows that the time of nirvana has arrived and the assembly is pure, firm in faith and discernment, penetrated with the Law of the Void, profound in meditation, then he will gather together all bodhisattvas and śrāvakas to preach this sutra to them. In the world there is no second vehicle to attain extinction; there is only the One Buddha-vehicle for attaining extinction. Know, bhikshus! The tact of the Tathāgata reaches deeply into the natures of all living beings and knows that they are bent on the pleasures of trifling things and deeply attached to the five desires. For the sake of these he preaches nirvana. If they hear it, they will receive it in faith.

"Suppose there is a fearful region, five hundred yojanas [in extent], through which lies a perilous and difficult road, far from the abodes of men. [Suppose] there is a large company wishing to pass along that road to the Place of Jewels, and they have a guide, wise and astute, who knows well the perilous road, where it is open and where closed, and who leads the company that wish to cross this arduous [region]. [Suppose] the company he leads become tired on the way and say to the leader: 'We are utterly exhausted and moreover afraid and cannot go any farther; the road before us stretches far; let us turn back.' The leader, [a man] of much tact, reflects thus: 'These [people] are to be pitied. How can they give up such great treasure and want to turn back?' Reflecting thus, by a device, in the midst of the perilous road, he mystically makes a city over three hundred yojanas in extent and says to the company: 'Do not fear, and do not turn back. Here is this great city in which you may rest and follow your own desires. If you enter this city, you will speedily be at rest; and if you [then] are able to go forward to the Place of Jewels, you proceed.'

"Thereupon the exhausted company greatly rejoice in their minds and praise [their] unexampled [fortune]: 'Now indeed we escape this evil way; let us speedily be at ease.' Then the company proceed into the magic city, imagining they have arrived at their destination, and are settled in comfort. When the leader perceives that the company are rested and are no longer fatigued, he makes the magic city disappear, and says to the company: 'Come along, all of you, the Place of Jewels is at hand. I [only] created this past large city for you to rest in.'

"Bhikshus! So is it with the Tathāgata. At present he is your great leader acquainted with all the distresses, the evils, the perils, and the long-continued [processes of] mortality, from which you must be rid and removed. If living beings only hear of One Buddha-vehicle, they will not desire to see the Buddha nor wish to approach him, but think thus: 'The Buddha-way is long and far; only after the long suffering of arduous labor can the end be reached.' The Buddha, knowing that their minds are feeble and low, by his tact, when they are on the way, to give them rest, preaches the two [stages] of nirvana.[10] If [those] beings dwell in [these] two stages, then the Tathāgata proceeds to tell them: 'You have not yet accomplished your task. The place where you are dwelling is near the Buddha-wisdom. Take note and ponder that the nirvana which you have attained is not the real [one]! It is only that the Tathāgata, through his tactfulness, in the One Buddha-vehicle discriminates and speaks of three.' It is just as when that leader, in order to give rest [to his company], magically makes a great city and after they are rested informs them, saying: 'The Place of Jewels is at hand; this city is not real, but only my magic production.' "

At that time the World-honored One, desiring to proclaim this teaching over again, spoke thus in verse:

"The Buddha Universal Surpassing Wisdom
For ten kalpas sat on the wisdom throne,
The Buddha-law still unrevealed,
Still unaccomplished the Buddha-way.
Heavenly gods and dragon kings,
Asuras and other beings
Constantly rained celestial flowers
To pay homage to that buddha.
The gods beat their celestial drums
And made all kinds of music.
Fragrant breezes sweep away the faded flowers,
While raining others of fresh beauty.

10. See p. 44, fn. 30; also, the two stages of śrāvaka and pratyekabuddha.

When ten minor kalpas had passed,
Then he accomplished the Buddha-way.
Gods and men in the world
All were ecstatic in mind.
The sixteen sons of that buddha,
All with their followers,
Thousands of myriads of koṭis around them,
All went to the buddha.
Bending low at the buddha's feet,
They begged him to roll the Law-wheel:
'Holy Lion! With rain of the Law,
Fill us and all others!'
Hard it is to meet a world-honored one;
He appears but once in long ages,
And [then] to awaken the living
He shakes all things.
In the worlds of the eastern quarter,
Five hundred myriad koṭis of domains,
Brahma palaces shone with light
Such as never was before.
All the Brahmas, seeing this sign,
Sought till they reached the buddha.
They honored him, strewing flowers,
And offered him their palaces,
Entreating him to roll the Law-wheel
And extolling him in verse.
The buddha, knowing the time had not yet come,
Received their entreaty but sat in silence.
From three [other] quarters[11] and four directions,[12]
The zenith and the nadir [they] likewise [came],
Strewing flowers, offering their palaces,
And begging the buddha to roll the Law-wheel:
'Hard it is to meet a world-honored one;
Be pleased, in thy great[13] compassion,
Widely to open the gates of the sweet dew

11. West, south, and north.
12. The intermediate points of the compass.
13. Some copies have 本 "original" instead of 大 "great."

And roll the supreme Law-wheel!'
The world-honored one of infinite wisdom,
Receiving the entreaty of that throng,
Proclaimed for them the various laws of
The Four Noble Truths and Twelve Causes:
'Ignorance on to age and death,
All exist because of birth.
All such distresses as these,
All of you must know.'
While this law was being proclaimed,
Six hundred myriad koṭis of nayutas
[Of beings] ended all their distresses,
All becoming arhats.
The second time he preached the Law
Thousands of myriads, as the sands of the Ganges,
Not following ordinary methods,
Also became arhats.
From that time forth the Way-attainers
Were incalculable in number;
To count them for myriads of koṭis of kalpas
Would not reach their end.
Then the sixteen royal sons
Who left home as śrāmaṇeras
Unitedly entreated the buddha:
'Proclaim the Law of the Great-vehicle!
We and our companies of followers
Would all accomplish the Buddha-way.
We would be like the World-honored One,
With wise and perfectly pure eyes.'
The buddha, knowing his sons' mind
And the doings of their former lives,
By countless reasonings
And various parables
Preached the Six Pāramitās
And the supernatural things,
Discriminated the real Law of
The way bodhisattvas walk,
And preached this Law-Flower Sutra

In verses [numerous] as the sands of the Ganges.
When the buddha had preached the sutra,
In a quiet room he entered meditation;
With concentrated mind he sat in one place
For eighty-four thousand kalpas.
All those śrāmaṇeras,
Perceiving he would not yet emerge from meditation,
To infinite koṭis of beings
Expounded the buddha's supreme wisdom,
Each sitting on a Law throne,
Preaching this Great-vehicle sutra;
And, after the buddha's rest,
Proclaimed and aided his teaching of the Law.
The number of living saved by
Each of those śrāmaṇeras was
Six hundred myriad koṭis of beings,
As [many as] the sands of the Ganges.
After that buddha was extinct,
Those hearers of the Law,
In every one of the Buddha-lands,
Were [re]born along with their teachers.[14]
These sixteen śrāmaṇeras,
Perfectly practicing the Buddha-way,
Now dwell in the ten directions,
Each having attained Perfect Enlightenment.
Those who then heard the Law
All dwell with the buddhas.
Those who [still] remain śrāvakas
Are gradually taught in the Buddha-way.
I was amongst the sixteen
And formerly preached to you.
Therefore, by my tactfulness,
I lead you on to Buddha-wisdom.
Because of this former connection,
I now preach the Law-Flower Sutra
To cause you to enter the Buddha-way.

14. The sixteen royal sons.

Be careful not to harbor fear!
Suppose there be a perilous way,
Cut off and full of venomous beasts,
Without either water or grass,
A region of terror to men.
An innumerable multitude, thousands of myriads,
Wish to pass along this perilous way,
A road indeed far-reaching,
Through five hundred yojanas.
Then appears a leader
Of strong sense and wise,
Clear-headed and of resolute mind,
Who in peril saves from all danger.
[But] those people all become exhausted
And speak to the leader, saying:
'We now are weary and worn
And want to turn back from here.'
The leader reflects [thus]:
'These fellows are much to be pitied.
How can they want to turn back
And miss such great treasure?'
At that instant he thinks of a device:
'Let me exert supernatural power
And make a great magic city
Splendidly adorned with houses,
Surrounded with gardens and groves,
Streamlets and bathing pools,
Massive gates and lofty towers,
Full of both men and women.'
Having made this transformation,
He pacifies them, saying: 'Do not fear!
Enter all of you into this city,
And let each enjoy himself at will.'
When those people had entered the city,
Their hearts were full of joy;
All thought [only] of rest and ease
And considered they had been saved.
When the leader knew they were rested,

He assembled and addressed them, saying:
'Let all of you push forward!
This was only an illusory city.
Seeing you all worn out
And wanting to turn back midway,
I therefore by a device
Temporarily made this city.
Do you now diligently advance
Together to the Place of Jewels.'
I, too, in like manner,
Am the leader of all [beings].
Seeing the seekers of the Way
Midway becoming wearied
And unable to cross the perilous ways
Of mortality and earthly cares,
So I by my tactful powers
For their relief preached nirvana, saying:
'Your sufferings are ended;
You have finished your work.'
When I knew you had reached nirvana
And all become arhats,
Then I gathered you all together
And preached to you the real Law.
Buddhas by their tactful powers
Separately preach the three vehicles;
[But] there is only the One Buddha-vehicle;
It is for the resting-place that two are preached.[15]
Now I preach to you the truth;
What you have reached is not the [real] extinction.
For the sake of [obtaining] the Buddha's perfect knowledge,
Exert yourselves with the utmost zeal!
[When] you have proved the perfect knowledge,
The ten powers, and so on of the Buddha-laws,
And perfected the thirty-two signs,
Then that is the real extinction.
The buddhas, the leaders,

15. Or "[Only] for the sake of a [temporary] resting place is a second preached."

For the sake of giving rest call it nirvana,
But perceiving this rest [should be] ended,
They lead them [on] into Buddha-wisdom."

HERE ENDS
THE THIRD FASCICLE

CHAPTER VIII

The Five Hundred Disciples Receive the Prediction of Their Destiny

AT THAT TIME Pūrṇa, son of Maitrāyaṇī,[1] having heard the Buddha preach in such wise, tactful, and opportune fashion, and having heard the prediction of the great disciples' Perfect Enlightenment; having, moreover, heard the stories of their former destinies, and also having heard of the sovereign, transcendent powers of the buddhas; having [thus] received such unexampled [teaching], his heart was purified and in ecstasy. Immediately he rose from his seat, went before the Buddha, prostrated himself at his feet, then withdrew to one side, gazing upon his honored countenance without for a moment turning away his eyes, and reflected thus: "Wonderful is the World-honored One. Rare are his doings according to the many kinds of earthly dispositions. By tactful wisdom, he preaches the Law to and lifts all beings out of every condition to let them get rid of selfish attachment. No words of ours can declare the Buddha's

1. One of the ten disciples of the Buddha, noted for his eloquence. Pūrṇa means "full"; Maitrāyaṇī means "benevolence" and is said to be his mother's name, but Kern suggests that it means the fifteenth day of the moon and that the whole title indicates the full moon (see SBE vol. 21, p. 194 n).

merits. Only the Buddha, the World-honored One is able to know the natural inclinations of our inmost hearts."[2]

Thereupon the Buddha addressed the bhikshus, [saying]: "Do you see this Pūrṇa, son of Maitrāyaṇī? I have always styled him the very first among all the preachers of the Law and constantly praised his varied merits. He has been zealous in guarding and helping to proclaim my Law. Among the four groups he has been able to display and teach it with profit and delight [to them]. Perfectly interpreting the Righteous Law of the Buddha, he has greatly benefited his fellow followers of brahma-conduct. Aside from the Tathāgata, no one is able to equal the lucidity of his discourse. Do not think that it is only my Law which Pūrṇa is able to guard and help to proclaim. He also under ninety koṭis of buddhas in the past guarded and helped to proclaim the Righteous Law of the buddhas. Among those preachers of the Law he was also the foremost. And in regard to the Law of the Void preached by the buddhas, he was clear-minded and penetrating; he attained the four degrees of unhindered wisdom; he has ever been able to preach the Law with judgment and in purity, without doubt and perplexity. Perfect in transcendent bodhisattva-powers, he maintained brahma-conduct to the end of his life. All the people of those buddha-periods spoke of him as 'the true disciple' [śrāvaka]. Thus Pūrṇa, by such tactfulness, has benefited innumerable hundreds and thousands of living beings and converted innumerable asaṃkhyeyas of people to achieve Perfect Enlightenment. For the sake of purifying [his] buddha-land, he has constantly done a buddha's work and instructed the living. Bhikshus! Pūrṇa also was the foremost among the preachers of the Law under the Seven Buddhas[3] and now is again the foremost among the preachers of the Law under me.

"Among the preachers of the Law under future buddhas[4] in this

2. After this paragraph Dharmaraksha's translation has a parable in prose and verse that is not found in the extant Sanskrit text.

3. The Seven Buddhas are Vipaśyin, Śikhin, Viśvabhū, Krakucchanda, Kanakamuni, Kāśyapa, and Sakyamuni. The first three are the last three of a thousand buddhas who appeared during the Glorious kalpa in the past; the last four are the first four of a thousand buddhas who appear during the present kalpa of the sages. Kern writes: "The seven so-called Mānushi-Buddhas; a rather transparent disguise of the fact that in cosmological mythology there are seven Manus, rulers of certain periods" (see SBE vol. 21, p. 193 n).

4. The coming 996 buddhas (after Sakyamuni).

Virtuous kalpa,[5] he will also be the foremost and will guard and help to proclaim the Buddha-law. Also in the future he will guard and help to proclaim the Law of incalculable, infinite buddhas, instructing and benefiting innumerable living beings to cause them to achieve Perfect Enlightenment. For the sake of purifying [his] buddha-land he will ever diligently and zealously instruct the living. Gradually fulfilling the bodhisattva-course, after infinite asaṃkhyeya kalpas, in that land he will attain Perfect Enlightenment and his title will be Radiance of the Law Tathāgata, Worshipful, All Wise, Perfectly Enlightened in Conduct, Well Departed, Understander of the World, Peerless Leader, Controller, Teacher of Gods and Men, Buddha, World-honored One.

"That buddha will make [his] buddha-land of a three-thousand-great-thousandfold universe [of worlds as many] as the sands of the Ganges, with the precious seven for its earth, its ground level as the palm of the hand, free from hills and valleys, runnels and ditches, and its midst filled with terraces of the precious seven. The palaces of its gods will be situated nearby in the sky, where men and gods will meet and behold each other. There will be no evil ways and no womankind, [for] all living beings will be born transformed and have no carnal passion. They will attain to the great transcendent [powers]: their bodies will emit rays of light; they will fly anywhere at will; their will and memory will be firm; they will be zealous and wise, all golden-hued, and adorned with the thirty-two signs. All the beings in his domain will always have two [articles of] food—one the food of joy in the Law, the other the food of gladness in meditation. There will be a host of infinite asaṃkhyeyas and thousands of myriads of koṭis of nayutas of bodhisattvas who have attained the great transcendent [faculties] and the four [degrees] of unhindered wisdom, and who have excellent ability in instructing all kinds of beings. His śrāvakas cannot be told by counting and calculation, and all will attain perfection in the six transcendent [faculties], the three clear [views], and the eight emancipations. The domain of that buddha will be adorned and perfected with such boundless excellencies as these. His kalpa will be named Jewel Radiance and his domain named Excellent Purity. The lifetime of that buddha will be infinite asaṃkhyeya

5. Or the kalpa of the sages. This is the present kalpa, during which a thousand buddhas appear.

kalpas, and the Law will remain for long. After the extinction of that buddha, stupas of the precious seven will be [erected] throughout all that domain."

At that time the World-honored One, desiring to proclaim this teaching over again, spoke thus in verse:

"Bhikshus! Listen to me attentively!
The Way [my] Buddha-son has walked,
Through well studying tactfulness,
Is beyond conception.
Knowing how all enjoy mere trifles
And are afraid of the greater wisdom,
The bodhisattvas therefore become
Śrāvakas or pratyekabuddhas.
By numberless tactful methods
They convert the various kinds of beings,
Saying: 'We are but śrāvakas,
Far removed from the Buddha-way.'
They release innumerable beings,
All completing [their course];
Even the lowly disposed and the neglectful
Gradually become buddhas.
Inwardly hiding their bodhisattva-deeds,
Outwardly they appear as śrāvakas.
With few desires and disliking mortal life,
They truly purify their buddha-land.
They show themselves possessed of human passions[6]
And seem to hold heretical views.
Thus do my disciples
Tactfully save all beings.
If I fully explained
The varied [future] transformations,
Beings who heard of them
Would be perplexed and puzzled.
Now this Pūrṇa
Under thousands of koṭis of former buddhas

6. Or "They show to all they [too] have the three poisons."

Has diligently maintained his course,
And proclaimed and protected the Buddha-law.
He has sought supreme wisdom
And under the buddhas
Has shown himself the superior disciple
In learning and wisdom.
In preaching he has been fearless,
Able to cause all beings to rejoice;
He has ever been tireless
In aiding Buddha-tasks.
Having achieved the great transcendent [faculties],
Acquired the four unhindered [powers of] wisdom,
And known the faculties [of others], keen or dull,
He has always preached the pure Law.
Expounding such principles as these,
He has taught thousands of koṭis of beings,
Leading them to rest in the Great-vehicle Law,
And himself purified his buddha-land.
In future he shall also worship
Infinite, numberless buddhas,
Protect and aid in proclaiming the Righteous Law,
And himself purify his buddha-land.
Constantly with tactful methods
He shall fearlessly preach the Law
And lead incalculable beings
To attain perfect knowledge;
And worshiping the tathāgatas,
And guarding the treasury of the Law,
He shall afterward become a buddha
Whose title will be Law Radiance.
His domain, named Excellent Purity,
Will be formed of the precious seven,
And his kalpa be called Jewel Radiance.
His bodhisattvas, a great host,
Infinite koṭis in number,
All accomplished in great transcendent [faculties]
And perfect in dread powers,
Will fill that domain to the full.

Numberless also will be his śrāvakas
With the three clear [views] and eight emancipations,
Who have attained the four unhindered wisdoms.
Such will be his monks.
All the living in that domain
Will be free from carnal passions,
Pure and born by transformation,
Adorned with all the signs.
Joy in the Law and pleasure in meditation
Shall be their food, with no thought of other;
No womankind will be there,
Nor any evil ways.
The Bhikshu Pūrṇa,
Complete in all his merits,
Shall gain this pure land
Where the wise and sages abound.
Such are the boundless things of which
I have now but briefly spoken."

Then the twelve hundred arhats of self-reliant mind reflected thus: "Delighted are we to gain this unprecedented [experience]. If the World-honored One would predict for each of us [our future destiny] as for the other great disciples, how glad we should be!" The Buddha, knowing the thoughts in their minds, addressed Mahā-Kāśyapa, [saying]: "These twelve hundred arhats: let me now in their presence and in order predict [for them] Perfect Enlightenment. Amongst this assembly, my great disciple Kauṇḍinya Bhikshu, after paying homage to sixty-two thousand koṭis of buddhas, will become a buddha whose title will be Universal Light Tathāgata, Worshipful, All Wise, Perfectly Enlightened in Conduct, Well Departed, Understander of the World, Peerless Leader, Controller, Teacher of Gods and Men, Buddha, World-honored One. Of [the rest of] those arhats, five hundred—Uruvilvā-Kāśyapa, Gayā-Kāśyapa, Nadī-Kāśyapa, Kālodāyin, Udāyin, Aniruddha, Revata, Kapphiṇa, Vakkula, Cunda, Svāgata, and others—all will attain to Perfect Enlightenment, all with the same title, namely, Universal Light."

At that time the World-honored One, desiring to proclaim this teaching over again, spoke thus in verse:

"Kauṇḍinya Bhikshu
Will see innumerable buddhas,
And after asaṃkhyeya kalpas have passed,
Accomplish Perfect Enlightenment.
Ever emitting great light,
Perfect in the transcendent [powers],
His fame spread over the universe,
Revered by all [beings],
Ever preaching the supreme Way,
His title will be Universal Light.
Pure will be his domain;
His bodhisattvas all will be brave;
All mounted on wonderful buildings,
They will travel through all lands
With unsurpassed offerings,
To present them to the buddhas.
Having made these offerings,
Their hearts will greatly rejoice
And soon return to their own domain;
Such will be their supernatural powers.
That buddha's life will be six myriad kalpas;
His Righteous Law will remain twice his lifetime,
The Counterfeit Law double that.
His Law ended, gods and men will sorrow.
Five hundred other bhikshus
One by one shall become buddhas
With the same title, Universal Light;
In turn [each] shall predict, [saying]:
'After my extinction
So and so shall become buddha;
The world which he instructs
Shall be as mine of today.'
The splendid purity of their domain
And its transcendent powers,
Its bodhisattvas and śrāvakas,
Its Righteous Law and its Counterfeit,
The length of its kalpa period,
All will be as that above stated.

Kāśyapa! You now know
Of these five hundred self-reliant ones.
The other band of śrāvakas
Will also be like them.
To these, who are not in this assembly,
Do you proclaim my words."

Thereupon the five hundred arhats present before the Buddha, having received [this] prediction, ecstatic with joy, instantly rose from their seats, went before the Buddha, made obeisance at his feet, repented their errors, and rebuked themselves, [saying]: "World-honored One! We have constantly been thinking that we had attained final nirvana. Now we know that we were just like the foolish ones. Wherefore? Because we ought to have obtained the Tathāgata-wisdom, and yet were content with the inferior knowledge.

"World-honored One! It is as if some man goes to an intimate friend's house, gets drunk, and falls asleep. Meanwhile his friend, having to go forth on official duty, ties a priceless jewel within his garment as a present, and departs. The man, being drunk and asleep, knows nothing of it. On arising he travels onward till he reaches some other country, where for food and clothing he expends much labor and effort, and undergoes exceedingly great hardship, and is content even if he can obtain but little. Later, his friend happens to meet him and speaks thus: 'Tut! Sir, how is it you have come to this for the sake of food and clothing? Wishing you to be in comfort and able to satisfy all your five senses,[7] I formerly in such a year and month and on such a day tied a priceless jewel within your garment. Now as of old it is present there and you in ignorance are slaving and worrying to keep yourself alive. How very stupid! Go you now and exchange that jewel for what you need and do whatever you will, free from all poverty and shortage.'

"The Buddha also is like this. When he was a bodhisattva, he taught us to conceive the idea of perfect wisdom, but we soon forgot, neither knowing nor perceiving. Having obtained the arhat-way, we said we had reached nirvana;[8] in the hardship of [gaining] a living we

7. Literally, "five desires." See Glossary.
8. Literally, "extinction."

had contented ourselves with a mere trifle. [But] our aspirations after perfect wisdom still remain and were never lost, and now the World-honored One arouses us and speaks thus: 'Bhikshus! That which you have obtained is not final nirvana. For long I have caused you to cultivate the roots of buddha-goodness, and for tactful reasons have displayed a form of nirvana. But you have considered it to be the real nirvana you had obtained.' World-honored One! Now we know we are really bodhisattvas predicted to attain Perfect Enlightenment. For this cause we greatly rejoice in our unprecedented gain."

Thereupon Ājñāta-Kauṇḍinya and the others, desiring to announce this meaning over again, spoke thus in verse:

"We, hearing his voice
Predicting [for us] unsurpassed comfort,[9]
Rejoice in our unexpected [lot]
And salute the all-wise Buddha.
Now before the World-honored One
We repent our errors;
[Though] countless Buddha-treasures [awaited],
With but a trifle of nirvana
We, like ignorant and foolish people,
Were ready to be content.
It is like [the case of] a poor man
Who goes to the house of a friend.
That friend, being very rich,
Sets much fine food before him.
A priceless precious pearl
He ties in his inner garment,
Secretly giving it and departing
While he sleeps on unaware.
The man when he arises
Travels on to another country
In search of food and clothes to keep alive,
Suffering great hardships for his living,
Contented with ever so little,
Wishing for nothing better,

9. Perfect Enlightenment.

Never perceiving that in his inner garment
There is a priceless jewel.
The friend who gave him the jewel
Afterward sees this poor man
And, bitterly rebuking him,
Shows where the jewel is bound.
The poor man, seeing this jewel,
Is filled with a great joy;
Rich, in possession of wealth,
He can satisfy his five senses.
Such were also we.
For long has the World-honored One
Always pitied and taught us
To cultivate the highest aspiration;
But because of our ignorance,
We neither perceived nor knew it;
Gaining but a little of nirvana,
Contented, we sought no more.
Now the Buddha has awakened us,
Saying this is not real nirvana;
[Only] on attaining the highest Buddha-wisdom
Is there real nirvana.
Now, having heard from the Buddha
The prediction and its glory,[10]
And the command[11] we receive in turn,
Body and soul are full of joy."

10. Some read: "The prediction and the splendid adornment [of the land]."
11. Literally, "decision; to determine [to become a buddha]." It is also translated as "prediction."

CHAPTER IX

Prediction of the Destiny of Arhats, Training and Trained

AT THAT TIME Ānanda and Rāhula reflected thus: "We have thought to ourselves if [our future] were only foretold, how happy we should be!" Thereupon they rose from their seats, went before the Buddha, made obeisance at his feet, and together spoke to the Buddha, saying: "World-honored One! Let us in this also have a place. We have only the Tathāgata in whom to trust. We are known to and acknowledged by all the worlds, including gods, men, and asuras. Ānanda is always [thy] attendant, protecting and keeping the treasury of the Law, and Rāhula is the Buddha's son. If the Buddha sees [fit] to predict for us Perfect Enlightenment our desires will be fulfilled and the hopes of many will be satisfied."

Thereupon the two thousand śrāvaka disciples who were under training and no longer under training all rose from their seats, bared their right shoulders, went before the Buddha, with one mind folded their hands, and gazed upon the World-honored One, wishing as Ānanda and Rāhula [had wished], and stood there in line.

"Arhats, Training and Trained" means men studying and graduated, that is, under training and no longer under training. See p. 31, fn. 3.

Then the Buddha addressed Ānanda, [saying]: "In a future world you will become a buddha with the title of Sovereign Universal King of Wisdom [great as] Mountains and Oceans Tathāgata, Worshipful, All Wise, Perfectly Enlightened in Conduct, Well Departed, Understander of the World, Peerless Leader, Controller, Teacher of Gods and Men, Buddha, World-honored One. He shall pay homage to sixty-two koṭis of buddhas, protect and keep the treasury of the Law, and afterward attain Perfect Enlightenment, instructing twenty thousand myriad koṭis of bodhisattvas like the sands of the Ganges, causing them to accomplish Perfect Enlightenment. His domain will be named Never-lowered Victorious Banner. Its land shall be pure, with lapis lazuli for earth. His kalpa will be named World-filling Wonderful Sound. That buddha's lifetime will be immeasurable thousand myriad koṭis of asaṃkhyeya kalpas, so that even if a man counts and calculates it for thousands of myriads of koṭis of immeasurable asaṃkhyeya kalpas, it will be impossible to know it. [His] Righteous Law will abide in [his] world twice his lifetime and the Counterfeit Law again abide in [his] world double [the time] of the Righteous Law. Ānanda! This buddha, Sovereign Universal King of Wisdom [great as] Mountains and Oceans, will be extolled and his merits praised by universal unlimited thousand myriad koṭis of buddha-tathāgatas like the sands of the Ganges."

Then the World-honored One, desiring to proclaim this teaching over again, spoke thus in verse:

"I now declare among [you] monks that
Ānanda, keeper of the Law,[1]
Shall pay homage to buddhas
And afterward accomplish Perfect Enlightenment.
His title will be Wisdom [great as] Mountains and Oceans
Sovereign Universal Buddha-King.
His domain will be pure,
Named Never-lowered Victorious Banner.
He shall instruct bodhisattvas
As sands of the Ganges in number.

1. Ānanda is especially honored as the disciple who memorized and transmitted the teachings of the Buddha.

That buddha will have august powers,
His fame filling the universe;
His lifetime will be beyond calculation
Because of his compassion for the living;
His Righteous Law will be twice his lifetime
And the Counterfeit double that.
Many as the sands of the Ganges,
Countless living creatures
In that buddha's Law
Shall cultivate the seed of the Buddha-way."

Thereupon the eight thousand bodhisattvas in the assembly who had newly started [on the road] all reflected thus: "We have not yet heard [even] senior bodhisattvas receive such predictions as these; what can be the cause of these śrāvakas obtaining such decisions as these?" Then the World-honored One, knowing what the bodhisattvas were thinking in their minds, addressed them, saying: "Good sons! I and Ānanda together under the Buddha Firmament King at the same time conceived the thought of Perfect Enlightenment. Ānanda took constant pleasure in learning, [while] I was devoted to active progress. For this reason I have already attained Perfect Enlightenment, while Ānanda has been taking care of my Law, as he will take care of the Law-treasuries of future buddhas, and instruct and bring to perfection the host of bodhisattvas. Such was his original vow, and so he receives this prediction."

Ānanda, face to face with the Buddha, hearing his own prediction and the adornment of his domain, and that his vow had been fulfilled, was filled with joy at obtaining such unprecedented [news]. Instantly he remembered the Law-treasuries of unlimited thousand myriad koṭis of buddhas in the past, and understood them without difficulty as if he were now hearing them, recalling also his original vow.

Then Ānanda spoke thus in verse:

"The rare and World-honored One
Recalls to my mind the Law
Of innumerable buddhas in the past
As if I were hearing it today.

I now, having no more doubts,
Peacefully abide in the Buddha-way.
Tactfully will I serve
In caring for the Buddha's Law."

Then the Buddha addressed Rāhula: "In the world to come you will become a buddha entitled Treader on Seven-Jeweled Lotuses Tathāgata, Worshipful, All Wise, Perfectly Enlightened in Conduct, Well Departed, Understander of the World, Peerless Leader, Controller, Teacher of Gods and Men, Buddha, World-honored One. He shall pay homage to buddha-tathāgatas equal in number to the atoms of ten worlds, always becoming the eldest son of those buddhas, just as he is at present. The domain of this Treader on Seven-Jeweled Lotuses Buddha will be splendidly adorned; the number of kalpas of his lifetime, the disciples converted by him, the Righteous Law and Counterfeit Law, will be just the same as those of the Sovereign Universal King of Wisdom [great as] Mountains and Oceans; and of this buddha he will also become the eldest son. Afterward he will attain Perfect Enlightenment."

Thereupon the World-honored One, desiring to proclaim this teaching over again, spoke thus in verse:

"When I was a prince royal,
Rāhula was my eldest son.
Now that I have accomplished the Buddha-way,
He is the Law-heir receiving the Law.
In worlds to come,
Seeing infinite koṭis of buddhas,
To all he will be eldest son
And with all his mind seek the Buddha-way.
Of the hidden course of Rāhula
Only I am able to know.
At present as my eldest son
He is revealed to all.
Infinite thousand myriad koṭis
Are his merits, beyond calculation.
Peacefully abiding in the Buddha-law,
He seeks the supreme Way."

At that time the World-honored One looked upon the two thousand men under training and no longer under training, gentle in mind, tranquil and calm, who were observing the Buddha with all their mind. The Buddha addressed Ānanda, [saying]: "Do you see these two thousand men under training and no longer under training?"

"Yes, I see them."

"Ānanda! These men shall pay homage to buddha-tathāgatas innumerable as the atoms of fifty worlds, revere and honor them, and care for their treasuries of the Law; and finally, in the same hour, in domains in every direction, each will become a buddha. All will have the same title, namely, Jewel Sign Tathāgata, Worshipful, All Wise, Perfectly Enlightened in Conduct, Well Departed, Understander of the World, Peerless Leader, Controller, Teacher of Gods and Men, Buddha, World-honored One. Their lifetimes will be one kalpa, and the splendor of their domains, their śrāvakas and bodhisattvas, their Righteous Law and Counterfeit Law, all will be equal."

Then the World-honored One, desiring to proclaim this teaching over again, spoke thus in verse:

"These two thousand śrāvakas
Who are now in my presence,
I give to them the prediction that
In the future they will become buddhas.
The buddhas they worship will be
Numerous as the aforementioned atoms.
After caring for their Law-treasuries,
They will reach Perfect Enlightenment.
In domains in all directions
Each will have the same title;
Simultaneously sitting on the wisdom terrace,
They shall prove the supreme wisdom.
The name of all will be Jewel Sign;
Their domains and disciples,
Their Righteous Law and Counterfeit Law,
Will all be equal without difference.
All by transcendent [powers]
Shall everywhere save the living;

And their fame universally spreading,
They shall progress into nirvana."

Thereupon the two thousand men under training and no longer under training, hearing the Buddha's prediction, became ecstatic with joy and spoke thus in verse:

"World-honored One! Bright Lamp of Wisdom!
We, hearing [his] voice of prediction,
Are filled with joyfulness,
As if sprinkled with sweet dews."

CHAPTER X

A Teacher of the Law

AT THAT TIME the World-honored One addressed the eighty thousand great leaders through the Bodhisattva Medicine King, [saying]: "Medicine King! Do you see in this assembly innumerable gods, dragon kings, yakshas, gandharvas, asuras, garuḍas, kiṃnaras, mahoragas, human and nonhuman beings, as well as bhikshus, bhikshuṇīs, male and female lay devotees, seekers after śrāvakaship, seekers after pratyekabuddhahood, seekers after bodhisattvaship, and seekers after buddhahood? All such beings as these, in the presence of the Buddha, if they hear a single verse or a single word of the Wonderful Law-Flower Sutra and even by a single thought delight in it, I predict that they will all attain Perfect Enlightenment." The Buddha [again] addressed Medicine King: "Moreover, after the extinction of the Tathāgata, if there be any people who hear even a single verse or a single word of the Wonderful Law-Flower Sutra,

The title of this chapter refers to a doctor, master, or teacher of the Law. Kern's title is "The Preacher." At the beginning of this chapter Dharmaraksha's translation has the story of the holy wheel-rolling king Jeweled Canopy and one of his sons, Fine Canopy, who practiced under the Medicine King Tathāgata in a former world. This story, written in prose and verse, is not found in the extant Sanskrit text.

and by a single thought delight in it, I also predict for them Perfect Enlightenment. Again, let there be any who receive and keep, read and recite, expound and copy even a single verse of the Wonderful Law-Flower Sutra, and look upon this sutra with reverence as if it were the Buddha, and make offering to it in various ways with flowers, perfume, garlands, sandal powder, perfumed unguents, incense for burning, silk canopies, banners, flags, garments, and music, as well as revere it with folded hands: know, Medicine King, these people have already paid homage to ten myriad koṭis of buddhas and under the buddhas performed their great vows; therefore, out of compassion for all living beings they are born here among men.

"Medicine King! If there be any people who ask you what sort of living beings will become buddhas in future worlds, you should show them that those are the people who will certainly become buddhas in future worlds. Wherefore? If [my] good sons and good daughters receive and keep, read and recite, expound, and copy even a single word of the Law-Flower Sutra, and make offerings to it in various ways with flowers, perfumes, garlands, sandal powder, fragrant unguents, incense for burning, silk canopies, banners, flags, garments, and music, as well as revere it with folded hands, these people will be looked up to by all the worlds; and as you pay homage to tathāgatas, so should you pay homage to them. Know! These people are great bodhisattvas who, having accomplished Perfect Enlightenment and out of compassion for all living beings, are willingly born in this world, and widely proclaim and expound the Wonderful Law-Flower Sutra. How much more those who are perfectly able to receive, keep, and in every way pay homage to it! Know, Medicine King! These people will of themselves abandon the recompense of their purified karma, and after my extinction, out of pity for all living beings, will be born in the evil world and widely proclaim this sutra. If these good sons and good daughters, after my extinction, should be able [even] by stealth to preach to one person even one word of the Law-Flower Sutra, know these people are Tathāgata-apostles sent by the Tathāgata to perform Tathāgata-deeds. How much more so those who in great assemblies widely preach to others.

"Medicine King! Even if there be some wicked person who out of an evil mind, throughout a whole kalpa, appears before the Buddha and unceasingly blasphemes the Buddha, his sin is still light, [but] if anyone, even with a single ill word, defames the lay devotees or monks who read and recite the Law-Flower Sutra, his sin is extremely heavy. Medicine King! He who reads and recites the Law-Flower Sutra—know! That man has adorned himself with the adornment of the Buddha, and so is carried by the Tathāgata on his shoulder. Wherever he goes, he should be saluted with hands wholeheartedly folded, revered, worshiped, honored, and extolled, and offerings made to him of flowers, perfumes, garlands, sandal powder, perfumed unguents, incense for burning, silk canopies, banners, flags, garments, edibles and dainties, and music; he should be served with the most excellent offerings found amongst men. He should be sprinkled with celestial jewels, and offerings made of celestial jewels in heaps. Wherefore? Because, this man delighting to preach the Law, they who hear it but for a moment thereupon attain Perfect Enlightenment."

Then the World-honored One, desiring to proclaim this teaching over again, spoke thus in verse:

"Should one wish to abide in the Buddha-way
And accomplish intuitive wisdom,
He must always earnestly honor
The keepers of the Flower of the Law.
Should one wish quickly to attain
Every kind of wisdom,
He must receive and keep this sutra
And honor those who keep it.
Should one be able to receive and keep
The Wonderful Law-Flower Sutra,
Know, he is the Buddha's apostle,
[Who] has compassion for all living beings.
He who is able to receive and keep
The Wonderful Law-Flower Sutra,
Giving up his pure land,[1]
And, from pity for the living, being born here:
Know, such a man as this,
Free to be born where he will,
Is able, in this evil world,

1. Or "the pure [clear] position [he had attained]."

Widely to preach the supreme Law.
You should, with celestial flowers and perfumes,
Garments of heavenly jewels,
And heaps of wonderful celestial jewels,
Pay homage to [such] a preacher of the Law.
In evil ages after my extinction,
Those who are able to keep this sutra
Must be saluted and revered with folded hands,
As if paying homage to the World-honored One.
With the best of dainties and abundant sweets,
And every kind of garment,
This son of the Buddha should be worshiped
In the hope of even a momentary hearing.
In future ages, if anyone is able
To receive and keep this sutra,
I will send him to be amongst men
To perform the task of the Tathāgata.
If anyone in the course of a kalpa
Unceasingly cherishes a wicked heart
And, with angry mien, rails at the Buddha,
He commits an infinitely heavy sin.
But anyone who reads, recites, and keeps
This Sutra of the Law-Flower,
[Should one] abuse him even a moment,
His sin is still heavier.
Anyone who seeks after the Buddha-way
And for a [complete] kalpa,
With folded hands, in my presence
Extols me in numberless verses,
Because he thus extols the Buddha
Will acquire infinite merit.
[But] he who praises the bearers of the sutra,
His happiness will be even greater.
During eighty koṭis of kalpas,
With the most excellent color, sound,
Scent, flavor, and touch,
If one worships the sutra-bearers;
If, having thus worshiped,

He hears [it from them but] for a moment,
Then let him joyfully congratulate himself,
[Saying]: 'I have now obtained a great benefit.'
Medicine King! Now I say to you:
Of the sutras I have preached,
Amongst [all] these sutras,
The Law-Flower is the very foremost."

Thereupon the Buddha again addressed the Medicine King Bodhisattva-Mahāsattva, [saying]: "Infinite thousand myriad koṭis are the sutras I preach, whether already preached, now being preached, or to be preached in the future; and, among them all, this Law-Flower Sutra is the most difficult to believe and the most difficult to understand. Medicine King! This sutra is the mystic, essential treasury of all buddhas, which must not be distributed among or recklessly delivered to men. It is watched over by buddhas, world-honored ones, and from of yore it has never been revealed and preached. And this sutra while the Tathāgata is still here has [aroused] much enmity and envy; how much more after his extinction!

"Know, Medicine King! After the Tathāgata is extinct those who are able to copy, keep, read, recite, worship, and preach it to others will be invested by the Tathāgata with his robe, and will be protected and remembered by buddhas abiding in other regions. They shall have great powers of faith and the power of a resolute vow [and] the powers of virtuous character. Know, those people shall dwell with the Tathāgata, and the Tathāgata shall place his hand upon their heads.

"Medicine King! In every place where [this sutra] is preached or read or recited or copied or its volumes are kept, one should erect a caitya[2] of the precious seven, making it very high, spacious, and splendid. But there is no need to deposit relics. Wherefore? [Because] in it there is the whole body of the Tathāgata. This caitya[3] should be served, revered, honored, and extolled with all kinds of flowers, perfumes, garlands, silk canopies, banners, flags, music, and hymns. If any, seeing that caitya, salute and worship it, know that they all are

2. A caitya is a pagoda in which sutras are deposited. From this chapter on, the erecting of caityas instead of stupas, or pagodas for relics, is stressed.

3. The Sanskrit text has "stupa," signifying that this caitya should be honored as if it were a stupa.

near to Perfect Enlightenment. Medicine King! Many people there are, both laymen and monks, who walk in the bodhisattva-way, without, as it were, being able to see, hear, read, recite, copy, keep, and worship this Law-Flower Sutra. Know that those people are not yet rightly walking in the bodhisattva-way; but if any of them hear this sutra, then they shall be able to walk aright in the bodhisattva-way. If any living beings who seek after the Buddha-way either see or hear this Law-Flower Sutra, and after hearing it believe and discern, receive and keep it, you may know that they are near Perfect Enlightenment.

"Medicine King! It is like a man, extremely thirsty and in need of water, who searches for it by digging in a tableland. So long as he sees dry earth, he knows that the water is still far off. Continuing his labor unceasingly, he in time sees moist earth and then gradually reaches the mire. Then he makes up his mind, knowing that water is at hand. Bodhisattvas are also like this. If they have not heard, nor understood, nor been able to observe this Law-Flower Sutra, you may know that they are still far from Perfect Enlightenment. If they hear, understand, ponder, and observe it, you may assuredly know that they are near Perfect Enlightenment. Wherefore? [Because] the Perfect Enlightenment of every bodhisattva all belongs to this sutra. This sutra brings out the fuller meaning of the tactful or partial method in order to reveal the real truth.[4] The [treasury] of this Law-Flower Sutra is so deep and strong, so hidden and far away that no human being has been able to reach it. Now the Buddha has revealed it for instructing and perfecting bodhisattvas.

"Medicine King! If any bodhisattva, on hearing this Law-Flower Sutra, is startled, doubts, and fears, you may know that this is a bodhisattva neophyte. If any śrāvaka, on hearing this sutra, is startled, doubts, and fears, you may know him for an arrogant person.

"Medicine King! If there be any good son or good daughter who after the extinction of the Tathāgata desires to preach this Law-Flower Sutra to the four groups, how should he preach it? That good son or good daughter, entering into the abode of the Tathāgata, wearing the

4. That is, it opens wide the door, which has heretofore been only partially open, in order to reveal the truth in its reality; in other words, it opens the door to buddhahood for all—Hinayana, Mahayana, śrāvakas, pratyekabuddhas, bodhisattvas—and is the only sutra that does so. This doctrine is called "opening the temporary [truths] and revealing the real [truth]" or "opening the three [vehicles] and revealing the One [vehicle]."

robe of the Tathāgata, and sitting on the throne of the Tathāgata, should then widely proclaim this sutra to the four groups [of hearers].

"The abode of the Tathāgata is the great compassionate heart within all living beings; the robe of the Tathāgata is the gentle and forbearing heart; the throne of the Tathāgata is the voidness of all laws. Established in these, then with unflagging mind to bodhisattvas and the four groups [of hearers] he will preach this Law-Flower Sutra. Medicine King! I [though dwelling] in another realm will send spirit messengers[5] to gather together hearers of the Law for that [preacher] and also send spirit bhikshus, bhikshuṇīs, and male and female lay devotees to hear his preaching of the Law. All these spirit people, hearing the Law, shall unresistingly receive it in faith and obey it. If the preacher of the Law takes up his abode in a secluded place, then I will abundantly send gods, dragons, spirits, gandharvas, asuras, and others to hear him preach. Though I am in a different domain, I will from time to time cause the preacher of the Law to see me. If he forgets any detail of this sutra, I will return and tell him, that he may be in perfect possession of it."

At that time the World-honored One, desiring to proclaim this teaching over again, spoke thus in verse:

"In order to be rid of sloth,
Hearken to this sutra!
Rare is the chance of hearing it
And rare are those who receive it in faith.
It is like a thirsty man needing water,
Who digs in a tableland;
Still seeing dry and arid earth,
He knows water is yet far off.
Moist earth and mire gradually appearing,
He is assured that water is near.
Know, Medicine King!
Such is the case with those
Who hear not the Law-Flower Sutra;
They are far from the Buddha-wisdom.
Should they hear this profound sutra,

5. Literally, "transformed men"; that is, men who have been made to appear expediently through the supernatural power of the Buddha.

Which determines the Law for disciples
And is the king of all sutras,
And, hearing, truly ponder it,
Know that those people
Are near the Buddha-wisdom.
Should anyone preach this sutra,
Let him enter the Tathāgata abode,
Wear the Tathāgata robe,
And sit on the Tathāgata throne;
Undaunted amidst the multitude,
Let him openly expound and preach it.
With great compassion for his abode,
Gentleness and forbearance for his robe,
And the voidness of all laws for his throne,
Abiding in these, let him preach the Law.
If, when he preaches this sutra,
Some should with evil mouth abuse,
Or lay on swords, sticks, shards, or stones,
Think of the Buddha; let him be patient.
In thousands of myriads of koṭis of lands,
I appear with pure imperishable bodies,
And in infinite koṭis of kalpas
Preach the Law for all the living.
If anyone after my extinction
Is able to proclaim this sutra,
I will send him the four spirit groups
Of bhikshus and bhikshuṇīs,
Pure[-minded] men and women,
To worship him as teacher of the Law,
While I will draw living beings
And assemble them to hear [this] Law.
Should men seek to assail with ill [words],
With swords, sticks, shards, or stones,
I will send spirit people
To act as his protectors.
Should any preacher of [this] Law,
Dwelling alone in a secluded place,
In solitude where is no voice of man,

Read and recite this sutra,
Then I will appear to him
With a pure and luminous body.
Should he forget sentences or words,
I will tell him to his clear apprehension.
Whenever such a man, perfect in these merits,
Either preaches to the four groups
Or in seclusion reads and recites the sutra,
He will always see me.
When such a man is in seclusion,
I will send gods and dragon kings,
Yakshas, demons, spirits, and others
To be hearers of [this] Law.
That man will delight to preach the Law
And expound it without hindrance.
Because buddhas guard and mind him,
He can cause multitudes to rejoice.
Whoever is close to [such] a teacher of the Law
Will speedily attain the bodhisattva-way;
And he who becomes a pupil of that teacher
Will behold buddhas [numerous] as the sands of the Ganges."

CHAPTER XI

Beholding the Precious Stupa

AT THAT TIME in front of the Buddha a stupa of the seven precious things, five hundred yojanas in height and two hundred and fifty yojanas in length and breadth, sprang up from the earth and abode in the sky.[1] It was decorated with all kinds of precious things, splendidly adorned with five thousand parapets, thousands of myriads of recesses, and countless banners and flags; hung with jewel garlands, with myriads of koṭis of gem bells suspended on it; on every side exhaling the fragrance of tamālapattra sandalwood, filling the whole world. All its streamers and canopies were composed of the precious seven, gold, silver, lapis lazuli, moonstone, agate, pearl, and carnelian, reaching up to the palaces of the four heavenly kings. The

Kern's title for this chapter is "Apparition of a Stūpa," and the Chinese for Kern's "apparition" can be translated "manifestation" or "revelation," but the word is generally interpreted as meaning "beholding."

1. With regard to the Sanskrit *vaihāyasam antrarīkshe* here, Nanjio notes: "Kern translated the word *vaihāyasam* as 'a meteoric phenomenon,' reading it as the neuter gender, subject, and singular, and besides, saying in the footnote: 'Here, it would seem, the rainbow of seven colours. We shall see that the Stūpa has also another function, that of symbolising the celestial dhishṇya in which sun and moon are standing' [SBE vol. 21, p. 227 n]. But this has nearly the same meaning as the next word, *antarīkshe*, and is used as an adverb. Therefore it is right to translate it as Kumārajīva did."

thirty-three gods, raining celestial mandārava flowers, paid homage to the Precious Stupa. Other gods, dragons, yakshas, gandharvas, asuras, garuḍas, kiṃnaras, mahoragas, human and nonhuman beings, all these thousand myriad koṭis of beings, paid homage to the stupa with all kinds of flowers, perfumes, garlands, streamers, canopies, and music, revered, honored, and extolled it. Then from the midst of the Precious Stupa there came a loud voice, praising and saying:[2] "Excellent! Excellent! World-honored Sakyamuni! Thou art able to preach to the great assembly the Wonderful Law-Flower Sutra of universal and great wisdom, by which bodhisattvas are instructed and which the buddhas guard and mind. So is it, so is it, World-honored Sakyamuni! All that thou sayest is true."

Then the four groups, beholding the great Precious Stupa abiding in the sky and hearing the sound which proceeded from the stupa, were all [filled with] delight in the Law and with wonder at these unheard-of happenings; they rose up from their seats and, reverently folding their hands, withdrew to one side. Meanwhile, a bodhisattva-mahāsattva named Great Eloquence, perceiving uncertainty in the minds of all the world[s] of gods, men, asuras, and others, spoke to the Buddha, saying: "World-honored One! For what reason has this stupa sprung out of the earth and from its midst this voice proceeded?"

Then the Buddha told the Bodhisattva Great Eloquence: "In this stupa there is the whole body of the Tathāgata. Of yore in the past, innumerable thousand myriad koṭis of asaṃkhyeya worlds away in the east, there was a domain named Jewel Clear. In that [domain] there was a buddha entitled Abundant Treasures. When that buddha was treading the bodhisattva-way, he made a great vow, [saying]: 'After I become a buddha and am extinct, if in any country in the universe there be a place where the Law-Flower Sutra is preached, my stupa shall arise and appear there, in order that I may hearken to that sutra, bear testimony to it, and extol it, saying: "Excellent!"' When that buddha had finished his course, he, his extinction approaching, in the midst of gods, men, and a great host, instructed [his] bhikshus: 'Those who, after my extinction, desire to worship my whole body should erect a great stupa.' Wherever in the worlds of the universe the

2. The Tibetan version has a long preceding address, translated into Japanese by Oka, and then follows with the address given here. The former is not found in the extant Sanskrit text.

Law-Flower Sutra is preached, that buddha by the supernatural powers of his vow causes his stupa, containing his whole body, there to spring forth, and praises [the sutra], saying: 'Excellent! Excellent!' Great Eloquence! It is because just now the Tathāgata Abundant Treasures heard the Law-Flower Sutra preached that his stupa sprang up from the earth and he extolled [the sutra], saying: 'Excellent! Excellent!'"

Thereupon the Bodhisattva Great Eloquence, because of the divine power of the Tathāgata, said to the Buddha: "World-honored One! We earnestly desire to see this buddha's body." The Buddha addressed the Bodhisattva-Mahāsattva Great Eloquence [thus]: "This Buddha Abundant Treasures has a profound and grave vow: 'When my stupa appears in the presence of [any of the] buddhas for the sake of hearing the Law-Flower Sutra, if [he] desires to show my body to the four groups, let the buddhas who have emanated from that buddha and who are preaching the Law in the worlds in all directions return all together and assemble in one place, and then shall my body appear.' [So,] Great Eloquence, I must now assemble the buddhas who have emanated from me and who are preaching the Law in the worlds in all directions."

Great Eloquence replied to the Buddha: "World-honored One! We would also see the buddhas emanated from the World-honored One and worship and pay homage to them."

Then the Buddha sent forth a ray from the [circle of] white hair between his eyebrows, whereupon eastward there became visible all the buddhas in five hundred myriad koṭis of nayutas of domains [numerous] as the sands of the Ganges. All those domains had crystal for earth and jewel trees and precious cloth for adornment, were filled with countless thousand myriad koṭis of bodhisattvas, had jeweled canopies stretched [above them], and were covered with networks of jewels. All the buddhas in those domains were preaching the laws with ravishing voices. And innumerable thousand myriad koṭis of bodhisattvas were also seen, filling those domains and preaching to the multitude. So, too, was it in the southern, western, and northern quarters, in the four intermediate directions, in the zenith and the nadir, wherever shone the ray-signal from the [circle of] white hair.

Then the buddhas in all directions each addressed the host of [his] bodhisattvas, saying: "Good sons! We must now go to Sakyamuni

Buddha in the sahā-world and pay homage to the Precious Stupa of the Tathāgata Abundant Treasures."

Thereupon the sahā-world instantly became pure, with lapis lazuli for earth, adorned with jewel trees, cords made of gold marking the boundaries of its eight divisions, having no hamlets, villages, towns, cities, great seas, great rivers, mountains, streams, forests, and thickets, smoking with most precious incense, its ground strewn with mandārava flowers, spread with precious nets and curtains, and hung with all kinds of precious bells.

There only remained the assembled congregation, all [other] gods and men having been removed to other lands. Then those buddhas, each bringing a great bodhisattva as his attendant, arrived at the sahā-world, and each went to the foot of a jewel tree. Each of the jewel trees was five hundred yojanas high, adorned in turn with boughs, leaves, blossoms, and fruit; under all those jewel trees there were lion thrones five yojanas high, also decorated with magnificent jewels. Then each of those buddhas sat cross-legged on those thrones.

Thus all around him the three-thousand-great-thousandfold world was filled [with buddhas], though as yet, from but one point of the compass, the bodies which had emanated from Sakyamuni Buddha had not finished [arriving]. Then Sakyamuni Buddha, desiring to make room for the buddhas who had emanated from himself, in each of the eight directions of space transformed two hundred myriad koṭis of nayutas of domains, all of them pure, without hells, hungry spirits, animals, and asuras, and moreover removed their gods and men to other lands. The domains thus transformed also had lapis lazuli for earth and were ornate with jewel trees five hundred yojanas high, adorned in turn with boughs, leaves, blossoms, and fruit; under every tree was a jeweled lion throne five yojanas high, decorated with all kinds of gems; and there were no great seas or great rivers, nor any Mount Mucilinda, Mount Mahā-Mucilinda, Mount Iron Circle, Mount Great Iron Circle,[3] Mount Sumeru, and so on, all these kings of mountains which always form one buddha-land; their jeweled ground was even and smooth; everywhere jewel-decked awnings were spread and streamers and canopies hung, while most precious incense was burning, and precious celestial flowers everywhere covered

3. Four mountains surrounding Mount Sumeru.

the ground. Sakyamuni Buddha, in order that the buddhas who were coming might be seated, in each of the eight directions transformed two hundred myriad koṭis of nayutas of domains, making them all pure, without hells, hungry spirits, animals, and asuras, and removing [their] gods and men to other lands. The domains thus transformed also had lapis lazuli for earth and were ornate with jewel trees five hundred yojanas high, adorned in turn with boughs, leaves, blossoms, and fruit; under every tree was a jeweled lion throne five yojanas high, decorated with great jewels; and there were no great seas or great rivers, nor any Mount Mucilinda, Mount Mahā-Mucilinda, Mount Iron Circle, Mount Great Iron Circle, Mount Sumeru, and so on, these kings of mountains which always form one buddha-land; their jeweled ground was even and smooth; everywhere jewel-decked awnings were spread, and streamers and canopies hung, while most precious incense was burning, and precious celestial flowers everywhere covered the ground.

At that moment the bodies which had emanated eastward from Sakyamuni, [namely] the buddhas who were each preaching the Law in a hundred thousand myriad koṭis of nayutas of [eastern] domains [numerous] as the sands of the Ganges, arrived and assembled. In like manner in turn the buddhas from all the ten directions all arrived and assembled and took their seats in the eight directions. Thereupon each direction was filled with buddha-tathāgatas from [its] four hundred myriad koṭis of nayutas of domains. Then all the buddhas, each under a jewel tree, seated on a lion throne, sent their attendants to make inquiries of Sakyamuni Buddha, each sending a double handful of jewel flowers, and saying to them: "Good sons! Do you go and visit Mount Gṛdhrakūṭa, the abode of Sakyamuni Buddha, and, according to our words, say: 'Art thou free from disease and distress? Art thou at ease in thy physical powers? And are all the groups of thy bodhisattvas and śrāvakas at peace?' Strew the Buddha in homage with these jewel flowers and say thus: 'Such and such a buddha joins in wishing that this Precious Stupa be opened.'" All the buddhas sent their messengers in like manner.

Then Sakyamuni Buddha, beholding the buddhas who had emanated from him assembled together, each seated on his lion throne, and hearing that those buddhas unitedly desired the Precious Stupa to be opened, straightway rose up from his throne and abode in the sky.

All the four groups stood up, folded their hands, and with all their mind gazed at the Buddha. Thereupon Sakyamuni Buddha with the fingers of his right hand opened the door of the Stupa of the Precious Seven, when there went forth a great sound, like the withdrawing of the bolt on opening a great city gate. Thereupon all the congregation saw the Tathāgata Abundant Treasures sitting on the lion throne in the Precious Stupa, with his undissipated body whole and as if he were in meditation. And they heard him saying: "Excellent! Excellent! Sakyamuni Buddha! Speedily preach this Law-Flower Sutra. I have come hither in order to hear this sutra."

Then the four groups, seeing the buddha who had passed away and been extinct for immeasurable thousand myriad koṭis of kalpas speak such words as these, praised this unprecedented [marvel] and strewed on the Buddha Abundant Treasures and on Sakyamuni Buddha heaps of celestial jewel flowers. Thereupon the Buddha Abundant Treasures within the Precious Stupa shared half his throne with Sakyamuni Buddha, speaking thus: "Sakyamuni Buddha! Take this seat!" Whereon Sakyamuni Buddha entered the stupa and, sitting down on that half throne, folded his legs. Then the great assembly, seeing the two Tathāgatas sitting cross-legged on the lion throne in the Stupa of the Precious Seven, each reflected thus: "The Buddhas are sitting aloft and far away. Would that the Tathāgatas by their transcendent powers might cause us together to take up our abode in the sky." Immediately Sakyamuni Buddha, by his transcendent powers, received all the great assembly up into the sky, and with a great voice universally addressed the four groups, saying: "Who are able to publish abroad the Wonderful Law-Flower Sutra in this sahā-world? Now indeed is the time. The Tathāgata not long hence must enter nirvana. The Buddha desires to bequeath this Wonderful Law-Flower Sutra so that it may ever exist."

At that time the World-honored One, desiring to proclaim this meaning over again, spoke thus in verse:

"The holy world-honored lord,
Albeit for long extinct
And in his Precious Stupa,
Yet comes [to hear] the Law.
How [then] should anyone not be

Zealous for the Law's sake?
This buddha has been extinct
For countless kalpas,
[Yet] in place after place he hears the Law
Because of its rareness.
That buddha made a vow:
'After my extinction,
I will go anywhere
Forever to hear this Law.'
And innumerable buddhas
Emanated from my body,
As the sands of the Ganges,
Have come to hear the Law
And to behold the extinct Tathāgata
Abundant Treasures.
Each, leaving his wonderful land
And his host of disciples,
Gods, men, and dragons,
And all their offerings,
Has come here to this place
So that the Law may long abide.
In order to seat these buddhas,
By my transcendent powers
I have removed innumerable beings
And cleared [my] domain.
The buddhas, one by one,
Have arrived under the jewel trees,
As lotus flowers adorn
A clear and cool pool.
Under those jewel trees,
On the lion thrones,
The buddhas are seated,
Brilliant and resplendent,
As, in the darkness of night,
Great torches gleam.
From them proceeds a mystic fragrance
Spreading afar over all lands;
All beings perfumed thereby

Are beside themselves with joy;
It is just as when a great wind
Blows over the [fragrant] bushes.
By this expedient
I cause the Law long to abide.
To this great assembly I say:
'After my extinction,
Whoever is able to guard and keep,
Read and recite this sutra,
Let him before the Buddha
Himself declare his vow!'
The Buddha Abundant Treasures,
Albeit extinct for long,
By [reason of] his great vow
[Will sound forth] the lion's roar.[4]
Let the Tathāgata Abundant Treasures
And also me myself
And my assembly of emanated buddhas[5]
Know this resolve.
Of all my Buddha-sons,
Let him who is able to protect the Law
[Sound] forth a great vow
To make it long abide!
He who is able to protect
The Law of this sutra
Will be deemed to have worshiped
Me and Abundant Treasures,
This Buddha Abundant Treasures,
Who abides in the Precious Stupa
And ever wanders everywhere
For the sake of this sutra.
He will moreover have worshiped
All my emanated buddhas here,
Who adorn and make resplendent
All the worlds.

4. The buddha's voice.

5. The Buddha Abundant Treasures, the Buddha Sakyamuni, and all the buddhas emanated from Sakyamuni are called the three groups of buddhas.

If he preaches this sutra,
Then he is deemed to have seen me
And the Tathāgata Abundant Treasures,
Also my emanated buddhas.
All my good sons!
Let each carefully ponder that!
This is a difficult task,
Needing the taking of a great vow.
All the other sutras,
Numerous as the sands of the Ganges,
Though one expounded them,
It still could not be counted hard.
If one took up Sumeru
And hurled it to another region
Of numberless buddha-lands,
Neither would that be hard.
If one were with his toes
To move a great-thousandfold world
And hurl it afar to another land,
That also would not be hard.
If one, standing on the Summit of All Beings,[6]
Were to expound to all beings
The countless other sutras,
That also would not be hard.
But if one, after the Buddha's extinction,
In the midst of an evil world
Is able to preach this sutra,
This indeed is hard.
Though there be a man who
Grasps the sky in his hand
And wanders about with it,
That is still not hard.
But after my extinction,
Whether himself to copy and keep
Or cause another to copy it,
That indeed is hard.

6. The highest heaven, called the Summit of All Existence.

If one took the great earth,
Put it on his toenail,
And ascended to the Brahma heaven,
That would still not be hard.
But after the Buddha's extinction,
In the midst of an evil world
To read aloud this sutra for but a moment,
That indeed will be hard.
Though one, in the final conflagration,[7]
Carried a load of dry hay,
And entered it unseared,
That would still not be hard.
But after my extinction,
If anyone keeps this sutra
And proclaims it but to one man,
That indeed will be hard.
If one could keep the eighty-four thousand
Sections of the Law[8]
And the twelve divisions of sutras,[9]
Expound them to others,
And cause those who heard
To gain the six transcendent [powers],
Though he had such power as this,
That would still not be hard.
But after my extinction, if anyone
Hears and receives this sutra
And inquires into its meaning,
That indeed will be hard.
If one could preach the Law

7. The conflagration at the end of the world.
8. It is said that all living beings have eighty-four thousand faults, so the Buddha taught the same number of laws or remedies.
9. The Mahayana sutras are classified into twelve divisions, while the Hinayana sutras are divided into nine (see p. 63, fn. 23). The twelve divisions of the Mahayana sutras are (1) sutras; (2) *geya*, or repetitional chants; (3) *vyākaraṇa*, or predictions regarding the destiny of the Buddha's disciples; (4) *gāthā*, or detached stanzas; (5) *udāna*, or impromptu discourses; (6) *nidāna*, or reasonings; (7) *avadāna*, or parables; (8) *itivṛttaka*, or former things: (9) *jātaka*, or birth stories; (10) *vaipulya*, or amplified and diffuse scriptures; (11) *adbhuta-dharma*, or the unprecedented laws; and (12) *upadeśa*, or dogmatic discussions.

And cause thousands, myriads, koṭis,
Countless, innumerable beings,
As [many as] the sands of the Ganges,
To become arhats
And perfect the six transcendent [powers],
Even to confer such a benefit as this
Would still not be hard.
But after my extinction,
If anyone is able to keep
Such a sutra as this,
That will indeed be hard.
I, on account of the Buddha-way,
In innumerable lands
From the beginning till now
Have widely preached many sutras;
But amongst them all
This sutra is the chief, and
If anyone is able to keep it,
Then he keeps the Buddha's body.
All my good sons!
Let him who, after my extinction,
Is able to receive and keep,
Read and recite this sutra,
Now in the presence of the Buddha
Announce his own vow!
This sutra [so] difficult to keep,
If anyone keeps it a short time,
I shall be pleased,
And so will all the buddhas.
Such a one as this
Will be praised by all the buddhas;
Such a one is brave;
Such a one is zealous;
Such a one is named Law-keeper
And dhūta-observer;
Speedily shall he attain
The supreme Buddha-way.
He who, in coming generations,

Can read and keep this sutra
Is truly a Buddha-son
Dwelling in the stage of pure goodness.
After the Buddha's extinction,
He who can expound its meaning
Will be the eye of the world
For gods and men.
He who, in the [final] age of fear,
Can preach it even for a moment
By all gods and men
Will be worshiped."

HERE ENDS
THE FOURTH FASCICLE

CHAPTER XII

Devadatta

AT THAT TIME the Buddha addressed the bodhisattvas, the celestial beings, and the four groups,[1] [saying]: "Through innumerable kalpas of the past, I have tirelessly sought the Law-Flower Sutra; during many kalpas I was long a king and vowed to

The extant Sanskrit text, two other Chinese translations, and the Tibetan version of the Lotus Sutra include the Devadatta section of the text in chapter 11. Kumārajīva's version divides chapter 11 into two parts, making a new chapter, the twelfth, begin here with the title "Devadatta." Some have asserted that Kumārajīva did not translate this chapter, and it is said not to have been included in his Chinese text for some time. But Chih-i, founder of the T'ien-t'ai sect, supported the opposite view, saying that he had seen an old original copy of Kumārajīva's translation containing the translation of this portion.

Devadatta, "gift of the devas," was one of Sakyamuni's cousins but became his rival and enemy. He is said to have fallen into hell because he committed the five worst sins. That the Buddha in this chapter predicts that Devadatta will become a buddha indicates that all beings, however evil, can become buddhas. In addition, in the latter half of this chapter it is also proclaimed that the daughter of a dragon king will become a buddha, indicating that all women can also attain buddhahood. Generally speaking, apart from this sutra Buddhism does not recognize that women can become buddhas. Thus two great doctrines, the possibility of the worst men and also of women attaining buddhahood, are taught in this chapter.

1. This can also be translated as "gods, men, [and] the four groups"—monks, nuns, and male and female lay devotees.

seek the supreme Bodhi,[2] my mind never faltering. Desiring to fulfil the Six Pāramitās, I earnestly bestowed alms with an unsparing mind —elephants, horses, the rare seven,[3] countries, cities, wives, children, male and female slaves, servants and followers, head, eyes, marrow, brain, the flesh of my body, hands, and feet, unsparing of body and life. At that time people's lifetime was beyond measure. For the sake of the Law, I gave up the throne of my domain, deputed my government to the crown prince, and with beating drum and open proclamation, sought everywhere for the truth, [promising]: 'Whoever is able to tell me of a Great-vehicle, I will all my life provide for him and be his footman.' At that time a certain hermit came to [me] the king and said: 'I have a Great-vehicle named Wonderful Law-Flower Sutra. If you will not disobey me, I will explain it to you.' [I] the king, hearing what the hermit said, became ecstatic with joy and instantly followed him, providing for his needs, gathering fruit, drawing water, collecting fuel, laying his food, even turning my body into his seat and bed, yet never feeling fatigue of body or mind. While I thus served a millennium passed, [and] for the sake of the Law, I zealously waited on him that he should lack nothing."

Then the World-honored One, desiring to proclaim this meaning over again, spoke thus in verse:

"I remember in past kalpas,
When, to seek the Great Law—
Though I was a king in the world,
Yet coveted not earthly pleasures[4]—
With toll of bell, I proclaimed to the four quarters:
'Whoever possesses the Great Law,
If he will expound it to me,
To him I will become servant.'
Then there was the sage Asita,
Who came and said to the great king:
'I possess the wonderful Law
Rarely [heard] in the world.
If you are able to practice it,

2. Perfect Enlightenment.
3. The precious seven. See Glossary.
4. Literally, "the pleasures of the five desires." See Glossary.

I will preach it to you.'
Then the king, hearing the sage's word,
Conceived great joy in his heart
And thereupon followed him,
Providing for his needs,
Gathering fuel, fruit, and gourds,
And in season reverently offering them.
Keeping the Wonderful Law in my heart,
Body and mind were unwearied;
Universally for all living beings
I diligently sought the Great Law,
Not indeed for my own sake,
Not for the delight of the five desires.
So I, king of a great domain,
By zealous seeking obtained this Law
And at last became a buddha.
Now, therefore, I preach it to you."

The Buddha said to all the bhikshus: "The former king was myself and the sage at that juncture was the present Devadatta himself. Through the good friendship of Devadatta I was enabled to become perfect in the Six Pāramitās, in kindness, compassion, joy, and indifference,[5] in the thirty-two signs, the eighty kinds of excellence, the deep golden-hued [skin], the ten powers, the four kinds of fearlessness, the four social laws,[6] the eighteen special unique characteristics, the transcendent powers of the Way, the attainment of Perfect Enlightenment, and the widespread saving of the living—all this is due to the good friendship of Devadatta. I declare to all you four groups: Devadatta, after his departure and innumerable kalpas have passed, will become a buddha, whose title will be King of the Gods Tathāgata, Worshipful, All Wise, Perfectly Enlightened in Conduct, Well Departed, Understander of the World, Peerless Leader, Controller, Teacher of Gods and Men, Buddha, World-honored One, and whose

5. *Maitrī*, kindness or benevolence; *karuṇā*, compassion; *muditā*, joy; and *upekshā*, indifference, or the state of absolute indifference attained by renouncing any exercise of the mental faculties. These four are termed the four kinds of infinite mind or infinite virtues (see also p. 52, fn. 1).

6. The four guiding rules for human society: almsgiving, kind speech, helpful conduct, and mutual service.

world will be named Divine Way. At that time the Buddha King of Gods shall dwell in the world for twenty intermediate kalpas. He shall widely preach the Wonderful Law for all the living, and living beings [numerous] as the sands of the Ganges will attain arhatship; innumerable beings will devote themselves to pratyekabuddhahood; and living beings [numerous] as the sands of the Ganges, devoting themselves to the supreme Way, will attain to the assurance of no [re]birth[7] and reach the [stage] of never falling back [into mortal life]. Then after the parinirvāṇa of the Buddha King of Gods, the Righteous Law will dwell in his world during twenty intermediate kalpas. For his complete body relic, a stupa of the precious seven shall be erected, sixty yojanas in height and forty yojanas in length and width. All the gods and people, with various flowers, sandal powder, incense for burning, perfumed unguents, garments, garlands, banners, flags, jeweled canopies, music, and song, shall respectfully salute and pay homage to the wonderful Stupa of the Precious Seven. Innumerable living beings will attain arhatship; incalculable living creatures will awaken to pratyekabuddhahood; and inconceivable [numbers of] the living will be aroused to Bodhi and reach the [stage] of never falling back [into mortality]."

The Buddha said to the bhikshus: "If there be in a future world any good son or good daughter to hear this Devadatta chapter of the Wonderful Law-Flower Sutra with pure heart and believing reverence, and is free from doubt, such a one shall not fall into the hells or become a hungry spirit or animal, [but shall] be born into the presence of the buddhas of the universe. Wherever he be born he will always hear this sutra; and if he be born amongst men or gods, he will enjoy marvelous delight. As to the Buddha into whose presence [he is born], his birth shall be by emanation from a lotus flower."

Thereupon a bodhisattva-attendant, from a region beneath, of the World-honored One Abundant Treasures, named Wisdom Accumulation, said to the Buddha Abundant Treasures: "Let us return to our own land!" But Sakyamuni Buddha said to Wisdom Accumulation: "Good son! Wait a while! Here is the Bodhisattva Mañjuśrī. [First] meet and discuss with him the Wonderful Law and then return to your own land." Thereupon Mañjuśrī, sitting on a thousand-petal

7. Literally, "the patience of no [re]birth," interpreted as the assurance of no (re)-birth. This is the stage at which a bodhisattva has transcended life and death.

lotus flower as large as a carriage wheel, with the bodhisattvas who accompanied him also sitting on jeweled lotus flowers, unaided sprang up from the great ocean, out of the palace of the Sāgara Dragon [King]. Taking up his place in the sky, he advanced to the Divine Vulture Peak, alighted from his lotus flower, went before the Buddha, and reverently made obeisance at the feet of the two World-honored Ones. When he had expressed his reverence he went over to Wisdom Accumulation, and after they had asked after each other's welfare, they withdrew and sat to one side. The Bodhisattva Wisdom Accumulation asked Mañjuśrī: "Virtuous sir! Since you went to the dragon palace how many beings have you converted?" Mañjuśrī answered: "Their numbers are immeasurable; they cannot be calculated, nor expressed in words, nor fathomed by the mind. Just wait a moment! One must bring the proof." Before he had finished speaking numberless bodhisattvas sitting on jeweled lotus flowers sprang up from the sea, advanced to the Divine Vulture Peak, and took up their place in the sky. All these bodhisattvas had been converted and saved by Mañjuśrī, had become perfect in bodhisattva-deeds, and together discussed and expounded the Six Pāramitās. Those in the sky, who had formerly been śrāvakas, told of [their former] śrāvaka-deeds. [But] now they all maintained the spiritual principle of the Great-vehicle. Then said Mañjuśrī to Wisdom Accumulation: "Such has been the result of my course of instruction in the ocean." Then the Bodhisattva Wisdom Accumulation extolled him thus in verse:

"Most wise, virtuous, brave, and strong one!
Thou hast converted innumerable beings,
As now this great assembly
And I have all seen.
Expounding the principle of Reality
And revealing the One-vehicle Law,
Extensively hast thou led living beings
To attain with speed Bodhi."

Mañjuśrī replied: "That which I in the midst of the ocean always proclaimed was no other than the Wonderful Law-Flower Sutra." Wisdom Accumulation asked Mañjuśrī: "This sutra is very profound and subtle, the pearl of all the sutras, a rare thing in the world. Is there any being who, diligently and zealously practicing this sutra, can attain speedily buddhahood?" Mañjuśrī replied: "There is the daughter of the Dragon King Sāgara, just eight years old, wise and of keen faculties, well acquainted with the karma arising from the roots of action of all creatures, who has obtained dhāraṇī, has been able to receive and keep all the most profound and mystic treasuries revealed by buddhas, and has deeply entered into meditations and penetrated into all laws. In a moment of time,[8] she resolved on Bodhi and attained nonrelapse [into mortality]. She has unembarrassed powers of argument and a compassionate mind for all the living as if they were [her] children; her merits are complete and the thoughts of her mind and explanations of her mouth are both subtle and great. Kind and compassionate, virtuous and modest, gentle and beautiful in her disposition, she has been able to attain Bodhi."

The Bodhisattva Wisdom Accumulation said: "I have seen [how] Sakyamuni Tathāgata, during innumerable kalpas, in doing arduous and painful deeds, accumulating merit, and heaping up virtue, sought the Way of Bodhi ceaselessly and without rest. I have observed that in the three-thousand-great-thousandfold world there is not even [a spot] as small as a mustard seed where he has not laid down his body and life as a bodhisattva for the sake of the living; and only after that did he attain Bodhi. It is incredible that this girl, in but a moment, should become perfectly enlightened."

Before he had ceased talking, the daughter of the dragon king suddenly appeared before [them] and after making reverent obeisance [to the Buddha] withdrew to one side, extolling him in verse:

"Profound of insight into sin and blessedness,
He illuminates the universe;
His spiritual body, ethereal and pure,
Has the thirty-two perfect signs;
With the eighty kinds of excellence
Is his spiritual body adorned:
He to whom gods and men look up,
Dragons and spirits pay reverence,
And all species of living beings

8. *Kshaṇa*, an instantaneous point of time.

Do worship and honor.
That, having heard [the Truth], I attained Bodhi
Only the Buddha may bear witness.
I will reveal the teaching of the Great-vehicle
Which delivers creatures from suffering."

Thereupon Śāriputra said to the daughter of the dragon: "You state that in no length of time you attained the supreme Way. This thing is hard to believe. Wherefore? [Because] the body of a woman is filthy and not a vessel of the Law. How can she attain supreme Bodhi? The Buddha-way is so vast that only after passing through innumerable kalpas, enduring hardship, accumulating good works, and perfectly practicing the Perfections can it be accomplished. Moreover, a woman by her body still has five hindrances: she cannot become first, king of the Brahma-heaven; second, Śakra; third, a Māra-king; fourth, a holy wheel-rolling king; and fifth, a buddha. How then could a woman's body so speedily become a buddha?"

Now, the dragon's daughter possessed a precious pearl worth a three-thousand-great-thousandfold world, which she held up and presented to the Buddha, and which the Buddha immediately accepted. The dragon's daughter then said to the Bodhisattva Wisdom Accumulation and the honored Śāriputra: "I have offered my pearl, and the World-honored One has accepted it—was this action speedy?" They answered: "Most speedy." The daughter said: "By your supernatural powers behold me become a buddha even more rapidly than that!"

At that moment the entire congregation saw the dragon's daughter suddenly transformed into a male, perfect in bodhisattva-deeds, who instantly went to the world Spotless in the southern quarter, where [she] sat on a precious lotus flower, attaining Perfect Enlightenment, with the thirty-two signs and the eighty kinds of excellence, and universally proclaiming the Wonderful Law to all living creatures in the universe.

Then the sahā-world of bodhisattvas, śrāvakas, the eight groups of gods and dragons, and human and nonhuman beings, all from afar beholding the dragon's daughter become a buddha and universally preach the Law to gods, men, [and others] amongst that congregation, all rejoiced greatly and made reverent salutation from afar.

The countless multitude, on hearing [her preach] the Law, were aroused to apprehension and attained never sliding back [into mortality]. The countless multitude also received their prediction of the [perfect] Way. The world Spotless made the sixfold movement. Three thousand living beings in the sahā-world took up their abode in the stage of never returning [to mortality], while three thousand living beings set their minds on Bodhi and obtained their prediction [of attaining it].

The Bodhisattva Wisdom Accumulation and Śāriputra and all the congregation silently believed.

CHAPTER XIII

Exhortation to Hold Firm

AT THAT TIME the Bodhisattva-Mahāsattva Medicine King and the Bodhisattva-Mahāsattva Great Eloquence, with their retinue of twenty thousand bodhisattvas, all in the presence of the Buddha, made this vow, saying: "Be pleased, World-honored One, to be without anxiety! After the extinction of the Buddha we will keep, read, recite, and preach this sutra. In the evil age to come living beings will decrease in good qualities, while they will increase in utter arrogance [and] in covetousness of gain and honors, [and will] develop their evil qualities and be far removed from emancipation. Though it may be difficult to teach and convert them, we, arousing our utmost patience, will read and recite this sutra, keep, preach, and copy it, pay every kind of homage to it, and spare not our body and life."

Thereupon the five hundred arhats in the assembly, whose future

The title of this chapter can also be translated "Exhortation to Firmness." Some copies have only "Firmness." In this chapter two themes are presented: first, the vow of the twenty thousand bodhisattvas to propagate this sutra, according to the Buddha's command; and second, the exhortation to propagate this sutra by which the eighty myriad koṭis of nayutas of bodhisattvas are encouraged.

had been predicted, addressed the Buddha, saying: "World-honored One! We also vow to publish abroad this sutra in other lands." Again the eight thousand arhats, training and trained, whose future had been predicted, rising up from their seats and folding their hands toward the Buddha, made this vow, saying: "World-honored One! We also will publish abroad this sutra in other lands. Wherefore? Because in this sahā-world men abound in wickedness, cherish the utmost arrogance, [and] are of shallow virtue, defiled with hatreds, crooked with suspicions, and insincere in mind."

Then the sister of the Buddha's mother, the Bhikshuṇī Mahāprajāpatī, with six thousand bhikshuṇīs, training and trained, rose up from their seats, with one mind folded their hands, [and] gazed up to the honored face without removing their eyes for a moment. Then the World-honored One addressed the Gautamī:[1] "Why, with sad countenance, do you gaze at the Tathāgata? Are you not thinking to say that I have not mentioned your name and predicted for you Perfect Enlightenment? Gautamī! I have already inclusively announced that [the future of] all śrāvakas is predicted. Now you, who desire to know your future destiny, shall, in the world to come, become a great teacher of the Law in the laws of the sixty-eight thousand koṭis of buddhas,[2] and these six thousand bhikshuṇīs, training and trained, will all become teachers of the Law. Thus you will gradually become perfect in the bodhisattva-way and will become a buddha entitled Loveliness Tathāgata, Worshipful, All Wise, Perfectly Enlightened in Conduct, Well Departed, Understander of the World, Peerless Leader, Controller, Teacher of Gods and Men, Buddha, World-honored One. Gautamī! This Buddha Loveliness and the six thousand bodhisattvas will in turn be predicted to [attain] Perfect Enlightenment."

Thereupon the mother of Rāhula, the Bhikshuṇī Yaśodharā, reflected thus: "The World-honored One in his predictions has left my name alone unmentioned." [Then] the Buddha said to Yaśodharā: "You, in the laws of the hundred thousand myriads of koṭis of buddhas in the world to come, by your doing of bodhisattva-deeds shall become a great teacher of the Law, gradually become perfect in the

1. Gautamī is the general term for women of the Śākya clan, while Gautama is that for men. Here she is styled Gautamī in the sense of "Lady."

2. Literally, this seems to mean: "You shall, in the sixty-eight thousand koṭis of Buddha-laws, be a great Law-teacher."

Buddha-way, and in the domain Good become a buddha entitled The Perfect Myriad-rayed Tathāgata, Worshipful, All Wise, Perfectly Enlightened in Conduct, Well Departed, Understander of the World, Peerless Leader, Controller, Teacher of Gods and Men, Buddha, World-honored One. The lifetime of that buddha will be innumerable asaṃkhyeya kalpas."

Then the Bhikshuṇī Mahāprajāpatī and the Bhikshuṇī Yaśodharā, together with all their retinue, all rejoiced greatly, having obtained [such] unprecedented [felicity], and immediately before the Buddha spoke thus in verse:

"World-honored leader!
Comforter of gods and men!
We, hearing thy prediction,
Have perfect peace in our hearts."

After uttering this verse the bhikshuṇīs spoke to the Buddha, saying: "World-honored One! We also are able to publish abroad this sutra in lands in other regions."

Thereupon the World-honored One looked upon the eighty myriads of koṭis of nayutas of bodhisattva-mahāsattvas. All these bodhisattvas were of [the stage] avaivartika, who rolled the never-retreating Law-wheel and had attained to the dhāraṇīs. Immediately they rose from their seats, went before the Buddha, with one mind folded their hands, and reflected thus: "If the World-honored One commands us to keep and expound this sutra, we will proclaim abroad this Law as the Buddha has taught it." Again they reflected thus: "The Buddha now is silent; we are not commanded; what shall we do?"

Then these bodhisattvas, respectfully obeying the Buddha's will and themselves desiring to fulfill their original vow, before the Buddha raised a lion's roar and uttered a vow, saying: "World-honored One! After the extinction of the Tathāgata we will compass and travel through the worlds in all directions, in order to lead all the living to copy this sutra, receive and keep, read and recite it, expound its meaning, practice it as their law, and rightly keep it in mind, all by the Buddha's might. Be pleased, World-honored One, [though] in another quarter, to behold and guard us from afar!"

Then the bodhisattvas all together unanimously raised their voices, speaking thus in verse:

"Be pleased to be without anxiety!
After the Buddha's extinction,
In the [last] dreadful evil age,
We will proclaim abroad [this sutra].
Though in their ignorance many
Will curse and abuse us
And beat us with swords and staves,
We will endure it all.
Bhikshus in that evil age will be
Heretical, suspicious, warped,
Claiming to have attained when they have not,
And with minds full of arrogance.
Others in the āraṇya
Will wear patched garments[3] in seclusion,
Pretending that they walk the true path
And scorning [other] people;
Greedily attached to gain,
They will preach the Law to laymen
And be revered by the world
As arhats of the six transcendent [powers];
These men, cherishing evil minds,
Ever thinking of earthly things,
Assuming the name of āraṇyas,
Will love to calumniate us,
Saying such things of us as
'All these bhikshus,
From love of gain,
Preach heretical doctrine;
They have themselves composed this sutra
To delude the people of the world;
For the sake of acquiring fame,
They make a specialty of this sutra.'
Always in the assemblies,

3. Monk's garments made of patches.

In order to ruin us,
To kings and ministers,
To Brahmans and citizens,
And to the other groups of bhikshus,
They will slanderously speak evil of us,
Saying: 'These are men of false views,
Who proclaim heretical doctrines.'
But we, from reverence for the Buddha,
Will endure all these evils.
By these contemptuously addressed as
'All you buddhas!'—
Even such scorn and arrogance
We will patiently endure.
In the evil age of the corrupt kalpa,
Abounding in fear and dread,
Devils will take possession of them
To curse, abuse, and insult us.
But we, revering and believing in the Buddha,
Will wear the armor of perseverance;
For the sake of preaching this sutra
We will endure all these hard things.
We will not love body and life,
But only care for the supreme Way.
We will, throughout all ages to come,
Guard what the Buddha bequeaths.
World-honored One! Thou knowest that,
In the corrupt age, vicious bhikshus,
Knowing not the laws so tactfully preached
As opportunity served by the Buddha,
Will abuse and frown upon us;
Repeatedly shall we be driven out,
And exiled afar from the monasteries.
Such evils will be our ills
For remembering the Buddha's command,
But [we] will endure all these things.
Wherever in villages and cities
There be those who seek after the Law,
We will all go there and

Preach the Law bequeathed by the Buddha.
We are the World-honored One's apostles
And, amidst a multitude having nothing to fear,
Will rightly preach the Law.
Be pleased, O Buddha, to abide in peace.
In the presence of the World-honored One
And the buddhas come from all directions,
We thus make our vow,
And the Buddha knows our hearts."

CHAPTER XIV

A Happy Life

AT THAT TIME the Bodhisattva-Mahāsattva Mañjuśrī, the Law-king's son, spoke to the Buddha, saying: "World-honored One! Rare indeed are such bodhisattvas as these! Reverently according with the Buddha, they have made great vows that in the evil age to come they will protect, keep, read, recite, and preach this Law-Flower Sutra. World-honored One! How are these bodhisattva-mahāsattvas to be able to preach this sutra in the evil age to come?"

The Buddha addressed Mañjuśrī: "If any bodhisattva-mahāsattva desires to preach this sutra in the evil age to come, he should be steadfast in the four methods: first, steadfast in the bodhisattva's spheres of action and intimacy, so that he may be able to preach this sutra to living beings. Mañjuśrī! Why is it called a bodhisattva-mahāsattva's sphere of action? If a bodhisattva-mahāsattva abides in a state of patience, is gentle and agreeable, is neither hasty nor overbearing, and his mind [is] imperturbed; if, moreover, he has no laws by which to act,[1] but sees all things in their reality, nor proceeds along the un-

1. Literally, "in regard to laws, he has none by which to act." Here "laws" is interpreted as meaning the extremes of the realistic and nihilistic schools; thus the passage indicates the Middle Path between these two extremes.

divided way[2]—this is termed a bodhisattva-mahāsattva's sphere of action. Why is [the other] termed a bodhisattva-mahāsattva's sphere of intimacy? A bodhisattva-mahāsattva is not intimate with kings, princes, ministers, and rulers; nor intimate with heretics, the brahmacārins, Nirgranthas,[3] and so on; nor with composers of worldly and outside literature or poetry; nor with Lokāyatas[4] and Anti-Lokāyatas;[5] nor does he resort to brutal sports, boxing, and wrestling, nor to the various juggling performances of nartakas[6] and others; nor does he consort with caṇḍālas,[7] keepers of pigs, sheep, fowl, and dogs, hunters, fishermen, and [those engaged in] these evil pursuits; whenever such people as these sometimes come to him, he preaches the Law to them expecting nothing [in return]. Further, he does not consort with bhikshus, bhikshuṇīs, and male and female lay devotees who seek after śrāvakaship, nor does he address them; neither in a room, nor in the place of promenade, nor in the hall does he dwell or stay with them; if at times they come to him he takes the opportunity of preaching the Law expecting nothing [in return].

"Mañjuśrī! Again a bodhisattva-mahāsattva should not preach the Law to women, displaying an appearance capable of arousing passionate thoughts, nor have pleasure in seeing them; if he enters the homes of others, he does not converse with any girl, virgin, widow, and so forth, nor again does he become on friendly terms with any hermaphrodite; he does not enter the homes of others alone; if for some reason he must enter there alone, then with single mind he thinks of the Buddha; if he preaches the Law to women, he does not display his teeth in smiles nor let his breast be seen, nor even for the sake of the Law does he ever become intimate, how much less for other reasons. He takes no pleasure in keeping young pupils, śrāmaṇeras, and children, nor has he pleasure in being with them as teacher; but ever preferring meditation and seclusion, he cultivates and controls his

2. This can also be translated as "does not follow out or investigate [these laws]," but the T'ien-t'ai sect interprets the sentence in the sense of not being bound by the Law of the Middle Path.

3. These are nude ascetics, the Jains.

4. Lokāyatas are heretics who accord with the ways of the world.

5. The opposite of the Lokāyata, being utterly opposed to the world.

6. Dancers, singers, and actors.

7. One who kills; a butcher, fisherman, hunter, and so on; one who belongs to the lowest caste.

mind. Mañjuśrī! This is termed the first [grade or] sphere of intimacy [of a bodhisattva].

"Further, a bodhisattva-mahāsattva contemplates all existences as void—appearances as they really are,[8] neither upside down, nor moving, nor receding, nor turning, just like space, of the nature of nothingness, cut off from the course of all words and expressions, unborn, not coming forth, not arising, nameless, formless, really without existence, unimpeded, infinite, boundless, unrestrained, only existing by causation, and produced through perversion [of thought].

"Therefore I say constantly to delight in the contemplation of things [or laws] such as these is termed a bodhisattva-mahāsattva's second sphere of intimacy."

Thereupon the World-honored One, desiring to proclaim this teaching over again, spoke thus in verse:

"If there be any bodhisattva
Who, in the future evil age,
With fearless mind
Desires to preach this sutra,
He must occupy his [proper] sphere of action
And his [proper] sphere of intimacy,
Constantly avoiding kings
And princes,
Ministers and rulers,
Brutal and dangerous performers,
Caṇḍālas,
Heretics, brahmacārins;
Nor does he consort with
Men of arrogance
Who are fond of studying
The Tripiṭaka of Hinayana,
With commandment-breaking bhikshus,
Arhats [only] in name,
Or with bhikshuṇīs
Fond of jocularity,
Or with female disciples

8. Kern reads; "duly established as they are in reality." Burnouf adds: *"privées de toute essence."* Nanjio and Oka read: "established as they really are."

Who, through sensuousness,
Seek present nirvana.
He consorts with none of them.
But if such people as these,
In goodness of mind,
Come to the bodhisattva
To hear the Buddha-way,
Then the bodhisattva,
With fearless mind,
Cherishing no expectation,[9]
[Should] preach the Law to them.
Widows and virgins
And all sorts of eunuchs
He never approaches
For close friendship;
Nor does he consort with
Butchers and meat mincers,
Hunters and fishermen,
Who slaughter for gain;
Those who vend meat for a living
And procurators,
With such people as these
He should not consort.
With brutal wrestlings,
Amusements and plays,
Whores and so forth
He should have no intimacy whatever.
He should not, alone in a screened-off place,
Preach the Law to a woman;
If he has to preach the Law [to her]
He will avoid jocularity.
[When] he enters a hamlet in quest of food,
Let him take along [another] bhikshu;
If there be no [other] bhikshu,
Let him with single mind think of the Buddha.
These then are what are called

9. Not looking for reward.

The spheres of action and of intimacy.
Maintaining these two spheres,
He can teach with peace and joy.
And again [if] he does not observe
Laws, higher, middle, or lower,
Active or passive,
Laws real or unreal;
Also [if] he does not discriminate,
'This is a man' or 'This a woman';
[If] he discovers no laws
Nor recognizes nor sees them;
This then is called
A bodhisattva's sphere of action.
All laws [or things] are
Void and nonexistent,
Without permanence,
Neither beginning nor ending;
This is named the sphere
To which wise men resort.
The perverse discriminate
All laws as either existing or nonexisting,
Real or unreal,
Produced or unproduced.
Let [the bodhisattva] abide in seclusion,
Cultivate and control his mind,
And be firmly fixed and immovable
As Mount Sumeru;
Contemplating all laws
As though they were not,
As if they were space,
Without solidity,
Neither produced nor coming forth,
Motionless and unreceding,
Ever remaining a unity.
This is named the [proper] sphere of intimacy.
If any bhikshu,
After my extinction,
Enters this sphere of action

And sphere of intimacy,
When he preaches this sutra
He will have no timidity or weakness.
When the bodhisattva at times
Enters a quiet room
And in perfect meditation
Contemplates things in their true meaning,
And, rising up from his meditation,
To kings of nations,
Princes, ministers and people,
Brahmans and others
Reveals, expounds,
And preaches this sutra,
His mind shall be at ease
And free from timidity and weakness.
Mañjuśrī!
This is called a bodhisattva's
Steadfastness in the first method.[10]
He is [then] able, in future generations,
To preach the Law-Flower Sutra.

"Again, Mañjuśrī! After the extinction of the Tathāgata, in [the period of] the Decline of the Law, he who desires to preach this sutra should abide in the pleasant ministry [of speech].[11] Wherever he orally proclaims or reads the sutra, he takes no pleasure in telling of the errors of others of the sutras; neither does he despise other preachers; nor speaks of the good and evil, the merits and demerits of other people; nor singles out śrāvakas by name and publishes their errors and sins, nor by name praises their excellences; nor does he beget an invidious mind. By keeping well such a cheerful heart as this, those who hear will offer no opposition to him. To those who ask difficult questions, he does not answer with the law of the small vehicle [but] only with the Great-vehicle, and explains it to them that they may obtain perfect knowledge."

10. The first of the four methods, that is, of deed, word, thought, and vow. It is termed the pleasant practice or ministry of body or of deeds.

11. The second of the four methods, that is, the pleasant practice or ministry of the mouth, lips, or speech.

Thereupon the World-honored One, desiring to proclaim this teaching over again, spoke thus in verse:

"The bodhisattva ever delights
And is at ease in preaching the Law;
In a clean and pure spot,
Setting up [his] pulpit,
He anoints himself with oil,
Having bathed away uncleanliness,
Puts on a new, clean robe,
All clean within and without;
Calmly seated on the Law throne,
He teaches as he is questioned.
If there be any bhikshus
And bhikshuṇīs,
Male lay disciples
And female lay disciples,
Kings and princes,
Their retainers and people,
He preaches the mystic principle to them
With a gentle countenance.
If there be any difficult question,
He answers according to its meaning.
By reasonings and parables
He expounds and discriminates it.
By this tactful method,
He stirs them all to earnestness,
To steady advance
And entry on the Buddha-way.
He rids [himself] of a lazy mind
And slackness of thought;
He is free from all worries
And with kindly heart proclaims;
Day and night he ever propounds
The teaching of the supreme Way,
By various reasonings
And innumerable parables,
Revealing it to the living,

And causing them all to rejoice.
Garments and provision for sleep,
Drink, food, and medicines—
For all these things
He has no anticipation.
Only with single mind he thinks of
The cause of [his] preaching the Law,
Resolved on accomplishing the Buddha-way
And causing all others likewise so to do;
This then is [his] great profit
And joy and service.
After my extinction,
If there be any bhikshu
Who is able to proclaim
This Wonderful Law-Flower Sutra,
His mind will be free from envy,
From distresses and obstacles,
And from grief and sorrow,
As well as from the abuse of men.
Further, he will be free from fear,
From laying on of swords and staves;
Nor will he be driven away,
Because he is steadfast in forbearance.
The wise man, in such ways as these,
Rightly cultivates his mind,
Being able to dwell at ease,
As I have said above.
The merit of that man,
Though thousands of myriads of koṭis of kalpas
Were reckoned in illustration,
Is incapable of full expression.

"Again, Mañjuśrī! The bodhisattva-mahāsattva who, in the corrupt ages to come, when the Law is about to perish, receives and keeps, reads and recites this sutra, does not cherish an envious and deceitful mind; nor does he slight and abuse [other] learners of the Buddha-way and seek out their excesses and shortcomings. If there be bhikshus, bhikshuṇīs, male and female lay disciples who seek after śrāvakaship, or seek after pratyekabuddhahood, or seek after the bodhisattva-way, he does not distress them, causing them doubts and regrets, saying to them: 'You are far removed from the Way and will never be able to attain to perfect knowledge. Wherefore? Because you are unstable people and remiss in the Way.' Moreover, he should not indulge in discussions about the laws or engage in disputations; but in regard to all the living he should think of them with great compassion; in regard to the tathāgatas he should think of them as benevolent fathers; in regard to the bodhisattvas he should think of them as his great teachers; in regard to the universal great bodhisattvas he should ever from his deepest heart revere and worship them. In regard to all living beings, he should preach the Law equally, so as to accord with the Law, neither more nor less; even for those who deeply love the Law, he will not preach more [than it].

"Mañjuśrī! When this bodhisattva-mahāsattva, in the last age when the Law is about to perish, has accomplished this third pleasant ministry [of thought],[12] and preaches this sutra, nothing will be able to disturb him. He will find good fellow students who will read and recite this sutra with him. He will also find a great multitude come and hear him, who after hearing are able to observe it, after observing are able to recite it, after reciting are able to preach it, after preaching are able to copy or cause others to copy it, and who will pay homage to the sutra, revering, honoring, and extolling it."

Then the World-honored One, desiring to proclaim this teaching over again, spoke thus in verse:

"If one would preach this sutra,
Let him renounce an envious, angry, proud,
Deceitful, or false mind,
And ever do upright deeds;
He should disparage none,
And never for diversion discuss the laws,
Nor cause others doubt or regret,
Saying: 'You will never become buddhas.'
This Buddha-son in preaching the Law
Will ever be gentle, patient,

12. The third pleasant practice or ministry is of the mind or thought.

And compassionate to all,
With never a thought of slackness.
To the great bodhisattvas everywhere,
Who walk the Way in pity for all,
He should beget a reverent mind,
[Thinking]: 'These are my great teachers.'
To all world-honored buddhas
He should feel as to peerless fathers,
And suppressing his haughty spirit,
Should preach the Law without hindrance.
Such is the third method.
Let the wise man guard it.
Such a single-hearted pleasant ministry
Will be revered by countless hosts.

"Again, Mañjuśrī! The bodhisattva-mahāsattva, in the last ages to come when the Law is about to perish, who keeps this Law-Flower Sutra should beget a spirit of great charity to laymen and monks, and beget a spirit of great compassion for those not [yet] bodhisattvas. And he should reflect thus: 'Such people as these have suffered great loss; the Law preached, as opportunity served, by the tactful method of the Tathāgata they have neither heard nor known nor apprehended nor inquired for nor believed in nor understood. Though those people have not inquired for, nor believed in, nor understood this sutra, when I have attained Perfect Enlightenment, wherever I am, by my transcendental powers and powers of wisdom, I will lead them to abide in this Law.'

"Mañjuśrī! This bodhisattva-mahāsattva who, after the extinction of the Tathāgata, has accomplished this fourth method,[13] when he preaches this Law will be free from errors. He will ever be worshiped, revered, honored, and extolled by bhikshus, bhikshuṇīs, male and female lay devotees, by kings and princes, by their ministers and people, by Brahmans and citizens, and by others; all the gods in the sky also, in order to hear the Law, will always follow and attend on him; if he be in a village or city or secluded forest and someone comes desiring to put difficult questions to him, the gods day and night, for the sake of the Law, will constantly guard and protect him, so that he

13. The fourth method is termed the pleasant practice or ministry of the vow.

shall be able to cause all his hearers to rejoice. Wherefore? Because this sutra is that which all past, future, and present buddhas watch over by their divine powers.

"Mañjuśrī! In countless countries even the name of this Law-Flower Sutra cannot be heard; how much less can it be seen, received, and kept, read and recited.

"Mañjuśrī! It is like a powerful holy wheel-rolling king who desires by force to conquer other domains. When minor kings do not obey his command, the wheel-rolling king calls up his various armies and goes to punish them. The king, seeing his soldiers who distinguish themselves in the war, is greatly pleased and, according to their merit, bestows rewards, either giving fields, houses, villages, or cities, or giving garments or personal ornaments, or giving all kinds of treasures, gold, silver, lapis lazuli, moonstones, agates, coral, amber, elephants, horses, carriages, litters, male and female slaves, and people; only the [crown] jewel on his head he gives to none. Wherefore? Because only on the head of a king may this sole jewel [be worn], and if he gave it, all the king's retinue would be astounded. Mañjuśrī! The Tathāgata is also like this. By his powers of meditation and wisdom he has taken possession of the domain of the Law and rules as king over the triple world. But the Māra kings are unwilling to submit. The Tathāgata's wise and holy generals fight with them. With those who distinguish themselves he, too, is pleased, and in the midst of his four hosts preaches the sutras to them, causing them to rejoice, and bestows on them the meditations, the emancipations, the faultless roots and powers, and all the wealth of the Law. In addition, he gives them the city of nirvana, saying that they have attained extinction, and attracts their minds so that they all rejoice; yet he does not preach to them this Law-Flower Sutra. Mañjuśrī! Just as the wheel-rolling king, seeing his soldiers who distinguish themselves, is so extremely pleased that now at last he gives them the incredible jewel so long worn on his head, which may not wantonly be given to anyone, so also is it with the Tathāgata. As the great Law-king of the triple world, teaching and converting all the living by the Law, when he sees his wise and holy army fighting with the Māra of the five mental processes, the Māra of earthly cares, and the Māra of death,[14] and

14. These three—the five aggregates, cares, and death—and the fourth Māra, who dwells in the highest heaven of the Realm of Desire, are called the four Māras.

[doing so] with great exploits and merits, exterminating the three poisons, escaping from the triple world, and breaking [through] the nets of the Māras, then the Tathāgata also is greatly pleased, and now [at last] preaches this Law-Flower Sutra which has never before been preached, and which is able to cause all the living to reach perfect knowledge, though all the world greatly resents and has difficulty in believing it. Mañjuśrī! This Law-Flower Sutra is the foremost teaching of the tathāgatas and the most profound of all discourses. I give it to you last of all, just as that powerful king at last gives the brilliant jewel he has guarded for long. Mañjuśrī! This Law-Flower Sutra is the mysterious treasury of the buddha-tathāgatas, which is supreme above all sutras. For long has it been guarded and not prematurely declared; today for the first time I proclaim it to you all."

At that time the World-honored One, desiring to proclaim this teaching over again, spoke thus in verse:

"Ever acting patiently,
Pitying all beings,
Such a one can proclaim
The sutra the Buddha extols.
In the last ages to come,
They who keep this sutra,
Whether laymen or monks
Or not [yet] bodhisattvas,
Must have [hearts of] compassion;
[For] those who do not hear
Nor believe this sutra
Suffer great loss.
I, attaining the Buddha-way,
By tactful methods
Preach this sutra to them
That they may abide in it.
It is like a powerful
Wheel-rolling king
Who to his war-distinguished soldiers
Presents many rewards,
Elephants, horses, carriages, litters,
Personal ornaments,

As well as fields and houses,
Villages and cities;
Or bestows garments,
Various kinds of jewels,
Slaves and wealth,
Bestowing all with joy.
[But] only for one heroic
And of rare exploits
Does the king take from his head
The [crown] jewel to give him.
Thus is it also with the Tathāgata;
He is the king of the Law,
[Possessed of] great powers of patience
And the treasury of wisdom;
He, with great benevolence,
Transforms the world with his Law.
Seeing all human beings
Suffering from pains and distresses,
Seeking for deliverance,
Fighting against the Māras,
He to all these living beings
Has preached various laws,
And in great tactfulness
Has preached these [numerous] sutras;
Finally knowing the creatures
Have attained their [developed] powers,
At last he to them
Preaches this Law-Flower,
As the king took from his head
The jewel and gave it.
This sutra is preeminent
Among all the sutras.
I have always guarded
And not prematurely revealed it.
Now indeed is the time
To preach it to you all.
After my extinction,
Whoever seeks the Buddha-way

And desires imperturbedly
To proclaim this sutra
Should relate himself to
The four rules[15] such as these.
He who reads this sutra
Will be ever free from worry
And free from pain and disease;
His countenance will be fresh and white;
He will not be born poor,
Humble, or ugly.
All creatures will delight to see him
As a longed-for saint;
Heavenly cherubim
Will be his servants.
Swords and staves will not be laid on him;
Poison cannot harm him.
If anyone curses him,
[That man's] mouth will be closed.
Fearlessly he will roam
Like a lion king.
The radiance of his wisdom
Will shine like the sun.
If he should dream,
He will see only the wonderful,
Seeing the tathāgatas
Seated on lion thrones,
Preaching the Law to hosts
Of surrounding bhikshus;
Seeing also dragon spirits,
Asuras, and others,
In number as the sands of the Ganges,
Who worship him with folded hands;
And he sees himself
Preaching the Law to them.

15. Kern has "four qualities. . . . The qualities are such as follows." In Chinese the four rules are generally interpreted as the aforementioned four methods relating to deed, word, thought, and vow. Nanjio's and Oka's translations agree with the Chinese interpretation.

He will also see the buddhas,
With the sign of the golden body,
Emitting boundless light,
Illuminating all beings,
And with Brahma-voice
Expounding the laws.
[While] the Buddha to the four groups
Is preaching the supreme Law,
He will find himself in the midst,
Extolling the Buddha with folded hands;
He will hear the Law with joy,
Pay homage to him,
Attain the dhāraṇīs,
And prove the truth of never retreating.[16]
The Buddha, knowing his mind
Has entered deep into the Buddha-way,
Will then predict that he will accomplish
Supreme, Perfect Enlightenment,
[Saying]: 'You, my good son,
Shall in the age to come
Obtain infinite wisdom,
The Great Way of the Buddha:
A domain splendidly pure,
Of extent incomparable,
And with [its] four hosts
With folded hands hearing the Law.'
He will also find himself
In mountain groves,
Exercising himself in the good Law,
Proving reality,
And deep in meditation
Seeing the universal buddhas.
Golden colored are those buddhas,
Adorned with a hundred blessed signs;
[He who] hears and preaches to others

16. Literally, "the wisdom of not retreating," or not withdrawing, or non-apostasy. "Not retreating" is interpreted as the three kinds of not retreating, that is, in stage, practice, and memory.

Ever has good dreams like these.
Again he will dream he is a king
Who forsakes his palace and kinsfolk
And exquisite pleasures of the senses
To go to the wisdom throne;
At the foot of a Bodhi tree,
He sits on the lion throne;
After seeking the Way for seven days,
He attains the wisdom of buddhas;
Having attained the supreme Way,
He arises and, rolling the Law-wheel,
To the four hosts preaches the Law
For thousands of myriads of koṭis of kalpas.
After preaching the faultless Wonderful Law
And saving innumerable creatures,
He shall then enter nirvana,
As a lamp is extinct when its smoke ends.
If anyone in the evil ages to come
Preaches this preeminent Law,
He will obtain the great blessing
Of such rewards as the above."

CHAPTER XV

Springing Up out of the Earth

AT THAT TIME the bodhisattva-mahāsattvas who had come from other lands, numerous as the sands of eight Ganges, arose in the great assembly, and with folded hands saluted and spoke to the Buddha, saying: "World-honored One! If the Buddha will allow us, after his extinction, diligently and zealously to protect and keep, read and recite, copy and worship this sutra in this sahā-world, we would preach it abroad in this land." Thereupon the Buddha addressed all the host of those bodhisattva-mahāsattvas: "Enough! My good sons! There is no need for you to protect and keep this sutra. Wherefore? Because in my sahā-world there are in fact bodhisattva-mahāsattvas [numerous] as the sands of sixty thousand Ganges; each one of these bodhisattvas has a retinue [numerous] as the sands of sixty

According to Chih-i, the first fourteen chapters of the sutra comprise the "subordinate or temporary doctrine" because the Primal or Eternal Buddha is not yet revealed. The following fourteen chapters, from chapter 15 to the end, are called the "fundamental doctrine" because the Eternal Buddha is revealed in chapter 16, "Revelation of the [Eternal] Life of the Tathāgata," the essential and central teaching of this sutra. In the present chapter, which is the introduction to the fundamental doctrine, the so-called originally converted bodhisattvas appear as the chosen messengers who alone are able to preach this sutra in the latter days to come.

thousand Ganges; these persons are able, after my extinction, to protect and keep, read and recite, and preach abroad this sutra."

When the Buddha had thus spoken, all the earth of the three-thousand-great-thousandfold land of the sahā-world trembled and quaked, and from its midst there issued together innumerable thousand myriad koṭis of bodhisattva-mahāsattvas. All these bodhisattvas with their golden-hued bodies, thirty-two signs, and boundless radiance had all before been dwelling in [infinite] space[1] below this sahā-world. All these bodhisattvas, hearing the voice of Sakyamuni Buddha preaching, sprang forth from below. Each one of these bodhisattvas was the commander of a great host, leading a retinue as the sands of sixty thousand Ganges; moreover, others led retinues [numerous] as the sands of fifty thousand, forty thousand, thirty thousand, twenty thousand, ten thousand Ganges; moreover, down to the sands of one Ganges, the sands of half a Ganges, a quarter of it, down to a fraction of a thousand myriad koṭis of nayutas; moreover, a thousand myriad koṭis of nayutas of followers; moreover, myriads of koṭis of followers; moreover, a thousand myriad, a hundred myriad, or even a myriad; moreover, a thousand, a hundred, or even ten; moreover, those who lead five, four, three, two, or one disciples; moreover, one who is alone, happy in the practice of isolation. Such [bodhisattvas] as these are immeasurable, illimitable, beyond the powers of comprehension by calculation or comparison.

When these bodhisattvas had emerged from the earth, each went up to the wonderful Stupa of the Precious Seven in the sky, where were the Tathāgata Abundant Treasures and Sakyamuni Buddha. On their arrival they made obeisance, with faces to the ground, to both the World-honored Ones, and going to the buddhas seated on the lion thrones under the jewel trees, they also saluted them, three times making procession round them on their right, with folded hands revering them, and extolling them with all kinds of bodhisattva hymns. Then they stood to one side, with delight gazing upon both the World-honored Ones.

From the time that these bodhisattva-mahāsattvas first issued from the earth and extolled the buddhas with all kinds of bodhisattva

1. Sanskrit *ākāśa* (space, ether) is often used as a synonym for *śūnyatā* (void).

hymns, in the interval there had passed fifty minor kalpas. During all this time Sakyamuni Buddha sat in silence, and silent also were the four groups; [but] the fifty kalpas, through the divine power of the Buddha, seemed to the great multitude as half a day. At that time the four groups, also by the divine power of the Buddha, saw the bodhisattvas who everywhere fill the space of innumerable hundred thousand myriad koṭis of domains. Among the host of those bodhisattvas there were the four leading teachers: the first was named Eminent Conduct, the second named Boundless Conduct, the third named Pure Conduct, and the fourth named Steadfast Conduct.[2] These four bodhisattvas are of their hosts the chief heads and leaders. In front of [their] great hosts, each of them with folded hands looked toward Sakyamuni Buddha and inquired of him, saying: "World-honored One! Hast thou few ailments and few troubles, and art thou at ease? Are those whom thou must save readily receiving thy teaching? Do they cause the World-honored One not to become weary?"

Thereupon the four great bodhisattvas spoke thus in verse:

"Is the World-honored One at ease,
With few ailments and few troubles?
In instructing all the living beings,
Is he free from weariness?
And are all the living
Readily accepting his teaching?
Do they cause the World-honored One
Not to get tired?"

Then the World-honored One, in the great assembly of the bodhisattvas, spoke thus: "So it is, so it is, my good sons! The Tathāgata is at ease, with few ailments and few troubles. These beings are easy to transform and I am free from weariness. Wherefore? Because all these beings for generations have constantly received my instruction and worshiped and honored the former buddhas, cultivating roots of goodness. All these beings, from first seeing me and hearing my preaching, received it in faith and entered the Tathāgata wisdom, ex-

2. These four bodhisattvas are called the four great primarily or eternally evolved bodhisattvas.

cept those who had previously practiced and learned the small vehicle; [but] even such people as these I have now caused to hear this sutra and enter the Buddha-wisdom."

Thereupon these great bodhisattvas spoke thus in verse:

"Good, good!
Great Hero, World-honored One!
All these living creatures
Are easily transformed [by thee],
Are able to inquire into
The profound wisdom of buddhas,
And, hearing, to believe and discern.
We congratulate thee."

Then the World-honored One extolled these supreme chiefs, the great bodhisattvas, [saying]: "Good, good! My good sons! You may [rightly] be minded to congratulate the Tathāgata."

Then Maitreya Bodhisattva and the host of [other] bodhisattvas, numerous as the sands of eight thousand Ganges, all reflected thus: "From of old we have never seen nor heard of such a host of great bodhisattva-mahāsattvas issuing from the earth, standing in the presence of the World-honored Ones, with folded hands worshiping and inquiring of the Tathāgata."

Then Maitreya Bodhisattva-Mahāsattva, being aware of the thoughts in the minds of all the bodhisattvas, numerous as the sands of eight thousand Ganges, and desiring also to resolve his own doubt, folded his hands toward the Buddha and asked him thus in verse:

"[These] innumerable thousand myriad koṭis,
[This] great host of bodhisattvas,
Are such as we have never seen before.
Be pleased to explain, Honored of Men,
From what places they have come,
For what reason they have assembled.
Huge of body, of transcendent [power],
Of wisdom inconceivable,
Firm of will and memory,

With great powers of long-suffering,
Whom all the living rejoice to see:
Whence have they come?
Each of these bodhisattvas
Leads on a retinue
Whose numbers are beyond compute,
Like the sands of the Ganges.
There are also the great bodhisattvas
Leading [followers numerous] as sixty thousand Ganges-sands.
Such mighty hosts
With one mind seek the Buddha-way.
These great leaders [in number]
As sixty thousand Ganges-sands
All come and worship the Buddha
And guard and keep this sutra.
Some, still more numerous,
Lead [followers numerous] as fifty thousand Ganges-sands,
As forty thousand, or thirty thousand,
As twenty thousand, down to ten thousand,
As a thousand or a hundred and so forth,
Down to the sands of one Ganges,
As half, one-third, one-fourth,
As one part of the myriad koṭis [of a Ganges' sands]:
Those who lead a thousand myriad nayutas,
Or a myriad koṭis of disciples,
Or even half a koṭi [of disciples];
These [leaders] are still more numerous than the above,
[The leaders of] a million or ten thousand,
A thousand or a hundred,
Or fifty or ten,
Or three, two, or one;
Single ones with no following,
Who enjoy solitariness,
Have all come together to the Buddha,
In numbers even greater than [the leaders] above.
Such are these great hosts that
If a man kept tally

Through kalpas numerous as Ganges-sands,
He still could not fully know them,
These great, majestic,
And zealous bodhisattva hosts.
Who has preached the Law to them,
Instructed and perfected them?
From whom did they get their start?
What Buddha-law have they extolled?
Whose sutra received, kept, and practiced?
What Buddha-way have they followed?
Such bodhisattvas as these,
With transcendent powers and great wisdom,
In all quarters of the riven earth,
All spring forth from its midst.
World-honored One! From of yore
We have never seen such things;
Be pleased to tell us the name
Of the domain from which they come.
Roaming constantly in many domains,
I have never seen such a host,
And amid all this host
I know not a single one
[Who] suddenly springs from the earth.
Be pleased to tell us its cause.
This great congregation now present,
Innumerable hundred thousand koṭis
Of these bodhisattvas and others,
All desire to know this matter.
Of all these bodhisattva hosts,
What is the course of their history?
World-honored One of measureless virtue!
Be pleased to resolve our doubts!"

Meanwhile, the buddhas who had emanated from Sakyamuni Buddha and had come from innumerable thousand myriad koṭis of domains in other quarters sat cross-legged on the lion thrones under the jewel trees in every direction. The attendants of these buddhas each beheld the great host of bodhisattvas who, in every direction of the three-thousand-great-thousandfold world, issued from the earth and dwelt in space. And each spoke to his own buddha, saying: "World-honored One! This great, countless, illimitable asaṃkhyeya host of bodhisattvas—whence have they come?"

Thereupon each of those buddhas told his own attendants: "Good sons! Wait a while! There is a bodhisattva-mahāsattva whose name is Maitreya, and who has been predestined by Sakyamuni Buddha as the next buddha; he has already asked about this matter. The Buddha is now going to reply to him, and from his reply you will hear for yourselves."

Thereupon Sakyamuni Buddha addressed Maitreya Bodhisattva: "Good, good! Ajita![3] You have well asked the Buddha concerning so great a matter. Do you all, with one mind, don the armor of zeal and exhibit a firm will, [for] the Tathāgata now intends to reveal and proclaim the wisdom of buddhas, the sovereign and supernatural power of buddhas, the lion-eagerness of buddhas, and the awe-inspiring forceful power of buddhas."

Then the World-honored One, desiring to proclaim this teaching over again, spoke thus in verse:

"Be zealous and of one mind.
I am about to expound this matter.
Have no doubts or disquietude.
Inconceivable is the Buddha-wisdom.
Do you now exert your faith;
Be steadfast in the virtue of endurance;
[For] the Law never heard before,
Now you all are about to hear.
I now [first] put your minds at ease;
Cherish neither doubt nor fear.
The Buddha has no words but the true;
His wisdom is beyond measure.
The supreme Law attained by him

3. Ajita, "unconquered," is a title of Maitreya. Maitreya, "The Kindly One," is a principal, though not historical, figure in the retinue of Sakyamuni Buddha. He is now in the Tushita heaven, awaiting his incarnation as the next buddha.

Is profound and beyond discrimination.
Such [Law] let me now expound,
And do you all, with one mind, listen."

Then the World-honored One, having spoken these verses, addressed Maitreya Bodhisattva: "Now I, in this great assembly, declare to you all. Ajita! All these great bodhisattva-mahāsattvas, in innumerable and numberless asaṃkhyeyas, who have issued from the earth and whom you have never seen before, I in this sahā-world, after attaining Perfect Enlightenment, instructed and led them, all these bodhisattvas, controlled their minds, and caused them to set their thoughts on the Way. All these bodhisattvas dwell in the space beneath this sahā-world, [where] they read, recite, penetrate, ponder, and discriminate the sutras, and correctly keep them in memory. Ajita! These good sons have not found pleasure in talking among the crowd [but] have found their pleasure in quiet places, in diligence and zeal; they have not relaxed, nor clung to abodes among men and gods, but have ever taken their pleasure in profound wisdom, without let or hindrance, have ever rejoiced in the law of buddhas, and with one mind have zealously sought supreme wisdom."

Then the World-honored One, desiring to proclaim this teaching over again, spoke thus in verse:

"Ajita! Know thou!
All these great bodhisattvas,
From numberless kalpas,
Have studied the Buddha-wisdom.
All of them are my converts,
Whom I have caused to desire the Great Way.
These are my sons
Who dwell in this [Buddha-]world,
Ever practicing the dhūta deeds,
Joyfully devoted to quiet places,
Shunning the clamor of the crowds,
With no pleasure in much talk.
Such sons as these
Are learning the Law of my Way,
Always zealous day and night

For the sake of seeking the Buddha-way;
They dwell in space
Beneath the sahā-world.
Firm in their power of will and memory,
Ever diligently seeking after wisdom,
They preach all kinds of wonderful laws,
Having no fear in their minds.
I, [near] the city of Gayā,
Sitting beneath the Bodhi tree,
Accomplished Perfect Enlightenment;
And rolling the supreme Law-wheel,
I have then taught and converted them
And caused them first to aspire to the Way.
Now all abide in the never-relapsing [state]
And all will become buddhas.
What I now speak is the truth;
Believe me with single minds!
I from a long distant past
Have instructed all this host."

Then the Bodhisattva-Mahāsattva Maitreya and the numberless bodhisattvas and others were seized with doubt and perplexity, wondering at this rare [thing], and reflected thus: "How has the World-honored One, in so short a time, instructed such innumerable, countless asaṃkhyeyas of great bodhisattvas and caused them to abide in Perfect Enlightenment?" Then, addressing the Buddha, they said: "World-honored One! The Tathāgata, when he was a prince, left the Śākya palace and not far from the city of Gayā took his seat on the wisdom terrace, and attained to Perfect Enlightenment. From that time but forty years have passed. World-honored One! In so short a time how hast thou done such great Buddha-deeds, and by Buddha-power and Buddha-merit taught such an innumerable host of great bodhisattvas to attain Perfect Enlightenment? World-honored One! This host of great bodhisattvas, even if a man counted them through thousands of myriad koṭis of kalpas, he could not come to an end or reach their limit. All these from the far past under innumerable and countless buddhas have planted their roots of goodness and accomplished the bodhisattva-way, constantly living the noble life. World-honored One! Such a matter as this the world will find it hard to believe.

"It is just as if there were a man of fine complexion and black hair, twenty-five years old, who pointed to centenarians and said: 'These are my sons,' and as if those centenarians also pointed to the youth and said: 'This is our father who begot and reared us.' This matter is hard of belief. So also is it with the Buddha, whose attainment of the Way is really not long since. Yet this great host of bodhisattvas, for numberless thousands of myriads of koṭis of kalpas, for the sake of the Buddha-way have devoted themselves with zeal; they have entered deep into, come out of, and dwelt in infinite hundred thousand myriad koṭis of contemplations, have attained the great transcendent [faculties], and for long have practiced brahma-conduct; have been well able, step by step, to learn all kinds of good laws; they are skillful in question and answer, are treasures amongst men and of extreme rareness in all worlds. Today the World-honored One has just said that when he attained the Buddha-way he from the beginning caused them to aspire [to enlightenment], instructed and led, and caused them to proceed toward Perfect Enlightenment. It is not long since the World-honored One became a buddha, yet he has been able to do this great, meritorious deed. Though we still believe that what the Buddha opportunely preached and the words the Buddha uttered have never been false, and also the Buddha's knowledge is all perceived by us, yet if newly converted bodhisattvas hear this statement after the Buddha's extinction, they may not receive it in faith and this will give rise to causes of wrong action to the destruction of the Law. So, World-honored One, be pleased to explain it, removing our doubts, and so that all [thy] good sons in future generations, on hearing this matter, shall also not beget doubt."

Thereupon Maitreya Bodhisattva, desiring to announce this meaning over again, spoke thus in verse:

"The Buddha of old from the Śākya race
Left his home and near Gayā
Took his seat under the Bodhi tree;
From then it has not been long.
These sons of the Buddha,
Immeasurable in their number,

Have long pursued the Buddha-way,
And are firm in transcendent wisdom power;
They have ably learned the bodhisattva way,
And are as untainted with worldly things
As the lotus flower in the water;
Issuing from the earth,
All have a reverent mind
As they stand before the World-honored One.
This matter is hard to conceive;
How can it be believed?
It is but recently the Buddha has attained the Way,
And the things he has accomplished abound.
Be pleased to remove all doubts;
Explain and tell us the real [meaning]!
It is as if a young, strong man,
Just twenty-five years old,
Indicated centenarian sons
With white hair and wrinkled faces,
[Saying], 'These are begotten by me,'
The sons also saying, 'This is our father.'
The father young and the sons old—
The whole world will not believe it.
So is it with the World-honored One;
Very recently he has attained the Way.
[Yet] all these bodhisattvas are
Firm in will, dauntless, and strong,
And from innumerable kalpas
Have followed the bodhisattva-way;
Skilled in answering hard questions,
Their minds are free from fear;
Decided in their patient mind,
Dignified and majestic,
They are extolled by universal buddhas;
Well able to reason and preach,
They rejoice not in the crowd,
But ever love to dwell in meditation;
For the sake of seeking the Buddha-way,
They dwell in the space [region] below.

We, hearing it from the Buddha,
Have no doubts on this matter;
[But] we beg that the Buddha, for future [hearers],
Will explain that they may understand.
If any should doubt
And disbelieve this sutra,
He would fall into the evil path.
Be pleased to expound for them now
How these innumerable bodhisattvas
In so short a time
Have been instructed and converted
And abide in the never-retreating stage."

HERE ENDS
THE FIFTH FASCICLE

CHAPTER XVI

Revelation of the [Eternal] Life of the Tathagata

AT THAT TIME the Buddha said to the bodhisattvas and all the great assembly: "Believe and discern, all you good sons, the veracious word of the Tathāgata." Again he said to the great assembly: "Believe and discern the veracious word of the Tathāgata." And again he said to all the great assembly: "Believe and discern the veracious word of the Tathāgata." Then the great host of bodhisattvas, Maitreya at their head, folded their hands and said to the Buddha: "World-honored One! Be pleased to expound the matter, and we will believingly receive the Buddha's words." Thus they spoke three times, repeating the words: "Be pleased to expound the matter, and we will believingly receive the Buddha's words."

Then the World-honored One, perceiving that the bodhisattvas thrice without ceasing repeated their request, addressed them, saying: "Listen then all of you attentively to the secret, mysterious, and supernaturally pervading power[1] of the Tathāgata. All the worlds of gods,

The revelation of the eternal life of the Buddha in this chapter is among the most essential of the Buddha's teachings.

1. According to Chih-i, by "secret" is meant that the one body of the Buddha is three bodies, and by "mysterious" that the three bodies are in the one. Spiritually or

men, and asuras consider: 'Now has Sakyamuni Buddha come forth from the palace of the Śākya clan, and seated at the training place of enlightenment, not far from the city of Gayā, has attained Perfect Enlightenment.' But, my good sons, since I veritably became Buddha [there have passed] infinite, boundless hundreds of thousands of myriads of koṭis of nayutas of kalpas. For instance, suppose there were five hundred thousand myriad koṭis of nayutas of asaṃkhyeya three-thousand-great-thousandfold worlds; let someone grind them to atoms, pass eastward through five hundred thousand myriad koṭis of nayutas of asaṃkhyeya countries, and then drop one of those atoms; suppose he thus proceeded eastward till he had finished those atoms—what do you think, my good sons, is it possible to imagine and calculate all those worlds so as to know their number?" Maitreya Bodhisattva and the others all said to the Buddha: "World-honored One! Those worlds are infinite, boundless, beyond the knowledge of reckoning and beyond the reach of thought. Not all the śrāvakas and pratyekabuddhas, with their faultless wisdom, would be able to imagine and know the bounds of those numbers. And to us also, who are dwelling in the stage of avaivartika, these matters are beyond apprehension. World-honored One! All such worlds as these are measureless and boundless."

Thereupon the Buddha addressed all those bodhisattva-mahāsattvas: "Good sons! Now I must clearly announce and declare to you. Suppose you take as atomized all those worlds where an atom has been deposited or where it has not been deposited, and [count] an atom as a kalpa, [the time] since I became Buddha still surpasses these by hundreds of thousands of myriads of koṭis of nayutas of asaṃkhyeya kalpas. From that time forward I have constantly been preaching and teaching in this sahā-world, and also leading and benefiting all living beings in other places in hundreds of thousands of myriads of koṭis of nayutas of asaṃkhyeya domains. Good sons! During this time

---

supernaturally pervading power, or power of spiritual or supernatural pervasion, or ubiquity, is the function of the three bodies, or *trikāya:* the *dharmakāya* (truth-body or Law-body), the *saṃbhogakāya* (reward-body or bliss-body), and the *nirmāṇakāya* (mutation-body or response-body). *Dharmakāya* indicates the buddhahood in its universality, *nirmāṇakāya* the buddhahood embodied or personalized, and *saṃbhogakāya* the buddhahood as spiritualized. Chih-i attributes the revelation of the *trikāya* in this form to this passage and emphasizes the unity of the trinity as consituting the only correct doctrine of the Buddha's person and reality.

I have ever spoken of myself as the Buddha Burning Light and other [buddhas], and also have told of their entering into nirvana. Thus have I tactfully described them all. Good sons! Whenever living beings come to me, I behold with a buddha's eyes all the faculties, keen or dull, of their faith and so on. And I explain to them, in stage after stage, according to their capacity and degree of salvation, my different names and the length of my lives, and moreover plainly state that I must enter nirvana. I also, in various tactful ways, preach the Wonderful Law which is able to cause all the living to beget a joyful heart. Good sons! Beholding the propensities of all the living toward lower things, so that they have little virtue and much vileness, to these men the Tathāgata declares: 'In my youth I left home and attained Perfect Enlightenment.' But since I verily became Buddha, thus have I ever been, and thus have I made declaration, only by my tactful methods to teach and transform all living beings, so that they may enter the Way of the Buddha. Good sons! All the sutras which the Tathāgata preaches are for the deliverance of the living. Whether speaking of himself or speaking of others, whether indicating himself or indicating others, and whether indicating his own affairs or the affairs of others,[2] whatever he says is all real and not empty air. Wherefore? [Because] the Tathāgata knows and sees the character of the triple world as it really is: [to him] there is neither birth nor death, or going away or coming forth; neither living nor dead; neither reality nor unreality; neither thus nor otherwise.[3] Unlike [the way] the triple world beholds the triple world, the Tathāgata clearly sees such things as these without mistake. Because all the living have various natures, various desires, various activities, various ideas and reasonings, [so] desiring to cause them to produce the roots of goodness, [the Tathāgata] by so many reasonings, parables, and discourses has preached his various truths. The Buddha-deeds which he does have never failed for a moment. Thus it is, since I became Buddha in the very far distant past, [that my] lifetime is of infinite asaṃkhyeya kalpas, forever existing and immortal. Good sons! The lifetime which I attained by pursuing the

2. The Chinese text accords with Burnouf's translation. Kern has "either under his own appearance or another's, either on his own authority or under the mask of another" (SBE vol. 21, p. 301).

3. This can also be read: "it is neither born nor dies, or disappears or comes forth; it has no secular existence and no extinction; it is neither real nor unreal, neither thus nor otherwise."

bodhisattva-way is not even yet accomplished but will still be twice the previous number [of kalpas]. But now, in this unreal nirvana, I announce that I must enter the [real] nirvana. In this tactful way the Tathāgata teaches all living beings. Wherefore? If the Buddha abides long in the world, men of little virtue who do not cultivate the roots of goodness and are [spiritually] poor and mean, greedily attached to the five desires, and are caught in the net of [wrong] reflection and false views—if they see the Tathāgata constantly present and not extinct, [they] will then become puffed up and lazy, and unable to conceive the idea that it is hard to meet [the Buddha] or a mind of reverence [for him]. Therefore the Tathāgata tactfully teaches: 'Know, bhikshus, the appearance of buddhas in the world is a rare occurrence.' Wherefore? In the course of countless hundreds of thousands of myriad koṭis of kalpas, some men of little virtue may happen to see a buddha or none may see him. For this reason I say: 'Bhikshus! A tathāgata may rarely be seen!' All these living beings, hearing such a statement, must certainly realize the thought of the difficulty of meeting a buddha and cherish a longing and a thirst for him; then will they cultivate the roots of goodness. Therefore the Tathāgata, though he does not in reality become extinct, yet announces [his] extinction. Again, good sons! The method of all buddha-tathāgatas is always like this in order to save all the living, and it is altogether real and not false.

"Suppose, for instance, a good physician, who is wise and perspicacious, conversant with medical art, and skillful in healing all sorts of diseases. He has many sons, say ten, twenty, even up to a hundred. Because of some matter he goes abroad to a distant country. After his departure, his sons drink his other poisonous medicines, which send them into a delirium, and they lie rolling on the ground. At this moment their father comes back to his home. Of the sons who drank the poison, some have lost their senses, others are [still] sensible, but on seeing their father [approaching] in the distance they are all greatly delighted, and kneeling, salute him, asking: 'How good it is that you are returned in safety! We, in our foolishness, have mistakenly dosed ourselves with poison. We beg that you will heal us and give us back our lives.' The father, seeing his sons in such distress, in accordance with his prescriptions seeks for good herbs altogether perfect in color, scent, and fine flavor, and then pounds, sifts, and mixes them and gives them to his sons to take, speaking thus: 'This excellent medicine, with color, scent, and fine flavor altogether perfect, you may [now] take, and it will at once rid you of your distress so that you will have no more suffering.' Those amongst the sons who are sensible, seeing this excellent medicine with color and scent both good, take it immediately and are totally delivered from their illness. The others, who have lost their senses, seeing their father come, though they are also delighted, salute him, and ask him to heal their illness, yet when he offers them the medicine, they are unwilling to take it. Wherefore? Because the poison has entered deeply, they have lost their senses, and [even] in regard to this medicine of excellent color and scent they acknowledge that it is not good. The father reflects thus: 'Alas for these sons, afflicted by this poison, and their minds all unbalanced. Though they are glad to see me and implore to be healed, yet they are unwilling to take such excellent medicine as this. Now I must arrange an expedient plan so that they will take this medicine.' Then he says to them: 'You should know that I am now worn out with old age and the time of my death has now arrived. This excellent medicine I now leave here. You may take it and have no fear of not being better.' After thus admonishing them, he departs again for another country and sends a messenger back to inform them: 'Your father is dead.' And now, when those sons hear that their father is dead, their minds are greatly distressed and they thus reflect: 'If our father were alive he would have pity on us, and we should be saved and preserved. But now he has left us and died in a distant country. [Now] we feel we are orphans and have no one to rely on.' Continuous grief brings them to their senses, and they recognize the color, scent, and excellent flavor of the medicine and thereupon take it, their poisoning being entirely relieved. The father, hearing that the sons are all recovered, seeks an opportunity and returns so that they all see him. All my good sons! What is your opinion? Are there any who could say that this good physician had committed the sin of falsehood?"

"No, World-honored One!"

The Buddha [then] said: "I also am like this. Since I became Buddha, infinite boundless hundred thousand myriad koṭis of nayutas of asaṃkhyeya kalpas ago, for the sake of all living beings, by my tactful power, I have declared that I must enter nirvana, yet there is none who can lawfully accuse me of the error of falsehood."

At that time the World-honored One, desiring to proclaim this teaching over again, spoke thus in verse:

"Since I attained buddhahood,
The kalpas through which I have passed
Are infinite thousands of myriads
Of koṭis of asaṃkhyeya years.
Ceaselessly preached I the Law and taught
Countless koṭis of creatures
To enter the Way of the Buddha;
Since then are unmeasured kalpas.
In order to save all creatures,
By tactful methods I reveal nirvana,
Yet truly I am not [yet] extinct
But forever here preaching the Law.
I forever remain in this [world],
Using all my spiritual powers
So that all perverted creatures,
Though I am near, yet fail to see me.
All looking on me as extinct
Everywhere worship my relics,
All cherishing longing desires,
And beget thirsting hearts of hope.
[When] all creatures have believed and obeyed,
In [character] upright, in mind gentle,
Wholeheartedly wishing to see the Buddha,
Not caring for their own lives,
Then I with all the Saṃgha
Appear together on the Divine Vulture Peak.
And then I tell all creatures
That I exist forever in this [world],
By the power of tactful methods
Revealing [myself] extinct and not extinct.
[If] in other regions there are beings
Reverent and with faith aspiring,
Again I am in their midst
To preach the supreme Law.
You, not hearing of this,

Only say I am extinct.
I behold all living creatures
Sunk in the sea of suffering,
Hence I do not reveal myself
But set them all aspiring,
Till, when their hearts are longing,
I appear to preach the Law.
In such supernaturally pervading power,
Throughout asaṃkhyeya kalpas
[I am] always on the Divine Vulture Peak
And in every other dwelling place.
When all the living see, at the kalpa's end,
The conflagration when it is burning,
Tranquil is this realm of mine,
Ever filled with heavenly beings,
Parks, and many palaces
With every kind of gem adorned,
Precious trees full of blossoms and fruits,
Where all creatures take their pleasure;
All the gods strike the heavenly drums
And evermore make music,
Showering mandārava flowers
On the Buddha and his great assembly.
My Pure Land will never be destroyed,
Yet all view it as being burned up,
And grief and horror and distress
Fill them all like this.
All those sinful creatures,
By reason of their evil karma,
Throughout asaṃkhyeya kalpas,
Hear not the name of the Precious Three.
But all who perform virtuous deeds
And are gentle and of upright nature,
These all see that I exist
And am here expounding the Law.
At times for all this throng
I preach the Buddha's life is eternal;
To those who at length see the Buddha

I preach that a buddha is rarely met.
My intelligence-power is such,
My wisdom-light shines infinitely,
My life is of countless kalpas,
From long-cultivated karma obtained.
You who have intelligence,
Do not in regard to this beget doubt
But bring it forever to an end,
For the Buddha's words are true, not false.
Like the physician who with clever device,
In order to cure his demented sons,
Though indeed alive announces [his own] death,
[Yet] cannot be charged with falsehood,
I, too, being father of this world,
Who heals all misery and affliction,
For the sake of the perverted people,
Though truly alive, say [I am] extinct;
[Lest,] because always seeing me,
They should beget arrogant minds,
Be dissolute and set in their five desires,
And fall into evil paths.
I, ever knowing all beings,
Those who walk or walk not in the Way,
According to the right principles of salvation
Expound their every Law,
Ever making this my thought:
'How shall I cause all the living
To enter the Way supreme
And speedily accomplish their buddhahood?'"

CHAPTER XVII

Discrimination of Merits

AT THAT TIME when the great congregation heard the Buddha proclaim that such were the number of kalpas and the length of his lifetime, innumerable, countless living beings obtained great benefit.

Then the World-honored One said to the Bodhisattva-Mahāsattva Maitreya: "Ajita! While I proclaimed the duration of the Tathāgata's life, sixty-eight hundred thousand koṭis of nayutas of living beings, [numerous as] the sands of the Ganges, have attained to the assurance of [their] nonrebirth; again a thousand times more bodhisattva-mahāsattvas have attained the dhāraṇī-power of hearing and keeping [the Law];[1] again, bodhisattva-mahāsattvas, numerous as the atoms of a world, have attained the faculty of eloquent and unembarrassed discussion; again, bodhisattva-mahāsattvas numerous as the atoms of

When the eternal life of the Buddha was revealed in chapter 16, all the hearers, whether the former converts who issued from the earth or his immediate disciples, attained various degrees of meritoriousness according to the difference in their capacities. This chapter defines the degrees of merit.

1. Literally, "the door, or method, of the hearing and keeping of dhāraṇī [by means of which they hear and keep the Law]." This is the first of the four fearlessnesses of a bodhisattva.

a world have attained to hundreds of thousands of myriad koṭis of the dhāraṇī of infinite revolutions;[2] again, bodhisattva-mahāsattvas numerous as the atoms of a three-thousand-great-thousandfold world have been enabled to roll forward the never-retreating Law-wheel; again, bodhisattva-mahāsattvas numerous as the atoms of a middle-two-thousandfold domain have been enabled to roll forward the pure Law-wheel; again, bodhisattva-mahāsattvas numerous as the atoms of a small-thousandfold domain after eight rebirths will attain Perfect Enlightenment; again, bodhisattva-mahāsattvas numerous as the atoms of four four-continent worlds[3] after four births will attain Perfect Enlightenment; again, bodhisattva-mahāsattvas numerous as the atoms of three four-continent worlds after three births will attain Perfect Enlightenment; again, bodhisattva-mahāsattvas numerous as the atoms of two four-continent worlds after two births will attain Perfect Enlightenment; again, bodhisattva-mahāsattvas numerous as the atoms of one four-continent world after one birth will attain to Perfect Enlightenment; again, living beings numerous as the atoms of eight worlds have all aspired to Perfect Enlightenment."

When the Buddha had told of those bodhisattva-mahāsattvas obtaining [such] great benefits of the Law, from the sky there rained down mandārava and mahā-mandārava flowers, scattering over the innumerable hundreds of thousands of myriads of koṭis of buddhas on lion thrones below the jewel trees, scattering also over Sakyamuni Buddha and the long-extinct Abundant Treasures Tathāgata [seated] on the lion throne in the Stupa of the Precious Seven, and also scattering over all the great bodhisattvas and the host of the four groups; it also rained incense of fine sandalwood, aloes, and so forth; in the sky the heavenly drums resounded of themselves with exquisite deep resonance; there rained down also thousands of kinds of celestial garments, and in every direction[4] there hung down necklaces, pearl necklaces, maṇi necklaces, and felicitous-pearl necklaces; censers of

2. The dhāraṇī of numberless revolutions or evolutions is the power to discriminate manifold phenomena without error. By this discrimination a bodhisattva destroys all his perplexities and exhibits many Buddha-laws.

3. A world of four continents surrounding its central mountain, Sumeru. The four continents are Pūrvavideha in the east, Avaragodānīya in the west, Jambudvīpa in the south, and Uttarakuru in the north.

4. Literally, "in the nine quarters," that is, the eight points of the compass and the center.

many jewels, burning priceless incense, moved everywhere of their own accord to pay homage to the great congregation. Over each buddha, bodhisattvas held canopies, one above another, right up to the Brahma heaven. All these bodhisattvas with exquisite voices sang countless praise-hymns extolling the buddhas.

Thereupon Maitreya Bodhisattva rose from his seat and humbly bared his right shoulder, folded his hands toward the Buddha, and spoke thus in verse:

"The Buddha has preached the rare Law
Never heard [by us] before.
Great is the power of the World-honored One
And his lifetime beyond estimation.
Numberless Buddha-sons,
Hearing the World-honored One in detail
Tell of those who obtained the Law-benefit,
Have been filled with joy.
Some are steadfast in the never-retreating stage,
Some have attained to the dhāraṇīs,
Some to unembarrassed eloquence
Or to controlling myriads of koṭis of revolutions.
There are bodhisattvas numerous as the atoms
Of a great-thousandfold world,
Each of them able to roll
The unretreating Law-wheel;
And bodhisattvas numerous as the atoms
Of a middle-thousandfold world,
Each of them able to roll
The unsullied Law-wheel;
And bodhisattvas numerous as the atoms
Of a small-thousandfold world,
Each of whom, after eight rebirths,
Will accomplish the Buddha-way.
Again there are bodhisattvas,
Numerous as the atoms of four, three, two
Worlds of four continents like this,
Who will become buddhas after those numbers of rebirths.
Or bodhisattvas numerous as the atoms

Of one four-continent world,
Who after one more birth
Will accomplish perfect knowledge.
Such living beings as these,
Hearing the duration of the Buddha's life,
Will obtain infinite, perfect,
And pure reward.
Also there are the living, numerous
As the atoms of eight worlds, who,
Hearing the Buddha's announcement of his lifetime,
Have all aspired to the supreme [truth].
The World-honored One, by preaching the infinite
And inconceivable Law,
Has benefited many,
Boundlessly as space.
Divine mandārava flowers rain down
And mahā-mandāravas.
Śakras and Brahmas [numerous] as sands of the Ganges
From countless buddha-lands have come,
Raining sandal and aloes, which
Fall blended and commingled;
Like birds flying below the sky
They reverently bestrew the buddhas.
The celestial drums in space
Roll forth of themselves their wondrous sounds.
A thousand myriad kinds of divine robes
Whirl around in their descent.
Exquisite bejeweled censers,
Burning priceless incense,
Move all around of their own accord
In homage to the world-honored ones.
Hosts of great bodhisattvas
Hold canopies of the precious seven,
Of wondrous height and of myriads of koṭis of varieties,
One above another up to the Brahma heaven.
Before each one of the buddhas
Jeweled streamers hang fluttering;
Also with thousands of myriads of stanzas

They [celebrate] the tathāgatas in song.
Such a variety of things as these
We have never known before.
Hearing the Buddha's lifetime is infinite,
All beings are gladdened.
The Buddha's fame throughout the universe
Widely refreshes the roots of goodness
Of all living beings,
Aiding their desire for supreme [truth]."

Thereupon the Buddha addressed Maitreya Bodhisattva-Mahāsattva: "Ajita! Those living beings who have heard that the lifetime of the Buddha is of such long duration and have been able to receive but one thought of faith and discernment—the merits they will obtain are beyond limit and measure. Suppose there be any good son or good daughter who, for the sake of Perfect Enlightenment, during eight hundred thousand koṭis of nayutas of kalpas practices the five pāramitās: dāna-pāramitā, sīla-pāramitā, kshānti-pāramitā, vīrya-pāramitā, and dhyāna-pāramitā, prajñā-pāramitā being excepted; these merits compared with the above-mentioned merits are not equal to even the hundredth part, the thousandth part, or one part of a hundred thousand myriad koṭis of it; indeed, neither numbers nor comparisons can make it known. If any good son or good daughter possesses such merit as this, there is no such thing as failing [to obtain] Perfect Enlightenment."

Thereupon the World-honored One, desiring to proclaim this teaching over again, spoke thus in verse:

"Though a man, seeking the Buddha-wisdom,
During eighty myriad koṭis
Of nayutas of kalpas
Were to perform the five pāramitās,
And during those kalpas
Give alms and offerings to buddhas,
Pratyekabuddhas, and disciples,
As well as to bodhisattvas—
Rare and precious food and drink,
Superior clothing and bed furniture,

Monasteries built of sandalwood and
Adorned with gardens and groves,
Such alms as these,
Wonderful in variety—
Were he to maintain them through all those kalpas
As meritorious gifts to the Buddha-way;
Moreover, though he were to keep the commandments
Purely, without flaw or fault,
And seek the supreme Way
Which all buddhas praise;
Or were he patiently to endure insult,
Stand firm in the stage of gentleness,
And though evils came upon him,
Keep his mind undisturbed;
Were he by [other] believers
Filled with utmost arrogance
To be scorned and distressed,
Yet able to bear even this;
Or were he to be diligent and zealous,
Ever strong in will and memory,
And during measureless koṭis of kalpas
With all his mind continue unremitting,
And during numberless kalpas
Dwell in secluded places,
Whether resident or vagrant,
Avoiding sleep and ever concentrating his mind;
Were [he], by this means,
To be able to beget meditations
And for eighty myriad koṭis of kalpas
Calmly remain in them with unperturbed mind;
Were [he], maintaining this single-minded happiness,
Willingly to seek the supreme Way, [saying]:
'I will attain all knowledge
And go on to the utmost point of meditation':
Were such a man for hundreds of thousands of
Myriads of koṭis of kalpas
To perform such deeds of merits
As those above expounded;

Yet any good son or daughter
Who, hearing me declare my [eternal] life,
Believes it with but a single thought,
This one's reward surpasses his.
If anyone be entirely free
From all doubts and misgivings
And in his deepest heart believes it but a moment,
Such shall be his reward.
If there be bodhisattvas
Who have followed [good] ways for innumerable kalpas
And hear of my announcement of my [eternal] life,
They will be able to receive it in faith;
Such men as these
Will bow their heads in receiving this sutra
And say: 'May we in the future
Have long life to save all the living;
And just as the present World-honored One
Who, King of the Śākyas,
On his wisdom terrace raises the lion's roar,
Preaching the Law without fear,
So may we in future ages,
Honored and revered by all,
When sitting on the wisdom terrace,
In like manner tell of the duration of life!'
If there be any of profound spirit,
Pure and upright,
Learned and able to uphold [the truth],
Who understand the meaning of the Buddha's word,
Such men as these
Will have no doubts about this teaching.

"Again, Ajita! If anyone hears of the duration of the Buddha's lifetime and apprehends its meaning, the merit obtained by this man will be beyond limit and he will advance to the supreme wisdom of tathāgatas; how much more will [this be the case with] the one who is devoted to hearing this sutra, or causes others to hear it, or himself keeps it, or causes others to keep it, or himself copies it, or causes others to copy it, or with flowers, incense, garlands, banners, flags, silk canopies, and lamps of fragrant oil and ghee pays homage to the sutra; this man's merit will be infinite and boundless and able to bring forth perfect knowledge. Ajita! If any good son or good daughter, hearing of my declaration of the duration of my lifetime, believes and discerns it in his inmost heart, such a one will see the Buddha always on Mount Gṛdhrakūṭa surrounded by a host of great bodhisattvas and śrāvakas, and preaching the Law. And he will see this sahā-world whose land is lapis lazuli, plain and level, its eight roads marked off with jambūnada gold, lined with jewel trees; it has towers, halls, and galleries all made of jewels, in which dwell together its bodhisattva host. If anyone is able so to behold, you may know that this is the sign of profound faith and discernment.

"And again, if [anyone], after the extinction of the Tathāgata, hears this sutra, and does not defame but rejoices over it, you may know that he has had the sign of deep faith and discernment; how much more the one who reads and recites, receives and keeps it—this man carries the Tathāgata on his head.[5] Ajita! Such a good son or good daughter need no more erect stupas, temples, or monasteries for me, nor make offerings of the four requisites to the monks.[6] Wherefore? [Because] this good son or good daughter who receives and keeps, reads and recites this sutra has already erected stupas, built monasteries, and made offerings to the monks, that is to say, has erected, for the Buddha's relics, stupas of the precious seven, high and broad, and tapering up to the Brahma heaven, hung with flags and canopies and precious bells, and with flowers, perfumes, garlands, sandal powder, unguents, incense, drums, instruments, pipes, flutes, harps, all kinds of dances and plays—singing and lauding with wondrous notes—he has already made these offerings for innumerable thousands of myriads of koṭis of kalpas. Ajita! If anyone, after my extinction, hears this sutra, and is able either to receive and keep, or himself copy or cause others to copy it, he has [already] erected monasteries and built red sandalwood temples of thirty-two shrines, tall as eight tāla trees, lofty, spacious, splendid, in which abide hundreds, thousands of bhikshus; [adorned also with] gardens, groves, and bathing pools, promenades and meditation cells; with clothing, victuals, bedding, medicaments,

5. Kern has "carries it on his shoulder," that is, holds it in high esteem and treats it with care.

6. Garments, food and drink, bed furnishings, and medicines.

and all aids to pleasure provided to the full therein. Such monasteries and such numbers of temples, hundreds of thousands of myriads of koṭis, countless in their number, he has here in my presence offered to me and to [my] bhikshus. Therefore I say if anyone after the extinction of the Tathāgata receives and keeps, reads and recites it, preaches it to others, either himself copies it or causes others to copy it, and pays homage to the sutra, he need no longer erect stupas and temples or build monasteries and make offerings to the monks. How much less he who is able to keep this sutra and add thereto almsgiving, morality, forbearance, zeal, concentration, and wisdom. His merit will be most excellent, infinite and boundless; even as space, which, east, west, south, and north, the four intermediate directions, the zenith and nadir, is infinite and boundless, so also the merit of this man will be infinite and boundless, and he will speedily reach perfect knowledge. If anyone[7] reads and recites, receives and keeps this sutra, preaches it to other people, or himself copies it, or causes others to copy it; moreover, is able to erect caityas and build monasteries, and to serve and extol the śrāvaka-monks, and also, with hundreds of thousands of myriads of koṭis of ways of extolling, extols the merits of the bodhisattvas; also [if he] to other people, with various reasonings according to its meaning, expounds this Law-Flower Sutra; again [if he] is able to keep the commandments in purity, amicably to dwell with the gentle, to endure insult without anger, to be firm in will and thought, ever to value meditation, to attain profound concentration, zealously and boldly to support the good, to be clever and wise in ably answering difficult questionings; Ajita, again, if after my extinction there be good sons and good daughters who receive and keep, read and recite this sutra, who possess such excellent merits as these, you should know that those people have proceeded toward the wisdom terrace and are near Perfect Enlightenment, sitting under the tree of enlightenment. Ajita! Wherever those good sons or good daughters sit or stand or walk, in that place [you] should erect a caitya; all gods and men should pay homage to it as a stupa of [the relics of] the Buddha."

Thereupon the World-honored One, desiring to proclaim this teaching over again, spoke thus in verse:

7. The Chinese can also be translated "such a man," but the reading given is that which is usual in Japan. Cf. Kern, SBE vol. 21, p. 323.

"If anyone, after my extinction,
Is able respectfully to keep this sutra,
This man's happiness will be infinite
As is above explained.
Such a one will have made perfectly
All kinds of offerings
And erected stupas for relics,
Adorned with the precious seven,
With banner towers, high and broad,
Tapering up to the Brahma-heaven,
With thousands of myriads of koṭis of gem-bells,
Stirred by the wind to mystic music.
For innumerable kalpas
He will have paid homage to these stupas
With flowers, incense, and garlands,
With celestial garments and playing of music,
With perfumed oil and ghee lamps burning
And illuminating all around.
In the evil ages of the Law's decay,
He who can keep this sutra
Will have, as above [shown],
Perfectly made all kinds of offerings.
If anyone can keep this sutra,
It will be as if the Buddha were present
And he, with ox-head sandalwood,
Built monasteries to serve him,
Consisting of thirty-two halls,
Eight tāla trees in height,
With superior food and fine garments,
Beds and all complete,
With abodes for hundreds and thousands;
With gardens, groves, and bathing pools,
With walks and meditation cells,
All beautifully adorned.
If anyone has the mind of faith and discernment,
Receives, keeps, reads, recites, and copies,
Or moreover causes others to copy,

And pays homage to the sutra,
Strewing flowers, incense, and sandal powder,
And uses perfumed oil of sumana
And campaka and atimuktaka
For constant burning;
He who pays such homage to it
Will obtain infinite merit;
Just as space is boundless,
So will it be with his merits;
How much more with one who keeps this sutra,
Gives alms and keeps the commandments,
Is long-suffering and delights in meditation,
Not irascible, nor speaking ill,
Reverent to caityas and sanctuaries,
Humble toward the bhikshus,
Far removed from haughtiness,
Ever pondering on wisdom,
Not angry when asked about difficulties
But compliantly explaining them;
If he is able to do these deeds,
His merits cannot be estimated.
If one meets such a Law-teacher
Who has accomplished such virtues,
Let him strew divine flowers upon him,
Cover him with divine clothing,
And salute him by bowing to his feet,
With a mind as if thinking of the Buddha.
Moreover, let him reflect thus:
'Soon he will be going to the Bodhi tree
To achieve perfection and effortlessness,
Widely benefiting gods and men.'
Wherever he dwells and stays,
Walks, sits, or lies,
Or preaches but a stanza [of this sutra],
In that place erect a stupa,
Adorn it and make it beautiful,
And in all ways pay homage to it.

When a Buddha-son dwells in such a place,
It means that the Buddha himself uses it
And ever abides in it,
Walking, or sitting, or lying down."

CHAPTER XVIII

The Merits of Joyful Acceptance

AT THAT TIME Maitreya Bodhisattva-Mahāsattva spoke to the Buddha, saying: "World-honored One! If there be a good son or good daughter who, hearing this Law-Flower Sutra, accepts it with joy, how much happiness will he obtain?"

And he spoke [it again] in verse:

"After the extinction of the World-honored One,
If anyone, hearing this sutra,
Is able to accept it with joy,
How much happiness will he obtain?"

Then the Buddha addressed Maitreya Bodhisattva-Mahāsattva: "Ajita! If, after the extinction of the Tathāgata, any bhikshu, bhikshuṇi, upāsaka, upāsikā, or other wise person, whether old or young, on hearing this sutra has accepted it with joy, and coming out of the assembly goes elsewhere to dwell either in a monastery or solitary place, or in a city, street, hamlet, or village, to expound [what] he has heard, according to his ability, to his father, mother, kindred, good friends, and acquaintances; and all these people, having heard it, accept it with joy and again go on to transmit the teaching; these others, having heard it, also accepting it with joy, and transmitting the teaching, and so on in turn to the fiftieth [person]—Ajita! I will now tell you about the merit of that fiftieth good son or good daughter, who joyfully receives [the truth]. Do you hearken well!

"It is as [the number of] all the living creatures in the six states [of existence], in four hundred myriad koṭis of asaṃkhyeyas of worlds, born in the four [ways], egg-born, womb-born, humidity-born, or born by metamorphosis, whether they are formed or formless, whether conscious or unconscious, or neither conscious nor unconscious; footless, two-footed, four-footed, or many-footed—it is as the sum of all these living creatures. Suppose someone, seeking [their] happiness, provides them with every article of pleasure they may desire, giving each creature the whole of a Jambudvīpa, gold, silver, lapis lazuli, moonstone, agate, coral, amber, and all sorts of wonderful jewels, with elephants, horses, carriages, and palaces and towers built of the precious seven, and so forth. This great master of gifts thus bestows gifts for full eighty years and then reflects thus: 'I have bestowed on all these beings articles of pleasure according to their desires, but now they have all grown old and worn, over eighty years of age, with hair gray and faces wrinkled, and death is not far off—I ought to instruct and guide them in the Buddha-law.' Thereupon, gathering together those beings, he proclaims to them the Law's instruction; and by his revealing, teaching, benefiting, and rejoicing, they all in a moment become srota-āpannas, sakṛdāgāmins, anāgāmins, and arhats,[1] free from all imperfections, having all acquired mastery of profound meditation and completed the eight emancipations. What is your opinion? May the merits obtained by this great master of gifts be considered many or not?" Maitreya said to the Buddha: "World-honored One! The merits of this man are very many, infinite and boundless. Even though this master of giving had only made gifts of all those articles of pleasure to those creatures, his merits would be infinite; how much more when he causes them to attain arhatship?"

1. These are the four merits or fruits: (1) srota-āpanna, literally, "one who has entered the stream [leading to nirvana]"; (2) sakṛdāgāmin, literally, "returning," or being reborn once more; (3) anāgāmin, literally, "not returning," or no more rebirth; and (4) arhat. See also Glossary.

Then said the Buddha to Maitreya: "I will now speak clearly to you. The merits attained by this man in bestowing those means of happiness to all beings in the six states [of existence] of four hundred myriad koṭis of asaṃkhyeyas of worlds and causing them to attain arhatship do not compare with the merits of that fiftieth person who, hearing a single verse of the Law-Flower Sutra, receives it with joy; they are not up to one hundredth, or one thousandth, or one fraction of a hundred thousand myriad koṭis; the power of figures or comparisons cannot express it. Ajita! If the merits of such a fiftieth person who in turn hears the Law-Flower Sutra and accepts it with joy are indeed so infinite, boundless, and numberless, how much more is the happiness of him who among the first hearers in the assembly receives it joyfully, surpassing [happiness] still more infinite, boundless, and beyond number or compare.

"Again, Ajita! If anyone, for the sake of this sutra, goes to a monastery and, either sitting or standing, hears and receives it even for a moment, by reason of that merit in his next bodily rebirth he will acquire the most excellent kind of elephants, horses and carriages, jeweled palanquins and litters, and ride in celestial cars. If again there be anyone who sits down in the place where [this] Law is preached, and when others come persuades them to sit down and hear it, or shares his seat with others, that person's merit, on his bodily rebirth, will give him a Śakra's seat, or a Brahma's, or the seat of a sacred wheel-rolling king. Ajita! If, moreover, anyone says to another: 'There is a sutra named the Flower of the Law; let us go together and listen to it,' and if he who is persuaded hears it but for a moment, that person's merit, after his bodily rebirth, will cause him to be born in the same place with bodhisattvas [who have attained] dhāraṇī. He will be of keen faculties and wise; for hundreds of thousands of myriads of ages he will never be dumb nor have unpleasant breath; [will] ever be free from ailments of the tongue or ailments of the mouth; his teeth will never be dirty and black, nor yellow, nor in gaps, nor fall out, nor irregular, nor crooked; his lips will not be pendulous or twisted and shrunk, not coarse and rough, nor have sores and pustules, not be cracked and broken or awry and out of shape, neither thick nor big, neither sallow nor black, having nothing loathsome; his nose will not be flat or crooked and distorted; the color of his face will not be black, nor will it be narrow and long or ever be hollow and crooked, having nothing whatever unpleasing; his lips, tongue, and teeth all will be beautiful; his nose long, high, and straight; his face round and full; his eyebrows high and long; his forehead broad, even, and upright. His sign of manhood will be perfect. In whatever age he is born, he will see the Buddha, hear the Law, and receive the teaching in faith. Ajita! Just notice this—if the merit obtained from persuading one person to go and hear the Law is such as this, how much more is that of one who with his whole mind hears and reads it, in the assembly interprets it to the people, and practices what it preaches."

Thereupon the World-honored One, desiring to proclaim this teaching over again, spoke thus in verse:

"If anyone in an assembly
Hears this sutra,
Though only one stanza,
And joyfully proclaims it to others,
And thus its teaching rolls on
Till it reaches the fiftieth [hearer],
The happiness obtained by this last
I now will explain.
Suppose a great benefactor
Who provides for a countless throng
During full eighty years
According to all their desires,
Then sees them decayed and old,
Gray-haired and faces wrinkled,
Teeth sparse and forms withered,
And thinks their death approaches;
'Now,' says he, 'I must teach them
To obtain the fruits of the right way.'
Then by tactful methods he
Teaches them the true Law of nirvana:
'All worlds are unstable,
Like water bubbles or will-o'-the-wisp.
Do you all hasten to beget
A spirit turning in disgust from them.'
All of them on hearing this truth
Attain arhatship,

Perfect in the six transcendent [faculties],
Three clear [views], and eight emancipations.
The last, the fiftieth [person],
Who hears one verse and rejoices—
This man's felicity surpasses that [benefactor's]
Beyond the power of comparison.
If a hearer whose turn is [so remote]
Has such boundless felicity,
How much greater his who, in the congregation,
First hears it with joyfulness.
Let a man exhort but one person
And bring him to listen to the Law-Flower,
Saying: 'This sutra is profound and wonderful,
Hard to meet in thousands of myriads of kalpas.'
Persuaded, he goes to listen
And hears it but for a moment;
The reward of such a persuader
Let me now define.
Age by age his mouth will never suffer,
His teeth not be gapped, yellow, or black,
Nor his lips thick, awry, or cracked,
With no loathsome appearance;
His tongue neither dried up, black, nor shrunk;
His nose high, long, and straight;
His forehead broad, level, and upright;
A joy for men to behold;
No fetid breath from his mouth, but
The scent of the utpala flower
Ever exhaling from his lips.
[Or] suppose one on purpose visits a monastery
To hear the Law-Flower Sutra,
And hearing it but a moment rejoices;
Let me now tell of his happiness.
He will hereafter be born among gods and men,
Have fine elephants, horses and carriages,
Jeweled palanquins and litters,
And ride in celestial aerial cars.
If, in the place of preaching,

He begs men to sit and hear the sutra,
Because of this felicity he will attain
The seat of a Śakra, a Brahma, a wheel-rolling king.
How much more with him who single-minded
Hears and expounds its meaning
And practices according to [its] teaching—
His happiness is beyond limit."

CHAPTER XIX

The Merits of the Preacher

THEN THE BUDDHA addressed the Bodhisattva-Mahāsattva Ever Zealous: "If any good son or good daughter receives and keeps this Law-Flower Sutra, or reads, or recites, or expounds, or copies it, that person will obtain eight hundred merits of the eye, twelve hundred merits of the ear, eight hundred merits of the nose, twelve hundred merits of the tongue, eight hundred merits of the body, and twelve hundred merits of the mind; with these merits he will dignify his six organs, making them all serene. That good son or good daughter, with the natural pure eyes received at birth from his parents, will see whatever exists within and without the three-thousand-great-thousandfold world, mountains, forests, rivers, and seas, down to the Avīci hell and up to the Summit [of Existence], and also see all the living beings in it, as well as see and know in detail all their karma causes and rebirth states of retribution."

Thereupon the World-honored One, desiring to proclaim this teaching over again, spoke thus in verse:

"If one, in the great assembly,
With fearless mind,

Preaches this Law-Flower Sutra—
Hearken to his merits.
That man will obtain eight hundred
Surpassing merits of vision;
Because of these endowments
His eyes will be entirely serene.
With the eyes received from his parents
He will see all the three-thousandfold world,
Within and without, Mount Meru,
Sumeru and its Iron Circle,
And the other mountains and forests,
Great oceans, rivers, and waters,
Down to the Avīci hell,
Up to the Summit of Existence;
The living beings in its midst
All will be seen by him;
Though not yet having attained divine vision,
His eyes of flesh have powers like these.

"And again, Ever Zealous! If any good son or good daughter receives and keeps this sutra, or reads or recites or expounds or copies it, he will obtain twelve hundred merits of the ear. With this serene ear he will hear, in the three-thousand-great-thousandfold world, downward to the Avīci hell, upward to the Summit of Existence, within and without, all various words and sounds, the sounds of elephants, of horses, of cows, of carriages, of wailing, of lamentation, of conchs, of drums, of gongs, of bells, of laughter, of speech, of men, of women, of boys, of girls, of the lawful, of the unlawful, of suffering, of pleasure, of common people, of holy men, of comfort, of discomfort, of gods, of dragons, of yakshas, of gandharvas, of asuras, of garuḍas, of kimnaras, of mahoragas, of fire, of water, of wind, of the hells, of the animals, of hungry spirits, of bhikshus, of bhikshuṇīs, of śrāvakas, of pratyekabuddhas, of bodhisattvas, and of buddhas—essentially speaking, whatever sounds there may be within and without the three-thousand-great-thousandfold world; though he has still not obtained the heavenly ear, yet by the natural pure ears received at birth from his parents all these he will hear and know. And thus he discriminates all these various sounds without harm to his organ of hearing."

Thereupon the World-honored One, desiring to proclaim this teaching over again, spoke thus in verse:

"His ears, received from parents,
Are serene and untainted.
By these ordinary ears he hears
The sounds in the three-thousandfold world,
The sounds of elephants, horses, carts, and oxen,
The sounds of gongs, bells, conchs, and drums,
The sounds of lutes and harps,
The sounds of pipes and flutes,
The sounds of pure and lovely song;
He can listen without being under their control.
He hears the sounds of countless kinds of men,
And can understand all he hears;
He hears also the sounds of gods,
And mystic voices of singing;
Hears sounds of men and women,
And sounds of youths and maidens.
In mountains, streams, and gorges,
The sounds of kalavinkas,
Jīvakajīvakas and other birds,
All these sounds he hears.
The bitter pains of the hosts in hell
And the sounds of their sufferings;
The hungry spirits driven by hunger
And the sounds of their importunity;
The asuras and others
Inhabiting the ocean shores,
When they converse together,
Bellow forth their cries.
Such a preacher as this,
Calmly dwelling amidst this,
Hears from afar all these sounds
Without harm to his organ of hearing.

In the worlds in all directions,
Birds and beasts cry to each other,
And the preacher here abiding
Hears them in every detail.
All the Brahma heavens above,
From those of Light Sound[1] and Universal Purity[2]
To the heaven [called] the Summit of Existence—
The sounds of their conversation
The preacher here abiding
Hears in every detail.
All the host of bhikshus
And of bhikshuṇīs
Reading or reciting the sutra,
Or preaching it to others,
The preacher here abiding
Hears them in every detail.
Again there are the bodhisattvas
Who read and recite this sutra Law
Or preach it unto others,
Collating and expounding its meaning—
All such sounds as these
He hears in every detail.
The buddhas, great and holy honored ones,
Transformers of all living beings,
Who, in their great assemblies,
Proclaim the mystic Law—
He who keeps this Law-Flower
Hears in every detail.
In the three-thousand-great-thousandfold world,
Its sounds within and without,
Downward to the Avīci hell,
Upward to the Summit heaven,
All these sounds he will hear
Without harm to his organ of hearing,
And because his ears are acute,
He can discriminate and know them all.

1. The highest of the second realm of meditation heavens.
2. The highest of the third realm of meditation heavens.

He who keeps this Law-Flower,
Though not yet possessed of heavenly ears
And only using his natural ears,
Has already such merits as these.

"Moreover, Ever Zealous! If any good son or good daughter receives and keeps this sutra, or reads, or recites, or expounds, or copies it, he will attain eight hundred merits of the nose; and by means of this serene organ, in the three-thousand-great-thousandfold world, zenith and nadir, within and without, he will smell all kinds of fragrance, the fragrance of sumana flowers, of jātika flowers, of mallika flowers, of campaka flowers, of pāṭala flowers, of red lotus flowers, of blue lotus flowers, of white lotus flowers, of flowering trees, of fruit-bearing trees, of sandalwood, of aloes, of tamālapattras, of tagaras, and of thousands of myriads of blended perfumes, powdered, granular, or in unguents. He who keeps this sutra, while abiding in this place, can discern all these. Again, he will discern the odors of all living beings, the odor of elephants, of horses, of cattle, goats, and so on; of men, of women, of youths, of maidens, and of grass, trees, bushes, and woods; near or far, whatever odor there be, he will perceive it all and discern without mistake. He who keeps this sutra, though abiding here, will also perceive the odor of the gods in the heavens, of pārijāta and kovidāra, of mandārava flowers, of mahāmandārava flowers, of mañjūshaka flowers, of mahā-mañjūshaka flowers, of all kinds of powdered sandalwood and aloes, and of many mingled flowers—all the odors exhaled from such mingled celestial perfumes he will never fail to perceive and know. And he will perceive the odor of the bodies of gods, the odor of Śakra Devendra in his Surpassing Palace, indulging his five desires and disporting himself joyfully; or when he is in his Wonderful Law Hall preaching the Law to the gods of the Trāyastriṃśa; or when he wanders for pleasure in his gardens; also the odor of the bodies of the other male and female gods; from afar will he perceive them. Thus proceeding to the Brahma world, up to the Summit of Existence, he will also smell all the odors of the bodies of the gods. Besides, he will smell the incense burned by the gods; and the odor of śrāvakas, of pratyekabuddhas, of bodhisattvas, and of the bodies of buddhas—from afar will he smell all these and know where they abide. Though he smells these odors, yet his organ of smell will not be harmed nor mistaken; and if he wishes to define them to others, his memory will not err."

Thereupon the World-honored One, desiring to proclaim this teaching over again, spoke thus in verse:

"The nose of this man being serene,
[The odor of] everything in this world,
Be it fragrant or be it fetid,
In full detail he smells and knows.
Sumana and jātika,
Tamālapattra and sandal,
Aloes and cinnamon,
Odors of flowers and fruits,
Odors of all the living,
Odors of men and women:
The preacher, dwelling afar,
Smells them and knows their place.
All-powerful wheel-rolling kings,
Minor wheel-rollers and their sons,
All their ministers and courtiers:
He, by smell, knows their place.
The jewels they wear upon them,
The treasures [hidden] in the earth,
The precious queens[3] of wheel-rolling kings:
He, by smell, knows their place.
From the things adorning people,
Their clothes and necklaces,
And the perfumes they use for anointing,
He, by smell, knows their persons.
The gods, whether walking or seated,
Their playing and magic powers,
He who keeps this Law-Flower,
By smell, can know in detail.
The scent of tree flowers and fruits
And the fragrance of ghee oil:

3. Literally, "the precious women"; one of the seven treasures of a wheel-rolling king. A wheel-rolling king's seven treasures are the precious wheel, the elephant, the horse, the jewel, the queen, the treasurer, and the head of the army.

He who keeps this Law-Flower,
Abiding here, well knows their place.
Mountain gorges and cliffs,
Diffusion of sandal-tree blossoms,
And all the beings there dwelling
He, by smell, can perfectly know.
The oceans within the iron rim,
The living within their lands:
He who keeps this sutra
By [their] smell knows their place.
Asuras, male and female,
And all their tribe and followers,
When they quarrel or play together
He, by smell, is able to discern.
Prairies or ravines where [roam]
Lions, elephants, tigers, wolves,
Bisons, buffaloes, and their kind:
He, by smell, knows their place.
If there be a woman with child,
Who discerns not yet its sex,
Male, female, organless, or inhuman,
He, by smell, can discern it.
By his power of smell
He knows if the newly pregnant
Will succeed or not in being
Joyfully delivered of happy children.
By his perceptive power of smell
He knows the thoughts of men and women,
Their minds of lust, foolishness, or anger,
And also knows the doers of goodness.
All the treasures hidden in the earth,
Gold, silver, and jewels
Heaped in copper vessels,
By smell he can clearly distinguish.
All sorts of [jeweled] necklaces,
Of price beyond all knowledge—
By smell he knows their value,
Their source, and their location.

The flowers of the [various] heavens,
Mandāravas, mañjūshakas,
And pārijāta trees,
By smell he can clearly distinguish.
The palaces of the heavens,
Whether upper, middle, or lower,
Adorned with every precious flower,
By smell he can clearly distinguish.
The heavenly gardens, groves, surpassing palaces,
Studies, and Wonderful Law halls,
And those who take their pleasure in them,
By smell he can clearly distinguish.
Whenever the gods are hearing the Law,
Or indulging the five desires,
Coming, going, walking, sitting, lying—
By smell he can clearly distinguish.
The garments the goddesses wear,
Adorned and perfumed with beautiful flowers,
As they ramble about for pleasure,
By smell he can clearly distinguish.
So is it in turn ascending
Even up to the Brahma worlds;
Those in meditation and out of it
By smell he can clearly distinguish.
From the gods Light Sound and Universal Purity
To the god Summit of All Existence,
From their birth to their disappearance:
By smell he can all distinguish.
All the host of bhikshus
Ever progressing in the Law,
Whether seated or walking about,
Reading and reciting the sutra,
Or, beneath trees in the forest,
Devoting themselves to meditation—
The keeper of [this] sutra, by smell,
Knows their every location.
Bodhisattvas firm of will,
In meditation, or reading the sutra,

Or preaching the Law to others—
By smell he can all distinguish.
The world-honored in every direction,
By all beings revered,
Who pity all and preach the Law—
By smell he can all distinguish.
The living who, in a buddha's presence,
Hear the sutra and rejoice together,
And act according to the Law—
By smell he can all distinguish.
Though not yet possessed of a bodhisattva's
Faultless, Law-begotten organ of smell,
Yet this keeper of the sutra
First obtains this faculty of smell.

"Further, Ever Zealous! If any good son or good daughter receives and keeps this sutra, and either reads, or recites, or expounds, or copies it, he will obtain twelve hundred merits of the tongue. Whatever pleasant or unpleasant, sweet or not sweet, bitter or astringent things meet his tongue will become of the finest flavor, like celestial nectar; nothing will be unpleasant. If, in the assembly, he uses his organ of the tongue to preach, it will send forth a profound and beautiful voice that can enter their hearts, giving them pleasure and joy; and celestial sons and daughters, Śakras, Brahmas, and the gods, hearing what this profound and beautiful voice proclaims and the order of his discourse, will all come and listen to him; dragons also and female dragons, yakshas and female yakshas, gandharvas and female gandharvas, asuras and female asuras, garuḍas and female garuḍas, kiṃnaras and female kiṃnaras, mahoragas and female mahoragas will all come to hear the Law, to approach, revere, and pay homage to him; bhikshus also and bhikshuṇīs, upāsakas and upāsikās, kings and princes with their ministers and followers, minor wheel-rolling kings and great wheel-rolling kings with their seven treasures and their thousand princes and with their internal and external retinue, riding in their palatial chariots, will all come to listen to his Law. Because this bodhisattva so excellently preaches the Law, Brahmans, citizens, and the people in his country will follow, attend on, and pay homage to him to the end of their bodily life. And śrāvakas, pratyekabuddhas, bodhisattvas, and buddhas will always delight to see him. In whatever quarter this man abides, the buddhas will all preach toward him, and he will be able to receive and keep all the Buddha-law and also to utter the profound and beautiful sound of the Law."

Then the World-honored One, desiring to proclaim this teaching over again, spoke thus in verse:

"Pure is this man's organ of tongue,
Never receiving ill flavors:
Whatsoever he eats,
All becomes as nectar.
With lovely voice, profound and pure,
In the assembly he preaches the Law;
With reasonings and parables,
He leads on the minds of the living.
All his hearers rejoice
And make him the best of offerings.
Gods, dragons, and yakshas,
Asuras and others,
All with reverent minds
Come in company to hear his Law.
If this preacher desires
To make his lovely voice
Fill the three-thousandfold world,
He is able at will to achieve it.
Great and minor wheel-rolling kings
With their thousand princes and followers,
With folded hands and reverent minds,
Constantly come to hear his Law.
Gods, dragons, and yakshas,
Rākshasas and piśācakas
Also with joyful mind
Constantly rejoice to come and worship.
Brahma and Māra,
Iśvara and Maheśvara
And all such heavenly host
Come constantly to him.
Buddhas and their disciples,

Hearing the sound of his preaching,
Ever mind and protect him,
At times revealing themselves to him.

"Further, Ever Zealous! If any good son or good daughter receives and keeps this sutra, and either reads, or recites, or expounds, or copies it, he will obtain eight hundred merits of the body; he will obtain a pure body like pure crystal which all the living delight to see. Because of the purity of his body, the living beings of the three-thousand-great-thousandfold world, as they are born or die, superior or inferior, fine or ugly, born in good or in bad conditions, all will be displayed in [his body]. And Mount Iron Circle, Mount Great Iron Circle, Mount Meru, Mount Mahā-Meru, and other royal mountains, and the living beings in them, will all be displayed in [his body]. Downward to the Avīci hell, upward to the Summit of All Existence, all things and living beings will be displayed in [his body]. Śrāvakas, pratyekabuddhas, bodhisattvas, and buddhas preaching the Law will all display their forms and images in his body."

Then the World-honored One, desiring to proclaim this teaching over again, spoke thus in verse:

"If [anyone] keeps the Law-Flower Sutra,
His body will be utterly pure,
As that pure lapis lazuli;
All the living will delight to see it.
And as in a pure, bright mirror
Every image is seen,
The bodhisattva, in his pure body,
Sees everything in the world.
He himself alone sees clearly
What others do not see.
In the three-thousandfold world
All the common multitude,
Gods, men, asuras,
Beings in hell, demons, animals—
All such forms and images
Appear there in his body.
The palaces of the gods,

To the Summit of All Existence,
The Iron Circle and Meru,
Mount Mahā-Meru,
Great oceans and waters,
All appear in his body.
Buddhas and śrāvakas,
Buddha-sons, bodhisattvas,
Alone or preaching among the multitude,
All appear [in him].
Though not yet possessed of the flawless,
Mystic, spiritual body,
Yet in his pure ordinary body
Everything is revealed.

"Further, Ever Zealous! If any good son or good daughter, after the extinction of the Tathāgata, receives and keeps this sutra, or reads, or recites, or expounds, or copies it, he will obtain twelve hundred merits of thought. With this pure organ of thought, on hearing even a single verse or sentence he will penetrate its infinite and boundless meanings. Having discerned those meanings, he will be able to preach on that single sentence or verse for a month, four months, even a year. And that which he preaches, according to its several meanings, will not be contrary to the truth. If he refers to popular classics, maxims for ruling the world, means of livelihood, and so forth, all will coincide with the True Law. The beings in the six destinies of the three-thousand-great-thousandfold world, whatever is passing through their minds, whatever are the movements of their minds, whatever arguments are diverting their minds—he knows them all. Though such a one has not yet obtained faultless wisdom, yet his organ of thought will be pure like this. Whatever he ponders, estimates, and speaks, all will be the Buddha-law, nothing but truth, and also that which former buddhas have taught in the sutras."

Then the World-honored One, desiring to proclaim this meaning over again, spoke thus in verse:

"The thought of this man is pure,
Lucid, acute, unturbid;

By this mystic organ of thought
He knows all laws, high, low, and mean;
On hearing a single verse
He penetrates its infinite meanings,
And orderly preaches them as Law
For a month, four months, or a year.
All the living creatures of
This world, within and without,
Gods, dragons, human beings,
Yakshas, demons, spirits, others,
Those in the six destinations:
Whatever they may be thinking—
In reward for keeping the Law-Flower,
Instantly he knows them all.
The numberless buddhas of the universe,
With their hundreds of felicitous signs,
Who preach to all the living—
He hears and retains it all.
He ponders the infinite
And preaches the Law without limit,
Never forgets or makes a mistake,
Because he keeps the Law-Flower.
Knowing the form of all laws,
Perceiving their ordered meaning,
Comprehending the terms and words,
He explains them according to knowledge.
Whatever this man preaches
Is the Law of former buddhas;
And because he proclaims this Law,
He is fearless of the throng.
A keeper of the Law-Flower Sutra
Has an organ of thought like this.
Though not yet possessed of faultlessness,
He has such a foretoken as this.
This man, keeping this sutra,
Stands firm on a rare foundation;
By all living beings rejoiced in,

Beloved and reverenced,
He is able, with thousands of myriads
Of kinds of skillful expressions,
To interpret and preach to them
Through keeping the Law-Flower Sutra."

HERE ENDS
THE SIXTH FASCICLE

CHAPTER XX

The Bodhisattva Never Despise

AT THAT TIME the Buddha addressed the Bodhisattva-Mahāsattva Great Power Obtained:[1] "Now you should know that if bhikshus, bhikshuṇīs, upāsakas, and upāsikās keep the Law-Flower Sutra, and if anyone curses, abuses, and slanders them, he will receive such great punishment as before announced; but those who attain merits such as those previously announced, their eyes, ears, noses, tongues, bodies, and thoughts will be clear and pure.

"Great Power Obtained! In a past period of olden times, infinite, boundless, inconceivable, and asaṃkhyeya kalpas ago, there was a buddha named King of Majestic Voice Tathāgata, Worshipful, All Wise, Perfectly Enlightened in Conduct, Well Departed, Understander of the World, Peerless Leader, Controller, Teacher of Gods and Men, Buddha, World-honored One, whose kalpa was named

The translation of the name of the Bodhisattva Never Despise follows the T'ien-t'ai tradition. Kern translated the bodhisattva's Sanskrit name, Sadāparibhūta, as "always contemned" (*sadā* and *paribhūta*) and "always not-contemned, never contemned" (*sadā* and *aparibhūta;* see SBE vol. 21, p. 357 n). Dharmaraksha's Chinese translation reads "always contemned or despised." Here, according to the T'ien-t'ai reading, the name is rendered as "never despise."

1. He who has obtained or is endowed with great power or authority.

Free from Decline and his domain All Complete. That buddha, King of Majestic Voice, in that world preached to gods, men, and asuras. To those who sought to be śrāvakas he preached response to the Law of the Four Noble Truths for escape from birth, old age, disease, and death, [leading] finally to nirvana; to those who sought to be pratyekabuddhas he preached response to the Law of the Twelve Causes; to bodhisattvas he by means of Perfect Enlightenment preached response to the Six Pāramitās for the perfecting of Buddha-wisdom. Great Power Obtained! The lifetime of this buddha, King of Majestic Voice, was forty myriad koṭis of nayutas of kalpas, as many as the sands of the Ganges. The number of kalpas during which the Righteous Law remained in the world was equal to the atoms in a Jambudvīpa; and the number of kalpas during which the Counterfeit Law remained was equal to the atoms in four continents. After that buddha had abundantly benefited all living beings, he became extinct. After the Righteous Law and Counterfeit Law had entirely disappeared, in that domain there again appeared a buddha. He was also entitled King of Majestic Voice Tathāgata, Worshipful, All Wise, Perfectly Enlightened in Conduct, Well Departed, Understander of the World, Peerless Leader, Controller, Teacher of Gods and Men, Buddha, World-honored One. Thus in succession there were twenty thousand koṭis of buddhas who all had the same title. After the extinction of the first Tathāgata King of Majestic Voice and after the end of the Righteous Law, during [the period of] the Counterfeit Law bhikshus of utmost arrogance obtained the chief power. At that period there was a bodhisattva-bhikshu named Never Despise. Great Power Obtained! For what reason was he named Never Despise? [Because] that bhikshu paid respect to and commended everybody whom he saw, bhikshu, bhikshuṇī, upāsaka, upāsikā, speaking thus: 'I deeply revere you. I dare not slight and contemn you. Wherefore? [Because] you all walk in the bodhisattva-way and are to become buddhas.' And that bhikshu did not devote himself to reading and reciting the sutras but only to paying respect, so that when he saw afar off [a member of the] four groups, he would specially go and pay respect to them, commending them, saying: 'I dare not slight you, because you are all to become buddhas.' Amongst the four groups, there were those who, irritated and angry and muddy-minded, reviled and abused him, saying: 'Where did this ignorant bhikshu come from, who [takes it on] himself to say, "I do not slight you," and who predicts us as destined to become buddhas? We need no such false prediction.' Thus he passed many years, constantly reviled but never irritated or angry, always saying, 'You are to become buddhas.' Whenever he spoke thus, the people beat him with clubs, sticks, potsherds, or stones. But, while escaping to a distance, he still cried aloud: 'I dare not slight you. You are all to become buddhas.' And because he always spoke thus, the haughty bhikshus, bhikshuṇīs, upāsakas, and upāsikās styled him Never Despise.

"When this bhikshu was drawing near his end, from the sky he heard and was entirely able to receive and retain twenty thousand myriad koṭis of verses of the Lotus-Flower Sutra, which the Buddha King of Majestic Voice had formerly preached. Whereupon he obtained as above clearness and purity of the eye-organ and of the organs of ear, nose, tongue, body, and thought. Having obtained the purity of these six organs, he further prolonged his life for two hundred myriad koṭis of nayutas of years, and widely preached this Law-Flower Sutra to the people. Then the haughty four orders of bhikshus, bhikshuṇīs, upāsakas, and upāsikās who had slighted and contemned this man and given him the [nick]name Never Despise, seeing him possessed of great transcendent powers, of power of eloquent discourse, and of power of excellent meditation, and having heard his preaching, all believed in and followed him. This bodhisattva again converted thousands of myriads of koṭis of beings to Perfect Enlightenment.

"After the end of his lifetime, he met two thousand koṭis of buddhas who were all entitled Sun Moon Light, and under their Law he preached this Law-Flower Sutra. Because of this, he again met two thousand koṭis of buddhas, all equally entitled Sovereign Light King of the Clouds.[2] Because under the Law of those buddhas he received, kept, read, recited, and preached this sutra to all the four groups, he obtained clearness and purity of the common eye and of the organs of ear, nose, tongue, body, and thought, and among the four groups preached the Law fearlessly.

2. That is, Lightning King. Chapter 7 gives his name as Sovereign Cloud King. In the extant Sanskrit text, Dundubhisvararāja (literally, "Drum Sound King," that is, "Thunder") comes between the two kings Candrasvararāja (literally, "Moon Sound King") and Meghasvararāja (literally, "Cloud Sound King"). He is also included in Dharmaraksha's translation.

"Great Power Obtained! This Bodhisattva-Mahāsattva Never Despise paid homage to such numerous buddhas as these, revering, honoring, and extolling them; and after cultivating the roots of goodness, again he met thousands of myriads of koṭis of buddhas and also under the Law of those buddhas preached this sutra; his merits being complete, he then became a buddha. Great Power Obtained! What is your opinion? Can it be that the Bodhisattva Never Despise was at that time somebody else? He was [really] I myself. If I in my former lives had not received and kept, read and recited this sutra and preached it to others, I should not have been able so soon to attain Perfect Enlightenment. Because under former buddhas I received and kept, read and recited this sutra and preached it to others, I so soon attained Perfect Enlightenment.

"Great Power Obtained! At that time the four groups, bhikshus, bhikshuṇīs, upāsakas, and upāsikās, with angry minds slighted and contemned me, therefore for two hundred koṭis of kalpas they never met a buddha, never heard the Law, never saw a saṃgha, and for a thousand kalpas underwent great sufferings in the Avīci hell. After their sin was brought to an end, they again met the Bodhisattva Never Despise, who taught and converted them to Perfect Enlightenment. Great Power Obtained! What is your opinion? Those four groups at that time, who constantly slighted that bodhisattva—can they indeed be somebody else? They are now in this assembly—the five hundred bodhisattvas Bhadrapāla and the others, the five hundred bhikshuṇīs Lion Moon and the others, the five hundred upāsakas Thinking of Buddha and the others,[3] who all never retreat from Perfect Enlightenment. Know, Great Power Obtained! This Law-Flower Sutra greatly benefits all bodhisattva-mahāsattvas and enables them to reach Perfect Enlightenment. Therefore all bodhisattva-mahāsattvas, after the extinction of the Tathāgata, should ever receive and keep, read and recite, expound and copy this sutra."

Then the World-honored One, desiring to proclaim this teaching over again, spoke thus in verse:

3. Some read this as "the five hundred bhikshus Lion Moon and others, and the five hundred upāsakas Buddha Thinking Nun and others." The extant Sanskrit text has "upāsikās" instead of "upāsakas." Kern has "lay devotees," saying in a note, "*upāsaka*, masculine; this does not suit" (SBE vol. 21, p. 360 n).

"In the past there was a buddha
Styled King of Majestic Voice,
Boundless in divine wisdom,
Leader of all creatures;
Gods, men, dragons, spirits
All paid homage to him.
After this buddha's extinction,
When the Law drew near its end,
There existed a bodhisattva
Whose name was Never Despise.
At that time the four groups
Were devoted to [material] things.
The Bodhisattva Never Despise
On approaching them
Would address them thus:
'I may not despise you;
You are followers of the Way
And will all become buddhas.'
When they had heard it, they
Contemned or reviled him.
Bodhisattva Never Despise
Bore it all patiently.
When his sins were expiated
And his end was drawing near,
He heard this sutra
And his organs were clarified.
By his transcendent power
He prolonged his period of life
And again, to all the people,
Widely preached this sutra.
The groups [formerly] devoted to things
All received from this bodhisattva
Instruction and perfection,
Being led to abide in the Buddha-way.
Never Despise, his lifetime ended,
Met with countless buddhas,
And through his preaching of this sutra

Obtained inestimable happiness.
Gradually perfecting his merits,
He soon accomplished the Buddha-way.
The Never Despise of that time
Is really I myself.
The four groups of that time,
Attached to [earthly] things,
Who heard Never Despise say,
'You are to become buddhas,'
And who because of this
Met with countless buddhas,
Are the bodhisattvas of this assembly,
The host of five hundred,
And also the four sections
Of pure believers, men and women,
Who are now before me
Listening to the Law.
I, in my former lives,
Exhorted these people
To hear and receive this sutra,
The peerless Law,
And revealed and taught it to men,
That they might abide in nirvana.
Age by age have [I] received and kept
This so [wonderful] a sutra.
During myriads of koṭis and koṭis of kalpas
Of inconceivable reach,
Rare are the times that have heard
This Law-Flower Sutra.
During myriads of koṭis and koṭis of kalpas
Of inconceivable reach,
Buddhas, world-honored ones,
At rare times preach this sutra.
Therefore let his followers,
After the Buddha's extinction,
On hearing such a sutra as this,
Not conceive doubt or perplexity.

But let them wholeheartedly
Publish abroad this sutra,
And age by age meeting buddhas,
They will speedily accomplish the Buddha-way."

CHAPTER XXI

The Divine Power of the Tathagata

AT THAT TIME the bodhisattva-mahāsattvas, equal to the atoms of a [great-]thousandfold world, who had sprung up from the earth, all before the Buddha with one mind folded their hands, looked up into his noble countenance, and spoke to the Buddha, saying: "World-honored One! After the extinction of the Buddha, in whatever lands the transformed body of the World-honored One exists, wherever he is extinct, we will widely preach this sutra. Wherefore? [Because] we also ourselves wish to obtain this truly pure Great Law in order to receive and keep, read and recite, explain, copy, and make offerings to it."

Thereupon the World-honored One, before Mañjuśrī and the other countless hundred thousand myriad koṭis of bodhisattva-mahāsattvas, as well as of bhikshus, bhikshuṇīs, upāsakas, upāsikās, gods, dragons, yakshas, gandharvas, asuras, garuḍas, kiṃnaras, mahoragas, human and nonhuman beings, and so on,[1] [before] all these creatures, revealed

1. The extant Sanskrit text here has the following sentences, not found in any Chinese translation, as the words of these countless beings to the World-honored One: ". . . said unto the Lord: We also, O Lord, will promulgate this Dharmaparyāya after the complete extinction of the Tathāgata. While standing with an

his great divine power, putting forth his broad and far-stretched tongue till it reached upward to the Brahma world, every pore radiating the light of infinite and numberless colors, all shining everywhere throughout all directions of the universe. Under all the jewel trees the buddhas, each seated on a lion throne, also in like manner put forth their broad and far-stretched tongues radiating infinite light.

While Sakyamuni Buddha and all the [other] buddhas under the jewel trees were revealing their divine powers, hundreds of thousands of years had fully passed. After that they drew back their tongues, coughed simultaneously, and snapped their fingers in unison. These two sounds reached through every direction of buddha worlds, all their lands being shaken in six ways. In the midst of these [worlds] all living beings, gods, dragons, yakshas, gandharvas, asuras, garuḍas, kiṃnaras, mahoragas, human and nonhuman beings, and the other creatures, by reason of the divine power of the Buddha, all saw in this sahā-world the infinite, boundless hundred thousand myriad koṭis of buddhas seated on the lion thrones under all the jewel trees, and saw Sakyamuni Buddha together with the Tathāgata Abundant Treasures seated on lion thrones in the midst of the stupa, and also saw the infinite, boundless hundred thousand myriad koṭis of bodhisattva-mahāsattvas, and the four groups who reverently surround Sakyamuni Buddha. After beholding this they were all greatly delighted, obtaining that which they had never experienced before. At the same time all the gods in the sky sang with exalted voices: "Beyond these infinite, boundless hundreds of thousands of myriads of koṭis of asaṃkhyeya worlds, there is a realm named sahā. In its midst is a buddha, whose name is Sakyamuni. Now, for the sake of all bodhisattva-mahāsattvas, he preaches the Great-vehicle Sutra called the Lotus Flower of the Wonderful Law, the Law by which bodhisattvas are

invisible body in the sky, O Lord, we will send forth a voice, and plant the roots of goodness of such creatures as have not (yet) planted roots of goodness. Then the Lord addressed the Bodhisattva Mahāsattva Viśishṭacāritra, who was the very first of those afore-mentioned Bodhisattvas Mahāsattvas followed by a troop, a great troop, masters of a troop: Very well, Viśishṭacāritra, very well; so you should do; it is for the sake of this Dharmaparyāya that the Tathāgata &c., and the wholly extinct Lord Prabhūtaratna, the Tathāgata, &c., both seated on the throne in the centre of the Stūpa, commenced smiling to one another and . . ." (Quoted from Kern, SBE vol. 21, pp. 363–64).

instructed and which the buddhas watch over and keep in mind. You should with all your utmost heart joyfully follow it and should pay homage and make offerings to Sakyamuni Buddha."

All those living beings, after hearing the voice in the sky, folded their hands toward the sahā-world and thus exclaimed: "Namaḥ Sakyamuni Buddha! Namaḥ Sakyamuni Buddha!" [Then] with various flowers, incense, garlands, canopies, as well as personal ornaments, gems, and wonderful things, they all from afar strewed the sahā-world. The things so strewn from every quarter were like gathering clouds, transforming into a jeweled canopy, covering all the place above the buddhas. Thereupon the worlds of the universe were united as one buddha-land.

At that time the Buddha addressed Eminent Conduct and the host of other bodhisattvas: "The divine powers of buddhas are so infinite and boundless that they are beyond thought and expression. Even if I, by these divine powers, through infinite, boundless hundred thousand myriad koṭis of asaṃkhyeya kalpas, for the sake of entailing it, were to declare the merits of this sutra, I should still be unable to reach the end of those [merits]. Essentially speaking, all the laws belonging to the Tathāgata, all the sovereign, divine powers of the Tathāgata, all the mysterious, essential treasuries of the Tathāgata, and the very profound conditions of the Tathāgata, all are proclaimed, displayed, revealed, and expounded in this sutra. Therefore you should, after the extinction of the Tathāgata, wholeheartedly receive and keep, read and recite, explain and copy, cultivate and practice it as the teaching. In whatever land, whether it be received and kept, read and recited, explained and copied, cultivated and practiced as the teaching; whether in a place where a volume of the sutra is kept, or in a temple, or in a grove, or under a tree, or in a monastery, or in a lay devotee's house, in a palace or a mountain, in a valley or in the wilderness, in all these places you must erect a caitya and make offerings. Wherefore? You should know that [all] these spots are the thrones of enlightenment. On these [spots] the buddhas attain Perfect Enlightenment; on these [spots] the buddhas roll the wheel of the Law; on these [spots] the buddhas [enter] parinirvāṇa."

At that time the World-honored One, desiring to proclaim this teaching over again, spoke thus in verse:

"All the buddhas, saviors of the world,
Dwelling in mighty divine penetration,
In order to gladden all creatures
Reveal their infinite powers divine.
Their tongues extend to the Brahma heavens,
Their bodies emit countless rays of light;
For those who seek the Way of the Buddha
They show this rare phenomenon.
The sound when the buddhas cough
And that of the snap of their fingers
Are heard throughout the whole universe,
And the earth in six ways shakes.
Because, after the Buddha's extinction,
It is possible to possess this sutra,
The buddhas all rejoice
And show infinite powers divine.
Now that this sutra is entailed
To him who keeps it, let praise,
Through kalpas infinite,
Be inexhaustible.
The merits of this man
Shall be boundless and without end
As space in every direction,
Which cannot find a limit.
He who can keep this sutra
Is one who already beholds me
And also the Buddha Abundant Treasures,
And all buddhas emanated [from me],
And sees besides the bodhisattvas
Whom I have instructed until now.
He who can keep this sutra
Will cause me and the [buddhas] emanated from me,
And the Buddha Abundant Treasures in nirvana,
All of us entirely to rejoice;
And the buddhas now in the universe,
And those of the past and the future,
He shall also see and serve

And cause to rejoice.
The mysterious laws that have been attained
By the buddhas each on his wisdom throne,
He who can keep this sutra
Must surely gain ere long.
He who can keep this sutra
Shall the meaning of the laws,
With their terms and expressions,
Delightedly expound without end,
Like the wind in the sky,
Which never has impediment.
After the Tathāgata is extinct [such a one],
Knowing [this] sutra that the Buddha has taught,
[Together with] its reasoning and process,
Shall expound it according to its true meaning.
Just as the light of the sun and moon
Can dispel the darkness,
So this man, working in the world,
Can disperse the gloom of the living
And cause numberless bodhisattvas
Finally to abide in the One-vehicle.
Therefore he who has wisdom,
Hearing the benefits of this merit,
After I am extinct,
Should receive and keep this sutra.
This man shall in the Way of the Buddha
Be fixed and have no doubts."

CHAPTER XXII

The Final Commission

AT THAT TIME Sakyamuni Buddha rose from his Law seat, manifesting supernatural powers, laid his right hand on the heads of the innumerable bodhisattva-mahāsattvas, and spoke thus: "I, for incalculable hundreds of thousands of myriads of koṭis of nayutas of kalpas, have practiced this rare Law of Perfect Enlightenment. Now I entrust it to you. Do you wholeheartedly promulgate this Law and make it increase and prosper far and wide."

In like manner three times he laid his hand upon the heads of the bodhisattva-mahāsattvas and spoke thus: "I, for incalculable hundreds of thousands of myriads of koṭis of nayutas of kalpas, have practiced this rare Law of Perfect Enlightenment. Now I entrust it to you. Do you receive and keep, read and recite, and proclaim this Law abroad that all living beings universally may hear and know it. Wherefore?

The extant Sanskrit text and all other Chinese translations place this chapter last in this sutra, but internal evidence supports the idea that Kumārajīva's version is correct in placing it here. This chapter contains the final sermon to the assembly in the sky, which begins in chapter 11; the remaining six chapters of the sutra give the later semons on Mount Gṛdhrakūṭa, the early sermons there being given in chapters 1 to 10. The sutra includes three assemblies in two places: two on Mount Gṛdhrakūṭa and one in the sky.

The Tathāgata is most benevolent and compassionate, not mean and stingy, and is able fearlessly to give the Buddha-wisdom, the Tathāgata-wisdom, and the Self-existent wisdom to all living beings. The Tathāgata is the great lord of giving to all living beings. Do you also follow and learn the Tathāgata's example, not being mean and stingy. If good sons or good daughters in ages to come believe in the Tathāgata-wisdom, do you proclaim this Law-Flower Sutra to them that they may hear and know it, in order that they may obtain the Buddha-wisdom. If there be living beings who do not believe in it, do you show, teach, benefit, and rejoice them with the other [tactful] profound laws of the Tathāgata. If you are able thus to act, then you will have repaid the grace of the buddhas."

Thereupon all the bodhisattva-mahāsattvas, having heard the Buddha give this address, were all filled with great joy and paid him added reverence, bowing themselves, bending their heads, and with folded hands saluting the Buddha, crying with united voice: "We will do all as the World-honored One has commanded. Yea, World-honored One! Have no anxiety." Three times in such manner did all the host of bodhisattva-mahāsattvas cry with united voice: "We will do all as the World-honored One has commanded. Yea, World-honored One! Have no anxiety."

Thereupon Sakyamuni Buddha caused all the emanated buddhas, who had come from all directions, each to return to his own land, saying: "Buddhas! Peace be unto you. Let the stupa of the Buddha Abundant Treasures be restored as before."

As these words were spoken, the innumerable emanated buddhas from all directions, who were seated on lion thrones under the jewel trees, as well as the Buddha Abundant Treasures, the host of infinite asaṃkhyeyas of bodhisattvas, Eminent Conduct and others, also the four groups of hearers, Śāriputra and others, and all the worlds, gods, men, asuras, and so on, hearing the preaching of the Buddha, rejoiced greatly.

CHAPTER XXIII

The Story of the Bodhisattva Medicine King

AT THAT TIME the Bodhisattva Star Constellation King Flower addressed the Buddha, saying: "World-honored One! Why does the Medicine King Bodhisattva wander in the sahā-world? World-honored One! What hundreds of thousands of myriads of koṭis of nayutas of distresses the Bodhisattva Medicine King has to suffer! Excellent [will it be], World-honored One, if you will be pleased to explain a little, so that the gods, dragon spirits, yakshas, gandharvas, asuras, garuḍas, kiṃnaras, mahoragas, human and non-human beings, and the bodhisattvas who have come from other lands, as well as these śrāvakas, hearing it will all rejoice."

Thereupon the Buddha addressed the Bodhisattva Star Constellation King Flower: "Of yore, in the past, kalpas ago incalculable as the sands of the Ganges River, there was a buddha entitled Sun Moon Brilliance Tathāgata, Worshipful, All Wise, Perfectly Enlightened in Conduct, Well Departed, Understander of the World, Peerless Leader, Controller, Teacher of Gods and Men, Buddha, World-honored One. That buddha had eighty koṭis of great bodhisattva-mahāsattvas

The title of this chapter, literally, is "the chapter of the former [fundamental] deed of the Bodhisattva Medicine King."

and a great assembly of śrāvakas [numerous] as the sands of seventy-two Ganges rivers. The lifetime of that buddha was forty-two thousand kalpas, and the lifetime of his bodhisattvas was the same. His domain had no women, no hells, no hungry ghosts, no animals, no asuras, and no disasters; its land was level as one's palm and made of lapis lazuli; it was adorned with jewel trees, covered with jewel curtains, hung with flags of jewel flowers, and jeweled vases and censers were [seen] everywhere in the country. Terraces were there of the precious seven, with trees for each terrace, the trees distant from it a full arrow's flight.[1] Under all these jewel trees bodhisattvas and śrāvakas were seated. Above each of these platforms were a hundred koṭis of gods performing celestial music and singing praises to the buddha in homage to him. Then that buddha preached the Law-Flower Sutra to the Bodhisattva Loveliness[2] and all the bodhisattvas and host of śrāvakas. This Bodhisattva Loveliness had rejoiced to follow the course of suffering and in the Law of the Buddha Sun Moon Brilliance had made zealous progress, wandering about single-mindedly seeking the Buddha for fully twelve thousand years, after which he attained the contemplation of revelation of all forms.[3] Having attained this contemplation he was very joyful and reflected thus, saying: 'My attainment of the contemplation of revelation of all forms is entirely due to the power [resulting] from hearing the Law-Flower Sutra. Let me now pay homage to the Buddha Sun Moon Brilliance and the Law-Flower Sutra.' No sooner did he enter into this contemplation than [he] rained from the sky mandārava flowers, mahā-mandārava flowers, and fine dust of hard and black sandalwood, which filled the sky and descended like a cloud; [he] rained also incense of inner-sea-shore sandalwood;[4] six karshas of this incense are worth a sahā-world. [All this he did] in homage to the Buddha.

"Having made this offering, he arose from contemplation and reflected within himself, thus saying: 'Though I by my supernatural power have paid homage to the Buddha, it is not as good as offering

1. An arrow's flight is considered to be 120, 130, 140, or 150 steps.

2. Literally, "whom all creatures delight to see."

3. In this contemplation the bodies or forms of all beings appear.

4. Literally, "this [south] shore of the [inner] sea [of Mount Sumeru]," where this kind of sandalwood is said to be found.

my body.' Thereupon he partook of many kinds of incense—sandalwood, kunduruka, turushka, pṛikkā, aloes, and resin incense—and drank the essential oil of campaka and other flowers. After fully twelve hundred years, he anointed his body with perfumed unguents, and in the presence of the Buddha Sun Moon Brilliance wrapped himself in a celestial precious garment, bathed in perfumed oil, and by his transcendent vow burned his own body. Its brightness universally illuminated worlds fully numerous as the sands of eighty koṭis of Ganges rivers, whose buddhas simultaneously extolled him, saying: 'Good, good! Good son! This is true zeal. It is called the True Law Homage to the Tathāgata. Offerings of flowers, scents, necklaces, incense, sandal powder, unguents, flags and canopies of celestial silk, and incense of inner-sea-shore sandalwood, offerings of such various things as these cannot match it, nor can the giving of alms, countries, cities, wives, and children match it. My good son! This is called the supreme gift, the most honored and sublime of gifts, because it is the Law homage to the tathāgatas.' After making this statement they all became silent.

"His body continued burning for twelve hundred years, after which his body came to an end.

"The Bodhisattva Loveliness, after making such a Law offering as this, on his death was again born in the domain of the Buddha Sun Moon Brilliance, being suddenly metamorphosed, sitting cross-legged in the house of King Pure Virtue, to [whom as] his father he forthwith spoke thus in verse:

'Know, O great king!
Sojourning in that other abode,
I instantly attained the contemplation of
The revelation of all forms,
And devotedly performed a deed of great zeal
By sacrificing the body I loved.'

"After uttering this verse, he spoke to his father, saying: 'The Buddha Sun Moon Brilliance is still existing as of yore. Having first paid homage to that buddha, I obtained the dhāraṇī of interpreting the utterances of all the living, and moreover heard this Law-Flower Sutra

[in] eight hundred thousand myriad koṭis [of] nayutas, kaṅkaras, bimbaras, akshobhyas of verses. Great king! I ought now to return and pay homage to that buddha.' Having said this, he thereupon took his seat on a tower of the precious seven, arose in the sky as high as seven tāla trees, and on reaching that buddha, bowed down to his feet, and folding his ten fingers, extolled the buddha in verse:

'Countenance most wonderful,
Radiance illuminating the universe:
Formerly I paid homage to thee,
Now again I return to behold.'

"Then the Bodhisattva Loveliness, having uttered this verse, spoke to that buddha, saying: 'World-honored One! The World-honored One is still present in the world.'

"Thereupon the Buddha Sun Moon Brilliance addressed the Bodhisattva Loveliness: 'My good son! The time of my nirvana has come. The time of my extinction has arrived. You may arrange my bed. Tonight I shall enter parinirvāṇa.' Again he commanded the Bodhisattva Loveliness: 'My good son! I commit the Buddha-law to you. And I deliver to you all [my] bodhisattvas and chief disciples, [my] Law of Perfect Enlightenment, also [my] three-thousand-great-thousandfold world [made] of the precious seven, [its] jewel trees and jewel towers, and my celestial attendants. I also entrust to you whatever relics may remain after my extinction. Let them be distributed and paid homage to far and wide. Let some thousands of stupas be erected.' The Buddha Sun Moon Brilliance, having thus commanded the Bodhisattva Loveliness, in the last division of the night entered into nirvana.

"Thereupon the Bodhisattva Loveliness, seeing the buddha was extinct, mourned, was deeply moved and distressed, and ardently longed for him. Then piling up a pyre of inner-sea-shore sandalwood, he paid homage to the body of that buddha and burned it. After the fire died out he gathered the relics, made eighty-four thousand precious urns, and erected eighty-four thousand stupas high as a threefold world, adorned with banner towers, hung with flags and canopies and with many precious bells. Then the Bodhisattva Loveliness again reflected within himself, saying: 'Though I have paid this homage, my mind is not yet satisfied. Let me pay still further homage to the relics.' Thereupon he addressed the bodhisattvas and chief disciples, as well as gods, dragons, yakshas, and all the host, saying: 'Pay attention with all your mind, [for] I am now about to pay homage to the relics of the Buddha Sun Moon Brilliance.' Having said this, he thereupon before the eighty-four thousand stupas burned his arms, with their hundred felicitous signs, for seventy-two thousand years in homage to him, and led a numberless host of seekers after śrāvakaship and countless asaṃkhyeyas of people to set their mind on Perfect Enlightenment, causing them all to abide in the contemplation of revelation of all forms.

"Then all those bodhisattvas, gods, men, asuras, and others, seeing him without arms, were sorrowful and distressed and lamented, saying: 'This Bodhisattva Loveliness is indeed our teacher and instructor, but now his arms are burned off and his body is deformed.' Thereupon the Bodhisattva Loveliness in the great assembly made this vow, saying: 'Having given up both my arms, I shall [yet] assuredly obtain a buddha's golden body. If this [assurance] be true and not false, let both my arms be restored as they were before.' As soon as he had made this vow, [his arms] were of themselves restored, [all] brought to pass through the excellence of this bodhisattva's felicitous virtue and wisdom. At that moment the three-thousand-great-thousandfold world was shaken in the six ways, the sky rained various flowers, and gods and men all attained that which they had never before experienced."

The Buddha [then] addressed the Bodhisattva Star Constellation King Flower: "In your opinion what say you, was the Bodhisattva Loveliness some other person? It was indeed the present Medicine King Bodhisattva. His self-sacrifice and gifts were of such countless hundred thousand myriad koṭis of nayutas in number as these. Star Constellation King Flower! If anyone with his mind set on and aiming at Perfect Enlightenment is able to burn the fingers of his hand or even a toe of his foot in homage to a buddha's stupa he will surpass him who pays homage with domains, cities, wives, children, and his three-thousand-great-thousandfold land with its mountains, forests, rivers, pools, and all its precious things.

"Again, if anyone offers a three-thousand-great-thousandfold world full of the seven precious things in homage to buddhas, great bodhisattvas, pratyekabuddhas, and arhats, the merit this man gains is not equal to the surpassing happiness of him who receives and keeps but a single fourfold verse of this Law-Flower Sutra.

"Star Constellation King Flower! Suppose just as amongst all brooks, streams, rivers, canals, and all other waters the sea is the supreme, so is it also with this Law-Flower Sutra; amongst all the sutras preached by tathāgatas it is the profoundest and greatest. And just as amongst all mountains—the earth mountains, the Black Mountains,[5] the Small Iron Circle Mountains, the Great Iron Circle Mountains, the ten precious mountains, and all other mountains—it is Mount Sumeru which is the supreme, so is it also with this Law-Flower Sutra; amongst all sutras it is the highest. Again, just as amongst all stars the princely moon is the supreme, so is it also with this Law-Flower Sutra; amongst thousands of myriads of koṭis of kinds of sutra-law it is the most illuminating. Further, just as the princely sun is able to disperse all darkness, so is it also with this sutra; it is able to dispel all unholy darkness. Again, just as amongst all minor kings the holy wheel-rolling king is supreme, so is it also with this sutra; amongst all the sutras it is the most honorable. Again just as what Śakra is amongst the gods of the thirty-three heavens, so is it also with this sutra; it is the king of all sutras. Again, just as the Great Brahma Heavenly King is the father of all living beings, so is it also with this sutra; it is the father of all the wise and holy men, of those training and the trained, and of the bodhisattva-minded. Again, just as amongst all the common people srota-āpanna, sakṛdāgāmin, anāgāmin, arhat, and pratyekabuddha are the foremost, so is it also with this sutra; amongst all the sutras preached by tathāgatas, preached by bodhisattvas, or preached by śrāvakas, it is the supreme. So is it also with those who are able to receive and keep this sutra—among all the living they are supreme. Amongst all śrāvakas and pratyekabuddhas, bodhisattvas are supreme; so is it also with this sutra; amongst all the sutras, it is the supreme. Just as the buddha is king of the laws, so is it also with this sutra; it is king amongst the sutras.

"Star Constellation King Flower! This sutra is that which can save all the living; this sutra can deliver all the living from pains and sufferings; this sutra is able greatly to benefit all the living and fulfill their

5. According to the *Abhidharma Kośa,* there are three such mountains in the northern quarter of the continent of Jambudvīpa.

desires. Just as a clear, cool pool is able to satisfy all those who are thirsty, as the cold who obtain a fire [are satisfied], as the naked who find clothing, as [a caravan of] merchants who find a leader, as children who find their mother, as at a ferry one who catches the boat, as a sick man who finds a doctor, as in the darkness one who obtains a lamp, as a poor man who finds a jewel, as people who find a king, as merchant venturers who gain the sea, and as a torch which dispels the darkness, so is it also with this Law-Flower Sutra; it is able to deliver all the living from all sufferings and all diseases, and is able to unloose all the bonds of mortal life.

"If anyone, hearing this Law-Flower Sutra, either himself copies or causes others to copy it, the limits of the sum of merit to be obtained cannot be calculated [even] by the Buddha-wisdom. If anyone copies this sutra and pays homage to it with flowers, scents, necklaces, incense, sandal powder, unguents, flags, canopies, garments, and various kinds of lamps, ghee lamps, oil lamps, lamps of scented oil, lamps of campaka oil, lamps of sumana oil, lamps of pāṭala oil, lamps of vārshika oil, and lamps of navamālikā oil, the merit to be obtained by him is equally inestimable.

"Star Constellation King Flower! If there be anyone who hears this chapter of the former deeds of the Medicine King Bodhisattva, he will also obtain infinite and boundless merits. If there be any woman who hears this chapter of the former deeds of the Medicine King Bodhisattva and is able to receive and keep it, she, after the end of her present woman's body, will not again receive [one]. If, after the extinction of the Buddha, in the last five hundred years,[6] there be any woman who hears this sutra and acts according to its teaching, at the close of this life she will go to the Happy World, where Amita Buddha dwells, encompassed by his host of great bodhisattvas, and will [there] be

6. According to the *Mahāsaṃnipāta Sūtra*, after the parinirvāṇa of Sakyamuni Buddha there would be five periods of five hundred years each: (1) the period in which people's minds are fixed on and devoted to salvation; (2) the period devoted to meditation; these two are the periods in which the Righteous Law in its purity is maintained; (3) the period of devotion to reading and intoning, or the letter of the Law; (4) the period of devotion to erecting stupas and temples; these two are the periods of the Counterfeit Law; and (5) the period of the disappearance of the White, or True, Law and of devotion to strife and division; this final five hundred years is the beginning of the period of the Decay of the Law.

born in the middle of a lotus flower upon a jeweled throne. Never again will he[7] be harassed by desire, nor be harassed by anger and foolishness, nor again be harassed by pride, envy, or uncleanliness, [but] will attain transcendent [powers] and the assurance of no [re]birth; and having obtained this assurance, his organ of the eye will be serene, by which serene organ of the eye he will see seven million two thousand koṭis of nayutas of buddha-tathāgatas equal to the sands of the Ganges river, when these buddhas from afar will unite in lauding him, saying: 'Excellent, excellent! Good son! You have been able to receive and keep, read and recite, and ponder this sutra in the Law of Sakyamuni Buddha and to expound it to others. The blessed merit you have obtained is infinite and boundless; fire cannot burn it, water cannot wash it away. Your merit is beyond the powers of a thousand buddhas to explain. You have now been able to destroy the Māra-marauders, to overthrow the [hostile] forces of mortality, and to crush all other enemies. Good son! Hundreds of thousands of buddhas, with their transcendent powers, together guard and protect you. Among the gods and men of all worlds none can equal you except the Tathāgata. The wisdom and meditation of śrāvakas, pratyekabuddhas, or even bodhisattvas does not equal yours.' Star Constellation King Flower! Such is the power of the merit and wisdom attained by this bodhisattva.

"If there be anyone who, hearing this chapter of the former deeds of the Medicine King Bodhisattva, is able joyfully to receive and applaud it, that man during his present life will ever breathe out the fragrance of the blue lotus flower, and from the pores of his body will ever emit the fragrance of ox-head sandalwood; and his merit will be as above stated. Therefore, Star Constellation King Flower, I commit to you this chapter of the former deeds of the Medicine King. In the last five hundred years, after my extinction, proclaim and spread it abroad in Jambudvīpa, lest it be lost and Māra the Evil [One], his Māra-people, gods, dragons, yakshas, kumbhāṇḍas, and others gain their opportunity. Star Constellation King Flower! Guard and protect this sutra by your transcendent powers. Wherefore? [Because] this sutra is good medicine for the diseases of the Jambudvīpa people. If a man be sick, on hearing this sutra his sickness will instantly disappear

7. The transformed woman. Following the extant Sanskrit text, the feminine gender now changes to the masculine.

and he will neither grow old nor die. Star Constellation King Flower! If you see anyone who receives and keeps this sutra, you should strew upon him blue lotus flowers full of sandal powder, and after strewing them thus reflect: 'This man ere long will accept the bundle of grass[8] and take his seat on the wisdom plot; he will break the Māra host, and blowing the conch of the Law and beating the drum of the Great Law, he will deliver all living beings from the sea of old age, disease, and death.' Therefore he who seeks the Buddha-way, on seeing a man who receives and keeps this sutra, should thus beget a reverent mind."

While this chapter of the former deeds of the Medicine King Bodhisattva was being preached, eighty-four thousand bodhisattvas attained the dhāraṇī of interpreting the utterances of all the living. The Tathāgata Abundant Treasures in the Precious Stupa extolled the Bodhisattva Star Constellation King Flower, saying: "Excellent, excellent, Star Constellation King Flower! You have accomplished inconceivable merits, for you have been able to ask Sakyamuni Buddha such things as these and have infinitely benefited all the living."

8. As the Buddha is said to have accepted a bundle of grass from Svastika the grass-cutter when on his way to the Bodhi tree prior to his enlightenment.

CHAPTER XXIV

The Bodhisattva Wonder Sound

THEN SAKYAMUNI Buddha emitted a ray of light from the protuberance [on his cranium],[1] the sign of a great man, and emitted a ray of light from the white hair-circle sign between his eyebrows, everywhere illuminating eastward a hundred and eight myriad koṭis of nayutas of buddha-worlds, equal to the sands of the Ganges. Beyond those numbers [of worlds] is a world named Adorned with Pure Radiance.[2] In that domain there is a buddha styled King Wisdom of the Pure Flower Constellation[3] Tathāgata, Worshipful, All Wise, Perfectly Enlightened in Conduct, Well Departed, Understander of the World, Peerless Leader, Controller, Teacher of Gods and Men, Buddha, World-honored One. Revered and surrounded by a great host of incalculable and countless bodhisattvas, he preached the Law to them. The ray of light from the white hair-circle of Sakyamuni Buddha shone throughout their domain.

1. A protuberance on a buddha's cranium forming a natural hair tuft; this is the first of the thirty-two signs of a buddha.

2. Kern has "embellish by the rays of the sun."

3. Literally, "the king of the constellation [called] pure flower and buddha of wisdom."

At that time in the domain Adorned With All Pure Radiance there was a bodhisattva whose name was Wonder Sound,[4] who for long had cultivated many roots of virtue, paid homage to and courted innumerable hundred thousand myriad koṭis of buddhas, and perfectly acquired profound wisdom. He had attained the contemplation of the wonderful banner sign, the contemplation of the Law-Flower, the contemplation of pure virtue, the contemplation of the Constellation King's sport, the contemplation of causelessness,[5] the contemplation of the knowledge seal, the contemplation of interpreting the utterances of all beings, the contemplation of collection of all merits, the contemplation of purity, the contemplation of supernatural sport, the contemplation of wisdom torch, the contemplation of the king of adornment, the contemplation of pure luster, the contemplation of the pure treasury, the contemplation of the unique, and the contemplation of sun revolution: such hundreds of thousands of myriads of koṭis of great contemplations as these had he acquired, equal to the sands of the Ganges. No sooner had the ray from Sakyamuni Buddha shone upon him than he said to the Buddha King Wisdom of the Pure Flower Constellation: "World-honored One! I should go to visit the sahā-world to salute, approach, and pay homage to Sakyamuni Buddha, as well as to see the Bodhisattva Mañjuśrī, son of the Law-king, the Bodhisattva Medicine King, the Bodhisattva Courageous Giver, the Bodhisattva Star Constellation King Flower, the Bodhisattva Mind for Higher Deeds,[6] the Bodhisattva King of Adornment, and the Bodhisattva Medicine Lord."

Then the Buddha King Wisdom of the Pure Flower Constellation addressed the Bodhisattva Wonder Sound: "Do not look lightly on that domain or conceive a low opinion of it. Good son! That sahā-world with its high and low [places] is uneven and full of earth, stones, hills, and filth; the body of the Buddha is short and small, and all the bodhisattvas are small of stature, whereas your body is forty-two

4. The Sanskrit *gadgada* means "stammering, stuttering" but is also used with the opposite meaning, "sounding beautiful or wonderful."

5. Not caused but causing; universal benevolence.

6. The extant Sanskrit text has "Viśishṭacāritra," which is rendered by Kumārajīva as "Eminent Conduct" in chapters 15, 21, and 22. According to his version Viśishṭacāritra disappears with the close of the assembly in chapter 22. This Bodhisattva Mind for Higher Deeds may therefore be another Viśishṭacāritra. Dharmaraksha's version has "Honorable Thought Conduct."

thousand yojanas [high] and my body six million, eight hundred thousand yojanas. Your body is of the finest order, [blessed with] hundreds of thousands of myriads of felicities, and of a wonderful brightness. Therefore on going there do not look lightly on that domain, nor conceive a low opinion of the Buddha, nor of the bodhisattvas, nor of [their] country."

The Bodhisattva Wonder Sound replied to that buddha: "World-honored One! That I now go to visit the sahā-world is all due to the Tathāgata's power, the Tathāgata's magic play, and the Tathāgata's adornment of merit and wisdom."

Thereupon the Bodhisattva Wonder Sound, without rising from his seat and without stirring his body, entered into contemplation. By the power of his contemplation, on Mount Gṛdhrakūṭa, not far distant from the Law seat, there appeared in transformation eighty-four thousand precious lotus flowers with stalks of jambūnada gold, leaves of white silver, stamens of diamond, and cups of kiṁśuka gems.

Thereupon Mañjuśrī, son of the Law-king, seeing those lotus flowers, said to the Buddha: "World-honored One! For what reason does this auspicious sign first appear? There are some thousands and myriads of lotus flowers with stalks of jambūnada gold, leaves of white silver, stamens of diamond, and with cups of kiṁśuka gems." Then Sakyamuni Buddha informed Mañjuśrī: "It is the Bodhisattva-Mahāsattva Wonder Sound who desires to come from the domain of the Buddha King Wisdom of the Pure Flower Constellation, with his company of eighty-four thousand bodhisattvas, to this sahā-world in order to pay homage to, draw nigh to, and salute me, and who also desires to pay homage to and hear the Law-Flower Sutra." Mañjuśrī said to the Buddha: "World-honored One! What roots of goodness has that bodhisattva planted, what merits has he cultivated, that he should be able to have such great transcendent power? What contemplation does he practice? Be pleased to tell us the name of this contemplation; we also desire diligently to practice it, [for] by practicing this contemplation, we may be able to see that bodhisattva—his color, form, and size, his dignity and behavior. Be pleased, World-honored One, by [thy] transcendent power, to let us see the coming of that bodhisattva."

Thereupon Sakyamuni Buddha told Mañjuśrī: "The Tathāgata Abundant Treasures, so long extinct, shall display to you the sign."

Instantly the Buddha Abundant Treasures addressed that bodhisattva: "Come, good son! Mañjuśrī, son of the Law-king, wishes to see you."

Thereupon the Bodhisattva Wonder Sound disappeared from that domain and started out along with his eighty-four thousand bodhisattvas. The countries through which they passed were shaken in the six [different] ways, lotus flowers of the precious seven rained everywhere, and hundreds of thousands of heavenly instruments resounded of themselves. That bodhisattva's eyes were like broad big leaves of the blue lotus. His august countenance surpassed the combined [glory] of hundreds of thousands of myriads of moons. His body was of pure gold color, adorned with infinite hundreds of thousands of meritorious [signs]; he was of glowing majesty, radiant and shining, marked with the perfect signs, and of a body strong as Nārāyaṇa's.[7] Entering a seven-jeweled tower, he mounted the sky seven tāla trees above the earth and, worshiped and surrounded by a host of bodhisattvas, came to Mount Gṛdhrakūṭa in this sahā-world. Arrived, he alighted from his seven-jeweled tower and, taking a necklace worth hundreds of thousands, went to Sakyamuni Buddha, at whose feet he made obeisance and to whom he presented the necklace, saying to the Buddha: "World-honored One! The Buddha King Wisdom of the Pure Flower Constellation inquires after the World-honored One: 'Hast thou few ailments and few worries? Art thou getting on at ease and in comfort? Are thy four [component] parts[8] in harmony? Are thy wordly affairs tolerable? Are thy creatures easy to save? Are they not overcovetous, angry, foolish, envious, arrogant; not unfilial to parents or irreverent to śramaṇas; not having perverted views or being of bad mind, unrestrained in their five passions? World-honored One! Are thy creatures able to overcome the Māra-enemies? Does the Tathāgata Abundant Treasures, so long extinct, [still] abide in the Stupa of the Precious Seven and come to listen to the Law?' [King Wisdom] also inquires of the Tathāgata Abundant Treasures: 'Art thou at ease and of few worries? Wilt thou be content to remain long?' World-honored One! We now would see the body of the Buddha Abundant Treasures. Be pleased, World-honored One, to show and let us see him."

Then said Sakyamuni Buddha to the Buddha Abundant Treasures:

7. "Firm and solid" or "the original man"; a title of Brahma as creator.

8. The four elements of which every body is composed: earth, water, fire, and wind.

"This Bodhisattva Wonder Sound desires to see you." Instantly the Buddha Abundant Treasures addressed Wonder Sound: "Excellent, excellent, that you have been able to come here to pay homage to Sakyamuni Buddha, to hear the Law-Flower Sutra, and to see Mañjuśrī and the others."

Thereupon the Bodhisattva Flower Virtue said to the Buddha: "World-honored One! This Bodhisattva Wonder Sound—what roots of goodness has he planted, what merits has he cultivated, that he possesses such transcendent powers?" The Buddha answered the Flower Virtue Bodhisattva: "In the past there was a buddha named King of Cloud Thundering[9] Tathāgata, Arhat, Samyaksaṃbodhi, whose domain was named Display of All Worlds and whose kalpa named Joyful Sight. The Bodhisattva Wonder Sound, for twelve thousand years, with a hundred thousand kinds of music, paid homage to the Buddha King of Cloud Thundering and offered up eighty-four thousand vessels of the precious seven. Being rewarded for this reason, he has now been born in the domain of the Buddha King Wisdom of the Pure Flower Constellation and possesses such transcendent powers. Flower Virtue! What is your opinion? The Bodhisattva Wonder Sound who at that time paid homage to the Buddha King of Cloud Thundering with music and offerings of precious vessels—was it some other person? It was indeed the present Bodhisattva-Mahāsattva Wonder Sound. Flower Virtue! This Bodhisattva Wonder Sound had before paid homage to and been close to innumerable buddhas, for long had cultivated roots of virtue, and had met hundreds of thousands of myriads of koṭis of nayutas of buddhas, [numerous] as the sands of the Ganges. Flower Virtue! You merely see here [one] body of the Bodhisattva Wonder Sound. But this bodhisattva appears in many kinds of bodies everywhere preaching this sutra to the living. Sometimes he appears as Brahma, or appears as Śakra, or appears as Īśvara, or appears as Maheśvara, or appears as a divine general, or appears as the divine king Vaiśravaṇa, or appears as a holy wheel-rolling king, or appears as one of the ordinary kings, or appears as an elder, or appears as a citizen, or appears as a minister, or appears as a Brahman, or appears as a bhikshu, bhikshuṇī, upāsaka, or upāsikā, or appears as the wife of an elder or a citizen, or appears as the wife of a minister, or ap-

9. "Cloud Thunder-sound King" or "King of Thundering in the Clouds." Kern has "the king of the drum-sound of the clouds."

pears as the wife of a Brahman, or appears as a youth or maiden, or appears as a god, dragon, yaksha, gandharva, asura, garuḍa, kiṃnara, mahoraga, man, or nonhuman being, and so on, and preaches this sutra. He is able to rescue whatever beings are in the hells, or hungry ghosts, or animals, and all in distress. Even in the inner courts of a king, transforming himself into a woman he preaches this sutra. Flower Virtue! This Bodhisattva Wonder Sound is one who is able to save and protect all the living in the sahā-world. This Bodhisattva Wonder Sound, thus transforming himself and appearing in these various ways, in this sahā-land preaches this sutra to all the living. In his [powers of] supernatural transformation and wisdom there is never any diminution. This bodhisattva in so many [ways of] wisdom has enlightened the sahā-world, so that every one of the living has obtained knowledge [of him]. In [other] worlds in every direction, [numerous] as the sands of the Ganges, he also does the same. To those whom he must save in the form of a śrāvaka, he appears in the form of a śrāvaka and preaches the Law. To those whom he must save in the form of a pratyekabuddha, he appears in the form of a pratyekabuddha and preaches the Law. To those whom he must save in the form of a bodhisattva, he appears in the form of a bodhisattva and preaches the Law. To those whom he must save in the form of a buddha, he then appears in the form of a buddha and preaches the Law. In such various ways as these, according to the way in which he should save [men] he appears to them. Even to those whom he must save by extinction, he reveals himself as extinct. Flower Virtue! Such is the great supernatural power and wisdom attained by the Bodhisattva-Mahāsattva Wonder Sound."

Thereupon the Bodhisattva Flower Virtue said to the Buddha: "World-honored One! This Bodhisattva Wonder Sound has [indeed] deeply planted [his] roots of goodness. World-honored One! In what contemplation does this bodhisattva abide, that he is able thus to transform and manifest himself according to circumstances, to save the living?" The Buddha answered Flower Virtue Bodhisattva: "Good son! That contemplation is named revelation of all forms. The Bodhisattva Wonder Sound, abiding in this contemplation, is able thus to benefit countless beings."

While this chapter of the Bodhisattva Wonder Sound was preached the eighty-four thousand who had come with the Bodhisattva Wonder Sound all attained the contemplation of revelation of all forms, and countless bodhisattvas in this sahā-world also attained this contemplation and dhāraṇī.

Then the Bodhisattva-Mahāsattva Wonder Sound, having paid homage to Sakyamuni Buddha and to the stupa of the Buddha Abundant Treasures, returned to his own land. The countries through which he passed were agitated in the six [different] ways, raining precious lotus flowers and performing hundreds of thousands of myriads of koṭis of kinds of music. Having arrived at his own domain, he, with the eighty-four thousand bodhisattvas around him, went to the Buddha King Wisdom of the Pure Flower Constellation and said to him: "World-honored One! I have been to the sahā-world, done good to its living beings, seen Sakyamuni Buddha, also seen the stupa of the Buddha Abundant Treasures, and worshiped and paid homage to them; I have also seen the Bodhisattva Mañjuśrī, son of the Law-king, as well as the Bodhisattva Medicine King, the Bodhisattva Attainer of Earnestness and Zeal,[10] the Bodhisattva Courageous Giver, and others, and caused those eighty-four thousand bodhisattvas to attain the contemplation of revelation of all forms."

While this chapter on the going and coming of the Bodhisattva Wonder Sound was preached, the forty-two thousand heavenly sons attained the assurance of no [re]birth, and the Bodhisattva Flower Virtue attained the contemplation termed Law-Flower.

HERE ENDS

THE SEVENTH FASCICLE

10. In the extant Sanskrit text this is an adjectival phrase modifying "the Bodhisattva Medicine King," so that it reads: "the Bodhisattva Medicine King, the attainer of earnestness and zeal."

CHAPTER XXV

The All-Sidedness of the Bodhisattva Regarder of the Cries of the World

AT THAT TIME the Bodhisattva Infinite Thought rose up from his seat, and baring his right shoulder and folding his hands toward the Buddha, spoke thus: "World-honored One! For what reason is the Bodhisattva Avalokiteśvara named Regarder of the Cries of the World?"

The Buddha answered the Bodhisattva Infinite Thought: "Good son! If there be countless hundred thousand myriad koṭis of living beings suffering from pain and distress who hear of this Bodhisattva Regarder of the Cries of the World, and with all their mind call upon his name, the Bodhisattva Regarder of the Cries of the World will instantly regard their cries, and all of them will be delivered.

"If there be any who keep the name of that Bodhisattva Regarder of the Cries of the World, though they fall into a great fire, the fire will not be able to burn them, by virtue of the supernatural power of that bodhisattva's majesty. If any, carried away by a flood, call upon his name, they will immediately reach the shallows. If there be hundreds of thousands of myriads of koṭis of beings who in search of gold, silver, lapis lazuli, moonstones, agate, coral, amber, pearls, and other treasures go out on the ocean, and if a black gale[1] blows their ships to drift upon the land of the rākshasa demons, and if amongst them there be even a single person who calls upon the name of the Bodhisattva Regarder of the Cries of the World, all those people will be delivered from the throes of the rākshasas. It is for this reason that [he] is named Regarder of the Cries of the World.

"If, again, there be any man on the verge of [deadly] harm who calls upon the name of the Bodhisattva Regarder of the Cries of the World, the sword of the attacker will instantly snap asunder and he will be set free. Even if the three-thousand-great-thousandfold world were full of yakshas and rākshasas seeking to afflict people, these wicked demons, hearing them call upon the name of the Bodhisattva Regarder of the Cries of the World, would not be able to see them with [their] wicked eyes, how much less to hurt them.

"If, moreover, there be anyone, guilty or not guilty, loaded with manacles, fetters, cangues, or chains, who calls on the name of the Bodhisattva Regarder of the Cries of the World, they shall all be snapped and broken off and he shall be freed.

"If the three-thousand-great-thousandfold world were full of enemies and robbers, and there were a merchant chief who led many merchants having charge of costly jewels along a perilous road, and among them one man speaks forth: 'Good sons! Be not afraid. With one mind do you invoke the title of the Bodhisattva Regarder of the Cries of the World, for this bodhisattva is able to give courage to all the living. If you invoke his name, you will be freed from these enemies and robbers.' On hearing this, if all the traders together with one voice cry, 'Namaḥ! Bodhisattva Regarder of the Cries of the World!' then, by invoking his name, they will be relieved. Infinite Thought! Such is the awe-inspiring supernatural power of the Bodhisattva Regarder of the Cries of the World.

"If any living beings much given to carnal passion keep in mind and revere the Bodhisattva Regarder of the Cries of the World, they will be set free from their passion. If any much given to irascibility keep in mind and revere the Bodhisattva Regarder of the Cries of the World, they will be set free from their irascibility. If any much given to infatuation keep in mind and revere the Bodhisattva Regarder of

1. Literally, "a black wind." There are six kinds of wind: black, red, blue, of heaven, of earth, and of fire.

the Cries of the World, they will be set free from their infatuation. Infinite Thought! Such are the abundant benefits conferred by the supernatural power of the Bodhisattva Regarder of the Cries of the World. Consequently, let all the living ever keep him in mind.

"If any woman desiring a son worships and pays homage to the Bodhisattva Regarder of the Cries of the World, she will bear a son happy, virtuous, and wise. If she desires a daughter, she will bear a daughter of good demeanor and looks, who of old has planted virtuous roots, beloved and respected by all. Infinite Thought! Such is the power of the Bodhisattva Regarder of the Cries of the World. If any of the living revere and worship the Bodhisattva Regarder of the Cries of the World, blessings will not be rudely rejected.

"Therefore, let all the living cherish the title of the Bodhisattva Regarder of the Cries of the World. Infinite Thought! Suppose anyone cherishes the names of bodhisattvas [numerous as] the sands of sixty-two koṭis of the Ganges, who all his life makes them offerings of food, drink, garments, bedding, and medicaments—what is your opinion—are not the merits of that good son or good daughter abundant?" Infinite Thought replied: "Extremely abundant!" The World-honored One, the Buddha, proceeded: "But if [any]one cherishes the title of the Bodhisattva Regarder of the Cries of the World, or only for a moment worships and reveres him, the blessings of these two men will be exactly equal without difference, and cannot be exhausted in hundreds of thousands of myriads of koṭis of kalpas. Infinite Thought! Such is the immeasurable, boundless degree of blessedness he will obtain who cherishes the name of the Bodhisattva Regarder of the Cries of the World."

The Bodhisattva Infinite Thought [again] said to the Buddha: "World-honored One! How is it that the Bodhisattva Regarder of the Cries of the World wanders in this sahā-world? How does he preach the Law to the living? What is the character of his tactfulness?"

The Buddha replied to the Bodhisattva Infinite Thought: "Good son! If the living in any realm must be saved in the body of a buddha, the Bodhisattva Regarder of the Cries of the World appears as a buddha and preaches to them the Law. To those who must be saved in the body of a pratyekabuddha, he appears as a pratyekabuddha and preaches to them the Law. To those who must be saved in the body of a śrāvaka, he appears as a śrāvaka and preaches to them the Law. To those who must be saved in the body of Brahma, he appears as Brahma and preaches to them the Law. To those who must be saved in the body of Śakra, he appears as Śakra and preaches to them the Law. To those who must be saved in the body of Īśvara, he appears as Īśvara and preaches to them the Law. To those who must be saved in the body of Maheśvara, he appears as Maheśvara and preaches to them the Law. To those who must be saved in the body of a great divine general, he appears as a great divine general and preaches to them the Law. To those who must be saved in the body of Vaiśravaṇa, he appears as Vaiśravaṇa and preaches to them the Law. To those who must be saved in the body of a minor king, he appears as a minor king and preaches to them the Law. To those who must be saved in the body of an elder, he appears as an elder and preaches to them the Law. To those who must be saved in the body of a citizen, he appears as a citizen and preaches to them the Law. To those who must be saved in the body of a minister of state, he appears as a minister and preaches to them the Law. To those who must be saved in the body of a Brahman, he appears as a Brahman and preaches to them the Law. To those who must be saved in the body of a bhikshu, bhikshuṇī, upāsaka, or upāsikā, he appears as a bhikshu, bhikshuṇī, upāsaka, or upāsikā and preaches to them the Law. To those who must be saved in the body of the wife of an elder, citizen, minister, or Brahman, he appears as a woman and preaches to them the Law. To those who must be saved in the body of a youth or maiden, he appears as a youth or maiden and preaches to them the Law. To those who must be saved in the body of a god, dragon, yaksha, gandharva, asura, garuḍa, kiṃnara, mahoraga, human or nonhuman being, he appears in every such form and preaches to them the Law. To those who must be saved in [the shape of] a diamond-holding god,[2] he appears as a diamond-holding god and preaches to them the Law. Infinite Thought! Such are the merits acquired by this Bodhisattva Regarder of the Cries of the World and the various forms in which he rambles through many lands to save the living. Therefore, do you with single mind pay homage to the Bodhisattva Regarder of the Cries of the World. This Bodhisattva-Mahāsattva Regarder of the Cries of the World is able to make

2. The god who holds the *vajra,* or diamond club. Five hundred such gods guard a buddha, protecting him from all foes.

fearless those in anxiety and distress. For this reason all in this sahā-world give him the title Bestower of Fearlessness."

The Bodhisattva Infinite Thought said to the Buddha: "World-honored One! Let me now make an offering to the Bodhisattva Regarder of the Cries of the World."

Thereupon he unloosed from his neck a necklace of pearls worth a hundred thousand pieces of gold and presented it to him, making this remark: "Good sir! Accept this pious gift of a pearl necklace." But the Bodhisattva Regarder of the Cries of the World would not accept it.

Again the Bodhisattva Infinite Thought addressed the Bodhisattva Regarder of the Cries of the World: "Good sir! Out of compassion for us, accept this necklace." Then the Buddha said to the Bodhisattva Regarder of the Cries of the World: "Out of compassion for this Bodhisattva Infinite Thought and the four groups, and for the gods, dragons, yakshas, gandharvas, asuras, garuḍas, kiṃnaras, mahoragas, human and nonhuman beings, and others, accept this necklace." Then the Bodhisattva Regarder of the Cries of the World, having compassion for all the four groups and the gods, dragons, human and nonhuman beings, and others, accepted the necklace, and dividing it into two parts, offered one part to Sakyamuni Buddha and offered the other to the stupa of the Buddha Abundant Treasures.

"Infinite Thought! With such sovereign supernatural powers does the Bodhisattva Regarder of the Cries of the World wander through the sahā-world."

Then the Bodhisattva Infinite Thought made inquiry thus in verse:[3]

"The World-honored One with all the mystic signs!
Let me now again inquire of him:
For what cause is this Buddha-son named
Regarder of the Cries of the World?"

3. The following verses are not given by either Kumārajīva or Dharmaraksha. They are found in Kumārajīva's version as the interpolation of a later translator, Jñānagupta, who used a Sanskrit text written on palm leaves, while Kumārajīva had used a text written on silk from Khotan. The Nepalese text has the poetry section, but it differs widely from Jñānagupta's. Chih-i has no comment on the verses, indicating that the version of the sutra that he used did not contain them. This section may have been an independent song in praise of Avalokiteśvara that was later incorporated into the sutra.

The Honored One with all the mystic signs answered Infinite Thought in verse:

"Listen to the deeds of the Cry Regarder,
Who well responds to every quarter;
His vast vow is deep as the sea,
Inconceivable in its eons.
Serving many thousands of koṭis of buddhas,
He has vowed a great pure vow.
Let me briefly tell you.
[He who] hears his name, and sees him,
And bears him unremittingly in mind,
Will be able to end the sorrows of existence.
Though [others] with harmful intent
Throw him into a burning pit,
Let him think of the Cry Regarder's power
And the fire pit will become a pool.
Or driven along a great ocean,
In peril of dragons, fishes, and demons,
Let him think of the Cry Regarder's power
And waves cannot submerge him.
Or if, from the peak of Sumeru,
Men would hurl him down,
Let him think of the Cry Regarder's power
And like the sun he will stand firm in the sky.
Or if, pursued by wicked men,
And cast down from Mount Diamond,[4]
He thinks of the Cry Regarder's power,
Not a hair shall be injured.
Or if, meeting with encompassing foes,
Each with sword drawn to strike him,
He thinks of the Cry Regarder's power,
All their hearts will turn to kindness.
Or if, meeting suffering by royal [command],
His life is to end in execution,

4. The same as Mount Iron Circle.

[And] he thinks of the Cry Regarder's power,
[The executioner's] sword will break in pieces.
Or if, imprisoned, shackled, and chained,
Arms and legs in gyves and stocks,
He thinks of the Cry Regarder's power,
Freely he shall be released.
Or if by incantation and poisons
One seeks to hurt his body,
And he thinks of the Cry Regarder's power,
All will revert to their originator.
Or if, meeting evil rākshasas,
Venomous dragons, and demons,
He thinks of the Cry Regarder's power,
At once none will dare to hurt him.
If, encompassed by evil beasts,
Tusks sharp and claws fearful,
He thinks of the Cry Regarder's power,
They will flee in every direction.
If, scorched by the fire-flame
Of the poisonous breath
Of boas, vipers, and scorpions,
He thinks of the Cry Regarder's power,
Instantly at his voice they will retreat.
Clouds thunder and lightning flashes,
Hail falls and rain streams:
He thinks of the Cry Regarder's power
And all instantly are scattered.
The living, crushed and harassed,
Oppressed by countless pains:
The Cry Regarder with his mystic wisdom
Can save [such] a suffering world.
Perfect in supernatural powers,
Widely practiced in wisdom and tact,
In the lands of the universe there is no place
Where he does not manifest himself.
All the evil states of existence,
Hells, ghosts, and animals,

Sorrows of birth, age, disease, death,
All by degrees are ended by him.
True regard, serene regard,
Far-reaching wise regard,
Regard of pity, compassionate regard,
Ever longed for, ever looked for!
Pure and serene in radiance,
Wisdom's sun destroying darkness,
Subduer of woes of storm and fire,
Who illumines all the world!
Law of pity, thunder quivering,
Compassion wondrous as a great cloud,
Pouring spiritual rain like nectar,
Quenching the flames of distress!
In disputes before a magistrate,
Or in fear in battle's array,
If he thinks of the Cry Regarder's power
All his enemies will be routed.
His is the wondrous voice, voice of the world-regarder,
Brahma-voice, voice of the rolling tide,
Voice all world-surpassing,
Therefore ever to be kept in mind,
With never a doubting thought.
Regarder of the World's Cries, pure and holy,
In pain, distress, death, calamity,
Able to be a sure reliance,
Perfect in all merit,
With compassionate eyes beholding all,
Boundless ocean of blessings!
Prostrate let us revere him."[5]

Thereupon the Bodhisattva Stage Holder[6] rose from his seat, and went before and said to the Buddha: "World-honored One! If any living being hears of the sovereign work and the all-sided transcendent powers [shown in] this chapter of the Bodhisattva Regarder of

5. The extant Sanskrit text here adds other verses, for which see Kern's translation.
6. Or "Earth Holder."

the Cries of the World, it should be known that the merits of this man are not a few."

While the Buddha preached this chapter of the All-sided One, the eighty-four thousand living beings in the assembly all set their minds upon Perfect Enlightenment, with which nothing can compare.

CHAPTER XXVI

Dharanis

AT THAT TIME the Medicine King Bodhisattva rose from his seat and, humbly baring his right shoulder, folded his hands toward the Buddha and spoke to the Buddha, saying: "World-honored One! If there be any good son or good daughter who is able to receive and keep the Law-Flower Sutra, either reading or reciting or studying or copying the sutra, what is the extent of the blessings obtained?"

The Buddha answered the Medicine King: "Suppose any good son or good daughter pays homage to eight hundred myriad koṭis of nayutas of buddhas, equal to the sands of the Ganges, in your opinion are not the blessings so obtained rather numerous?"

"Very numerous, World-honored One!" [was the reply]. The Buddha continued: "If any good son or good daughter is able, in regard to this sutra, to receive and keep but a single four-line verse, read and recite, understand its meaning, and do as it says, his merits will be still more numerous."

Thereupon the Medicine King Bodhisattva said to the Buddha: "World-honored One! To the preachers of the Law I will now give dhāraṇī spells[1] for their guard and protection." Whereupon he delivered the following spell:

"Anye manye mane mamane citte carite same samitā viśānte mukte muktame same avishame samasame jaye [kshaye] akshaye akshīṇe śānte samite dhāraṇī ālokabhāshe pratyavekshaṇi nidhiru abhyantaranivishṭe abhyantarapāriśuddhi utkule mutkule araḍe paraḍe sukāṅkshī asamasame buddhavilokite dharmaparīkshite saṃghanirghoshaṇi [nirghoshaṇī] bhayābhayaviśodhani mantre mantrākshayate rute rutakauśalye akshaye akshayavanatāye [vakkule] valoḍa amanyanatāye [svāhā].[2]

"World-honored One! These supernatural dhāraṇī spells have been spoken by buddhas numerous as the sands of sixty-two koṭis of Ganges rivers. If anyone does violence to the teacher of this Law, then he will have done violence to these buddhas."

Then Sakyamuni Buddha extolled the Medicine King Bodhisattva, saying: "Good, good, O Medicine King! Because you are compassionate and protect these teachers of the Law, you have pronounced these dhāraṇīs, which will abundantly benefit the living."

Thereupon the Bodhisattva Courageous Giver spoke to the Buddha, saying: "World-honored One! I, too, for the protection of these who read and recite, receive and keep the Law-Flower Sutra, will deliver dhāraṇīs. If these teachers of the Law possess these dhāraṇīs, neither yakshas, nor rākshasas, nor pūtanas, nor kṛityas, nor kumbhāṇḍas, nor hungry ghosts, nor others spying for their shortcomings can find a chance." Then, in the presence of the Buddha, he delivered the following spell:

"Jvale mahājvle ukke [tukku] mukku aḍe aḍāvati nṛtye nṛtyāvati iṭṭini viṭṭini ciṭṭini nṛtyeni nṛtyāvati [svāhā].[3]

"World-honored One! These supernatural dhāraṇī spells have

1. A spell or talismanic word, one of the four kinds of dhāraṇīs. There are four kinds of spells: (1) to heal disease, (2) to put an end to the consequences of sin, (3) to protect the sutras, and (4) for wisdom. The following spell is for the protection of this sutra.

2. The lists in Burnouf and Kern are somewhat different. Kern adds: "All these words are, or ought to be, feminine words in the vocative. I take them to be epithets of the Great Mother, Nature or Earth, differently called Aditi, Prajñā, Māyā, Bhavānī, Durgā. Anyā may be identified with the Vedic anyā, inexhaustible, and synonymous with aditi. More of the other terms may be explained as synonymous with prajñā (e.g. pratyavekshaṇī), with nature (kshaye akshaye), with the earth (dhāraṇī)" (SBE vol. 21, p. 371 n). Dharmaraksha translated the spell into Chinese and Oka into Japanese according to one of several interpretations.

3. Kern writes: "These terms are obviously names of the flame, mythologically

been spoken by buddhas numerous as the sands of the Ganges, and all approved. If anyone does violence to the teachers of this Law, he will have done violence to these buddhas."

Thereupon the Divine King Vaiśravaṇa, protector of the world, spoke to the Buddha, saying: "World-honored One! I, too, in compassion for the living and for the protection of these teachers of the Law, will deliver these dhāraṇīs." Whereupon he delivered the following spell:

"Aṭṭe [taṭṭe] naṭṭe vanaṭṭe anaḍe nāḍi kunaḍi [svāhā].

"World-honored One! By these supernatural spells I will protect the teachers of the Law. I will also myself protect those who keep this sutra, so that no corroding care shall [come] within a hundred yojanas."

Thereupon the Divine King Domain Holder,[4] who was present in this congregation, with a host of thousands of myriads of koṭis of nayutas of gandharvas[5] reverently encompassing him, went before the Buddha, and folding his hands said to the Buddha: "World-honored One! I, too, with supernatural dhāraṇī spells, will protect those who keep the Law-Flower Sutra." Whereupon he delivered the following spell:

"Agaṇe gaṇe gauri gandhāri caṇḍāli mātaṅgi [pukkaśi] saṃkule vrūsali sisi [svāhā].

"World-honored One! These supernatural dhāraṇī spells have been spoken by forty-two koṭis of buddhas. If anyone does violence to these teachers of the Law, he will have done violence to these buddhas."

Thereupon there were female rākshasas,[6] the first named Lambā, the second named Vilambā, the third named Crooked Teeth, the fourth named Flowery Teeth, the fifth named Black Teeth, the sixth named Many Tresses, the seventh named Insatiable, the eighth named Necklace Holder, the ninth named Kuntī, and the tenth named

---

called Agni's wife, the daughter of Daksha. As Śiva may be identified with Agni, the feminine words again are epithets of Durgā. Jvalā and mahājvalā are perfectly clear; ukkā is the Prākrit form of Sanskrit ulkā" (SBE vol. 21, p. 372 n).

4. The extant Sanskrit text has "Virūḍhaka" (Divine King Growth).
5. The extant Sanskrit text has "kumbhāṇḍas."
6. The wives and daughters of rākshasa demons.

Spirit Snatcher. These ten female rākshasas, together with the Mother of Demon Sons[7] and her children and followers, all went to the Buddha and with one voice said to the Buddha: "World-honored One! We, too, would protect those who read and recite, receive and keep the Law-Flower Sutra, and rid them of corroding care. If any spy for the shortcomings of these teachers of the Law, we will prevent their obtaining any chance." Whereupon in the presence of the Buddha they delivered the following spell:

"Iti me, iti me, iti me, iti me, iti me; ni me, ni me, ni me, ni me, ni me; ruhe, ruhe, ruhe, ruhe, [ruhe]; stuhe, stuhe, stuhe, stuhe, stuhe [svāhā].

"Let troubles come on our heads, rather than on the teachers of the Law; neither yakshas, nor hungry ghosts, nor pūtanas, nor kṛityas, nor vetaḍas, nor kashāyas, nor umārakas, nor apasmārakas, nor yaksha-kṛityas,[8] nor man-kṛityas;[9] nor fevers, whether for a single day, or quotidian, or tertian, or quartan, or weekly, or unremitting fevers; whether in male form, or female form, or form of a youth, or form of a maiden, even in dreams shall ever cause distress." Whereupon before the Buddha they spoke thus in verse:

"Whoever resists our spell
And troubles a preacher,
May his head be split in seven
Like an arjaka sprout;[10]
May his doom be that of a parricide,
His retribution that of an oil-expresser[11]
Or a deceiver with [false] measures and weights,
Or of Devadatta who brought schism into the Saṃgha;

7. Also called "Joyful Mother" or "Mother Who Loves Her Children." She is a female rākshasa, or rākshasī, who devoured others' babies every day until her own five hundred babies were hidden by Sakyamuni Buddha and she was converted. After her conversion she vowed to protect the Buddha-law and especially to guard babies.

8. A kṛitya in the form of a yaksha.

9. A kṛitya in human form.

10. It is said that if one touches an arjaka flower its petals open and fall into seven pieces. Kern identifies the plant as *Symplocos racemosa,* while Monier-Williams' dictionary has *Ocinum gratissimum.*

11. The crime of producing worms by grinding sesame and at the same time squeezing the worms. This is the crime of taking life.

He who offends these teachers of the Law,
Such shall be his retribution."

After these female rākshasas had uttered this stanza, they addressed the Buddha, saying: "World-honored One! We ourselves will also protect those who receive and keep, read and recite, and practice this sutra, and give them ease of mind, freedom from corroding care and from all poisons."

The Buddha addressed the rākshasa women: "Good, good! Even if you are only able to protect those who receive and keep the name of the Law-Flower, your happiness will be beyond calculation; how much more if you protect those who perfectly receive, keep, and pay homage to the sutra with flowers, necklaces, sandal powder, perfumes, incense, flags, canopies, and music, burning various kinds of lamps—ghee lamps, oil lamps of scented oil, lamps of oil of campaka flowers, lamps of oil of vārshika flowers, and lamps of oil of udumbara flowers, such hundreds of thousands of kinds of offerings as these. Kuntī! You and your followers should protect such teachers of the Law as these."

While this chapter of the dhāraṇīs was preached, sixty-eight thousand people attained the assurance of no [re]birth.

CHAPTER XXVII

The Story of King Resplendent

AT THAT TIME the Buddha addressed the great assembly: "Of yore, in a former eon, infinite, boundless, and inconceivable asaṃkhyeya kalpas ago, there was a buddha named Thunder Voice Constellation King of Wisdom,[1] Tathāgata, Arhat, Samyaksaṃbodhi, whose domain was named Adorned with Radiance, and whose kalpa was named Joyful Sight. Under the spiritual rule of that buddha there was a king named Resplendent. The wife of that king was called Pure Virtue, who had two sons, one named Pure Treasury, the other named Pure-Eyed. Those two sons possessed great supernatural power, blessedness, and wisdom, and had for long devoted themselves to the ways in which bodhisattvas walk, that is to say, donation pāramitā, keeping the precepts pāramitā, perseverance pāramitā, assiduity pāramitā, meditation pāramitā, wisdom pāramitā, tactfulness pāramitā, benevolence, compassion, joy, indifference, and the thirty-seven kinds of aids to the Way—all these they thoroughly understood. They had also attained the bodhisattva contemplation—

The literal translation of the title of this chapter is "The original affair of King Wonderfully Adorned."

1. Or "Constellation King of Flowery Wisdom with the Voice of Thunder."

the pure contemplation, the sun constellation contemplation, the pure light contemplation, the pure color contemplation,[2] the pure illumination contemplation, the ever resplendent contemplation, and the contemplation of the treasury of great dignity, in which contemplations they were thoroughly accomplished.

"Then that buddha, desiring to lead King Resplendent and having compassion for the living, preached this Law-Flower Sutra. Meanwhile the two sons, Pure Treasury and Pure-Eyed, went to their mother and, putting together their ten-fingered hands, spoke to her, saying: 'We beg you, mother, to go and visit the Buddha Thunder Voice Constellation King of Wisdom. We also would wait on, approach, serve, and worship him. Wherefore? [Because] that buddha among the host of gods and men is preaching the Law-Flower Sutra, and we ought to hear it.' The mother replied to her sons: 'Your father believes in the heretics and is deeply attached to the Brahman law. Do you go and speak to your father that he may go with us.'[3] Pure Treasury and Pure-Eyed, putting together their ten-fingered hands, said to their mother: 'We are sons of the Law-king, though born in this home of heretical views.' The mother spoke to her sons, saying: 'You should have sympathy for your father, and show him some supernatural deed so that seeing it his mind will become clear and he will perhaps permit us to go to that buddha.'

"Thereupon the two sons, with a mind for their father, sprang up into the sky seven tāla trees high, and displayed many kinds of supernatural deeds, walking, standing, sitting, and lying in the sky; the upper [part of their] bodies emitting water, the lower emitting fire, or the lower emitting water and the upper emitting fire; or enlarging themselves till they filled the sky, and again appearing small, or small and again appearing large; then vanishing from the sky and suddenly appearing on the earth, or entering into the earth as into water, or walking on water as on the earth; displaying such various supernatural deeds, they led their father, the king, to cleanse his mind to faith and discernment.

"When their father saw his sons [possessed of] such supernatural powers he was greatly delighted at so unprecedented an experience

2. This contemplation is not found in the extant Sanskrit text.

3. The Chinese can be read "that he may grant [us] to go together." Kern has "you will not obtain the permission."

and with joined hands [saluted] his sons, saying: 'Who is your master? Whose pupils are you?' The two sons replied: 'Great king! That Buddha Thunder Voice Constellation King of Wisdom, who is now under the seven-jeweled Bodhi tree, seated on the throne of the Law, preaching abroad the Law-Flower Sutra in the midst of the world-host of gods and men—he is our master, we are his pupils.' The father then said to his sons: 'I also would now like to see your master; let us go together.'

"On this the two sons descended from the sky, went to their mother, and with folded hands said to her: 'Our father the king has now believed and understood, and been able to set his mind on Perfect Enlightenment. We have done a buddha-deed for our father. Be pleased, mother, to permit us to leave home and under that buddha pursue the Way.'

"Then the two sons, desiring again to announce their wish, said to their mother in verse:

'Be pleased, mother, to release us
To leave home and become śramaṇas.
Hard it is to meet the buddhas,
And we would be followers of a buddha.
As the blossom of the udumbara,
Even harder is it to meet a buddha,
And hard it is to escape from hardships.
Be pleased to permit us to leave home.'

"Then the mother spoke, saying: 'I grant you permission to leave home; and why? Because a buddha is hard to meet.'

"On this the two sons said to their parents: 'Good, father and mother! We beg that you will now go to the Buddha Thunder Voice Constellation King of Wisdom, approach [him], and pay him homage. Wherefore? Because a buddha is as hard to meet as an udumbara flower, or as the one-eyed tortoise meeting the hole in the floating log.[4] But we, richly blessed through a former lot, have met the Buddha-law in this life. Therefore, father and mother, listen to us and let us go forth from home. Wherefore? [Because] buddhas are hard to meet and the occasion is also hard to encounter.'

4. According to chapter 15 of the *Samyutta Nikāya,* in the occean there is a blind

"At that juncture all the eighty-four thousand court ladies of King Resplendent became capable of receiving and keeping this Law-Flower Sutra. The Bodhisattva Pure-Eyed had for long been thorough in the Law-Flower contemplation. The Bodhisattva Pure Treasury had for infinite hundreds of thousands of myriads of koṭis of kalpas been thorough in the contemplation of free from evil paths, [which] sought to lead all the living away from all evil states of existence. The queen of that king had attained the contemplation of assemblage of buddhas and was able to know the secret resources of buddhas. Thus did the two sons with tact wisely convert their father, bringing his mind to believe, discern, and delight in the Buddha-law.

"Thereupon King Resplendent[5] accompanied by his ministers and retinue, Queen Pure Virtue accompanied by her fine court ladies and retinue, and the two sons of that king, accompanied by forty-two thousand people, at once set out together to visit the buddha. Arriving and prostrating themselves at his feet, they made procession around the buddha three times and then withdrew to one side.

"Then that buddha preached to the king, showing, teaching, profiting, and rejoicing him, so that the king was greatly delighted. Then King Resplendent and his queen unloosed the necklaces of pearls worth hundreds and thousands from their necks, and threw them upon the buddha, which in the sky were transformed into a four-columned jeweled tower; on the tower was a large jeweled couch spread with hundreds of thousands of myriads of celestial coverings, on which was the buddha sitting cross-legged, emitting a great [ray of] light. Whereupon King Resplendent reflected thus: 'Rare, dignified, extraordinary is the buddha's body, perfect in its supreme, refined coloring!'

"Then the Buddha Thunder Voice Constellation King of Wisdom addressed the four groups, saying: 'You see this King Resplendent standing before me with folded hands? This king, having become a bhikshu within my rule, and being zealous in observing the laws which aid the Buddha-way, shall become a buddha entitled Śālendra Tree King, whose domain will be named Great Luster, and his kalpa

---

tortoise infinite kalpas old, who rises to the surface once a century. In that ocean there is also a floating log with only one hole. What are the chances of the two meeting?

5. This can also be read: "The two sons having thus with tact wisely converted their father, . . . then King Resplendent . . ."

named Great High King. This Buddha Śālendra Tree King will have countless bodhisattvas and countless śrāvakas, and his domain will be level and straight. Such will be his merits.'

"The king at once made over his domain to his younger brother; the king together with his queen, two sons, and retinue forsook his home and followed the Way under the rule of [that] buddha. Having forsaken his home, for eighty-four thousand years the king was ever diligent and zealous in observing the Wonderful Law-Flower Sutra, and after these [years] passed attained the contemplation of adorned with all pure merits.

"Whereupon he arose in the sky to a height of seven tāla trees and said to that buddha: 'World-honored One! These my two sons have already done a buddha-deed by their supernatural transformations, changing my heretical mind, establishing me in the Buddha-law, and causing me to see the World-honored One. These two sons are my good friends, for out of a desire to develop the roots of goodness [planted] in my former lives and to benefit me, they came and were born in my home.'

"Thereupon the Buddha Thunder Voice Constellation King of Wisdom addressed King Resplendent, saying: 'So it is, so it is, it is as you say. Any good son or good daughter, by planting roots of goodness, will in every generation obtain good friends, which good friends will be able to do buddha-deeds, showing, teaching, profiting, and rejoicing him, and causing him to enter into Perfect Enlightenment. Know, great king! A good friend is the great cause whereby [men] are converted and led to see the buddha and aroused to Perfect Enlightenment. Great king! Do you see these two sons? These two sons have already paid homage to buddhas sixty-five [times] the hundreds of thousands of myriads of koṭis of nayutas of the sands of the Ganges, waiting upon and revering them; and among those buddhas received and kept the Law-Flower Sutra, having compassion for the living with their false views, and establishing them in right views.'

"King Resplendent thereupon descended from the sky and said to the buddha: 'World-honored One! Rare indeed is [the sight of] the Tathāgata; by his merits and wisdom the protuberance on his head shines brilliantly; his eyes are wide [open] and deep blue; the tuft between his eyebrows is white as the pearly moon; his teeth are white, even, close, and ever shining; his lips are red and beautiful as bimba fruit.' Then, when King Resplendent had extolled that buddha's so many merits, countless hundreds of thousands of myriads of koṭis of them, with all his mind he folded his hands before the tathāgata and again addressed that buddha, saying: 'Unprecedented is the World-honored One. The Tathāgata's teaching is perfect in its inconceivable and wonderful merits. The moral precepts which he promulgates are comforting and quickening. From this day onward I will not again follow my own mind, nor beget false views, nor a haughty, angry, or any other sinful mind.' Having uttered these words, he did reverence to the buddha and went forth."

[Sakyamuni] Buddha [then] said to the great assembly: "What is your opinion? This King Resplendent—could he be any other person? He is indeed the present Bodhisattva Flower Virtue. That Queen Pure Virtue is the Bodhisattva Shining Splendor now in the presence of the Buddha,[6] who out of compassion for King Resplendent and his people was born amongst them. These two sons are the present Medicine King Bodhisattva and Medicine Lord Bodhisattva. Those bodhisattvas Medicine King and Medicine Lord, having perfected such great merits, under countless hundred thousand myriad koṭis of buddhas, planted virtuous roots and perfectly attained qualities of goodness beyond conception. If there be anyone who is acquainted with the names of these two bodhisattvas, gods and men in all the world will pay him homage."

While the Buddha preached this chapter, "The Story of King Resplendent," the eighty-four thousand people departed from impurity and separated themselves from uncleanliness, and acquired pure spiritual eyes in regard to spiritual things.

6. The Japanese version reads: "the Bodhisattva Splendor Sign, whom the present Buddha formerly illuminated with his ray." She is said to be identical with the Bodhisattva Wonder Sound.

CHAPTER XXVIII

Encouragement of the Bodhisattva Universal Virtue

AT THAT TIME the Bodhisattva Universal Virtue, with sovereign supernatural power, majesty, and fame, accompanied by great bodhisattvas, unlimited, infinite, incalculable, came from the eastern quarter; the countries through which he passed were shaken, jeweled lotus flowers rained down, and countless hundred thousand myriad koṭis of kinds of music were performed. Encompassed also by a great host of countless gods, dragons, yakshas, gandharvas, asuras, garuḍas, kiṃnaras, mahoragas, men, nonhuman beings, and others, all displaying majestic supernatural powers, he arrived at Mount Gṛdhrakūṭa in the sahā-world. Having prostrated himself before Sakyamuni Buddha, he made procession around him to the right seven times and addressed the Buddha, saying: "World-honored One! I, in the domain of the Buddha Jeweled Majestic Superior King, hearing afar that the Law-Flower Sutra was being preached in this sahā-world, have come with this host of countless, infinite hundred thousand myriad koṭis of bodhisattvas to hear and receive it. Be pleased, World-honored One, to preach it to us, [and tell] how good sons and good daughters will be able to obtain this Law-Flower Sutra after the extinction of the Tathāgata."

The Buddha replied to the Bodhisattva Universal Virtue: "If any good son or good daughter acquires the four requisites, such a one will obtain this Law-Flower Sutra after the extinction of the Tathāgata: first, to be under the guardianship of the buddhas; second, to plant the roots of virtue; third, to enter [the stage of] correct congregation;[1] fourth, to aspire after the salvation of all the living. Any good son or good daughter who acquires such four requisites will certainly obtain this sutra after the extinction of the Tathāgata."

Then the Bodhisattva Universal Virtue said to the Buddha: "World-honored One! In the latter five hundred years of the corrupt and evil age, whoever receives and keeps this sutra I will guard and protect, eliminate the anxiety of falling away, and give ease of mind, so that no spy shall find occasion—neither Māra, nor Māra-sons, nor Māra-daughters, nor Māra-people, nor Māra-satellites, nor yakshas, nor rākshasas, nor kumbhāṇḍas, nor piśācakas, nor kṛityas, nor pūtanas, nor vetaḍas, nor other afflicters of men—that none may find occasion. Wherever such a one walks or stands, reading and reciting this sutra, I will at once mount the six-tusked white elephant king and with a host of great bodhisattvas go to that place and, showing myself, will serve and protect [him], comforting his mind, also thereby serving the Law-Flower Sutra. Wherever such a one sits, pondering this sutra, I will at once again mount the white elephant king and show myself to him. If such a one forgets [be it but] a single word or verse of the Law-Flower Sutra, I will teach it to him, read and recite it with him, and again cause him to master it. Thereupon he who receives and keeps, reads and recites the Law-Flower Sutra on seeing me will greatly rejoice and renew his zeal. Through seeing me, he will thereupon acquire the contemplation and dhāraṇīs named the dhāraṇī of revolution,[2] the dhāraṇī of hundreds of thousands of myriads of koṭis of revolutions,[3] and the dhāraṇī of skill in Law-sounds;[4] such dhāraṇīs as these will he acquire.

1. Kern's translation reads "come under 'the mass of disciplinary regulations,'" but the above is the generally accepted interpretation.

2. This is interpreted as "unhindered revolution," meaning to contemplate all phenomena as the void. It is the contemplation of the void.

3. This means to turn the void to phenomena, that is, to contemplate all beings as existing things. It is the contemplation of existence.

4. This is the contemplation of the Middle Path, that is, neither void nor existing, unifying the above two contemplations, which are conventional.

"World-honored One! If in the latter age, in the last five hundred years of the corrupt and evil age, the bhikshus, bhikshuṇīs, upāsakas, and upāsikās, seekers, receivers and keepers, readers and reciters, or copiers desire to put in practice this Law-Flower Sutra, they must with single mind devote themselves to it for three times seven days. After the three times seven days are fulfilled, I will mount the six-tusked white elephant and, together with countless bodhisattvas surrounding me, appear before those people in the form all the living delight to see, and preach to them, revealing, instructing, benefiting, and rejoicing them. Moreover, I will give them dhāraṇīs, and obtaining these dhāraṇīs, no human or nonhuman being can injure them, nor any woman beguile them. I myself also will ever protect them. Be pleased, World-honored One, to permit me to announce these dhāraṇī spells." Then in the presence of the Buddha he uttered a spell, saying:

"Adaṇḍe daṇḍapati daṇḍāvartani daṇḍakuśale daṇḍasudhāri sudhāri sudhārapati buddhapaśyane dhāraṇī āvartani saṃvartani saṃghaparīkshite saṃghanirghātani dharmaparīkshite sarvasattvarutakauśalyānugate siṃha-vikrīḍite [anuvarte vartani vartāli svāhā].[5]

"World-honored One! If there be any bodhisattvas who hear these dhāraṇīs, they shall be aware of the supernatural power of Universal Virtue. If while the Law-Flower Sutra proceeds on its course through Jambudvīpa there be those who receive and keep it, let them reflect thus: 'This is all due to the majestic power of Universal Virtue.' If any receive and keep, read and recite, rightly remember it, comprehend its meaning, and practice it as preached, let it be known that these are doing the works of Universal Virtue and have deeply planted good roots under numberless countless buddhas, and that their heads will be caressed by the hands of the tathāgatas. If they only copy it, these when their life is ended will be born in the heaven Trāyastriṃśa; on which occasion eighty-four thousand nymphs, performing all kinds of music, will come to welcome them, and they, wearing

5. Kern comments: "All terms are, or ought to be, vocatives of feminine words in the singular. Pati, as in Pāli pājāpati, Buddhistic Sansk. prajāpatī, interchanges with the ending vatī; not only in prajāvatī (e.g. in Lalita-vistara), but in some of the words occurring in the spell; so for daṇḍapati the Tibetan text has daṇḍāvati. As Śiva in Mahābhārata XII, 10361 is represented as the personified Daṇḍa, we may hold that all the names above belong to Śiva's female counterpart, Durgā. The epithet of Siṃha-vikrīḍitā is but a variation of Siṃhikā, one of the names of Dakshāyanī or Durgā in her quality of mother to Rāhu" (SBE vol. 21, p. 435 n).

seven-jeweled crowns, will joy and delight among those beautiful nymphs; how much more those who receive and keep, read and recite, rightly remember it, comprehend its meaning, and practice it as preached! If there be any who receive and keep, read and recite it, and comprehend its meaning, when their life is ended the hands of a thousand buddhas will be proffered, that they fear not, neither fall into any evil destiny, [but] go straight to Maitreya Bodhisattva in the Tushita heaven, [where] Maitreya Bodhisattva, possessed of the thirty-two signs, is surrounded by a host of great bodhisattvas and has hundreds of thousands of myriads of koṭis of nymph-followers, amongst whom they will be born. Such are their merits and benefits. Therefore the wise should with all their mind themselves copy it, or cause others to copy it, receive and keep, read and recite, rightly remember it, and practice it as preached. World-honored One! I now by my supernatural power will guard and protect this sutra so that, after the extinction of the Tathāgata, it may spread abroad without cease in Jambudvipa."

Then Sakyamuni Buddha extolled him, saying: "It is well, it is well, Universal Virtue, that you are able to protect and assist this sutra, and bring happiness and weal to the living in many places. You have already attained inconceivable merits and profound benevolence and compassion. From a long distant past have you aspired to Perfect Enlightenment and been able to make this supernatural vow to guard and protect this sutra. [And] I, by my supernatural power, will guard and protect those who are able to receive and keep the name of the Bodhisattva Universal Virtue. Universal Virtue! If there be any who receive and keep, read and recite, rightly remember, practice, and copy this Law-Flower Sutra, know that such are attending on Sakyamuni Buddha as if they were hearing this sutra from the Buddha's mouth; know that such are paying homage to Sakyamuni Buddha; know that the Buddha is praising them—'Well done'; know that the heads of such are being caressed by the hands of Sakyamuni Buddha; know that such are covered by the robe of Sakyamuni Buddha.[6] Such

6. There is no indication of the tense in the Chinese text. Kern has "have seen Śākyamuni," "have heard," "have paid homage," "the Tathāgata Śākyamuni will have laid his hands upon their head, and they will have decked the Lord Śākyamuni with their robes" (SBE vol. 21, p. 437).

as these will not again be eager for wordly pleasure, nor be fond of heretical scriptures and writings, nor ever again take pleasure in intimacy with such men or other evil persons, whether butchers, or herders of pigs, sheep, fowl, and dogs, or hunters, or panderers. But such as these will be right-minded, have correct aims, and be auspicious. Such will not be harassed by the three poisons, nor be harassed by envy, pride, haughtiness, and arrogance. Such will be content with few desires, and able to do the works of Universal Virtue. Universal Virtue! After the extinction of the Tathāgata, in the latter five hundred years, if anyone sees one who receives and keeps, reads and recites the Law-Flower Sutra, he must reflect thus: 'This man will ere long go to the wisdom-floor, destroy the host of Māra, attain Perfect Enlightenment, and rolling onward the Law-wheel, beating the Law-drum, blowing the Law-conch, and pouring the rain of the Law, shall sit on the lion throne of the Law amidst a great assembly of gods and men.' Universal Virtue! Whoever in future ages shall receive and keep, read and recite this sutra, such persons will no longer be greedily attached to clothes, bed things, drink, food, and things for the support of life; whatever they wish will never be in vain, and in the present life they will obtain their blessed reward. Suppose anyone slights and slanders them, saying, 'You are only madmen, pursuing this course in vain with never a thing to be gained.' The doom for such a sin as this is blindness generation after generation. If anyone takes offerings to and praises them, he will obtain visible reward in the present world. Again, if anyone sees those who receive and keep this sutra, and proclaims their errors and sins, whether true or false, such a one in the present life will be smitten with leprosy. If he ridicules them, generation after generation his teeth will be sparse and missing, his lips vile, his nose flat, his hands and feet contorted, his eyes asquint, his body stinking and filthy with evil scabs and bloody pus, dropsical and short of breath, and [with] every evil disease. Therefore, Univeral Virtue, if one sees those who receive and keep this sutra, he should stand up and greet them from afar just as if he were paying reverence to the Buddha."

While this chapter of the encouragement of the Bodhisattva Universal Virtue was being preached, innumerable incalculable bodhisattvas equal to the sands of the Ganges attained the dhāraṇī of the hundreds of thousands of myriads of koṭis of revolutions, and bodhisattvas equal to the atoms of a three-thousand-great-thousandfold world became perfect in the Way of Universal Virtue.

When the Buddha preached this sutra, Universal Virtue and the other bodhisattvas, Śāriputra and the other śrāvakas, and the gods, dragons, human and nonhuman beings, and all others in the great assembly greatly rejoiced together and, taking possession of the Buddha's words, made salutation to him and withdrew.

HERE ENDS
THE EIGHTH FASCICLE

The Sutra of Meditation on the Bodhisattva Universal Virtue

translated by
Kojiro Miyasaka
with revisions by
Pier P. Del Campana

THUS HAVE I HEARD. Once the Buddha was staying at the two-storied assembly hall in the Great Forest Monastery, Vaiśālī; then he addressed all the bhikshus, [saying]: "After three months, I shall surely enter parinirvāṇa." Thereupon the honored Ānanda rose from his seat, straightened his garment, and with joined palms and folded hands he made procession around the Buddha three times and saluted him, kneeling with folded hands, and attentively gazed at the Tathāgata without turning away his eyes for a moment. The elder Mahā-Kāśyapa and the Bodhisattva-Mahāsattva Maitreya also rose from their seats, and with folded hands saluted and gazed up at his honored face. Then the three great leaders with one voice spoke to the Buddha, saying: "World-honored One! After the extinction of the Tathāgata, how can living beings raise the mind of the bodhisattva, practice the sutras of Great Extent, the Great-vehicle, and ponder the world of one reality with right thought? How can they keep from losing the mind of supreme buddhahood? How, without cutting off their earthly cares and renouncing their five desires, can they also purify their organs and destroy their sins? How, with the natural pure eyes received at birth from their parents and without forsaking their five desires, can they see things without all impediment?"

The Buddha said to Ānanda: "Do you listen to me attentively! Do you listen to me attentively, ponder, and remember it! Of yore on Mount Gṛdhrakūṭa and in other places the Tathāgata had already extensively explained the way of one reality. But now in this place, to all living beings and others in the world to come who desire to practice the supreme Law of the Great-vehicle, and to those who desire to learn the works of Universal Virtue and to follow the works of Universal Virtue, I will now preach the Law that I have entertained. I will now widely make clear to you the matter of eliminating numerous sins from anyone who may happen to see or not see Universal Virtue. Ānanda! The Bodhisattva Universal Virtue was born in the eastern Pure Wonder Land, whose form I have already clearly and extensively explained in the Sutra of Miscellaneous Flowers.[1] Now I, in this sutra, will briefly explain it [again].

"Ānanda! If there be bhikshus, bhikshuṇīs, upāsakas, upāsikās, the eight groups of gods and dragons, and all living beings who recite the Great-vehicle, practice it, aspire to it, delight to see the form and body of the Bodhisattva Universal Virtue, have pleasure in seeing the stupa of the Buddha Abundant Treasures, take joy in seeing Sakyamuni Buddha and the buddhas who emanated from him, and rejoice to obtain the purity of the six organs, they must learn this meditation. The merits of this meditation will make them free from all hindrances and make them see the excellent forms. Even though they have not yet entered into contemplation, just because they recite and keep the Great-vehicle they will devote themselves to practicing it, and after having kept their minds continuously on the Great-vehicle for a day or three times seven days, they will be able to see Universal Virtue; those who have a heavy impediment will see him after seven times seven days; again, those who have a heavier one will see him after one birth; again, those who have a much heavier one will see him after two births; again, those who have a still heavier one will see him after three births. Thus the retribution of their karma is various and not equal. For this reason, I preach the teaching variously.

"The Bodhisattva Universal Virtue is boundless in the size of his

1. Another name for the *Avataṃsaka Sūtra.*

body, boundless in the sound of his voice, and boundless in the form of his image. Desiring to come to this world, he makes use of his free transcendent powers and shrinks his stature to the small size [of a human being]. Because the people in Jambudvīpa have the three heavy hindrances,[2] by his wisdom-power he appears transformed as mounted on a white elephant. The elephant has six tusks[3] and, with its seven legs,[4] supports its body on the ground. Under its seven legs seven lotus flowers grow. The elephant is white as snow, the most brilliant of all shades of white, so pure that even crystal and the Himalaya Mountains cannot be compared with it. The body of the elephant is four hundred and fifty yojanas in length and four hundred yojanas in height. At the end of the six tusks there are six bathing pools. In each bathing pool grow fourteen lotus flowers exactly the size of the pools. The flowers are in full bloom as the king of celestial trees. On each of these flowers is a precious daughter whose countenance is red as crimson and whose radiance surpasses that of nymphs. In the hand of that daughter there appear, transformed of themselves, five harps, and each of them has five hundred musical instruments as accompaniment. There are five hundred birds including ducks, wild geese, and mandarin ducks, all having the color of precious things, arising among flowers and leaves. On the trunk of the elephant there is a flower, and its stalk is the color of a red pearl. That golden flower is still a bud and has not yet blossomed. Having finished beholding this matter, if one again further repents one's sins, meditates on the Great-vehicle attentively with entire devotion, and ponders it in his mind incessantly, he will be able to see the flower instantly blossom and light up with a golden color. The cup of the lotus flower is a cup of kiṃśuka gems with wonderful Brahma jewels, and the stamens are of diamond. A transformed buddha[5] is seen sitting on the petals of the lotus flower with a host of bodhisattvas sitting on the stamens of the lotus flower. From the eyebrows of the transformed buddha a ray of light is sent forth and enters the elephant's trunk. This ray, having the color of a

2. Arrogance, envy, and covetousness.

3. Suggesting the purity of the six sense organs: eye, ear, nose, tongue, body, and mind.

4. Suggesting the absence of the seven evils: killing, stealing, committing adultery, lying, speaking ill of others, improper language, and having a double tongue.

5. The transformed body in which a buddha manifests himself in order to save sentient beings.

red lotus flower, emanates from the elephant's trunk and enters its eyes; the ray then emanates from the elephant's eyes and enters its ears; it then emanates from the elephant's ears, illuminates its head, and changes into a golden cup. On the head of the elephant there are three transformed men: one holds a golden wheel, another a jewel, and yet another a diamond-pounder. When he raises the pounder and points it at the elephant, the latter walks a few steps immediately. The elephant does not tread on the ground but hovers in the air seven feet above the earth, yet the elephant leaves on the ground its footprints, which are altogether perfect, marking the wheel's hub with a thousand spokes. From each [mark of] the wheel's hub there grows a great lotus flower, on which a transformed elephant appears. This elephant also has seven legs and walks after the great elephant. Every time the transformed elephant raises and brings down its legs, seven thousand elephants appear, all following the great elephant as its retinue. On the elephant's trunk, having the color of a red lotus flower, there is a transformed buddha who emits a ray from his eyebrows. This ray of light, as mentioned before, enters the elephant's trunk; the ray emanates from the elephant's trunk and enters its eyes; the ray then emanates from the elephant's eyes and again enters its ears; it then emanates from the elephant's ears and reaches its head. Gradually rising to the elephant's back, the ray is transformed into a golden saddle which is adorned with the precious seven. On the four sides of the saddle are the pillars of the precious seven, which are decorated with precious things, forming a jewel pedestal. On this pedestal there is a lotus-flower stamen bearing the precious seven, and that stamen is also composed of a hundred jewels. The cup of that lotus flower is made of a great jewel.

"[On the cup] there is a bodhisattva called Universal Virtue who sits cross-legged. His body, pure as a white jewel, radiates fifty rays of fifty different colors, forming a brightness around his head. From the pores of his body he emits rays of light, and innumerable transformed buddhas are at the ends of the rays, accompanied by the transformed bodhisattvas as their retinue.

"The elephant walks quietly and slowly, and goes before the follower [of the Great-vehicle], raining large jeweled lotus flowers. When this elephant opens its mouth, the precious daughters, dwelling in the bathing pools on the elephant's tusks, play music whose sound is mystic and extols the way of one reality in the Great-vehicle. Having seen [this wonder], the follower rejoices and reveres, again further reads and recites the profound sutras, salutes universally the innumerable buddhas in all directions, makes obeisance to the stupa of the Buddha Abundant Treasures and Sakyamuni Buddha, and salutes Universal Virtue and all the other great bodhisattvas. Then the follower makes this vow: 'Had I [received] some blessings through my former destinies, I could surely see Universal Virtue. Be pleased, honored Universal Fortune,[6] to show me your form and body!'

"Having thus made his vow, the follower must salute the buddhas in all directions six times[7] day and night, and must practice the law of repentance; he must read the Great-vehicle sutras and recite them, think of the meaning of the Great-vehicle and reflect over its practice, revere and serve those who keep it, see all people as if he were thinking of the Buddha, and treat living beings as if he were thinking of his father and mother. When he finishes reflecting thus, the Bodhisattva Universal Virtue will at once send forth a ray of light from the white hair-circle, the sign of a great man, between his eyebrows. When this ray is displayed, the body of the Bodhisattva Universal Virtue will be dignified as a mountain of deep gold, so well ordered and refined that it possesses all the thirty-two signs. From the pores of his body he will emit great rays of light which will illuminate the great elephant and turn it to the color of gold. All transformed elephants will also be colored gold and all transformed bodhisattvas will be colored gold. When these rays of light shine on the innumerable worlds in the eastern quarter, they will turn them all to the color of gold. So, too, will be it in the southern, western, and northern quarters, in the four intermediate directions, in the zenith and the nadir.

"Then in each quarter of all directions there is a bodhisattva who, mounting the six-tusked white elephant-king, is exactly equal to Universal Virtue. Like this, by his transcendent powers, the Bodhisattva Universal Virtue will enable all the keepers of the Great-vehicle sutras to see transformed elephants filling the infinite and

6. Another name for the Bodhisattva Universal Virtue.

7. The worship of the Buddha six times a day: at sunset, at the beginning of the night, in the middle of the night, at the end of the night, in the early morning, and at midday.

boundless [worlds] in all directions. At this time the follower will rejoice in body and mind, seeing all the bodhisattvas, and will salute them and speak to them, saying: 'Great merciful and great compassionate ones! Out of compassion for me, be pleased to explain the Law to me!' When he speaks thus, all the bodhisattvas and others with one voice will each explain the pure Law of the Great-vehicle sutras and will praise him in various verses. This is called the first stage of mind, in which the follower first meditates on the Bodhisattva Universal Virtue.

"Thereupon, when the follower, having beheld this matter, keeps the Great-vehicle in mind without forsaking it day and night, even while sleeping, he will be able to see Universal Virtue preach the Law to him in a dream. Exactly as if [the follower] were awake, [the Bodhisattva] will console and pacify the follower's mind, speaking thus: 'In the sutras you have recited and kept, you have forgotten this word or have lost this verse.' Then the follower, hearing Universal Virtue preach the profound Law, will comprehend its meaning and keep it in his memory without forgetting it. As he does like this day by day, his mind will gradually acquire spiritual profit. The Bodhisattva Universal Virtue will cause the follower to remember the buddhas in all directions. According to the teaching of Universal Virtue, the follower will rightly think and remember everything, and with his spiritual eyes he will gradually see the eastward buddhas, whose bodies are gold colored and very wonderful in their majesty. Having seen one buddha, he will again see another buddha. In this manner, he will gradually see all the buddhas everywhere in the eastern quarter, and because of his profitable reflection, he will universally see all the buddhas in all directions.

"Having seen the buddhas, he conceives joy in his heart and utters these words: 'By means of the Great-vehicle, I have been able to see the great leaders. By means of their powers, I have also been able to see the buddhas. Though I have seen these buddhas, I have yet failed to make them plain. Closing my eyes I see the buddhas, but when I open my eyes I lose [sight of] them.' After speaking thus, the follower should universally make obeisance, prostrating himself down to the ground toward the buddhas in all directions. Having made obeisance to them, he should kneel with folded hands and should speak thus: 'The buddhas, the world-honored ones, possess the ten powers, the fearlessnesses, the eighteen unique characteristics, the great mercy, the great compassion, and the three kinds of stability in contemplation.[8] These buddhas, forever remaining in this world, have the finest appearance of all forms. By what sin do I fail to see these buddhas?'

"Having spoken thus, the follower should again practice further repentance. When he has achieved the purity of his repentance, the Bodhisattva Universal Virtue will again appear before him and will not leave his side in his walking, standing, sitting, and lying, and even in his dreams will ceaselessly preach the Law to him. After awaking from his dreams, this person will take delight in the Law. In this manner, after three times seven days and nights have passed, he will thereupon acquire the dhāraṇī of revolution. Through acquiring the dhāraṇī, he will keep in his memory without losing it the wonderful Law which the buddhas and bodhisattvas have taught. In his dreams, he will also see constantly the Seven Buddhas of the past, among whom only Sakyamuni Buddha will preach the Law to him. These world-honored ones will each praise the Great-vehicle sutras. At that time the follower will again further rejoiçe and universally salute the buddhas in all directions. After he salutes the buddhas in all directions, the Bodhisattva Universal Virtue, abiding before him, will teach and explain to him all karmas and environments of his former lives, and will cause him to confess his black and evil sins. Turning to the world-honored ones, he should confess [his sins] with his own mouth.

"After he finishes confessing [his sins], then he will attain the contemplation of the revelation of buddhas to men.[9] Having attained this contemplation, he will plainly and clearly see the Buddha Akshobhya and the Kingdom of Wonderful Joy in the eastern quarter. In like manner he will plainly and clearly see the mystic lands of the buddhas in each of all directions. After he has seen the buddhas in all directions, he will have a dream: on the elephant's head is a diamond-man pointing his diamond-pounder at the six organs; after pointing it at the six organs, the Bodhisattva Universal Virtue will preach to the follower the law of repentance to obtain the purity of the six organs. In this way the follower will do repentance for a day or three times seven days. [Then] by the power of the contemplation

8. That is, the buddhas remain undisturbed regardless of the faith or lack of faith of those who hear the doctrine.

9. The contemplation in which the buddhas always reveal themselves to everyone.

of the revelation of Buddhas to men and by the adornment of the preaching of the Bodhisattva Universal Virtue, the follower's ears will gradually hear sounds without impediment, his eyes will gradually see things without impediment, and his nose will gradually smell odors without impediment. This is as preached extensively in the Wonderful Law-Flower Sutra. Having obtained the purity of the six organs, he will have joy of body and mind and freedom from evil ideas, and will devote himself to this Law so that he can conform to it. He will again further acquire a hundred thousand myriad koṭis of the dhāraṇī of revolution and will again see extensively a hundred thousand myriad koṭis of innumerable buddhas. These world-honored ones will all stretch out their right hands, laying them on the head of the follower, and will speak thus: 'Good! Good! You are a follower of the Great-vehicle, an aspirant to the spirit of great adornment, and one who keeps the Great-vehicle in his mind. When of old we aspired to buddhahood, we were also like you. Do you be zealous and do not lose the Great-vehicle! Because we practiced it in our former lives, we have now become the pure body of the All Wise. Do you now be diligent and not lazy! These Great-vehicle sutras are the Law-treasury of the buddhas, the eyes of the buddhas from all directions in the past, present, and future, and also the seed which produces the tathāgatas in the past, present, and future. He who keeps these sutras has the body of a buddha and does the work of a buddha; know that such is the apostle sent by the buddhas; such is covered by the robes of the buddhas, the world-honored ones; such is a true Law-heir of the buddhas, the tathāgatas. Do you practice the Great-vehicle and do not cut off the Law-seeds! Do you now attentively behold the buddhas in the eastern quarter!'

"When these words are spoken, the follower sees all the innumerable worlds in the eastern quarter, whose lands are as even as one's palm, with no mounds or hills or thorns, but with ground of lapis lazuli and with gold to bound the ways. So, too, is it in the worlds of all directions. Having finished beholding this matter, the follower will see a jewel tree which is lofty, wonderful, and five thousand yojanas high. This tree will always produce deep gold and white silver, and will be adorned with the precious seven; under this tree there will be a jeweled lion throne of itself; the lion throne will be two thousand yojanas high and from the throne will radiate the light of a hundred jewels. In like manner, from all the trees, the other jewel thrones, and each jewel throne will radiate the light of a hundred jewels. In like manner, from all the trees, the other jewel thrones, and each jewel throne will emerge of themselves five hundred white elephants on which all the Bodhisattva Universal Virtues mount. Thereupon the follower, making obeisance to all Universal Virtues, should speak thus: 'By what sin have I only seen jewel grounds, jewel thrones, and jewel trees, but have been unable to see the buddhas?'

"When the follower finishes speaking thus, [he will see that] on each of the jewel thrones there is a world-honored one sitting on a jewel throne and very wonderful in his majesty. Having seen the buddhas, the follower will be greatly pleased and will again further recite and study the Great-vehicle sutras. By the power of the Great-vehicle, from the sky there will come a voice, praising and saying: 'Good! Good! Good son! By the cause of the merit you have [acquired] practicing the Great-vehicle, you have seen the buddhas. Though you have now been able to see the buddhas, the world-honored ones, you cannot yet see Sakyamuni Buddha, the buddhas who emanated from him, and the stupa of the Buddha Abundant Treasures.'

"After hearing the voice in the sky, the follower will again zealously recite and study the Great-vehicle sutras. Because he recites and studies the sutras of Great Extent, the Great-vehicle, even in his dreams he will see Sakyamuni Buddha staying on Mount Gṛdhrakūṭa with the great assembly, preaching the Law-Flower Sutra and expounding the meaning of one reality. After the teaching is preached, with repentance and a thirsting heart of hope, he will wish to see the Buddha. Then he must fold his hands, and kneeling in the direction of Mount Gṛdhrakūṭa, he must speak thus: 'Tathāgata, the world's hero forever remains in this world. Out of compassion for me, please reveal yourself to me.'

"After he has spoken thus, he will see Mount Gṛdhrakūṭa adorned with the precious seven and filled with countless bhikshus, śrāvakas, and a great assembly; this place is lined with jewel trees, and its jewel ground is even and smooth; there a wonderfully jeweled lion throne is spread. [On it sits] Sakyamuni Buddha, who sends forth from his eyebrows a ray of light, which shines everywhere throughout all directions of the universe and passes through the innumerable worlds in all directions. The buddhas emanated from Sakyamuni Buddha in all directions where this ray reaches assemble like a cloud at one time, and preach extensively the Wonderful Law—as [it is said] in the Wonderful Law-Flower Sutra.[10] Each of these emanated buddhas, having a body of deep gold, is boundless in the size of his body and sits on his lion throne, accompanied by countless hundreds of koṭis of great bodhisattvas as his retinue. The practice of each bodhisattva is equal to that of Universal Virtue. So, too, is it in the retinue of the countless buddhas and bodhisattvas in all directions. When the great assembly have gathered together like a cloud, they will see Sakyamuni Buddha, who from the pores of his whole body emits rays of light in each of which a hundred koṭis of transformed buddhas dwell. The emanated buddhas will emit rays of light from the white hair-circles, the sign of a great man, between their eyebrows, streaming on the head of Sakyamuni Buddha. Beholding this aspect, the emanated buddhas will also emit from all the pores of their bodies rays of light in each of which transformed buddhas, numerous as the atoms of the sands of the Ganges, abide.

"Thereupon the Bodhisattva Universal Virtue will again emit the ray of light, the sign of a great man, between his eyebrows, and put it into the heart of the follower. After this ray has entered into his heart, the follower himself will remember that under the countless hundreds and thousands of buddhas in the past he received and kept, read and recited the Great-vehicle sutras, and he will himself plainly and clearly see his former lives. He will possess the very faculty of transcendent remembrance of former states of existence.[11] Immediately attaining a great enlightenment, he will acquire the dhāraṇī of revolution and a hundred thousand myriad koṭis of dhāraṇīs. Rising from his contemplation, he will see before himself all the emanated buddhas sitting on lion thrones under all the jewel trees. He will also see the ground of lapis lazuli springing up from the lower sky like heaps of lotus flowers; between each flower there will be bodhisattvas, numerous as the atoms [of the sands of the Ganges] and sitting cross-legged. He will also see the bodhisattvas who emanated from Universal Virtue, extolling and expounding the Great-vehicle among their assembly. Then the bodhi-

10. See pp. 197 ff.

11. One of the six transcendent powers. These are mysterious powers of the Buddha and arhats that can be gained by meditation and wisdom.

sattvas with one voice will cause the follower to purify his six organs.

"One bodhisattva's preaching will say: 'Do you reflect on the Buddha'; another's preaching will say: 'Do you reflect on the Law'; yet another's preaching will say: 'Do you reflect on the Saṃgha'; still another's preaching will say: 'Do you reflect on the precepts'; still another one's preaching will say: 'Do you reflect on gift-giving'; yet another's preaching will say: 'Do you reflect on the heavens.' And the preaching will further say: 'Such six laws are the aspiration to buddhahood and are the ones that beget the bodhisattvas. Before the buddhas, do you now confess your previous sins and repent them sincerely.'

"In your innumerable former lives, by reason of your organ of the eye, you have been attached to all forms. Because of your attachment to forms, you hanker after all dust.[12] Because of your hankering after dust, you receive a woman's body and you are pleasurably absorbed in all forms everywhere you are born age after age. Forms harm your eyes and you become a slave of human affections. Therefore forms cause you to wander in the triple world. Such fatigue of your wandering there makes you so blind that you can see nothing at all. You have now recited the sutras of Great Extent, the Great-vehicle. In these sutras the buddhas of all directions preach that their forms and bodies are not extinct. You have now been able to see them—is this not true? The evil of your eye-organ often does much harm to you. Obediently following my words, you must take refuge in the buddhas and Sakyamuni Buddha, and confess the sins due to your organ of the eye, saying: 'Law-water of wisdom-eye possessed by the buddhas and the bodhisattvas! Be pleased, by means of it, to wash me and to let me become pure!'

"Having finished speaking thus, the follower should universally salute the buddhas in all directions, and turning to Sakyamuni Buddha and the Great-vehicle sutras, he should again speak thus: 'The heavy sins of my eye-organ of which I now repent are such an impediment and are so tainted that I am blind and can see nothing at all. May the Buddha be pleased to pity and protect me by his great mercy! The Bodhisattva Universal Virtue on board the ship of the great Law ferries the company of the countless bodhisattvas everywhere in all direc-

12. Suggesting illusions, because the illusions preventing living beings from attaining knowledge are as innumerable as atoms of dust.

tions. Out of compassion for me, be pleased to permit me to hear the law of repenting the evil of my eye-organ and the impediment of my bad karma!'

"Speaking thus three times, the follower must prostrate himself down to the ground and rightly reflect on the Great-vehicle without forgetting it. This is called the law repenting the sin of the organ of the eye. If there be anyone who calls upon the names of the buddhas, burns incense, strews flowers, aspires to the Great-vehicle, hangs silks, flags, and canopies, speaks of the errors of his eyes, and repents his sins, such a one in the present world will see Sakyamuni Buddha, the buddhas who emanated from him, and countless other buddhas, and will not fall into the evil paths for asaṃkhyeya kalpas. Thanks to the power and to the vow of the Great-vehicle, such a one will become an attendant [of the buddhas], together with all the bodhisattvas of dhāraṇī. Anyone who reflects thus is one who thinks rightly. If anyone reflects otherwise, such is called one who thinks falsely. This is called the sign of the first stage of the purification of the eye-organ.

"Having finished purifying the organ of the eye, the follower should again further read and recite the Great-vehicle sutras, kneel and repent six times day and night, and should speak thus: 'Why can I only see Sakyamuni Buddha and the buddhas who emanated from him, but cannot see the Buddha's relics of his whole body in the stupa of the Buddha Abundant Treasures? The stupa of the Buddha Abundant Treasures exists forever and is not extinct. I have defiled and evil eyes. For this reason, I cannot see the stupa.' After speaking thus, the follower should again practice further repentance.

"After seven days have passed, the stupa of the Buddha Abundant Treasures will spring out of the earth. Sakyamuni Buddha with his right hand opens the door of the stupa, where the Buddha Abundant Treasures is seen deep in the contemplation of the universal revelation of forms. From each pore of his body he emits rays of light as numerous as the atoms of the sands of the Ganges. In each ray there dwells one of the hundred thousand myriad koṭis of transformed buddhas. When such a sign appears, the follower will rejoice and make procession around the stupa with praising verses. When he has finished making procession around it seven times, the Tathāgata Abundant Treasures with a great voice praises him, saying: 'Heir of the Law! You have truly practiced the Great-vehicle and have obediently followed Universal Virtue, repenting [the sins of] your eye-organ. For this reason, I will go to you and bear testimony to you.' Having spoken thus, the Tathāgata extols the Buddha, saying: 'Excellent! Excellent! Sakyamuni Buddha! Thou art able to preach the Great Law, to pour the rain of the Great Law, and to cause all the defiled living to accomplish their buddhahood.' Thereupon the follower, having beheld the stupa of the Buddha Abundant Treasures, again goes to the Bodhisattva Universal Virtue, and folding his hands and saluting him, speaks to him, saying: 'Great Teacher! Please teach me the repentance of my errors.'

"Universal Virtue again speaks to the follower, saying: 'Through many kalpas, because of your ear-organ, you dangle after external sounds; your hearing of mystic sounds begets attachment to them; your hearing of evil sounds causes the harm of one hundred and eight illusions. Such retribution of your hearing evils brings about evil things and your incessant hearing of evil sounds produces various entanglements. Because of your perverted hearing, you will fall into evil paths, faraway places of false views, where the Law cannot be heard. At present you have recited and kept the Great-vehicle, the ocean-store of merits. For this reason, you have come to see the buddhas in all directions, and the stupa of the Buddha Abundant Treasures has appeared to bear testimony to you. You must yourself confess your own errors and evils and must repent all your sins.'

"Then the follower, having heard thus, must again further fold his hands, and prostrating himself down to the ground, he must speak thus, saying: 'All Wise, World-honored One! Be pleased to reveal yourself and bear testimony to me! The sutras of Great Extent are the masters of compassion. Be pleased to look upon me and hear my words! Until my present life, for many kalpas, because of my ear-organ, I have been attached to hearing [evil] sounds, like glue sticking to grass; my hearing of evil sounds causes the poison of illusions which are attached to every condition and I am not able to rest even for a little while; my raising evil sounds fatigues my nerves and makes me fall into the three evil ways. Now having for the first time understood this, I confess and repent it, turning to the world-honored ones.' Having finished repenting thus, the follower will see the Buddha Abundant Treasures emitting a great ray of light which is gold-colored and universally illuminates the eastern quarter as well as the worlds in all directions, where the countless buddhas appear with their bodies of pure gold color. In the sky of the eastern quarter there comes a voice uttering thus: 'Here is a buddha, the world-honored one named Excellent Virtue, who also possesses innumerable emanated buddhas sitting cross-legged on lion thrones under jewel trees. All these world-honored ones who enter into the contemplation of the universal revelation of forms speak to the follower, praising him and saying: "Good! Good! Good son! You have now read and recited the Great-vehicle sutras. That which you have recited is the mental stage of the Buddha." '

"After these words have been spoken, the Bodhisattva Universal Virtue will again further preach to the follower the law of repentance, saying: 'In the innumerable kalpas of your former lives, because of your attachment to odors, your discrimination and your perception are attached to every condition and you fall into birth and death. Do you now meditate on the cause of the Great-vehicle! The cause of the Great-vehicle is the Reality of All Existence.'

"Having heard these words, the follower should again further repent, prostrating himself down to the ground. When he has repented, he should exclaim thus: 'Namaḥ Sakyamuni Buddha! Namaḥ stupa of the Buddha Abundant Treasures! Namaḥ all the buddhas emanated from Sakyamuni Buddha!' Having spoken thus, he should universally salute the buddhas in all directions, exclaiming: 'Namaḥ the Buddha Excellent Virtue in the eastern quarter and the buddhas who emanate from him!' The follower should also make obeisance to each of these buddhas as wholeheartedly as if he saw them with his naked eyes, and should pay homage to them with incense and flowers. After paying homage to the buddhas, he should kneel with folded hands and extol them with various verses. After extolling them, he should speak of the ten evil karmas and repent all his sins. Having repented, he should speak thus, saying: 'During the innumerable kalpas of my former lives, I yearned after odors, flavors, and contacts and produced all [manner of] evils. For this reason, for innumerable lives I have continuously received states of evil existence including hells, hungry spirits, animals, and faraway places of false views. Now I confess such evil karmas, and taking refuge in the buddhas, the kings of the Righteous Law, I confess and repent my sins.'

"Having repented thus, the follower must again read and recite the

Great-vehicle sutras without negligence of body and mind. By the power of the Great-vehicle, from the sky there comes a voice saying: 'Heir of the Law! Do you now praise and explain the Law of the Great-vehicle, turning to the buddhas in all directions, and before them do you yourself speak of your errors! The buddhas, the tathāgatas, are your merciful fathers. Do you yourself speak of the evils and bad karmas produced by your organ of the tongue, saying: "This organ of the tongue, moved by the thought of evil karmas, causes me to praise false speaking, improper language, ill speaking, a double tongue, slandering, lying, and words of false views, and also causes me to utter useless words. Because of such many and various evil karmas I provoke fights and dissensions and speak of the Law as if it were not the Law. I now confess all such sins of mine." '

"Having spoken thus before the world's heroes, the follower must universally revere the buddhas in all directions, prostrating himself down to the ground, and folding his hands and kneeling salute them, and he must speak thus, saying: 'The errors of this tongue are numberless and boundless. All the thorns of evil karmas come from the organ of the tongue. This tongue causes the cutting off of the wheel of the Righteous Law. Such an evil tongue cuts off the seeds of merits. Preaching of meaningless things is frequently forced upon [others]. Praising false views is like adding wood to a fire and further wounding living beings [who already suffer] in raging flames. It is like one who dies drinking poison without [showing] sores or pustules. Such reward of sins is evil, false, and bad, and causes me to fall into the evil paths during a hundred or a thousand kalpas. Lying causes me to fall into a great hell. I now take refuge in the buddhas of the southern quarter and confess my errors and sins.'

"When the follower reflects thus, there will come a voice from the sky saying: 'In the southern quarter there is a buddha named Sandalwood Virtue who also possesses countless emanated buddhas. All these buddhas preach the Great-vehicle and extinguish sins and evils. Turning to the innumerable buddhas and the great merciful world-honored ones in all directions, you must confess such sins, false evils, and repent them with a sincere heart.' When these words have been spoken, the follower should again salute the buddhas, prostrating himself down to the ground.

"Thereupon the buddhas will send forth rays of light which illuminate the follower's body and cause him naturally to feel joy of body and mind, to raise a great mercy, and to reflect on all things extensively. At that time the buddhas will widely preach to the follower the law of great kindness, compassion, joy, and indifference, and also teach him kind words to make him practice the six ways of harmony and reverence.[13] Then the follower, having heard this royal teaching, will greatly rejoice in his heart and will again further recite and study it without laziness.

"From the sky there again comes a mystic voice, speaking thus: 'Do you now practice the repentance of body and mind! [The sins of] the body are killing, stealing, and committing adultery, while [the sins of] the mind are entertaining thoughts of various evils. Producing the ten evil karmas and the five deadly sins is just like [living as] a monkey, like birdlime and glue, and the attachment to all sorts of conditions leads universally to the [passions of the] six sense organs of all living beings. The karmas of these six organs with their boughs, twigs, flowers, and leaves entirely fill the triple world, the twenty-five abodes of living beings, and all places where creatures are born. Such karmas also increase ignorance, old age, death, and the twelve sufferings, and infallibly reach through to the eight falsenesses and the eight circumstances.[14] Do you now repent such evil and bad karmas!' Then the follower, having heard thus, asks the voice in the sky, saying: 'At what place may I practice the law of repentance?'

"Thereupon the voice in the sky will speak thus, saying: 'Sakyamuni Buddha is called Vairocana Who Pervades All Places, and his dwelling place is called Eternally Tranquil Light,[15] the place which is composed of permanency-pāramitā, and stabilized by self-pāramitā, the place where purity-pāramitā extinguishes the aspect of existence, where bliss-pāramitā does not abide in the aspect of one's body and

13. The six ways of harmony and reverence practiced by those who seek enlightenment.

14. Eight places or circumstances in which one is unable to see the Buddha or to listen to the Law. These are the conditions of hell, animals, hungry spirits, the heaven of long life, remote places, the state of being blind or deaf, secular prejudice, and the period of the absence of the Buddha.

15. The expressions "Vairocana Who Pervades All Places" and "Eternally Tranquil Light," like those that follow, signify the transcendence of all limitations of time and space, based on the idea of *śūnya,* or the void. Positively, it means the absolute universality of the Buddha and the Buddha-land.

mind, and where the aspects of all the laws cannot be seen as either existing or nonexisting, the place of tranquil emancipation or prajñā-pāramitā. Because these forms are based on permanent law, thus you must now meditate on the buddhas in all directions.'

"Then the buddhas in all directions will stretch out their right hands, laying them on the head of the follower, and will speak thus: 'Good! Good! Good son! Because you have now read and recited the Great-vehicle sutras, the buddhas in all directions will preach the law of repentance. The bodhisattva practice is not to cut off binding and driving[16] nor to abide in the ocean of driving. In meditating on one's mind, there is no mind one can seize, except the mind that comes from one's perverted thought. The mind presenting such a form rises from one's false imagination like the wind in the sky, which has no foothold. Such a form of the law neither appears nor disappears. What is sin? What is blessedness? As one's own mind is void of itself, sin and blessedness have no existence.[17] In like manner all the laws are neither fixed nor going toward destruction. If one repents like this, meditating on his mind, there is no mind he can seize. The law also does not dwell in the law. All the laws are emancipation, the truth of extinction, and quiescence. Such an aspect is called the great repentance, the greatly adorned repentance, the repentance of the non-sin aspect, and the destruction of discrimination. He who practices this repentance has the purity of body and mind not fixed in the law [but free] as flowing water. Through each reflection, he will be able to see the Bodhisattva Universal Virtue and the buddhas in all directions.'

"Thereupon all the world-honored ones, sending forth the ray of light of great mercy, preach the law of nonaspect to the follower. He hears the world-honored ones preaching the Void of the first principle. When he has heard it, his mind becomes imperturbable. In due time, he will enter into the real bodhisattva standing." The Buddha addressed Ānanda: "To practice in this manner is called repentance. This is the law of repentance which the buddhas and great bodhisattvas in all directions practice."

16. This is a term denoting defilement because defilement binds human beings to transmigration and also drives them to the world of suffering. The bodhisattva practice is the middle way between excessive austerity and excessive indulgence.

17. The state of nonattachment, that is, *śūnya*. When a person reaches the state of nonattachment the problem of good and evil is eliminated.

The Buddha addressed Ānanda: "After the extinction of the Buddha, if all his disciples should repent their evil and bad karmas, they must only read and recite the Great-vehicle sutras. These sutras of Great Extent are the eyes of the buddhas. By means of the sutras the buddhas have perfected the five kinds of eyes.[18] The three kinds of the Buddha's bodies grow out [of the sutras] of Great Extent. This is the seal of the Great Law with which the ocean of nirvana is sealed. From such an ocean are born the three kinds of pure bodies of the Buddha. These three kinds of the Buddha's bodies are the blessing-field for gods and men, and the supreme object of worship. If there be any who recite and read the sutras of Great Extent, the Great-vehicle, know that such are endowed with the Buddha's merits and, having extinguished their longstanding evils, are born of the Buddha's wisdom."

At that time the World-honored One spoke thus in verse:

"If one has evil in his eye-organ
And his eyes are impure with the impediment of karmas,
He must only recite the Great-vehicle
And reflect on the first principle.
This is called the repentance of the eye,
Ending all bad karmas.
His ear-organ hears disordered sounds
And disturbs the principle of harmony.
This produces in him a demented mind,
Like [that of] a foolish monkey.
He must only recite the Great-vehicle
And meditate on the void nonaspect of the Law,
Ending all the longstanding evils,
So that with the heavenly ears he may hear [sounds] from all directions.
His organ of smell is attached to all odors,

18. The five kinds of eyes are (1) the eye of those who have a material body; (2) the divine eye of celestial beings in the Realm of Form; (3) the eye of wisdom, by which the followers of the two vehicles perceive the nonsubstantiality of things; (4) the eye of the Law, by which the bodhisattvas perceive all teachings in order to lead human beings to enlightenment; and (5) the Buddha's eye, the four kinds of eyes enumerated above existing in the Buddha's body.

Causing all contacts according to lusts.
His nose thus deluded
Gives birth to all dust [of illusions] according to his lusts.
If one recites the Great-vehicle sutras
And meditates on the fundamental truth of the Law,
He will become free from his longstanding evil karmas,
And will not again produce them in his future lives.
His organ of the tongue causes five kinds
Of bad karmas of evil speech.
Should one wish to control them by himself,
He must zealously practice mercy,
And considering the true principle of quiescence of the Law,
He should not conceive discriminations.
His organ of thought is like [that of] a monkey,
Never resting even for a little while.
Should one desire to subdue this organ,
He must zealously recite the Great-vehicle,
Reflecting on the Buddha's greatly enlightened body,
The completion of his power, and his fearlessness.
The body is the master of its organs,
As wind causes dust to roll,
Wandering in its six organs,
Freely without obstacles.
If one desires to destroy these evils,
To be removed from the longstanding illusions of dust,
Ever dwelling in the city of nirvana,
And to be at ease with mind tranquil,
He should recite the Great-vehicle sutras
And reflect on the mother[19] of bodhisattvas.
Innumerable surpassing means of tactfulness
Will be obtained through one's reflection on reality.
Such six laws
Are called [the purification of] the six sense organs.
The ocean of impediment of all karmas
Is produced from one's false imagination.

19. The doctrine of the Great-vehicle as the mother and supporter of the bodhisattvas.

Should one wish to repent of it
Let him sit upright and meditate on the true aspect [of reality].
All sins are just as frost and dew,
So wisdom's sun can disperse them.
Therefore with entire devotion
Let him repent of his six sense organs."

Having spoken these verses, the Buddha addressed Ānanda: "Do you now repent of these six organs, keep the law of meditating on the Bodhisattva Universal Virtue, and discriminate and explain it widely to all the gods of the universe and men. After the extinction of the Buddha, if all his disciples receive and keep, read and recite, and expound the sutras of Great Extent, whether in a quiet place or in a graveyard, or under a tree, or in a place of the āraṇya, they must read and recite [the sutras of] Great Extent, and must think of the meaning of the Great-vehicle. By virtue of the strong power of their reflecting on the sutras, they will be able to see myself, the stupa of the Buddha Abundant Treasures, the countless emanated buddhas from all directions, the Bodhisattva Universal Virtue, the Bodhisattva Mañjuśrī, the Bodhisattva Medicine King, and the Bodhisattva Medicine Lord. By virtue of their revering the Law, these buddhas and bodhisattvas, abiding in the sky with various wonderful flowers, will extol and revere those who practice and keep the Law. By virtue of their only reciting the sutras of Great Extent, the Great-vehicle, the buddhas and bodhisattvas will day and night pay homage to those who keep the Law."

The Buddha addressed Ānanda: "I as well as the bodhisattvas in the Virtuous kalpa and the buddhas in all directions, by means of our thinking of the true meaning of the Great-vehicle, have now rid ourselves of the sins of birth and death during hundreds of myriad koṭis of asaṃkhyeya kalpas. By means of this supreme and wonderful law of repentance, we have each become the buddhas in all directions. If one desires to accomplish Perfect Enlightenment rapidly and wishes in his present life to see the buddhas in all directions and the Bodhisattva Universal Virtue, he must take a bath to purify himself, wear clean robes, and burn rare incense, and must dwell in a secluded place, where he should recite and read the Great-vehicle sutras and think of the meaning of the Great-vehicle."

The Buddha addressed Ānanda: "If there are living beings who desire to meditate on the Bodhisattva Universal Virtue, they must meditate thus. If anyone meditates thus, such is called one who meditates rightly. If anyone meditates otherwise, such is called one who meditates falsely. After the extinction of the Buddha, if all his disciples obediently follow the Buddha's words and practice repentance, let it be known that these are doing the work of Universal Virtue. Those who do the work of Universal Virtue see neither evil aspects nor the retribution of evil karmas. If there be any living beings who salute the buddhas in all directions six times day and night, recite the Great-vehicle sutras, and consider the profound Law of the Void of the first principle, they will rid themselves of the sins of birth and death [produced] during hundreds of myriad koṭis of asaṃkhyeya kalpas in the [short] time it takes one to snap his fingers. Anyone doing this work is a real Buddha-son who is born from the buddhas. The buddhas in all directions and the bodhisattvas will become his preceptors. This is called one who is perfect in the precepts of the bodhisattvas. Without going through the ceremony of confession, he will of himself accomplish bodhisattvahood and will be revered by all the gods and men.

"At that time, if the follower desires to be perfect in the precepts of the bodhisattva, he must fold his hands, dwell in the seclusion of the wilds, universally salute the buddhas in all directions, and repent his sins, and must himself confess his errors. After this, in a calm place, he should speak to the buddhas in all directions, saying thus: 'The buddhas, the world-honored ones, remain forever in this world. Because of the impediments of my karmas, though I believe in [the sutras of] Great Extent, I cannot clearly see the buddhas. I have now taken refuge in the buddhas. Be pleased, Sakyamuni Buddha, All Wise and World-honored One, to be my preceptor! Mañjuśrī, possessor of great compassion! With your wisdom, be pleased to bestow on me the laws of pure bodhisattvas! Bodhisattva Maitreya, supreme and great merciful sun! Out of your compassion for me, be pleased to permit me to receive the laws of the bodhisattvas! Buddhas in all directions! Be pleased to reveal yourselves and bear testimony to me! Great bodhisattvas! Through calling each upon your names, be pleased, supreme great leaders, to protect all living beings and to help us! At present I have received and kept the sutras of Great Extent. Even if I should lose my life, fall into hell, and receive innumerable sufferings, I would never slander the Righteous Law of the buddhas. For this reason and by the power of this merit, Sakyamuni Buddha! Be now pleased to be my preceptor! Mañjuśrī! Be pleased to be my teacher! Maitreya in the world to come! Be pleased to bestow on me the Law! Buddhas in all directions! Be pleased to bear witness to me! Bodhisattvas of great virtues! Be pleased to be my friends! I now, by means of the profound and mysterious meaning of the Great-vehicle sutras, take refuge in the Buddha, take refuge in the Law, and take refuge in the Saṃgha.'

"The follower must speak thus three times. Having taken refuge in the Three Treasures, next he must himself vow to receive the sixfold laws.[20] Having received the sixfold laws, next he must zealously practice the unhindered brahma-conduct, raise the mind of universally saving all living beings, and receive the eightfold laws.[21] Having made such vows in the seclusion of the wilds, he must burn rare incense, strew flowers, pay homage to all the buddhas, the bodhisattvas, and [the sutras of] Great Extent, the Great-vehicle, and must speak thus, saying: 'I have now raised the aspiration to buddhahood: may this merit save all the living!'

"Having spoken thus, the follower should again further prostrate himself before all the buddhas and the bodhisattvas, and should think of the meaning of [the sutras of] Great Extent. During a day or three times seven days, whether he be a monk or a layman, he has no need of a preceptor nor does he need to employ any teacher; even without [attending the ceremony of] the jñapti-karman, because of the power [coming] from his receiving and keeping, reading and reciting the Great-vehicle sutras and because of the works which the Bodhisattva Universal Virtue helps and inspires him to do—they are in fact the eyes of the Righteous Law of the buddhas in all directions—he will be able, through this Law, to perform by himself the five kinds of Law-bodies: precepts, meditation, wisdom, emancipation, and knowledge of emancipation. All the buddhas, the tathāgatas, have been born of this Law and have received the prediction [of their enlightenment] in

20. The five Buddhist precepts (not to take life, not to steal, to refrain from wrong sexual activity, not to lie, and not to drink intoxicants) and not to speak of other people's faults.

21. The six precepts enumerated in fn. 20 plus not to conceal one's faults and not to emphasize other people's shortcomings rather than their good points.

the Great-vehicle sutras. Therefore, O wise man! Suppose that a śrāvaka breaks the threefold refuge, the five precepts, and the eight precepts,[22] the precepts of bhikshus, of bhikshuṇīs, of śrāmaṇeras, of śrāmaṇerikās, and of śikshamāṇās and their dignified behavior, and [also suppose] that because of his foolishness, evil, and bad and false mind he infringes many precepts and the rules of dignified behavior. If he desires to rid himself of and destroy these errors, to become a bhikshu again and to fulfill the laws of monks, he must diligently read the sutras of Great Extent, considering the profound Law of the Void of the first principle, and must bring this wisdom of the Void to his heart; know that in each one of his thoughts such a one will [gradually] end the defilement of all his longstanding sins without any remainder—this is called one who is perfect in the laws and the precepts of monks and fulfills their dignified behavior. Such a one will be served by all gods and men. Suppose any upāsaka violates his dignified behavior and does bad things. To do bad things means, namely, to proclaim the errors and sins of the Buddha-laws, to discuss evil things perpetrated by the four groups, and not to feel shame even in committing theft and adultery. If he desires to repent and rid himself of these sins, he must zealously read and recite the sutras of Great Extent and must think of the first principle. Suppose a king, a minister, a Brahman, a citizen, an elder, a state official, all of these persons seek greedily and untiringly after desires, commit the five deadly sins, slander the sutras of Great Extent, and perform the ten evil karmas. Their recompense for these great evils will cause them to fall into evil paths faster than the breaking of a rainstorm. They will be sure to fall into the Avīci hell. If they desire to rid themselves of and destroy these impediments of karmas, they must raise shame and repent all their sins."

The Buddha spoke, saying: "Why is it called a law of repentance of Kshatriyas and citizens? The law of repentance of Kshatriyas and citizens is that they must constantly have the right mind, not slander the Three Treasures nor hinder the monks nor persecute anyone practicing brahma-conduct; they must not forget to practice the law of the six reflections; they must again support, pay homage to, and surely

22. The five precepts (see p. 368 fn. 20 and Glossary) plus the following three: to avoid perfume, dancing, and the theater; not to sit or sleep in an adorned chair; and not to eat after noon.

salute the keeper of the Great-vehicle; they must remember the profound doctrine of sutras and the Void of the first principle. One who thinks of this law is called one who practices the first repentance of Kshatriyas and citizens. Their second repentance is to discharge their filial duty to their fathers and mothers and to respect their teachers and seniors—this is called one who practices the law of the second repentance. Their third repentance is to rule their countries with the Righteous Law and not to oppress their people unjustly—this is called one who practices the third repentance. Their fourth repentance is to issue within their states the ordinance of the six days of fasting[23] and to cause their people to abstain from killing wherever their powers reach. One who practices such a law is called one who practices the fourth repentance. Their fifth repentance is to believe deeply the causes and results of things, to have faith in the way of one reality, and to know that the Buddha is never extinct—this is called one who practices the fifth repentance."

The Buddha addressed Ānanda: "If, in future worlds, there be any who practices these laws of repentance, know that such a man has put on the robes of shame, is protected and helped by the buddhas, and will attain Perfect Enlightenment before long." As these words were spoken, ten thousand divine sons acquired pure spiritual eyes, and also the great bodhisattvas, the Bodhisattva Maitreya and others, and Ānanda, hearing the preaching of the Buddha, all rejoiced and did [as the Buddha commanded].

23. The days of purification, on which offerings are made to the dead. The eighth, fourteenth, fifteenth, twenty-third, twenty-ninth, and thirtieth days of the month, on which laymen observe the eight precepts, are called the *roku sainichi,* or six days of fasting, in Japanese.

Glossary

Abhidharma Kośa A commentary, or *śāstra,* on Buddhist doctrine, attributed to Vasubandhu (fifth century A.D.).

Abundant Treasures The extinct buddha who appears in order to testify to the truth of Sakyamuni Buddha's teaching of the Lotus Flower of the Wonderful Law, though he himself does not preach the Law. He is said to be the *Dharmakāya,* or truth-body, of Sakyamuni, while the truth of the Wonderful Law is Sakyamuni's *saṃbhogakāya,* or reward-body, and Sakyamuni himself is the *nirmāṇakāya,* or mutation-body. See page 249, note 1. *See also* Stupa of the Precious Seven, *trikāya.*

Akanishthā The heaven of final form; the highest of the eighteen heavens of the Realm of Form.

Akshobhya The buddha of the realm of Wonderful Joy in the east.

akshobhya One hundred *bimbaras.* See *bimbara.*

Amita Also called Amitābha (Infinite Light) or Amitāyus (Infinite Life). The buddha of the Pure Land, Sukhāvatī, or "Highest Joy," in the west; the principal buddha of the Pure Land (Jōdo) sect of Buddhism in Japan.

anāgāmin *See* four merits.

Ānanda A cousin of Sakyamuni and one of the Buddha's ten great disciples. He was famous for his excellent memory and is supposed to have memorized all the Buddha's sermons, which were later recorded as sutras.

Aniruddha A cousin of Sakyamuni and one of the Buddha's ten great disciples.

apasmāraka A blue-colored demon.

āraṇya A general term for a Buddhist monastery.

arhat Literally, "man of worth, honorable one." (1) One who is free from all cravings and thus from rebirth. (2) One of the titles of the Buddha. (3) The highest stage attained by a Hīnayāna Buddhist. *See also* four holy states.

arjaka A kind of flower which, when touched, opens and falls apart in seven pieces. Identified as *Symplocos racemosa* (Kern) and *Ocinum gratissimum* (Monier-Williams).

asaṃkhyeya Countless.

asura A titan or spirit that may be either good or evil. The *asuras* are the enemies of the *devas* and are the mightiest of all demons. They comprise the fourth class of sentient beings. *See also* six states of existence.

atimuktaka A variety of sweet-smelling flower.

avaivartika See *avivartika.*

Avalokiteśvara *See* Regarder of the Cries of the World.

Avīci hell The hell of "no interval" (*avīci*), or uninterrupted hell; the last of the eight great hot hells, whose sufferers die and are reborn incessantly.

avivartika Also *avaivartika, avinivartanīya.* "Not turning back" or "not sliding back," that is, going straight to nirvana.

ayuta One hundred *koṭis.* See *koṭi.*

bhikshu Literally, "beggar." A religious mendicant who has left home and renounced all possessions in order to follow the way of the Buddha, and who has become a fully ordained monk.

bhikshuṇī A Buddhist nun observing the same rules as a *bhikshu.* See *bhikshu.*

bimba A kind of fruit.

bimbara Also *vi(ṃ)vara.* One hundred *kaṅkaras.* See *kaṅkara.*

Bodhi Wisdom, enlightenment, buddhahood. (1) The wisdom of the Buddha's enlightenment. (2) Nirvana. (3) The way to nirvana. (4) The Buddhist Way.

bodhisattva *Bodhi,* buddhahood; *sattva,* living being. (1) A being in the final stage prior to attaining buddhahood. (2) One who seeks enlightenment not only for himself but for all sentient beings.

bodhisattva-*mahāsattva* A perfected bodhisattva, greater (*mahā*) than any being (*sattva*), especially in saving other beings; a perfected being who falls short of buddhahood only because, in order to save others, he has voluntarily not yet entered nirvana.

Bodhi tree The appellation of the tree under which Sakyamuni was seated in meditation when he attained enlightenment. *See also* Bodhi, Gayā.

Boundless Conduct One of the four great perfected bodhisattvas who attend Sakyamuni Buddha and protect the Lotus Sutra and its devotees. The other three are Eminent Conduct, Pure Conduct, and Steadfast Conduct. Together they are called the four great primarily evolved or eternally evolved bodhisattvas.

Brahma One of the three major deities of Hinduism, along with Vishnu and Śiva; in Buddhism, he is the lord of the Realm of Form.

brahmacārin Literally, "descendant of purity." A young male Brahman who is a student of the Vedas under a preceptor or who practices chastity; a young male Brahman before marriage. *See also* Brahman.

Brahman A member of the priestly caste, highest of the four major castes of India.

buddha A title meaning "one who is enlightened," or "enlightened one."

buddha-nature The potential for attaining buddhahood, or potential for enlightenment, innate in every sentient being. *See also* buddha-seed.

buddha-seed The buddha-nature innate in all living beings. There are two aspects to the buddha-seed: (1) the natural seed, or nature-seed, which all living beings, even those in hell, possess, but which has no independent power to appear of itself; (2) the vehicle-seed, by which the natural seed is caused to appear. The vehicle-seed is the One Buddha-vehicle Law revealed in the Lotus Sutra. *See* Buddha-vehicle.

Buddha-vehicle Also called the One-vehicle. The vehicle leading to Perfect Enlightenment and buddhahood, and transcending both Hīnayāna and Mahāyāna. See also page 60, note 14.

caitya A pagoda in which sutras are deposited. *See also stūpa.*

cakravartin *See* wheel-rolling king.

campaka A sweet-smelling flower from which a perfumed oil is made.

City of Royal Palaces Rājagṛha, the capital city of the ancient kingdom of Magadha in Central India.

Counterfeit Law The second of the three stages through which the Law passes in each buddha-period. In the first stage, that of the Righteous Law, the Law remains perfect; in the second it is a mere copy without power, remaining in form alone; and in the third and final period, that of the Decline of the Law, the Law vanishes and a new buddha appears in the world to preach the Righteous Law again.

Deer Park A park in Benares (Sanskrit, Vārāṇasī), where the Buddha preached his first sermon to five fellow mendicants—Ājñāta-Kauṇḍinya, Aśvajit, Vāshpa, Mahānāman, and Bhadrika—shortly after his enlightenment.

deva A celestial or heavenly deity.

Devadatta A cousin of Sakyamuni, who followed him at first but later turned against him and tried to have him killed. See also page 207, unnumbered footnote.

dhāraṇī Literally, "wholly grasping." (1) A magic spell or incantation. (2) Special powers. (3) The virtues that adhere to all good laws.

Dharma *See* Law.

dharma *See* law.

dhūta An ascetic practice or precept. There are twelve *dhūtas,* or mendicant's duties: (1) living in a forest, (2) taking whatever seat may be offered, (3) living on alms, (4) using only one seat for both meditation and eating, (5) wearing coarse garments, (6) not eating at unregulated times, (7) wearing clothes made of discarded rags, (8) having only three robes, (9) living in or near a cemetery, (10) living under a tree, (11) living in the open air, (12) sleeping in a seated posture.

Diamond, Mount Another name for Mount Iron Circle. *See* Great Iron Circle, Mount.

Divine Vulture Peak *See* Gṛdhrakūṭa, Mount.

eighteen characteristics The eighteen unique qualities characterizing a buddha: (1) faultless in body, (2) faultless in speech, (3) faultless in mind and thought, (4) having no unsteadiness of mind, (5) impartiality, (6) perfect resignation, (7) imperishable aspiration to save all living beings, (8) unfailing zeal, (9) unfailing memory of all teachings of all buddhas past, present, and future, (10) unfailing contemplation, (11) unfailing wisdom, (12) unfailing freedom from all hindrances, (13) all bodily deeds being in accord with wisdom, (14) all deeds of speech being in accord with wisdom, (15) all deeds of thought being in accord with wisdom, (16) unhindered knowledge of the past, (17) unhindered knowledge of the future, (18) unhindered knowledge of the present.

eight emancipations (1) Emancipation from the conception that notions have both subjective and objective realities corresponding to them; (2) emancipation from the conception that notions have no subjective but do have objective realities corresponding to them; (3) emancipation from the conception of any realities whatsoever, whether subjective or objective; (4) emancipation through the recognition that unreality is unlimited; (5) emancipation through the recognition that knowledge is unlimited; (6) emancipation through the recognition of absolute nonexistence; (7) emancipation through a state of mind in which there is neither consciousness nor unconsciousness; (8) emancipation through a state of mind in which there is final extinction of both sensation and consciousness. These are mental operations. There are also eight moral emancipations from vice and passion, gained through observing the eight sections of the *Prātimoksha Sūtra*, that is, the *vinaya*, or precepts and rules of conduct. In addition, there are eight mystic emancipations, or dwellings of the mind successively in eight different localities, corresponding to the above-listed eight mental operations.

Eightfold Path Right views, right thinking, right speech, right action, right living, right endeavor, right memory, right meditation.

eight guardians The eight kinds of nonhuman beings, both divine and demonic, that protect Buddhism: *devas, nāgas, yakshas, gandharvas, asuras, garuḍas, kiṃnaras,* and *mahoragas.*

Eminent Conduct *See* Boundless Conduct.

five aggregates The five *skandhas,* the elements or attributes of which every human being is comprised: (1) form, or the body; (2) receptivity, sensation, feeling; (3) conception; (4) volition, or various mental activities; (5) consciousness. The union of these five aggregates dates from the moment of birth and constitutes the individual.

five desires (1) The desires of the five senses—sight, hearing, smell, taste, and touch; (2) the desires for wealth, sex, food, fame, and sleep.

five Law-bodies Precepts, meditation, wisdom, emancipation, knowledge of emancipation.

five *pāramitās* The first five of the Six *Pāramitās.* See *pāramitā,* Six *Pāramitās.*

five precepts The five basic Buddhist precepts: (1) not to take life, (2) not to steal, (3) to refrain from wrong sexual activity, (4) not to lie, (5) not to drink intoxicants.

five transcendent faculties (1) The celestial eye (instantaneous viewing of any object in any universe); (2) the celestial ear (the ability to apprehend any sound produced in any universe); (3) the minds of others (intuitive knowledge of the minds of all other beings); (4) the destiny of the karma-abodes (knowledge of all former lives of oneself and of others); (5) freedom of will (the power of spirit over matter). There is also a sixth transcendent faculty, the elimination of faults (supernatural knowledge of the finality or end of all faults).

four evil conditions Beings in hell, *pretas,* animals, and *asuras.*

four fearlessnesses of a buddha (1) Fearlessness in proclaiming all truth; (2) fearlessness in proclaiming the truth of perfection, or freedom from faults; (3) fearlessness in exposing obstacles to the truth; (4) fearlessness in proclaiming the way to end all suffering.

four fruits *See* four merits.

four groups The four classes of the Buddha's disciples: *bhikshus,* monks; *bhikshuṇīs,* nuns; *upāsakas,* male lay devotees; and *upāsikās,* female lay devotees.

four heavenly kings Four divine beings who protect the world from demons, each guarding one quarter of the compass surrounding Mount Sumeru. They are under the jurisdiction of Indra. Their names are Dhṛtarāshṭra Mahārājā, ruler of the east; Virūḍhaka Mahārājā, ruler of the south; Virūpāksha Mahārājā, ruler of the west; and Vaiśravaṇa Mahārājā, ruler of the north.

four holy states *Śrāvaka, pratyekabuddha,* bodhisattva, buddha.

four merits Also called the "four fruits" or "four rewards." (1) *Srota-āpanna,* one who has entered the stream (leading to nirvana); (2) *sakṛdāgāmin,* returning, or being reborn only once more; (3) *anāgāmin,* not returning, or not being reborn again; (4) *arhat.* See also *arhat.*

Four Noble Truths (1) All existence entails suffering. (2) Suffering is caused by ignorance, which gives rise to craving and illusion. (3) There is an end to suffering, and this state of no suffering is called nirvana. (4) Nirvana is attained through the practice of the Eightfold Path. This is one of the fundamental doctrines of all forms of Buddhism and was the content of the first sermon preached by the Buddha. *See also* Deer Park, Eightfold Path.

four rewards *See* four merits.

gandharva Literally, "feeding in fragrance." A celestial spirit living on Mount Gandha; *gandharvas* are the musicians of Indra.

garuḍa A fabulous bird with golden wings, king of all birds; the natural enemy of the *nāgas,* earth spirits that the *garuḍas* hunt for food.

gāthā Literally, "singly raising a chant." Stanzas of poetry in a sutra independent of the preceding prose passage. *See also geya.*

Gayā A city in Magadha, an ancient kingdom in Central India, situated about six miles from the Bodhi tree. *See also* Bodhi tree.

geya A passage of poetry in a sutra that repeats the sense of the preceding prose passage. *See also gāthā.*

Gṛdhrakūṭa, Mount Also called Divine Vulture Peak or simply Vulture Peak.

A mountain near present Rajgir, Bihar; its name is said to derive from the fact that its peak is shaped like a vulture, and also that many vultures are supposed to have lived on the mountain.

Great Extent, sutras of A general term for the Mahāyāna sutras.

Great Iron Circle, Mount One of four mountains around Mount Sumeru; the other three are Mount Iron Circle, Mount Mucilinda, and Mount Mahā-Mucilinda.

Great-vehicle The Mahāyāna; a Mahāyāna sutra. *See* Mahāyāna.

Hīnayāna Literally, "small vehicle" or "lesser vehicle." A derogatory name applied by Mahāyāna Buddhists to the Theravada school of Buddhism, an older and more conservative form of Buddhism based on the Pāli canon.

Indra In Hinduism, the deity controlling thunder, lightning, wind, and rain. He is the enemy of Māra and the *asuras*. In Buddhism Indra is identified with Śakra, and is lord of Trāyastriṃśa heaven. *See also* Trāyastriṃśa.

Iron Circle, Mount *See* Great Iron Circle, Mount.

Īśvara An epithet of Brahma.

jambū tree A mythical variety of tree growing in the northern part of Jambudvīpa.

Jambudvīpa The southern of the four continents surrounding Mount Sumeru. In it grows a great *jambū* tree with triangular leaves; the continent is said to be shaped like such a leaf, hence its name. This is the world of men. *See also* Sumeru, Mount.

jambūnada gold Gold found in the river running through the grove of *jambū* trees in Jambudvīpa.

jātika A variety of sweet-smelling flower.

jīvakajīvaka Also called *jīvajīva, jīvamjīvaka.* A mythical bird with two heads, famous for the sweetness of its song.

jñapti-karman *Jñapti* means "announcement, declaration," while *karman* refers to proceedings at a Buddhist assembly. This is the part of the Buddhist ordination ceremony in which the candidate confesses his past sins and vows to follow the Buddha's teachings.

kalavinka According to Kern, this word denotes a sparrow, but the corresponding Pāli word, *kuṛavīka,* is supposed to refer to the Indian cuckoo, the *koil,* which is the equivalent in Indian poetry of the nightingale in English verse.

kalpa An eon. The period during which a physical universe is formed and destroyed. There are small, medium, and great *kalpas.* The duration of a small *kalpa* is likened to the period required to remove all the poppy seeds from an area the size of a ten-mile-square city if one removed one poppy seed every three years, or the period required for a celestial maiden to wear away a ten-mile-cubic stone if she brushed it once with her garments every three years. When ten miles in the above examples is read as twenty miles, a medium *kalpa* is described; when read as thirty miles, a great *kalpa* is described. A small *kalpa* is also explained as the period during which the human lifespan increases by one year every hundred years from

10 to 84,000, then decreases at the same rate from 84,000 to 10. Twenty small *kalpas* constitute a medium *kalpa,* and four medium *kalpas* comprise a great *kalpa.* The second half of a *kalpa,* called the *kalpa* of decrease, is divided into three periods of calamity: famine, pestilence, and war. Such calamitous periods are called *kalpahashāyaḥ.* According to one explanation, the *kalpahashāyaḥ* is the period during which the following four kinds of corruption occur: (1) *Kleśakashāyaḥ,* the period during which all creatures, being bound by their own attachments, are filled with error, and evil laws replace good laws; (2) *Sattvakashāyaḥ,* the period during which all creatures degenerate, having no moral restraint; (3) *Dṛshtikashāyaḥ,* the period during which every doctrinal view is false; and (4) *Āyushkashāyaḥ,* the period during which the human lifespan becomes very short.

kaṅkara One trillion.

karma The results of actions, which produce effects that may be either good or bad.

karsha The equivalent of 176 or 280 grains troy.

kashāya A yellow-colored demon.

kiṃnara A fabulous being, half man and half animal; the *kiṃnaras* are the musicians of Indra and are subject to the four heavenly kings. *See also* four heavenly kings, Indra.

kimśuka A tree with red flowers, called the "red gem" or "macaw gem" because its flowers are as red as a macaw's beak. Kern identifies it as *Butea frondosa.*

koṭi An astronomical number variously interpreted as ten million, one hundred million, and so on.

kovidāra A kind of celestial tree.

kṛitya A kind of demon.

Kshatriya The warrior caste, second highest of the four major castes of India. Kings and other members of the ruling class, as well as warriors, were traditionally of this caste.

kumbhāṇḍa A kind of demon with an enormous scrotum.

kumuda A variety of red or white lotus flower.

kunduruka A milky resin from which a type of incense is made; "western incense."

Law Sanskrit, *Dharma.* The truth; the teaching of the Buddha.

law Sanskrit, *dharma.* A constituent element of the phenomenal world; phenomenon; event.

Law-body Sanskrit, *Dharmakāya.* The body of the truth as noumenon. *See* Abundant Treasures, *trikāya.*

Law-king Also, King of the Law. An epithet of every buddha.

lesser vehicle *See* Hīnayāna.

mahā-mañjūshaka One of the four heavenly flowers. The other three are *mandārava, mahā-mandārava,* and *mañjūshaka.*

Mahā-Meru, Mount *See* Sumeru, Mount.

Mahāprajāpatī The sister of Sakyamuni's mother; she was the first woman to be ordained a *bhikshuṇī,* or nun, and was the chief *bhikshuṇī.* She was also Sakyamuni's foster mother, bringing him up after his mother's death.

Mahā-Prajñā Great Wisdom.

mahāsattva Literally, "great being." *See* bodhisattva-*mahāsattva.*

Mahāyāna Literally, "great vehicle." One of the two major divisions of Buddhism, together with the Theravada (Hīnayāna) school. The more liberal and speculative of the two major schools; its scriptures are written in Sanskrit, Tibetan, and Chinese rather than Pāli.

Maheśvara An epithet of Śiva, one of the three major Hindu deities, along with Brahma and Vishnu. The creator of the world, who lives in Akanishthā heaven. *See also* Akanishthā.

mahoraga A boa spirit; a kind of demon.

Maitreya "The Kindly One." A perfected bodhisattva who is a principal figure in the retinue of Sakyamuni Buddha. He lives in Tushita heaven, awaiting his incarnation as the next buddha. *See also* Tushita.

mallika A variety of sweet-smelling flower.

mandārava See *mahā-mañjūshaka.*

maṇi A general term meaning "jewel."

mañjūshaka See *mahā-mañjūshaka.*

Mañjuśri A perfected bodhisattva characterized by great wisdom, who is supposed to have attended innumerable buddhas and to be always in attendance on Sakyamuni Buddha.

Māra Literally, "murderer," so called because he takes away the wisdom-life of all living beings; he is lord of the Realm of Desire.

Medicine King Sanskrit, Bhaiśajyarāja. A bodhisattva who in a former life made a vow to heal the physical and mental diseases of all beings; he has also provided many efficacious medicines for monks.

Meru, Mount *See* Sumeru, Mount.

Middle Path The middle way between the two extremes of existence and nonexistence.

nāga A kind of earth spirit. *See also garuḍa.*

Namaḥ Literally, "bend, incline, bow, submit"; often translated as "I pay homage to," "I submit myself to," or "I take refuge in."

navamālikā A sweet-smelling flower from which a perfumed oil is made.

nayuta One hundred *ayutas.* See *ayuta.*

nirvāṇa Literally, "extinction." Emancipation from all forms of existence; nonaction; the highest and absolute state of spiritual bliss.

One-vehicle *See* Buddha-vehicle.

padma A variety of red or white lotus flower.

pāramitā Literally, "arriving at the other shore." Perfection. *See also* Six *Pāramitās.*

pārijāta A kind of celestial tree.

parinirvāṇa Literally, "complete extinction." Perfect quietude, when all illusion is destroyed. This word is frequently used to signify the death of Sakyamuni.

pāṭala A variety of sweet-smelling flower.

piśācaka A vampire demon.

prajñāpāramitā Perfect wisdom.

pratyekabuddha One who attains enlightenment through completely apprehending the *nidānas,* that is, the twelve-link causal chain (*nidāna*) of existence. Also called "self-apprehended" because the *pratyekabuddha* attains buddhahood through his own independent practice, without a teacher. This is the third of the four holy states. *See also* Twelve Causes, Law of.

precious seven Sanskrit, *sapta ratnāni*. Gold, silver, lapis lazuli, crystal or moonstone, agate, ruby or pearl, carnelian. There are also other variations; cf. page 37.

Precious Stupa *See* Stupa of the Precious Seven.

Precious Three *See* Three Treasures.

preta A hungry spirit. The second lowest state of existence. *See* six states of existence.

pṛikkā Cloves.

puṇḍarīka A variety of white lotus flower.

Pure Conduct *See* Boundless Conduct.

Pure Land Sukhāvatī, "Highest Joy," the realm of Amita Buddha in the west. *See also* Amita.

pūtana A type of spirit that protects pregnant women.

Rāhula The son of Sakyamuni, and one of his major disciples.

rākshasa A demon that devours men; a general name for the demons who attend Vaiśravaṇa. *See also* Vaiśravaṇa.

Regarder of the Cries of the World Sanskrit, Avalokiteśvara; Chinese, Kuan-yin; Japanese, Kanzeon, Kannon. A perfected bodhisattva characterized by boundless compassion and mercy.

Righteous Law *See* Counterfeit Law.

Right Law *See* Counterfeit Law.

Sāgara Literally, "Ocean"; one of the eight great dragon-kings.

sahā-world The world of suffering; this world. *See also* three-thousand-great-thousandfold world.

Śakra *See* Indra.

Śakra Devendra "Mighty Lord of Devas." Another name for Indra. *See also* Indra.

sakṛdāgāmin *See* four merits.

Śākya The clan into which Gautama, Sakyamuni Buddha, was born; the ruling clan of ancient Kapilavastu in North India (present southern Nepal).

Śākyamuni Literally, "Sage of the Śākyas." The usual appellation of Gautama, the historical Buddha (c. 565–c. 486 B.C.).

samādhi Contemplation; meditation; complete concentration of the mind.

Saṃgha The monastic community of *bhikshus* or *bhikshuṇīs,* Buddhist monks or nuns, respectively; more generally, the community of Buddhist believers. *See also* Three Treasures.

Samyaksaṃbodhi The full, perfect enlightenment of the Buddha.

Śāriputra One of the ten chief disciples of the Buddha, known especially for his wisdom.

Seven Buddhas Vipaśyin, Śikhin, Viśvabhū, Krakucchanda, Kanakamuni, Kāśyapa, and Sakyamuni. The first three are the last three of a thousand buddhas who appeared during the previous *kalpa,* called Glorious, while the last four are the first four of a thousand buddhas to appear during the present *kalpa* of the sages.

Śikhin Another name of Brahma. *See* Brahma.

śikshamāṇā A *śrāmaṇera* eighteen to twenty years old, who practices the five precepts plus the additional one of not eating at unregulated hours. *See also* five precepts, *śrāmaṇera.*

Six *Pāramitās* The Six Perfections of a bodhisattva: (1) *dāna,* donation; (2) *sīla,* keeping the precepts; (3) *kshānti,* perseverance; (4) *vīrya,* assiduity; (5) *dhyāna,* meditation; (6) *prajñā,* wisdom.

six sense organs Eyes, ears, nose, tongue, body, mind.

six senses Sight, hearing, smell, taste, touch, thought.

six states of existence The six changing conditions of sentient beings; in descending order: *devas,* human beings, *asuras,* animals, *pretas,* and beings in hell.

small vehicle *See* Hīnayāna.

śramaṇa A monk or ascetic.

śrāmaṇera A male novice who has received the ten precepts, after which he may become a *śramaṇa.* See also *śramaṇa,* ten precepts.

śrāmaṇerikā A female novice. *See also śrāmaṇera.*

śrāvaka Literally, "one who hears" the voice of the Buddha and thereby reaches enlightenment; the lowest of the four holy states. *See also* four holy states.

srota-āpanna *See* four merits.

Steadfast Conduct *See* Boundless Conduct.

stūpa A pagoda or dagoba in which sacred relics are deposited. Originally a tomb, then a cenotaph, it is now for the most part merely a symbol of Buddhism.

Stupa of the Precious Seven The stupa in which the Buddha Abundant Treasures resides and within which he appears when he manifests himself to bear witness to the Lotus Flower of the Wonderful Law. *See also* Abundant Treasures, precious seven.

sumana A sweet-smelling flower from which a perfumed oil is made.

Sumeru, Mount The central mountain of every world; in this world it is situated at the center of four continents, Pūrvavideha in the east, Avaragodānīya in the west, Jambudvīpa in the south, and Uttarakuru in the north, each of which is governed by one of the four heavenly kings; Indra's heaven is located on its summit. *See also* four heavenly kings, Indra, Trāyastriṃśa.

Summit of All Existence The top or extreme limit of existence; the fourth and highest heaven of the Realm of Formlessness.

śūraṃgama-samādhi The contemplation, or *samādhi,* by which one can exterminate all illusions.

sūtra Literally, "thread" or "string." The scriptures containing the teachings of the

Buddha. Most of the major sutras were originally written in Pāli or Sanskrit, though some were written in Tibetan or Chinese.

tāla The name of a type of Indian tree with large leaves on which sutras used to be inscribed.

tamālapattra A kind of sandalwood tree.

Tathāgata Literally, "one who has thus gone," that is, one who has reached the truth and come to declare it; the highest epithet of a buddha.

ten directions North, south, east, west, the four intermediate compass points, zenith, and nadir.

ten powers Every buddha possesses the following ten powers: (1) the power to know right and wrong states; (2) the power to know the consequences of karma; (3) the power to know all meditations and contemplations; (4) the power to know the various higher and lower capabilities of sentient beings; (5) the power to know what sentient beings understand; (6) the power to know the basic nature and actions of sentient beings; (7) the power to know the causes and effects of sentient beings in all worlds; (8) the power to know the results of karmas in past lives; (9) the power of knowledge through supernatural insight; (10) the power of being free from all error, or infallibility in knowledge.

ten precepts The ten rules of discipline observed by a *śrāmaṇera* or *śrāmaṇerikā:* (1) not to kill, (2) not to steal, (3) to refrain from wrong sexual conduct, (4) not to lie, (5) not to drink intoxicants, (6) not to decorate the body or wear ornaments, (7) not to listen to music or view dancing or other theatrical performances, (8) not to sleep in a wide or raised bed, (9) not to eat except at regulated times, (10) not to keep money or jewels. *See also śrāmaṇera, śrāmaṇerikā.*

ten titles of a buddha Tathāgata, Worshipful, All Wise, Perfectly Enlightened in Conduct, Well Departed, Understander of the World, Peerless Leader, Controller, Teacher of Gods and Men, Buddha.

Theravada *See* Hīnayāna.

thirty-two signs The distinguishing characteristics of the body of a buddha; these are described in chapter 1 of the Sutra of Innumerable Meanings (pages 7–8).

three evil paths Beings in hell, *pretas,* and animals.

threefold refuge The vow of absolute allegiance to the Buddha, the Law, and the *Saṃgha. See also* Three Treasures.

three laws (1) The Four Noble Truths, (2) the Law of the Twelve Causes, (3) the Six *Pāramitās. See* Four Noble Truths, Six *Pāramitās,* Twelve Causes, Law of.

three poisons (1) Covetousness or sensual desire, (2) anger or ill will, (3) foolishness or delusion.

three precious things Sanskrit, *triratna. See* Three Treasures.

three-thousand-great-thousandfold world The chiliocosm. The three-thousand-great-thousandfold world is equal to one billion small worlds, each with a Mount Sumeru at its center and eight concentric continents, separated by eight seas. According to ancient Indian cosmology, the universe consists of an infinite number of worlds, all more or less on the same plan as our own, with the same number of mountains, continents, oceans, and so on, including the hells in the interior and the heavens above each world. The number of these worlds is incalculable, and they are grouped in various kinds of chiliocosms. A small chiliocosm consists of a thousand worlds and is encompassed by a gigantic wall. A middle chiliocosm consists of a thousand small chiliocosms and is bounded by a similar wall. A large chiliocosm consists of a thousand middle chiliocosms, again with a wall. The *Abhidharma Kośa* states that the distance between two worlds in a chiliocosm is 1,203,450 *yojanas*. See also *Abhidharma Kośa, yojana.*

three sufferings (1) The suffering of pain, mental or physical; (2) the suffering of decay; (3) the suffering of evolution, or of birth and death.

Three Treasures Sanskrit, *ratnatraya*. The Buddha; the Law, or teaching of the Buddha; and the *Saṃgha,* or monastic community.

three vehicles *Śrāvaka, pratyekabuddha,* and bodhisattva (the Buddha-vehicle).

three worlds The past, present, and future.

Trāyastriṃśa The heaven of the thirty-three heavenly cities. This is the heaven of Indra, and the second highest of the six heavens of the Realm of Desire. Situated atop Mount Sumeru, eighty thousand *yojanas* above this world, it consists of thirty-two cities of *devas,* eight on each of the four peaks of Mount Sumeru, and Indra's own heaven in the center. *See also* Indra.

trikāya The "three bodies" (*trikāya*) of the Buddha: (1) *Dharmakāya,* truth-body or Law-body; (2) *saṃbhogakāya,* reward-body or bliss-body; (3) *nirmāṇakāya,* mutation-body or response-body. According to the T'ien-t'ai interpretation, the *Dharmakāya* indicates the buddhahood in its universality, or the Eternal Buddha, as expounded in chapter 16 of the Lotus Sutra; the *nirmāṇakāya* the buddhahood embodied or personalized, that is, the historical Buddha, Sakyamuni; and the *saṃbhogakāya* the buddhahood in its glory. See page 249, note 1. *See also* Abundant Treasures.

Tripiṭaka Literally, "three baskets." The three divisions of the Buddhist scriptures: (1) the sutras; (2) the *vinaya,* or disiplinary rules and precepts; (3) the *śāstras,* doctrinal commentaries.

triple world *See* three worlds.

triratna The three precious things. *See* Three Treasures.

turushka A thyme-mixture incense.

Tushita The heaven inhabited by Maitreya Bodhisattva; the fourth of the six heavens of the Realm of Desire.

Twelve Causes, Law of Also called the twelve-link chain of causation or of dependent origination (Sanskrit, *pratītya-samutpāda*), each link of which gives rise to the following one: (1) ignorance, (2) actions, (3) consciousness, (4) name and form (mind and body), (5) the six entrances (the six sense organs), (6) contact, (7) sensation, (8) desire, (9) clinging, (10) existence, (11) birth, (12) old age and death. This doctrine is discussed in chapter 7 of the Lotus Sutra (page 158).

twenty-five abodes The four evil worlds (hell, *pretas,* animals, *asuras*), the four continents of the *sahā*-world, the six heavens of the Realm of Desire, the seven heavens of the Realm of Form (instead of the usual eighteen heavens; *see* Akanishthā), and the four heavens of the Realm of Formlesseness. *See also sahā*-world.

two vehicles (1) Hīnayāna and Mahāyāna; (2) *śrāvaka* and *pratyekabuddha.*

udumbara A mythical flower that blooms only once every three thousand years, heralding the advent of a *cakravartin* (world-ruler) or a buddha. *See also* wheel-rolling king.

umāraka A black-colored demon.

upadeśa Literally, "direction, instruction"; doctrinal treatises and discourses.

upāsaka A male lay devotee of Buddhism.

upāsikā A female lay devotee of Buddhism.

utpala A variety of blue lotus flower.

Vairocana A nonhistorical buddha who lives in the realm called Eternally Tranquil Light according to the Sutra of Meditation on the Bodhisattva Universal Virtue (see page 362).

Vaiśālī An ancient country in Central India; one of the sixteen large kingdoms of India in Sakyamuni's time. Its capital, also called Vaiśālī, was located at present Besarb, twenty-seven miles north of Patna.

Vaiśravaṇa One of the four heavenly kings; he governs the northern of the four continents surrounding Mount Sumeru. *See also* four heavenly kings.

Vārāṇasī Benares.

vārshika A sweet-smelling flower from which a perfumed oil is made.

vetaḍa A red-colored demon.

Void Sanskrit, *śūnya, śūnyatā.* Literally, "emptiness, void." The undifferentiated absolute.

wheel-rolling king Sanskrit, *cakravartin.* There are four such kings, each with a precious wheel of gold, silver, copper, or iron. The kings reign over the four great regions north, south, east, and west of Mount Sumeru. The king of the gold wheel rules the entire world; the king of the silver wheel the east, west, and south regions; the king of the copper wheel the east and south; and the king of the iron wheel the south alone. The coming of the king of the gold wheel in order to unify the world is one of the prophecies of the Buddha and is one of the strongest beliefs of some Buddhists.

World-honored One An epithet of a buddha.

yaksha A type of demon comprising the retinue of Vaiśravaṇa. *See also* Vaiśravaṇa.

Yaśodharā The wife of Sakyamuni before he left home to assume the life of a wandering ascetic, and the mother of Rāhula; she later became a *bhikshuṇī.*

yojana A unit of distance equivalent to 64, 120, or 160 kilometers.

法王子無憂藏法王子大辯藏法王子弥勒
菩薩導首菩薩藥王菩薩藥上菩薩花幢菩
薩華光幢菩薩陁羅尼自在王菩薩觀世音
菩薩大勢至菩薩常精進菩薩寶印首菩薩
寶積菩薩寶杖菩薩越三界菩薩毗摩颰羅
菩薩香象菩薩大香象菩薩師子吼王菩薩
師子遊戲世菩薩師子奮迅菩薩師子精進
菩薩勇鋭力菩薩師子威猛伏菩薩莊嚴菩
薩大莊嚴菩薩如是等菩薩摩訶薩八万人